Potsdamer Altertumswissenschaftliche Beiträge

Band 88

www.steiner-verlag.de/brand/Potsdamer-altertumswissenschaftliche-Beitraege

Utilitas in Roman Jurists' Legal Interpretation

Joanna Kulawiak-Cyrankowska

Franz Steiner Verlag

Printed with the generous support of the University of Łódź

UNIVERSITY
OF LODZ

Bibliographic information published by the German National Library:
The German National Library lists this publication in the Deutsche Nationalbibliografie;
detailed bibliographic information is available at
dnb.d-nb.de.

Maybachstraße 8, 70469 Stuttgart
service@steiner-verlag.de
www.steiner-verlag.de
Layout and production by Franz Steiner Verlag
Translation: Dagmara Łata
Typesetting: primustype Hurler GmbH, Notzingen
Print: Beltz Grafische Betriebe, Bad Langensalza
Printed on acid-free and age-resistant paper.
Printed in Germany.
ISBN 978-3-515-13668-6 (Print)
ISBN 978-3-515-13676-1 (E-Book)
DOI 10.25162/9783515136761

Moim Rodzicom, którym zawdzięczam wszystko i jeszcze więcej

Acknowledgements

Writing a doctoral thesis is quite a journey, and I doubt anyone could go through it alone. I was fortunate to have fantastic comrades along the way. While I owe thanks to many people who have supported me throughout this process, it would be impossible to name everyone here (though I could easily double the size of this book if I tried). Therefore, I will keep these acknowledgements brief and to the point.

My deepest gratitude goes to my supervisor, Professor Anna Pikulska-Radomska, for her unwavering guidance and insightful advice, which made possible not only this work but also my development as a scholar.

I am also profoundly thankful to my colleagues in the Department of Roman Law and the Department of Classical Philology at the University of Łódź. The support and camaraderie I received from you helped me grow in more ways than one. I am truly proud to be part of such amazing teams.

To Professors Anna Tarwacka and Maciej Jońca, the reviewers of this thesis, thank you for your thoughtful and constructive feedback, which played a crucial role in refining this work.

Special thanks to Professor Giuseppe Falcone for his critical and attentive reading, and for guiding me toward the perspective on Roman law research that I now hold dear.

To Dr. Antonio Villanueva Martínez, your support – both intellectual and personal – made all the difference.

Lastly, my deepest thanks go to my parents and my husband – there are no words that could adequately express my gratitude for your love, understanding, and encouragement throughout this and every other journey I embark on.

Table of Contents

Introduction

1. Research Subject

In one of his verses, Horace portrays *utilitas* as the mother of what is just and right (*Sat.* 1,3,98 *utilitas, iusti prope mater et aequi*). This poetic perspective highlights the profound influence that the concept of *utilitas* has had on legal thought. The term *utilitas*, signifying 'utility', 'usefulness', or 'interest', along with its derivatives, has been invoked in each epoch throughout the development of Roman law, appearing in both jurists' writings and emperors' constitutions[1]. *Utilitas* permeated almost every aspect of the *ius Romanum*[2]. To fully appreciate the extent of this phenomenon, consider that what we now define as 'applying the law'[3] was, in the Roman context, essentially 'using the law' or, more precisely, 'making use of it' as conveyed by the phrase *iure uti*. This phrase includes the verb *utor, uti* ('to use') from which the term *utilitas* is etymologically derived[4].

1 The term *utilitas* and its derivatives appear 1226 times in legal sources, as illustrated by the Table 1 in the Tables, Charts, and Graphs section.

2 Recognition of the criterion under study is notably expressed by Italian scholars, such as F. B. Cicala in *Il concetto dell'"utile' e sue applicazioni nel diritto romano*, Milano-Torino-Roma 1910, p. 9, where he asserts: 'il concetto dell'*utilitas* signoreggia in tuto il campo del diritto romano' ('the concept of *utilitas* dominates across the entire spectrum of Roman law'). Similarly, B. Biondi in *Il diritto romano cristiano. Vol. 2. La giustizia, le persone*, Milano 1952, p. 97, states: 'Il diritto classico e tutta la sapiente elaborazione giurisprudenziale non sono altro che il sistema, l'organizzazione, la disciplina dell'*utilitas*' ('The classical law and all the erudite jurisprudential elaboration are nothing more than a system, organization and discipline of *utilitas*'). While these scholars underscore the pivotal role of *utilitas* within Roman law, their opinions remain somewhat generalized. See also *Handlexikon zu den Quellen des römischen Rechts*, H. G. Heumann, E. Seckel (ed.), Jena 1926, pp. 541–542 s. v. *utilis, utilitas*.

3 G. Aricò Anselmo, *'Ius publicum'-'Ius privatum' in Ulpiano, Gaio e Cicerone*, 'AUPA' 1983, vol. 37, pp. 456–457.

4 This verb is derived from the older form **oitor*, attested by inscriptions. Cf. e.g. CIL 14,3584 = CIL 1,586 *oitile* = *utile*, CIL 1,583 *oetiles ioudices* = *utiles iudices*, CIL 9,3513 = CIL 1,756 *oeti* = *uti*. On etymology of terms see *Dictionnaire étymologique de la langue latine*, A. Ernout, A. Meillet (ed.), Paris 1951, p. 757, s. v. *utor*; W. M. Lindsay, *The Latin Language: An Historical Account of Latin Sounds, Stems, and Flexions*, Oxford 1984, p. 309§ 155; *Etymological Dictionary of Latin and the Other Italic Languages*, M. de Vaan (ed.), Leiden–Boston 2011, pp. 647–648, s. v. *utor*.

A deeper contemplation of Horace's idea reveals a thought-provoking puzzle: although it is ideal when righteousness, justice, and utility align, suggesting that utility is the source of the other two may misrepresent their true relationship, particularly in law, where *iustitia* and *aequitas* should take precedence.

This study examines the relationship between this poetic phrase and legal reasoning, particularly in the context of how Roman jurists interpreted the law. The central focus is, therefore, on *utilitas*, which manifested itself both in their thinking about the law and in the law itself. The Roman jurists, as legal practitioners, not only inherently embraced this criterion in their thinking, but also consistently prioritized the demands of legal practice when conflicts arose between legal rules and practical necessities[5]. Although scholars have extensively studied the pragmatic approach of Roman jurists, the deeper role of *utilitas* in their legal interpretation is still underexplored. Existing literature often overlooks non-legal sources, particularly rhetorical ones, which could offer a more comprehensive and theoretical perspective on *utilitas*. On the other hand, jurisprudence offers a wealth of examples of its practical application. While reconstructing the jurists' thought forms the core of this study, they are also considered as co-creators of intellectual life, not just as an elite group[6]. This approach allows for synthesis of both of these perspectives, presenting a complete picture of what the term *utilitas* encompassed.

While this work briefly introduces these issues, it does not aim to analyze every aspect of *utilitas* within Roman law. The focus here is on the abstract category without any limiting qualifications. Therefore, the concept of public good signified by the term *utilitas publica*, which has already been extensively studied[7], is discussed only to the

5 In this context, F. Schwarz writes about the dispute between *Denkrichtigkeit* and *Lebensrichtigkeit*, *Begriffsanwendung und Interessenwertung im klassischen römischen Recht*, 'Archiv für die civilistische Praxis' 1952, vol. 152, no. 3, p. 203. Similarly, M. Kaser, *Zur Methodologie der römischen Rechtsquellenforschung*, Wien-Köln-Graz 1972, p. 62. See also W. Rozwadowski, *Etiam clarum ius exigit interpretationem* [in:] *W poszukiwaniu dobra wspólnego: księga jubileuszowa Profesora Macieja Zielińskiego*, A. Choduń, S. Czepita (ed.), Szczecin 2010, p. 42.

6 P. Święcicka, *Formalność topicznego myślenia: problem 'reguł proceduralnych' dyskursu dogmatycznego rzymskich jurystów*, 'CPH' 2011, vol. 63, no. 2, p. 219, esp. n. 38 along with the literature cited therein. On elitism and influence of social factors (including origin) on the intellectual formation of jurists e.g. in W. Kunkel, *Die römischen Juristen: Herkunft und soziale Stellung*, Köln-Weimar-Wien 2001 and D. Mantovani, *Iuris scientia e honores. Contributo allo studio dei fattori sociali nella formazione giurisprudenziale del diritto romano (III–I sec. a.C.)* [in:] *Nozione formazione e interpretazione del diritto: dall'età romana alle esperienze moderne. Ricerche dedicate al professor Filippo Gallo*, vol. 1, S. Romano (ed.), 1997, pp. 617–680. See also M. Kuryłowicz, *Sacerdotes iustitiae* [in:] *Ecclesia et Status. Księga jubileuszowa z okazji 40-lecia pracy naukowej profesora Józefa Krukowskiego*, A. Dębiński, K. Orzeszyna, M. Sitarz (ed.), Lublin 2004, pp. 709–713. The wider context of the issue is presented in J. Pölönen, *The Case for a Sociology of Roman Law* [in:] *Law and Sociology*, M. Freeman (ed.), New York 2006, pp. 398–408 along with the literature cited therein.

7 On this issue e.g. A. Steinwenter, *Utilitas publica–Utilitas singulorum* [in:] *Festschrift Paul Koschaker mit Unterstützung der Rechts- und Staatswissenschaftlichen Fakultät der Friedrich-Wilhelms-Universität Berlin und der Leipziger Juristenfakultät zum 60. Geburtstag überreicht von seinen Fachgenossen,*

extent necessary to shed light on the role of *utilitas* in the jurisprudence interpretation of the law.

While the Romans owe the early stages of conceptualizing *utilitas* to the Greeks[8], who referred to it as τὸ συμφέρον, ἡ ὠφέλεια, τὸ χρήσιμον, or τὸ καλόν[9], this study incorporates Greek thought only insofar as it enhances understanding of the Roman aspect of this phenomenon. Given its significant place in the writings of Marcus Tullius Cicero, the initial time frame of the research is set at the Ciceronian period, namely the 1st century BCE. Earlier sources are referenced solely to provide historical or intellectual context for the events under examination.

This research delves into the works of Roman jurists[10], focusing primarily on the classical law period. This standard time frame for studying the writings of Roman jurisprudence is dictated by the state of preserved sources. In the *Digest of Justinian*, which

vol. 1, M. Kaser (ed.), Weimar 1939, pp. 84–102; J. Gaudemet, *Utilitas publica*, 'RHD' 1951, vol. 4, no. 29, pp. 465–499; T. Mayer-Maly, *Gemeinwohl und Naturrecht bei Cicero* [in:] *Völkerrecht und rechtliches Weltbild: Festschrift für Alfred Verdross*, F.A. Frhr. v. d. Heydte, I. Seidl-Hohenveldern, St. Verosta, K. Zemanek (ed.), Viena 1960, pp. 195–206; G. Jossa, *L''utilitas rei publicae' nel pensiero imperiale dell'epoca classica*, 'Studi Romani' 1963, vol. 11, no. 4, pp. 387–405; Idem, *L''utilitas rei publicae' nel pensiero di Cicerone*, 'Studi Romani' 1964, vol. 12, no. 3, pp. 269–288; G. Longo, *Utilitas publica*, 'Labeo' 1972, vol. 18, pp. 7–71; T. Mayer-Maly, *Gemeinwohl und Necessitas* [in:] *Rechtsgeschichte als Kulturgeschichte: Festschrift für Adalbert Erler zum 70 Geburtstag*, A. Fink et al. (ed.), Aalen 1976, pp. 135–145; T. Honsell, *Gemeinwohl und öffentliches Interesse im klassischen römischen Recht*, 'ZSS RA' 1978, vol. 95, no. 1, pp. 93–137; P. Hibst, *Utilitas publica, gemeiner Nutz, Gemeinwohl: Untersuchungen zur Idee eines politischen Leitbegriffes von der Antike bis zum späten Mittelalter*, Frankfurt am Main-New York 1991; R. Scevola, *'Utilitas publica', I. Emersione nel pensiero greco e romano*, Padova 2012; Idem, *'Utilitas publica', II. Elaborazione della giurisprudenza severiana*, Padova 2012; B. Sitek, *Utilitas publica z perspektywy prawa rzymskiego i polskiego*, 'Themis Polska Nova' 2014, vol. 1, no. 6, pp. 21–35; J.F. Stagl, *Die Funktionen der utilitas publica*, 'ZSS RA' 2017, vol. 134, no. 1, pp. 514–527; Idem, *Camino desde la servidumbre: Escritos sobre la servidumbre en la Antigüedad, su derrota y la amenaza de su retorno*, Madrid 2021, pp. 83–102.

8 The analysis of *utilitas publica* was started from presenting Greek reflections by, e.g., A. Steinwenter, *Utilitas publica…*, pp. 85–88; J. Gaudemet, *Utilitas publica*, pp. 466–467; R. Scevola, *'Utilitas publica', I. Emersione…*, pp. 11–285. See also P. Hibst, *Utilitas publica…*, pp. 122–131. G. Jossa, *L''utilitas rei publicae' nel pensiero imperiale…*, p. 392, maintains that Roman thought was impacted by the Stoic rather than Aristotelian influence up to the post-classical era. However, it is hard not to notice that the Stoic and Peripatetic vision of the issues analyzed here show many similarities. The problem of the common good and relationship between the benefits of the state and interests of individuals in the world of ancient Greece was carefully described by Scevola. The researcher devoted two large chapters to this problem (see *'Utilitas publica', I. Emersione…*): 'Da Omero a Solone. La tradizione greca in materia di utilità nella sfera pubblica' (pp. 11–139) and 'Utilità e giustizia nel discorso pubblico della πόλις e nel pensiero della comunità universale' (pp. 141–285).

9 *Novum lexicon manuale Graeco-Latinum et Latino-Graecum*, B. Hederich, G. Pinzger, F. Passovio (ed.), Lipsiae 1827, p. 749, s.v. *utilitas*.

10 *Utilitas* in the imperial constitutions of the 4th and 5th century was discussed by M. Navarra, *Utilitas publica-utilitas singulorum tra IV e V sec. D. C. Alcune osservazioni*, 'SDHI' 1997, vol. 63, pp. 269–291. The meaning of this criterion in later sources was also briefly addressed by N. Rampazzo, *Quasi praetor non fuerit. Studi sulle elezioni magistratuali in Roma repubblicana tra regola ed eccezione*, Napoli 2008, pp. 497–506.

constitutes the basis of knowledge on this subject, there are excerpts from the writings of thirty-eight Roman jurists. This includes three from the Republican era and two from the times of the Dominate. The rest hail from the Principate period, and it is primarily these jurists, though not all, who make references *ad utilitatem* in the context under examination. However, considering the common practice of jurists quoting their predecessors, it is likely that some *ad utilitatem* references appeared in earlier jurists' writings[11].

Noteworthy references to *utilitas* also appear in Gaius' *Institutes*, a legal textbook from the 2nd century CE, as well as in *Pauli Sententiae*. The dating of the latter work, however, presents some challenges. Although based on the writings of Julius Paulus, a jurist from the late 2nd century CE, the work is believed to have been composed at the end of the 3rd century CE, placing it within the post-classical period according to commonly applied periodization among Roman law scholars[12]. Here, a substantive approach guided the inclusion of certain excerpts from the *Pauli Sententiae* in this analysis. Thus, even though the majority of the jurisprudence sources examined here originate from the Principate, the research extends to the end of the 3rd century CE, marking a clear and definitive temporal boundary.

2. State of Research

The concept of *utilitas* in Roman law has garnered significant scholarly interest. This section provides an overview of existing research on this topic, setting the stage for defining the objectives of this work, which builds upon the insights gathered from these studies.

11 An example of such a reference can be found in Pap. D. 46,3,95,7. According to Papinian, Marcus Antistius Labeo and Lucius Plotius Pegasus held that the decision had to be adopted due to *utilitas* (*quod quidem Labeo et Pegasus putaverunt utilitatis causa recipiendum*). Later, the fragment is discussed in more detail. At this point, however, it should be noted that it is impossible to say whether the *ad utilitatem* reference came from the aforementioned jurists, or was a supplement introduced by Papinian. However, if the latter had been faithfully quoting the views of his predecessors, it could also entail at least a slight departure from the framework of the classical period, since Labeo was born at the end of the Republic (BCE). It should also be stated that in such doubtful situations, in the tables in the Tables, Charts, and Graphs section at the end of this study, the criterion of the author of the work from which the source was taken was considered decisive. Therefore, for instance, Labeo was not indicated as the author of this *utilitatis causa* decision even though it cannot be definitively ruled out that he nominally referred to this criterion.

12 Recently this opinion debated in I. Ruggiero, *Ricerche sulle Pauli Sententiae*, Milano 2017, assigning the *Sententiae* to Paulus or to his circle of disciples. Critically of this hypothesis in D. Liebs, *Ricerche sulle Pauli Sententiae (= Quaderni di ‚Studi Senesi' 145)*, 'ZSS RA' 2019, vol. 136, no. 1, pp. 465–466. It is not the role of this study to participate in the debate on the periodization of the work. As it turns out, references to *utilitas* in the *Pauli Sententiae* and in fragments of Paulus's works preserved in the *Digest of Justinian* serve the same function. However, since other jurists also referred to *utilitas* in their decisions, it is difficult to draw definitive conclusions about authorship from this fact. Therefore, in the text and the statistics at the end of this study, decisions from the *Pauli Sententiae* are attributed to (Pseudo-)Paulus.

The focus begins with literature on a particularly distinct manifestation of *utilitas* in jurists' interpretation: the decisions taken *utilitatis causa*, namely for the sake of utility. Their essence is as intriguing as it is evident to scholars of Roman law. Ulrich Leptien describes them as *die grundsatzwidrige Entscheidungen* ('decisions contrary to the principle'), contrasting them with categories such as *System und Grundsatz* ('system and principle')[13]. Similarly, Max Kaser characterizes these decisions as exceptions to the rules or principles[14]. Marialuisa Navarra refers to them as decisions *che si discostano da regole di portata generale, e che possono essere in apparente contradizzione con il 'sistema'* ('which deviate from the general rules, and which may be in apparent contradiction to the system'), also highlighting the category of exception: *una soluzione che fa eccezione ad una regola generale* ('a solution that creates an exception to the general rule')[15]. Hans Ankum views these decisions as 'dogmatically indefensible solutions'[16], sometimes referring to them as exceptions to the rules, seen as indefensible from a dogmatic standpoint[17]. Ankum employs various terms to elaborate on this, some describing the

13 On the *utilitatis causa* decisions, Leptien wrote his PhD thesis: *Utilitatis causa. Zweckmässigkeitsentscheidungen im römischen Recht*, Freiburg 1967 (in the mentioned context see pp. 237–240). Its fragment was then published as an article, *'Utilitatis causa'. Zweckmäßigkeitsentscheidungen im römischen Recht*, 'SDHI' 1969, vol. 35, pp. 51–72.

14 M. Kaser, *Das römische Privatrecht. 1. Abschnitt. Das altrömische, das vorklassische und klassische Recht*, München 1971, p. 212. Idem, *'Ius publicum' und 'ius privatum'*, 'ZSS RA' 1986, vol. 103, no. 1, p. 18.

15 M. Navarra, *Ricerche sulla 'utilitas' nel pensiero dei giuristi romani*, Torino 2002, p. 4. Cf. also p. 206: *la soluzione (...) in deroga a preesistenti regole di portata più generale* ('decision in deviation from the previously existing rules of a more general scope'). In this monograph the Italian researcher presents an extensive analysis of jurisprudence sources containing the expressions *utilitatis causa, propter utilitatem* and *utilitatis gratia*. She also prepared the tables illustrating the frequency of using the enumerated expressions in individual collections, including both jurists' decisions and imperial constitutions, as well as taking the presence of phrases in each jurist's works separately into account, p. 12. It should also be mentioned that the title of the monograph was noted as being too broad in relation to its actual content by H. Ankum, *Navarra, Marialuisa, Ricerche sulla utilitas nel pensiero dei giuristi romani*, 'ZSS RA' 2009, vol. 126, no. 1, p. 524, n. 5.

16 In 1968, Ankum published two influential studies on decisions made *utilitatis causa*: *'Utilitatis causa receptum'. On the pragmatical methods of the Roman lawyers* [in:] *Symbolae iuridicae et historicae Martino David dedicatae*, vol. 1, J.A. Ankum, R. Feenstra, W.F. Leemans (ed.), Leiden 1968, pp. 1–31, and *'Utilitatis causa receptum': sur la méthode pragmatique des juristes romains classiques*, 'RIDA' 1968, vol. 15, pp. 119–133. Leaving the specifics of the languages aside, both articles are basically similar in content. Later on, Ankum revisited the topic by entering into a discussion with Navarra. He contributed to the discourse by offering a detailed review and expanding upon the subject through two separate articles. See H. Ankum, *Navarra, Marialuisa, Ricerche ...*, pp. 524–536; Idem, *The functions of expressions with utilitatis causa in the works of the Classical Roman lawyers*, 'Fundamina: A Journal of Legal History' 2010, vol. 16, no. 1, pp. 5–22; Idem, *Utilitatis causa en los trabajos de los juristas clásicos romanos*, 'Revista chilena de derecho' 2016, vol. 43, no. 3, pp. 1121–1132.

17 The indicated pages contain either the author's initial thesis or his conclusions. See H. Ankum, *'Utilitatis causa receptum'. On the pragmatical methods...*, p. 28; Idem, *'Utilitatis causa receptum': sur la méthode...*, p. 132; Idem, *The functions...*, pp. 6 and 22; Idem, *Utilitatis causa...*, p. 1121.

applicable law[18] (*dogmatic, strict law, rules of dogmatics, strict dogmatic rules, the rule*), and others describing the interpretation process (*strict [dogmatic] reasoning, formal interpretation, strict literal interpretation, strict rules of logic*)[19]. He uses these terms interchangeably, indicating no clear line between outright opposition to the rules and deviation from their strict interpretation. Lastly, Benjamin Spagnolo and Joe Sampson define them as decisions deviating from the general principle embodied in the term *ratio*, viewing this notion in terms of logic[20] corresponding not so much (or not solely) to syllogistic schemes but rather to the rationality of a decision understood as consistency with the general legal order and its principles[21].

As we can see, the vision of the nature of *utilitatis causa* decisions is consistent[22] – a rarity in itself. However, the effects of these decisions akin to the actions of an absolute ruler, invite a deeper examination of the role and significance of *utilitas* in legal interpretation. Here, researchers offer various perspectives.

Ankum filled the expression *utilitatis causa* with the needs of everyday life and legal practice (*les exigences de la vie pratique; the needs of legal practice; las razones prácticas*)[23].

18 One should bear in mind the opinion of T. Giaro, who argued that Roman jurists were guided not by a juridical concept of the validity of the law, but by an axiological one, *Geltung und Fortgeltung des römischen Juristenrechts*, 'ZSS RA' 1994, vol. 111, no. 1, p. 80.

19 The terms taken from H. Ankum, *'Utilitatis causa receptum'. On the pragmatical methods…, passim*. The analogous terms are used by the author in French and Spanish articles. For instance: *une interprétation stricte, un raisonnement logique, le droit strict, raisonnement dogmatique, les règles de la théorie et de la logique, argumentation purement logique, la règle* and *las reglas lógico dogmáticas, las reglas de la dogmática, las (estrictas) reglas de la lógica, las reglas dogmáticas estrictas, una interpretación estricta, una regla*.

20 Cf. also P. Stein, *Interpretation and Legal Reasoning in Roman Law*, 'Chicago-Kent Law Review' 1995, vol. 70, no. 4, pp. 1552–1553.

21 B. Spagnolo, J. Sampson, *Principle and Pragmatism* [in:] *Principle and Pragmatism in Roman Law*, B. Spagnolo, J. Sampson (ed.), Oxford-New York 2020, pp. 3, 5–6.

22 Obviously, certain terminological diversity is notable. Leptien refers to the concept of 'principle'. Ankum and Navarra, in turn, use the term 'rule'. On the other hand, Spagnolo and Sampson, like Kaser before them, use both of these terms. Leaving aside any discussions about the content of each concept and their mutual relationships, it should be concluded that when researchers write about rules and principles, they mean the applicable legal norms. Regarding the term 'legal norm', one should share Giaro's observation that the Romans did not know this concept. This term, as indicating the law recognized as binding, is a paraphrase but it facilitates contemporary discussions, *Geltung …*, p. 70.

23 See both translations of sources and the statements in Ankum's studies quoted above. Heumann and Seckel similarly translated this expression as *Rücksicht auf praktische Bedürfnisse, auf die Verkehrssicherheit, Zweckmäßigkeit, Handlexikon…*, s. v. *utilitas* sub 3. Similarly also P. Stein, *Interpretation…*, p. 1553, who translated the term *utilitas communis* as 'general convenience'. See also L. Lombardi, *Saggio sul diritto giurisprudenziale*, Milano 1975, p. 28, who claims that *utilitas publica* should be understood rather in the empirical sense of opportunity and experience than in the ideal sense of common good or social justice. Rampazzo writes that the jurisprudence uses the category under study to achieve practical effects more suited to the needs of the community. See N. Rampazzo, *Quasi praetor…*, p. 492.

Assuming that the operational style of Roman jurists leaned more towards the jurisprudence of interests (*Interessenjurisprudenz*) rather than to the jurisprudence of concepts (*Begriffsjurisprudenz*)[24], he concluded that these decisions had been a manifestation of the legal method[25], which he described as pragmatism. According to him, in cases where logical and practical arguments led to the same results, preference was given to the former. However, when there was a discrepancy between logic and practice, the latter prevailed[26]. *Utilitatis causa* decisions were supposed to exemplify this approach, where the reference to the criterion under study could either indicate the reason for a decision, or serve as an argument for its acceptance[27]. In the first case, the decision fell within the realm of *ius receptum* – law universally accepted by jurists – while in the second, it reflected divergent juristic opinions and ongoing debates (*ius controversum*[28]).

24 These methods are the result of reflection of German civil lawyers in the 19th and early 20th centuries. In accordance with the assumptions of *Begriffsjurisprudenz*, a mathematical and logical way of thinking was promoted, aiming to define terms so precisely that decisions could be derived from them through deduction. *Interessenjurisprudenz*, on the other hand, sought practical solutions. In each legal relationship it was therefore necessary to establish the interests of the parties, and only then to decide whether the norm was applicable or not. On the basis of the Roman law, attempts to apply these methods as well by Seidl, as discussed below. Cf. E. Seidl, *Moderne zivilrechtliche Lehren als Erkenntnismittel der Rechtsgeschichte* [in:] *Das deutsche Privatrecht in der Mitte des 20. Jahrhunderts. Festschrift für Heinrich Lehmann zum 80. Geburtstag*, H. C. Nipperdey (ed.), Berlin 1956, pp. 97–112; Idem, *War Begriffsjurisprudenz die Methode der Römer?*, 'Archiv für Rechts- und Sozialphilosophie' 1957, vol. 43, no. 3, pp. 343–366. See also F. Schwarz, *Begriffsanwendung…*, pp. 193–215. Kaser was against transferring these concepts to the Roman context. See M. Kaser, *Das römische Privatrecht…*, p. 212.

25 H. Ankum, *The functions...*, pp. 2–6. This is also confirmed by the titles of the works. However, given the difference in the number of the noun ('*Utilitatis causa receptum*: sur la méthode pragmatique des juristes romains classiques' and '*Utilitatis causa receptum*. On the pragmatical methods of the Roman lawyers'), it is difficult to say whether Ankum ultimately meant a method or methods.

26 Ankum aligns closely with the views of Rudolf von Jhering, one of the most prominent representatives of the jurisprudence of interests. Cf. R. von Jhering, *Geist des römischen Rechts auf den verschiedenen Stufen seiner Entwicklung. Zweiter Theil*, Leipzig 1875, pp. 386–387, n. 528a: *die Jurisprudenz an hand der ratio iuris überall so weit vorschreiten soll, bis die utilitas in den Weg tritt und Protest einlegt* ('jurisprudence should develop on the basis of the *ratio iuris* everywhere until *utilitas* stands in the way and protests'). Jhering juxtaposes the terms *utilitas* and *ratio iuris* with each other and translates the former as *das praktische Bedürfnis* ('pracitical need', pp. 337, 365) and the latter as *das allgemeine Princip* ('general rule'; p. 337) or *die juristischen Consequenz oder Nothwendigkeit* ('legal consequence or necessity'; p. 365). See also T. Wischmeyer, *Zwecke im Recht des Verfassungsstaates: Geschichte und Theorie einer juristischen Denkfigur*, Freiburg 2015, p. 84.

27 In the first two studies by Ankum, this statement was the conclusion of the research. In the later ones, however, it was the starting point for a dispute with Navarra. See H. Ankum, *'Utilitatis causa receptum'. On the pragmatical methods…*, p. 28; Idem, *'Utilitatis causa receptum': sur la méthode pragmatique…*, p. 132; Idem, *The functions of expressions with utilitatis causa….*, p. 6; Idem, *Utilitatis causa en los trabajos…*, p. 1122. Alan Watson also shared a similar perspective on this view, *Narrow, Rigid and Literal Interpretation in the Later Roman Republic*, 'TR' 1969, vol. 37, p. 368.

28 See e. g. M. Bretone, *Ius controversum nella giurisprudenza classica*, 'Atti della Accademia Nazionale dei Lincei, Classe di Scienze Morali, Storiche e Filologiche' 2008, ser. 9, vol. 23, fasc. 3, pp. 755–879. Polish voice on that issue in P. Święcicka, *Prawo jurysprudencyjne jako prawniczy dyskurs argumentacyjny (zarys problematyki)*, 'ZP' 2011, vol. 11, no. 1, pp. 317–338.

This perspective, however, was not without its critics. Walter Selb opposed the characterization of pragmatism as a method underlying the renunciation of the system, proportion, and logic[29]. Leptien shared a partially similar perspective, contending that understanding the term *utilitatis causa* solely through such prism would exclude decisions aimed at implementing ethical values[30]. In essence, he accused Ankum's perspective of what Adam Szpunar, Polish civilian, regarded twenty years before him as the Achilles heel of jurisprudence of interests, describing this approach as follows: 'in the law, the teleological direction has undoubtedly fallen into one-sidedness, leading to a utilitarian view that forgets about the highest tasks of the law'[31]. So, while Leptien considered the category of *utilitas* to be pragmatic in its nature[32], he defined the *utilitatis causa* decisions somewhat differently than Ankum, referring to them as *Zweckmäßigkeitsentscheidungen/Zweckmäßigkeitsgründen,* namely decisions taken for teleological reasons[33]. According to him, these decisions were shaped to meet the requirements of practice, economy, society, as well as the world of values[34], and only as such did they justify deviating from a given rule.

A further distinction between the views of Ankum and Leptien on *utilitatis causa* decisions is that the former claimed that jurists were satisfied with the practical motive to justify their decisions, while the latter argued that they also needed a 'legal', namely dogmatic justification for their decisions. Leptien opined that *utilitas* was invoked to justify decisions that were more lenient than what would strictly adhere to binding legal rules, and he argued that for such a decision to be made, a solid dogmatic foundation should exist, preferably bolstered by other jurists' opinions. Thus, the reference to *utilitas* could not constitute the decision's foundation but rather served as an auxiliary instrument of legal argumentation[35]. He also claimed that one could refer *ad utilitatem,* as he put it somewhat enigmatically, 'in order to justify the interpretatively risky application of the written law' (*um eine auslegerisch riskante Anwendung des geschriebenen Rechts zu begründen*). However, he stated this phenomenon was rare due to the limited participation of statutory acts in the creation of the Roman legal order[36].

29 W. Selb, *Symbolae iuridicae et historicae Martino David dedicatae. Ediderunt J. A. Ankum, R. Feenstra, W. F. Leemans. Tomus primus: Ius Romanum. Tomus alter: Iura Orientis Antiqui* [review], 'ZSS RA' 1970, vol. 87, no. 1, p. 550.

30 U. Leptien, *'Utilitatis causa'...*, p. 62, n. 61. J. F. Stagl also claims that Ankum overestimated the practical aspect of the decisions, *Die Funktionen...*, p. 522, n. 60.

31 A. Szpunar, *Nadużycie prawa podmiotowego*, Kraków 1947, p. 6.

32 U. Leptien, *Utilitatis causa ...*, p. 235: *bedeutet utilitas nichts anderes und nicht mehr als Zweckmäßigkeit, Nützlichkeit oder Nutzen* ('*utilitas* does not mean anything else and nothing more than purposefulness, usefulness or benefit').

33 Similarly F. Schwarz, *Begriffsanwendung...*, p. 197, who translated this term as *Zweckmäßigkeitsgedanke* ('teleological thought').

34 U. Leptien, *Utilitatis causa...*, p. 241; Idem, *'Utilitatis causa'...*, p. 72.

35 Idem, *Utilitatis causa*, pp. 18, 19, 239; Idem, *'Utilitatis causa'...*, pp. 63–72.

36 Ibid., pp. 52–53.

As per Kaser[37], *utilitatis causa* decisions were to form a kind of a subordinate rule (*die Unterregel*), applicable to particular subgroups of cases and justified by the unique circumstances of each individual case. He employed various descriptions to outline the nature of this category in this context. On the one hand, he characterized it as reflecting a special interest of the individual case (*das Sonderinteresse des Einzelfalls*), allowing for exceptions to principles or general rules[38] if justified. On the other hand, in his extensive article on *ius publicum* and *ius privatum*, where he dedicated significant attention to the concept of *utilitas publica*, he concluded that the use of *utilitas*, representing *utilitas publica* even if the adjective was omitted, indicated a reference to the general principle according to which each regulation should aim to be as useful as possible for social life while remaining fair and in alignment with adopted values[39].

Yet another interpretation was offered by Navarra, who, without further justification, defined *utilitas* as the value underlying the legal order[40], avoiding, nevertheless, ethical connotations with regard to the content of this criterion. Her analyses focus primarily on defining the practical need motivating the introduction of a decision. Thus, her perspective appears to be more case-specific, aligning with Leptien's views and differing from Ankum's vision of *utilitas* as more homogenous. Navarra also saw *utilitatis causa* decisions as more than mere pragmatism reflections. She viewed them as an expression of unification and stabilization tendencies within the legal system[41]. Thus, referring to *utilitas* was to be an expression of the pursuit of systematization and certainty of the applicable law, both for educational purposes and to ensure greater consistency in judicial decisions[42]. According to Navarra, the criterion almost never served as an argument, but indicated a specific legal solution had gained approval among jurists, signifying its transition from *ius controversum* to *ius receptum*[43].

However, as Ankum rightly pointed out, this thesis cannot be upheld, if only for linguistic reasons[44]. While the phrase *utilitatis causa receptum* appears in some sources, there are also passages where the argumentative function of *utilitas* is beyond doubt, whether due to the overall context, or the syntactic construction. For instance, the expression *utilitatis causa* is sometimes accompanied by the *coniugatio periphrastica passiva*. Thus, when Paulus writes that *sententia propter utilitatem contrahentium admit-*

37 M. Kaser, *'Ius publicum'...*, pp. 28, 33.
38 M. Kaser, *Das römische Privatrecht...*, p. 212.
39 M. Kaser, *'Ius publicum'...*, pp. 18–19.
40 M. Navarra, *Ricerche ...*, p. 206 'valori dell'ordinamento, eminente tra i quali l'*utilitas*' ('values of the legal order, among which *utilitas* stands out').
41 This view could have been inspired by a PhD thesis by U. Leptien, *Utilitatis causa...*, p. 232.
42 M. Navarra, *Ricerche ...*, pp. 208–209. See also R. Scevola, *'Utilitas publica', II. Elaborazione ...*, pp. 378–379.
43 M. Navarra, *Ricerche...*, pp. 178–179, 183, 187–188, 207.
44 H. Ankum, *The functions of expressions with utilitatis causa...*, pp. 5–22; Idem, *Utilitatis causa en los trabajos...*, pp. 1121–1132.

tenda est ('the decision should be accepted for the utility of the parties')[45], it means the decision should be accepted but certainly not that it had already gained general acceptance[46]. Thus, this does not allow it to be considered part of *ius receptum*[47].

Certainly, the references to *utilitas* in jurisprudence writings extend beyond the scope of *utilitatis causa* decisions. Hence, Franz Wieacker included *utilitas* to the group of what he referred to as *offene Wertungen*, justifications for decisions that come from outside the legal order. According to him, *utilitas* was the equivalent of purposefulness (*die Zweckmäßigkeit*) and practicality (*die Praktikabilität*), although sometimes it could also carry an ethical message[48]. Tony Honoré also placed *utilitas* in the category of open arguments (*topoi* or *principles*). He viewed it as representing certain social values that, in the absence of any contrary reasons, supported adopting a particular solution, and only occasionally served to justify an exception to the rule[49].

As previously mentioned, Kaser considered *utilitatis causa* decisions as a special group of cases. In his view, *utilitas* (both on its own and with the adjective *publica*[50]), represented the abstract usefulness of the law (*die Nützlichkeit des Rechts*)[51] serving both to justify new legal institutions as well as to give grounds for resolving casuistic problems. In the latter case, *utilitas* paved the way for the correct interpretation according to the usefulness of the decision for the intended political and legal objectives[52].

One of the most critical assessments of *utilitas* was offered by Dieter Nörr. He argued that its meaning sometimes referred to the common good (*das Gemeinwohl*), and sometimes to the individual interest (*das Einzelinteresse*), but it was never more than an 'emotionally charged (empty) formula' – *die emotional geladene* (*Leer-*)*Formel* – serving as an attempt to justify the proposed decisions[53].

This statement may have prompted Thomas Honsell to explore the categories of 'common good' and 'public interest', of which *utilitas publica* was also a lexical expression[54]. He objected to considering it an empty formula, yet he emphasized that it did

45 Paul. D. 20,1,12.

46 This construction may also signal individual support for a proposed decision. Cf. e.g. Ulp. D. 35,3,3,10 (…) *et puto hoc probandum quod Pomponius, utilitatis gratia* ('and I believe that Pomponius' view should be accepted due to *utilitas*').

47 Ankum focused on this problem in two articles, which were a response to Navarra's study. See again H. Ankum, *The functions of expressions with utilitatis causa…*, pp. 5–22; Idem, *Utilitatis causa en los trabajos…*, pp. 1121–1132. Cf. also M.J. García Garrido, *Navarra, M., Ricerche sulla utilitas nel pensiero dei giuristi romani*, 'Iura' 2003, no. 54, p. 292, who found Navarra's hypothesis extremely interesting and equally difficult to prove on the basis of preserved sources.

48 F. Wieacker, *Offene Wertungen bei den römischen Juristen*, 'ZSS RA' 1977, vol. 94, no. 1, esp. pp. 6, 31.

49 A.M. Honoré, *Legal Reasoning in Rome and Today*, 'Cambrian Law Review' 1973, vol. 4, pp. 61, 66.

50 Ibid., pp. 17, 19, 32.

51 M. Kaser, *'Ius publicum'…*, p. 91.

52 Ibid., p. 24.

53 D. Nörr, *Rechtskritik in der Römischen Antike*, München 1974, pp. 136–138.

54 As he writes in *Gemeinwohl…*, p. 94: *Handelt es sich um Leerformeln und Scheinbegründungen?* ('Is it about empty formulas and apparent justifications?').

not represent a single principle under the law, and its content was always context-dependent. He pointed out that the reference *ad utilitatem publicam* could not only justify the deviations from the rules but also the introduction of other legal regulations. It could also serve as an argument for both broad and narrow interpretations. While he attributed to the analyzed category a more explanatory than a decisive role, he saw in it a guiding idea (*der Leitbegriff*) reflecting the method of Roman jurists, which he described, much like Ankum, as pragmatic (*die pragmatische Methode*)[55].

In addition to the aforementioned findings, it is important to highlight the conclusions of Roberto Scevola from his extensive study on *utilitas publica*. He claimed that this category served as a persuasive tool in resolving normative or interpretative conflicts, providing reinforcement for individual solutions, even in cases where their legal foundation might not be entirely definitive or beyond doubt. Furthermore, he highlighted that *utilitas publica* was employed as a means to deviate from ordinary rules, particularly when specific advantages for the imperial authority were at stake[56].

Jakob F. Stagl also presented his views on *utilitas publica*, asserting that it was based on the philosophy of values oriented towards the common good. According to him, it fulfilled three main functions in the area of the law and its application. First, it served to legitimize laws (*leges publicae*). Then, it was invoked to justify the specific *lex publica* for the purpose of its interpretation. Finally, it guided jurists in creating new law, and, as such, it constituted a theory for their method[57]. This statement was a response to Kaser, who argued that classical jurists did not developed any theory of legal reasoning (*die Rechtsfindung*) but were content with a teleological technique (*die zweckgerechten Technik*) in this regard[58].

Erwin Seidl's perspective marks a less frequently mentioned trend in the discussion on *utilitas*. Similar to Ankum, Seidl attempted to relate the methodological directions of the jurisprudence of concepts (*Begriffsjurisprudenz*) and the jurisprudence of interests (*Interessenjurisprudenz*)[59] to the thought of Roman jurists. According to Seidl, it was the thinking in the categories of *Begriffsjurisprudenz* that was to indicate the mainstream developed by Roman jurists. Therefore, referring *ad utilitatem*, representing an objective and context-dependent interest, to justify decisions, fill legal gaps, and define concepts, was rare. In other words, *utilitas* signalled deviations primarily from a certain order of thinking rather than from established rules[60].

Scholars have been particularly intrigued by the fact that references to *utilitas* (and thus *utilitatis causa* decisions) appear predominantly in the works of jurists from the

55 Ibid., esp. pp. 121–137.
56 R. Scevola, *'Utilitas publica', II. Elaborazione…*, p. 372.
57 J. Stagl, *Die Funktionen…*, pp. 514–523; Idem, *Camino…*, pp. 83–102.
58 M. Kaser, *Das römische Privatrecht…*, p. 212.
59 E. Seidl, *Moderne…*, pp. 97–112; Idem, *War Begriffsjurisprudenz…*, pp. 343–366. See also F. Schwarz, *Begriffsanwendung…*, pp. 193–215.
60 E. Seidl, *Moderne…*, pp. 103–112; Idem, *War Begriffsjurisprudenz…*, pp. 365–366.

classical period, especially its later phase. The exact reasons for this phenomenon remain uncertain. As said above, Navarra tried to justify it with attempts to systematize the law[61]. Ankum stated that the classical jurists were simply less 'dogmatic' than *veteres*[62]. Watson contested this view, attributing the lack of references to *utilitas* in Republican jurists' decisions to a small number of surviving records from that period[63]. Jean Gaudemet claimed that the jurists' general tendency to refer to this category resulted from the absolutist tendencies of the Severan dynasty and the shift of the political concept of the state[64]. Honoré, on the other hand, attributed the particular predilection of the Severan jurists for this category to a specific trend or fad[65].

3. Aim and Structure

Building on the existing research, this study addresses the gap in our understanding of *utilitas* by exploring its broader intellectual context and its varying interpretations within and beyond *utilitatis causa* decisions. The primary objective of this work is to delineate the concept of *utilitas* in legal thinking, and its impact on the legal interpretation. In contrast to the prevailing doctrinal approaches, this study seeks to contextualize *utilitas* within a broader intellectual framework by incorporating insights from ancient rhetorical and philosophical thought. The considerations will be drawn from the theses expressed in the subject literature that attempt to explain the nature of these decisions. For this reason, this study adopts a cascading structure guided not only by the need to identify to what extent pure pragmatism, or the teleological approach characterized the interpretations made by Roman jurists, but also by the question whether these categories can comprehensively expound upon the unique character of *utilitatis causa* decisions.

The work begins by defining the semantic scope of the term *utilitas*, and determining whether it conveys only a practical sense, or holds a broader meaning. Following this, the research delves into whether and when *utilitas* can be understood in teleological terms, and whether it relates to a specific method of legal interpretation. Subsequently, the study assesses the prevalence of the *ex utilitate* interpretation. Finally, the role of *utilitas* in the *utilitatis causa* decisions will be examined.

In Chapter One, '*Utilitas*: Terminological and Axiological Aspects', the meanings and contexts in which the term *utilitas* appears in legal sources will be briefly present-

61 M. Navarra, *Ricerche…*, pp. 205–209.

62 H. Ankum, *'Utilitatis causa receptum'. On the pragmatical…*, p. 6–7.

63 A. Watson, *Narrow…*, pp. 367–368.

64 J. Gaudemet, *Utilitas publica*, pp. 464–499. Roberto Scevola also associated this category (complemented with the adjective *publica*) with the ideology of political thought, *'Utilitas publica', II. Elaborazione…*, pp. 381–382.

65 A. M. Honoré, *Legal Reasoning…*, p. 61.

ed. Drawing insights from non-legal sources, this chapter will elucidate the semantic field of the analyzed category, including its interplay with other ethical values, the law, and justice. It will also examine whether the approach to the concept of *utilitas*, as presented in non-legal sources, can be reconciled with the jurisprudence writings.

Chapter Two, '*Utilitas* as a Guideline for Legal Interpretation', situates the examined criterion within the broader landscape of general principles of interpreting the law. In this aspect, attention will be devoted to understanding the relationship between the categories of *utilitas publica* and *utilitas singulorum*. The chapter will delve into jurisprudence writings where *utilitas* is directly invoked in the context of general legal theory, not representing examples of decisions made *utilitatis causa*, including famous Ulp. D. 1,1,1,2[66], Pap. D. 1,1,7,1[67], Paul. D. 1,1,11[68], or Mod. D. 1,3,25[69].

Chapter Three, '*Utilitatis causa* Interpretation', is dedicated to elucidating the essence of *utilitas*, and the rationale behind its nominal references in *utilitatis causa* decisions. This part seeks to determine whether *utilitas* was a unified and unifying criterion, as suggested by Arnaud Paturet[70], or whether the content and nature of the category was always context-dependent. In an attempt to unravel the adversative nature of these decisions, and to highlight their other characteristics, this chapter will contextualize them within the rhetorical theory of legal interpretation, and describe them through the prism of their relation to the initial norm.

Additionally, this study aims to supplement the corpus of *utilitatis causa* decisions. Until now, researchers have mainly focused on sources containing the noun *utilitas*, while often overlooking instances where its derivatives, such as *utilius* (*est*), or (*sententia*) *utilior*, were used in the same function. As each *utilitatis causa* decision tells a unique story, in order to preserve the legibility of the argument the decisions not raising any major interpretation difficulties will be quoted and briefly commented in the Appendix.

66 *Huius studii duae sunt positiones, publicum et privatum. publicum ius est quod ad statum rei Romanae spectat, privatum quod ad singulorum <u>utilitatem</u>: sunt enim quaedam publice <u>utilia</u>, quaedam privatim.*

67 *Ius praetorium est, quod praetores introduxerunt adiuvandi vel supplendi vel corrigendi iuris civilis gratia propter <u>utilitatem</u> publicam.*

68 *Ius pluribus modis dicitur: uno modo, cum id quod semper aequum ac bonum est ius dicitur, ut est ius naturale. altero modo, quod omnibus aut pluribus in quaque civitate <u>utile</u> est, ut est ius civile.*

69 *Nulla iuris ratio aut aequitatis benignitas patitur, ut quae salubriter pro <u>utilitate</u> hominum introducuntur, ea nos duriore interpretatione contra ipsorum commodum producamus ad severitatem.*

70 A. Paturet, *Ulpien D. 1.1.1.2 et la distinction ius publicum–ius privatum*, 'Global Jurist' 2013, vol. 13, no. 2–3, p. 122.

4. Methodology

The source material was selected from the resources of the *Romtext*[71] (legal sources) as well as *Classical Latin Texts*[72] and *Corpus Corporum – repositorium operum Latinorum apud universitatem Turicensem*[73] (non-legal sources) databases. Material selection was based on a lexical criterion, specifically the presence of the term *utilitas* or its derivatives within the content of the source. Synonymous terms and phrases, such as *commodum, (publice) interest,* or *(publice) expedit,* were not included in the analysis, as the aim of this research is to understand the category of *utilitas,* rather than the broader phenomena of 'interest', or 'benefit' in general.

This research employs a combination of legal, literary, and historical methods to thoroughly explore the multifaceted concept of *utilitas*. Given the nature of the *utilitatis causa* decisions, this work employed the formal-dogmatic method. Additionally, the induction method was applied, as it allowed for the generalization of the regularities characteristic of *utilitas,* as well as its fullest possible description. As a *Wortmonografie*[74], this study focuses on a philological analysis of sources, aiming to move beyond the simplistic conclusion that *utilitatis causa* decisions were merely more practical or useful.

One should also note that translating the central term of study itself presents a challenge, especially given the existence of multiple potential meanings that can be attributed to it. These meanings, particularly in the context of legal sources, are briefly explained in Chapter One. In this study, the Latin term is commonly used, and when translation is necessary (especially source translation) the word 'utility', as its English closest equivalent, is employed. This also applied to derivatives such as *utilis,* which is translated as 'useful'. These terms are used interchangeably to convey the same semantic field, although the meaning of the Latin term – as will soon be explained – is broader. When the term *utilitas* is accompanied by adjectives such as *publica* or *communis,* also the nearest English match, that is 'public', or 'common', is used for translation. To convey these concepts the term 'common good' is also used at times.

This research seeks to reconstruct the fragmented reflections of Roman jurists from the classical period, as preserved in the 6th-century *Digest of Justinian*. This effort presents two key challenges. The first is the issue of authenticity, which was addressed using Kaser's methodological assumption, known as the presumption of the authen-

71 The *Romtext* database by Hofrat Dr. Josef Menner was searched with software *Amanuensis V5.0.,* P. Riedlberger, G. Rosenbaum, München 2020. URL: http://www.riedlberger.de/08amanuensis.html. This and other web addresses quoted in the work were checked for availability as of the day 24.09.2024, unless stated otherwise.

72 *Classical Latin Texts.* A Resource Prepared by The Packard Humanities Institute (PHI), 2015. URL: http://latin.packhum.org/.

73 URL: http://mlat.uzh.ch/MLS/.

74 This way on her book in M. Navarra, *Ricerche…*, p. 1.

ticity of the sources[75]. Hence, in cases where there were no obvious doubts about to the originality of the account, it was considered authentic, and therefore free from later alterations[76]. However, a balanced approach was maintained to avoid assuming that there were no textual alterations while also avoiding bitter textual disputes. It is important to note that *utilitatis causa* decisions, which often contradict legal rules, are especially susceptible to being considered interpolated. Not surprisingly, their authenticity has often been questioned[77]. Navarra devoted special attention to this aspect of the *utilitatis causa* decisions, arguing for the classical origin of both the references to the *utilitas* category and, for the most part, the content of the entire accounts[78]. This perspective was also appreciated by Ankum[79], and this study, as it will soon turn out, strongly supports this view.

Another challenge in the field of research on legal thought, especially concerning abstract, ambiguous and potentially axiological concepts, is the so-called *duplices interpretationes*[80]. It can often be shown that the meaning of the source could have been different for a classical jurist than for a Justinian's commission. In these circumstances, it was necessary to subject the text to a critical linguistic and logical analysis and, above all, to attempt to present the analyzed concept in the context of the epoch to which it belonged. Therefore, the analysis of the sources was conducted in accordance with the principle of intersubjectivization of judgments, which involves examining the content of the accounts to reconstruct the meaning of the category within the specific period and circumstances of its creation[81]. Therefore, attempts were made to go beyond the narrative of legal sources and place the analyzed category in a broader cultural and intellectual context, particularly a philosophical and rhetorical one. When interpreting

75 M. Kaser, *Zur Methodologie…*, *passim*. See also W. Bojarski, *Remarks on Textual Reconstruction in Roman Law* [in:] *Le droit romain et le monde contemporain. Mélanges à la mémoire de Henryk Kupiszewski*, W. Wołodkiewicz, M. Zabłocka (ed.), Varsovie 1996, pp. 83–89.

76 Interesting remarks on the interpolationist approach have recently been presented in K. Sorka, *Interpolacje 'Digestów' justyniańskich. Rys historyczno-metodologiczny*, 'Forum Prawnicze' 2017, vol. 43, no. 5, pp. 54–68; Idem, *Veritatem esse quaerendam. Prawda w rzymskim procesie cywilnym*, Kraków 2021, pp. 21–22.

77 See e.g. G. Longo, *Utilitas publica*, pp. 7–71 and M. Bartošek, *Utilitas publica? Utilitas communis? Utilitas omnium?*, [in:] *Collectanea opusculorum ad iuris historiam spectantium Venceslao Vaněček septuagenario ab amicis discipulisque oblata: pocta akademiku Václavu Vaněčkovi k 70. narozeninám*, K. Malý (ed.), Praha 1975, pp. 331–352.

78 *Ricerche…*, *passim*. The author analyzes in this respect each of the quoted decisions, also presenting a research discussion of the context.

79 *Navarra, Marialuisa, Ricerche…*, p. 531. Cf. also reflections in E. Seidl, *Moderne…*, pp. 110–112. T. Honsell also assumed the authenticity of the sources, disregarding the criticism of the interpolations, *Gemeinwohl…* pp. 93–137. As noted in M. Kaser, *'Ius publicum'…*, p. 29, this did not prevent from building a coherent and convincing image of references to the category of common good.

80 A. Berger, *Encyclopedic Dictionary of Roman Law*, Philadelphia 1968, s. v. *duplex interpretatio*.

81 K. Zamorski, *Historia jako przedmiot poznania* [in:] *Przedmiot poznania politologii: podstawy dyscypliny nauki*, R. Skarzyński (ed.), Białystok 2014, pp. 97–99. The Polish researcher derived this principle from Robert Collingwood's thought, see *The Idea of History*, New York 1956.

individual decisions, it was no less important to carry out a palingenetic analysis of the sources. Moreover, the exegesis was sometimes supplemented by observations about the literary composition of the fragment.

At this point it should be noted that to some extent this work can also be classified into the field of the theory and philosophy of the law, just the one that is ancient. Therefore, in its content, and especially in Chapter Three, the terminology suitable for the above-mentioned areas is used. Although these are neither terms nor ancient categories[82], they made it possible to illustrate the subtleties of the category under study, and to resolve doubts as to its nature arising from earlier works. The use of modern terminology also enabled for proposing an alternative categorization of source texts[83].

In order to clarify the role of *utilitas*, this study examines both the starting point and the outcomes of jurists' interpretations. It also explores the relationship between these decisions and the rules from which they deviate, as well as their impact on the broader landscape of permitted, prescribed, and prohibited behaviors. However, adhering to the principle of William Ockham, this study does not intend to multiply entities without necessity. Since the *utilitatis causa* decisions have already been extensively analyzed, often with convergent conclusions, they were discussed primarily in terms of their significance for delineating the role of *utilitas* within the context of interpreting the law. Consequently, the reasons for deviating from a specific legal rule may, at times, remain unanswered in this study.

The excerpts quoted from the *Digest of Justinian* are from the Theodor Mommsen's and Paul Krüger's edition[84]. Minor editorial changes, such as punctuation and text capitalization, were made when necessary. The translations were placed right after the Latin or Greek excerpt[85], even if the translation choices are explained only on the following pages. While this approach may, to some extent, shape the reader's percep-

82 Previously, a similar reservation was made also in relation to the concept of a 'legal norm'.

83 The objective criterion adopted by Ankum and partially by Leptien only proves that the analyzed type of decisions can be found across all areas of the law. The approach proposed by Navarra seems to be no more effective. Due to the nature of the research, the Italian researcher was right not to treat jurisprudence as a monolith and began by dividing the sources according to the authors of decisions, assuming that the personalities of individual jurists could have influenced the way they referred to *utilitas*. However, it is difficult to justify the division proposed by the researcher according to the stylistic criterion, and categorization of fragments according to the synonymous phrases of *utilitatis causa, propter utilitatem* and *utilitatis gratia*. Cf. M. Navarra, *Ricerche…*, p. 14. A. Watson, K. Abou El Fadl, *Fox Hunting, Pheasant Shooting and Comparative Law*, 'The American Journal of Comparative Law' 2000, vol. 48, p. 20, also seem to attach greater importance to such categorization.

84 *Digesta Iustiniani Augusti*, vol. 1 and 2, Th. Mommsen, P. Krüger (ed.), Berolini 1870.

85 This is a tactic dictated by the observations presented in my short paper, *Tłumaczenie niezbędne? Garść uwag na temat języka łacińskiego w świecie polskiej romanistyki prawniczej* [in:] *Translatoryka i Translacje. Przekład w XXI wieku: wyzwania, możliwości, trendy*, Ł.J. Berezowski (ed.), Łódź 2020, pp. 31–38. For the convenience of the reader, it is also used when the same source is quoted again. At that time, however, the translation is placed in the footnote.

tion of the content of the source, any interpretation challenges within the text are thoroughly addressed, accompanied by an explanation of the translation choices. In the original Polish version of this work, prepared as a PhD thesis, the source translations are the author's own, unless otherwise stated. The English version, along with the sources, was translated by Dagmara Łata. The high quality of her work rendered unnecessary the pursuit of alternative translations. However, for comprehensive reference, a list of all translations into Polish used in the preparation of this work is included in the References.

1
Utilitas: Terminological and Axiological Aspects

1.1 *Utilitas* as an Ambiguous Concept

To understand the concept of *utilitas* in a legal context, it is essential to begin with a clear distinction between its various meanings in ancient thought. This section aims to unravel the complex meanings behind the Roman concept of *utilitas* and explore its multifaceted role in legal, economic, and ethical thought.

In *A Latin Dictionary* and the *Oxford Latin Dictionary*, under the entry *utilitas,* one can find terms such as 'use', 'usefulness', 'utility', 'serviceableness', 'service', 'expediency', 'benefit', 'profit', 'advantage', 'the quality or condition of being useful or advantageous', 'the interest', '(practical) convenience', 'validity', or 'effectiveness'[86]. Janusz Sondel, in his *Polish-Latin Dictionary for Lawyers and Legal Historians,* further extends this list to include the categories of 'good', 'value', 'righteousness' and 'appropriateness'[87]. Similarly, Marian Plezia, a Polish classicist, explicates the meaning of the adjective *utilis* as 'based on analogy, or on common sense in the absence of a relevant legal provision'[88]. Thus, it becomes immediately apparent that limiting *utilitas* to mere pragmatism or solely to material and economic utility would be an oversimplification[89].

86 *A Latin Dictionary,* C.T. Lewis, C. Short (ed.), Oxford 1917, p. 1946, s.v. *utilitas*; OLD, P.G.W. Glare (ed.), Oxford 1968, p. 2218, s.v. *utilitas*. Bartošek suggests that while the term *utilitas* is quite clear on its own, it gains more nuanced meanings when combined with adjectives such as *publica* or *communis, Utilitas publica?…,* p. 335. Further discussion on these concepts will be provided later.

87 J. Sondel, *Słownik łacińsko-polski dla prawników i historyków,* Kraków 2006, p. 972, s.v. *utilitas.*

88 M. Plezia (ed.) *Słownik łacińsko-polski,* vol. 5, Warszawa 2007, p. 510, s.v. *utilis* (*oitilis*). Cf. also OLD and *A Latin Dictionary,* s.v. *utilis.*

89 Conceptually, *utilitas* is associated with terms that are mostly economic in tone. Among synonymous terms, there are such expressions as: *beneficium* ('benefit', 'favor'), *fructus* ('fruits', 'harvest', 'the right to use benefits', 'use', 'getting benefits, 'income', 'profit', 'gain', 'advantage', 'reward', but also 'satisfaction', 'pleasure', 'gratification'), *id, quod interest* ('what brings benefits'), *lucrum* ('benefit', 'profit', and even 'greed', 'pursuit of profit', 'greed of profit'), *manubiae* ('loot, 'plunder', and metaphorically 'benefit', 'gain'), *praemium* ('loot', 'plunder', 'benefit', 'reward'), *praeda* ('loot', 'plunder', 'benefit', 'gain', and even 'theft' and 'illegal benefit'), *profectus* ('profit', 'gain'). It is not without rea-

The ambiguity inherent in the term *utilitas* made it a versatile concept, adaptable to the multifaceted needs of Roman legal reality[90]. In legal sources, *utilitas* takes on both abstract and concrete meanings, varying according to the specific context. It is often employed in relation to granting special protection to certain groups or individuals, including pupils (*utilitas pupillorum*[91]), minors (*utilitas impuberum*[92]), the mentally ill (*utilitas furiosum*[93]), or those receiving gratuitous gains (*utilitas alimentarii*[94]). It also appears in relation to protecting the interests of the parties in a dispute (*utilitas litigantium*[95], *utilitas absentium*[96]), including economic ones[97]. Similarly, the sources mention the benefits of other entities, such as *provincia*[98], *civitas*[99], or *annona*[100]. Finally, the term *utilitas publica* is also invoked in the context of protecting public places[101].

son that among the synonyms of the term *utilitas* one can point out to *bonum* ('profit', 'property', but also 'good', 'virtue', 'advantage', 'benevolence', 'grace', 'prosperity'), *commoditas* ('profit', 'benefit', and also 'facilitation', 'convenience', 'relevance', 'proportionality') and *commodum* ('benefit', 'profit', 'interest', 'convenience', 'reward', as well as 'good' and 'luck'), *habilitas* ('utility', 'relevance', 'ability'), *idoneitas* ('ability', 'utility', 'skilfulness', 'righteousness', 'reliability'), *expedientia* ('profit') and *expedimentum* ('problem solving', 'explanation'), coming from the verb *expedire* meaning among others 'be useful', 'be beneficial', 'be profitable', 'serve someone', *opportunitas* ('profit', 'benefit', 'need', but also ' convenience', 'possibility'), and even *ratio*, which can also mean 'profit' or 'interest' but explicitly implies rational mindset as well as *salus* ('safety, prosperity'). Cf. LTL, s.v. *expedientia, utilitas*; F. Wagner, *Lexicon Latinum*, Brugis 1878, p. 709, s.v. *utilitas*; in the context of the term *salus* see in particular *Deutsch-lateinisches Lexikon: aus den römischen Classikern zusammengetragen und nach den besten neuern Hülfsmitteln bearbeitet*, F.K. Kraft (ed.), Leipzig-Merseburg 1829, p. 1018, s.v. *Gemeinwohl*.

90 An alternative presentation of the contexts in which *utilitas* appears in jurisprudential sources was recently provided by D. Mantovani, *Giuristi romani e storia dell'economia antica. Elementi per una dialettica* [in:] *Il diritto allo stato puro? Le fonti giuridiche romane come documento della società antica*, C. Buzzacchi, I. Fargnoli (ed.), Milano 2021, pp. 182–207. Also, Rampazzo recently presented a concise thematic division of the examples in which *utilitas* occurs, along with a brief commentary, *Quasi praetor...*, pp. 507–521.

91 See e.g. Macer D. 1,21,4,pr.; Ulp. D. 12,3,4; Paul. D. 15,4,2,pr.; Tryph. D. 26,3,10; Ulp. D. 26,7,9,9; Paul. D. 26,7,12,1; Paul. D. 26,7,22; Aquila D. 26,7,34; Tryph. D. 26,7,54; Tryph. D. 27,1,45,4; Ulp. D. 27,4,1,6; Ulp. D. 27,4,3,pr.; Ulp. D. 27,9,5,10; Ulp. D. 29,2,42,pr.; Paul. D. 34,9,5,2. The examples quoted here and below are for illustrative purposes and may not be exhaustive. They are mainly based on the sources that use the *utilitas* noun and sometimes only its derivatives.

92 Ulp. D. 26,7,3,pr.; Paul. D. 27,10,11; Gai. D. 27,10,17.

93 Pap. D. 26,7,39,3.

94 Ulp. D. 2,15,8,24.

95 Ulp. D. 2,12,7; Paul. D. 50,16,81.

96 Ulp. D. 3,5,1.

97 Ulp. D. 10,4,9,8; Paul. D. 10,4,10; Ulp. D. 13,4,2,pr.; Ulp. D. 13,4,2,8.

98 Ulp. D. 1,16,10,pr.

99 Ulp. D. 12,1,27.

100 Marcian. D. 48,2,13; Papir. D. 48,12,3,1; Paul. D. 48,19,37 = P.S. 1,20a.

101 Paul. D. 43,1,2,1; Ulp. D. 43,8,2,2; Ulp. D. 43,8,2,44; Ulp. D. 43,9,1,1; Ulp. D. 43,23,1,7. See also R. Scevola, *'Utilitas publica', II. Elaborazione...*, pp. 75–180. In Polish literature, numerous studies on this issue were presented by R. Kamińska, *Ochrona dróg i rzek publicznych w prawie rzymskim w okresie Republiki i Pryncypatu*, Warszawa 2010; Eadem, *Organizacja 'cura urbis' w Rzymie w początkach Pryncypatu*, 'ZP' 2013, vol. 13, no. 1, pp. 73–95; Eadem, *W trosce o miasto. 'Cura urbis' w okresie Republiki*

Economic transactions were another domain were *utilitas* played a crucial role[102]. The sources mention concepts like *utilitas contrahentium*[103] representing the economic benefits that parties, or one of them, were entitled to, and at the same time establishing limits of liability for damages. Within this context, the benefits of the buyer (*utilitas emptoris*[104]), seller (*utilitas venditoris*[105]), lender (*utilitas commodantis*[106]), or creditor (*utilitas creditoris*[107]) are also mentioned. As part of the economic advantage, in addition to the generally understood profit[108], the following categories can be listed: *utilitas hereditatis*[109], *utilitas peculii*[110], *utilitas* brought by the land[111], or even the value of a slave[112].

i Pryncypatu, Warszawa 2015, pp. 73–95; Eadem, *Ochrona miejsc świętych w prawie rzymskim*, 'ZP' 2016, vol. 12, no. 1, pp. 79–93; Eadem, *Ochrona dróg publicznych przez urzędników rzymskich*, 'ZP' 2017, vol. 8, no. 2, pp. 75–96.

102 Paul. D. 14,3,17,2.

103 See S. Tafaro, *Regula e ius antiquum in D.50.17.23. Ricerche sulla responsabilità contrattuale*, Bari 1984, esp. pp. 123–131 and 215–218; M. Navarra, *'Utilitas contrahentium' e sinallagma* [in:] *La compravendita e l'interdipendenza delle obbligazioni nel diritto romano*, vol. 2, L. Garofalo (ed.), Padova 2007, pp. 225–255; L. Maganzani, *Il principio dell'utilitas contrahentium e il suo superamento nell'età del giusnaturalismo* [in:] *'Fides Humanitas Ius'. Studii L. Labruna*, vol. 5, C. Cascione, C. Masi Doria (ed.), Napoli 2007, pp. 3087–3095; G. Santucci, *'Utilitas contrahentium'. Note minime su una 'regula' che 'cacciata dalla porta rientrò dalla finestra'* [in:] *Modelli teorici e metodologici nella storia del diritto privato*, vol. 3, R. Fiori (ed.), Napoli 2008, pp. 277–312; B. Varonese, *L'utilitas contrahentium nei contratti reali gratuiti in diritto romano classico: un modello di responsabilità*, Padova 2012 (PhD thesis available online at: http://paduaresearch.cab.unipd.it/4367/1/Tesi_PDF_unita.pdf); B.L.C. Carrá, *Utilitas contrahentium: um princípio de responsabilidade civil romano para uma sociedade globalizada?*, 'Revista de Direito Civil Contemporâneo' 2016, vol. 3, no. 8, pp. 139–166. See also Ulp. D. 19,5,17,2; Paul. D. 20,1,12.

104 Paul. D. 19,1,21,3. Ulpian speaks in the same vein in D. 1,3,13, which is an excerpt of a commentary to the curule aedile's edict. While this passage is often interpreted in the context of general norms and law-making activity, Giuseppe Falcone offers a very convincing different interpretation in *D. 1.3.13 Pedio, Ulpiano e la 'lex contractus'*, 'Labeo' 1997, vol. 43, no. 2, pp. 240–258.

105 Pomp. D. 18,2,5; Ulp. D. 19,1,11,18.

106 Afr. D. 47,2,62(61),6.

107 Ulp. D. 43,4,1,5. See also Paul. D. 9,2,22.

108 Ulp. D. 13,4,4,pr.; Paul. D. 35,1,84; Pap. D. 35,2,5; Paul. D. 35,2,63,pr.; Ulp. D. 39,2,4,7; Ulp. D. 43,16,1,41.

109 Ulp. D. 5,3,20,pr.

110 Pap. D. 46,3,94,3.

111 Paul. D. 10,1,4,1; Ulp. D. 13,4,2,2. In a broader context Ner. D. 43,20,6.

112 Paul. D. 11,3,6.

Utilitas also indicated the general usefulness of things, or factual or legal status for a given individual or entity, usually in relation to a specific purpose[113]. For instance,

113 Since this category is relatively broad, quoting the content of the sources or their excerpts seems particularly useful at this point. See e. g. Ulp. D. 13,5,3,2 (…) *quam sententiam non invitus probarem: habet enim utilitatem, ut ex die obligatus constituendo se eadem die soluturum teneatur*; Ulp. D. 15,3,3,4 *Sed si mutua pecunia accepta domum dominicam exornavit tectoriis et quibusdam aliis, quae magis ad voluptatem pertinent quam ad utilitatem, non videtur versum, quia nec procurator haec imputaret, nisi forte mandatum domini aut voluntatem habuit* (…); Paul. D. 18,1,1,pr. *Origo emendi vendendique a permutationibus coepit. olim enim non ita erat nummus neque aliud merx, aliud pretium vocabatur, sed unusquisque secundum necessitatem temporum ac rerum utilibus inutilia permutabat, quando plerumque evenit, ut quod alteri superest alteri desit* (…); Ulp. D. 21,1,38,7 *Sed enim sunt quaedam, quae in hominibus quidem morbum faciunt, in iumentis non adeo: ut puta si mulus castratus est, neque morbi neque vitii quid habere videtur, quia neque de fortitudine quid eius detrahitur neque de utilitate, cum ad generandum numquam sit habilis* (…); Pap. D. 33,1,10,3 (…) *sumptus iumentorum non debebitur, quem actori domina praestare solita fuit utilitatis suae causa* (…); Ulp. D. 34,2,25,10 *Ornamenta muliebria sunt, quibus mulier ornatur, veluti inaures armillae viriolae anuli praeter signatorios et omnia, quae ad aliam rem nullam parantur, nisi corporis ornandi causa: quo ex numero etiam haec sunt: aurum gemmae lapilli, quia aliam nullam in se utilitatem habent* (…); Paul. D. 34,3,25 (…) *contra autem si debitor creditori leget, nullam utilitatem video, si sine quantitate leget* (…); Ulp. D. 38,15,2,3 *Si praeses provinciae in proxima fuit civitate, accedere debet ad utilitatem temporis ratio itineris, scilicet numeratione viginti milium passuum facta* (…); Ulp. D. 39,1,5,17 (…) *habet autem hoc remedium utilitatem* (…); Ulp. D. 39,2,7,2 (…) *respondit, si dominus aedium, quae ruerunt, vellet tollere, non aliter permittendum, quam ut omnia, id est et quae inutilia essent, auferret, nec solum de futuro, sed et de praeterito damno cavere eum debere* (…); Ulp. D. 43,13,1,7 *Sed et si alia utilitas vertatur eius, qui quid in flumine publico fecit (pone enim grande damnum flumen ei dare solitum, praedia eius depopulari), si forte aggeres vel quam aliam munitionem adhibuit, ut agrum suum tueretur eaque res cursum fluminis ad aliquid immutavit, cur ei non consulatur? plerosque scio prorsus flumina avertisse alveosque mutasse, dum praediis suis consulunt. oportet enim in huiusmodi rebus utilitatem et tutelam facientis spectari, sine iniuria utique accolarum*; Ulp. D. 43,15,1,1 *Ripas fluminum publicorum reficere munire utilissimum est* (…); Ven. D. 43,19,4,pr. *Veteres nominatim adiciebant, ut ea quoque, quae ad refectionem utilia essent, adportandi vis non fieret* (…), Ulp. D. 43,21,1,11 (…) *ego ceteros quidem impune prohiberi puto: at enim eum, qui operiat apertum vel contra, eum non puto prohibendum, nisi si quam maiorem utilitatem suam adversarius ostendat*; Ulp. D. 43,21,3,pr. (…) *ego et in specu contra, si non maior utilitas versetur adversarii*; Ulp. D. 45,1,81,1 *Si procurator sisti aliquem sine poena stipulatus sit, potest defendi non suam, sed eius, cuius negotium gessit, utilitatem in ea re deduxisse* (…); Ulp. D. 47,3,1,1 *Tigni autem appellatione continetur omnis materia, ex qua aedificium constet, vineaeque necessaria. unde quidam aiunt tegulam quoque et lapidem et testam ceteraque, si qua aedificiis sunt utilia (tigna enim a tegendo dicta sunt), hoc amplius et calcem et harenam tignorum appellatione contineri* (…); Ulp. D. 48,20,6 (…) *quod perquam nimiae diligentiae est, cum sufficiat, si quis non in usus proprios verterit, sed ad utilitatem officii patiatur deservire*; Paul. D. 49,14,47,1 (…) *hoc iniquum et inutile fisco videbatur, ut tamen suo periculo ipse eos quibus locaverat conveniret* (…); Ulp. D. 50,2,3,2 (…) *cessantibus vero his etiam spurii ad decurionatum et re et vita honesta recipientur: quod utique non sordi erit ordini, cum ex utilitate eius sit semper ordinem plenum habere*; Ulp. D. 50,4,3,5 *Quod pater non consensit honoribus sive muneribus filii, ne illius patrimonium oneri subiciatur, praestat defensionem, non civem patriae utilitatibus quatenus potest aufert*; Arcad. D. 50,4,18,11 (…) *hos ex albi ordine liberari, nisi sola laesi et inutilis corporis et infirmitate, specialiter sit expressum*; Ulp. D. 50,16,183 *'Tabernae' appellatio declarat omne utile ad habitandum aedificium, non ex eo quod tabulis cluditur*; Iav. D. 50,16,242,pr. *Malum navis esse partem, artemonem autem non esse Labeo ait, quia pleraeque naves sine malo inutiles essent, ideoque pars navis habetur* (…).

the sources mention things useful to the public and individuals[114], to the owner (*utiles domino*[115]), or to the land[116], utility of servitude (*utilitas servitutis*[117]), useful expenses (*impensae utiles*[118]), utility of pledge (*utilitas pignorum*[119]), and commodate (*utilitas commodati*[120]). Marcianus also discusses the category of *utilitas* in the context of statues and paintings being a subject of legacy, highlighting their potential usefulness when placed appropriately[121].

Utilitas also appears in strictly technical contexts. This category includes the concept of *tempus utile,* denoting the time during which a given entity could pursue their legal purpose – a timeframe that operates only within the legal reality and, unlike *tempus continuum,* is purely subjective[122]. Another significant category is the procedural protection measures derived from *utilitas,* with a central role played by *actiones utiles*[123]. These actions, created by the praetor or other jurisdiction-exercising officials through modifications to existing formulas, aimed to rectify situations not covered by the original ones[124]. *Actiones utiles* also encompass *actiones ficticiae,* namely actions adapted to situations not covered by the existing formula through legal fictions. In such cases an

114 Paul. D. 9,2,33,pr. (…) *Sextus quoque Pedius ait pretia rerum non ex affectione nec utilitate singulorum, sed communiter fungi* (…); Ulp. D. 38,17,2,44 (…) *nisi forte quis putet condicionem hanc quasi utilitati publicae obpugnantem remittendam* (…); Paul. D. 39,4,9,5 = P.S. 5,1a,6 (…) *alterum enim utilitas privatorum, alterum vigor publicae disciplinae postulat*; Ulp. D. 43,8,2,2 *Et tam publicis utilitatibus quam privatorum per hoc prospicitur* (…); Ulp. D. 43,8,2,22; (…) *refectio enim idcirco de communi fit, quia usum utilitatemque communem habet*; Pap. D. 50,5,8,4 *id est si ad publicam utilitatem respiciat rescissio prioris decreti*; Ulp. D. 50,10,5,1 *Fines publicos a privatis detineri non oportet. curabit igitur praeses provinciae, si qui publici sunt, a privatis separare et publicos potius reditus augere: si qua loca publica vel aedificia in usus privatorum invenerit, aestimare, utrumne vindicanda in publicum sint an vectigal eis satius sit imponi, et id, quod utilius rei publicae intellexerit, sequi*; Papir. D. 50,12,13,1 *Item rescripserunt condiciones donationibus adpositas, quae in rem publicam fiunt, ita demum ratas esse, si utilitatis publicae interest.*

115 Ner. D. 2,11,14; Ulp. D. 15,3,5,2. See also Gai. D. 7,1,56, where Gaius uses the expression *proprietas inutilis* and Gai. D. 33,2,8, where the same jurist refers to a similar concept using the phrase *nulla utilitas erit nudae proprietatis.* See also fragment of Pap. D. 47,2,81,1 in the context of *utilitas* of the owner in the event of *actio furti.*

116 Ulp. D. 25,1,3,pr.; Ulp. D. 25,1,3,1.

117 Ulp. D. 7,6,1,4; Lab. D. 8,1,16; Paul. D. 8,5,5.

118 Paul. D. 5,3,38; Iav. D. 23,5,18,pr.; Ulp. D. 25,1,1,pr.; Ulp. D. 25,1,5,3; Ulp. D. 25,1,7; Paul. D. 25,1,8; Paul. D. 25,1,10; Iul. D. 39,6,14; Paul. D. 50,16,79,1.

119 Ulp. D. 13,5,14,1.

120 Ulp. D. 13,6,5,2–3.

121 Marcian. D. 7,1,41,pr.

122 F.B. Cicala, *Il concetto…*, pp. 23–24.

123 Recently in J.D. Harke, *Actio utilis. Anspruchsanalogie im römischen Recht,* Berlin 2016. See also E. Valiño, *Actiones utiles,* Navarra 1974.

124 On a different note, Santoro asserts that the term *actio utilis* did not always have such a technical meaning. He rightly claims that the term *utilis* can also be understood as being rendered usable in a particular case – in this sense e.g. in G. 3,209. See R. Santoro, *Aspetti formulari della tutela delle convenzioni atipiche,* [in:] *Scritti Minori,* vol. 1, M. Varvaro (ed.), Torino 2009, esp. pp. 362–364; 380–382.

official presumed the existence of certain facts which, by the law, were necessary for the action to be granted[125].

Utilitas was also employed to evaluate actions or behaviors of an entity in relation to a specific economic, social or legal purpose. In this aspect, jurists use the terms like *utiliter agere* or *utiliter negotia gerere*, and a collection of sources dealing with *negotia utilia* is also related to this group. Depending on whether an entity managed to achieve an intended goal of establishing, modifying, or altering a legal relationship, the act could be classified as *negotium utile* or *negotium inutile*[126]. Importantly, this concept appears in the sources not only to define the effectiveness or ineffectiveness of legal acts but frequently serves to express the categories of their validity and invalidity, often also referred to by jurists with the use of verbs *valere* and *non valere*. This group includes activities performed *utiliter* (validly, or effectively) or *inutiliter* (invalidly, or ineffectively), though assigning particular meanings to these expressions is often a matter of interpretation.

Furthermore, *utilitas* often appears in the so-called *laudationes*, namely (pompous) praises of legal acts[127] – especially edicts[128], but also of other legal instruments[129], such as interdicts[130].

Lastly, there are sources that form the core of this study: those in which *utilitas* is situated in the domain of general theory of the law, including dozens of the so-called *utilitatis causa* decisions. This study attempts to determine what could it mean that, as Paulus writes, the *ius civile* was useful for all, or most citizens[131], and what could be

125 More on the issue in F. Mercogliano, *Actiones Ficticiae – Tipologie e Datazione*, Napoli 2001. Presenting just a general list, it should be noted that the same category of procedural protection measures also includes *iudicia utilia, interdicta utilia, exceptiones utiles, petitiones utiles*, and *replicationes utiles*. The sources that include expressions such as *utiliter agere, utiliter actionem experiri, actio utiliter competit, utiliter interdicto agi, utiliter interdici* and *utiliter replicari* should be interpreted in the same manner. Cf. F.B. Cicala, *Il concetto…*, pp. 25–27.

126 More specific examples can also be quoted. In the sources, for instance, one can meet the term *testamentum inutile* (e.g. Gai. D. 28,2,30), but also *legatum utile* or *inutile* (Gai. D. 30,66 and Gai. D. 30,5 respectively; these are only two of a very large number of examples found in Gaius' works), *utile* and *inutile fideicomissum* (e.g. Ulp. D. 30,77 and Valens D. 32,12 respectively), *inutilis substitutio* (e.g. Scaev. D. 36,1,78), *inutilis stipulatio* (e.g. Iul. D. 38,1,24), *inutilis nuntiatio* (e.g. Iul. D. 39,1,2), or *pactum inutile* (e.g. Iul. D. 45,1,56,1).

127 On this issue U. Babusiaux, *Zur Funktion der aequitas naturalis in Ulpians Ediktslaudationen* [in:] *Testi e problemi del giusnaturalismo romano*, D. Mantovani, A. Schiavone (ed.), Pavia 2007, pp. 603–644. See also T. Honsell, *Gemeinwohl…*, pp. 93–137 and M. Kaser, *'Ius publicum'…*, pp. 30–31 along with the literature cited therein.

128 Ulp. D. 3,5,1; Ulp. D. 4,9,1,1; Ulp. D. 9,3,1,1 Ulp. D. 14,1,1,pr.; Ulp. D. 14,4,1,pr.; Ulp. D. 43,8,2,44; Ulp. D. 43,9,1,1; Ulp. D. 47,6,1,pr.; Ulp. D. 47,9,1,1. *Laudationes edicti*, as one can see, were Ulpian's specialty.

129 Ulp. D. 35,1,7,pr., where Ulpian writes about *cautio Muciana*.

130 Paul. D. 43,1,2,1; Ulp. D. 43,3,1,3; Ulp. D. 43,8,2,44; Ulp. D. 43,9,1,1; Ulp. D. 43,18,1,1; Ulp. D. 43,19,3,12; Ulp. D. 43,21,1,1; Ulp. D. 43,22,1,7; Ulp. D. 43,23,1,7; Ven. D. 43,23,2.

131 Paul. D. 1,1,11.

the meaning of the phrase that a given decision was taken *utilitatis causa*, for the sake of *utilitas*.

As noted in Introduction, ongoing academic debate questions whether this category should be understood as purely pragmatic or if its meaning extends beyond pragmatism. Resolving this issue and defining the semantic field of the term cannot rely solely on the works of jurists, as the meaning of *utilitas* in this context cannot be exclusively deduced from jurisprudence sources. It is crucial to note that exploring this concept from a broader perspective is not only possible but also entirely justified. Notably, using *utilitas* as a means to deviate from established rules was not a technique exclusive to jurists. For instance, Cicero wrote that due to *utilitas*, a depositary was exempted from the obligation to return a sum given for safekeeping if the depositor later initiated an armed conflict with the Roman state[132]. Moreover, he recognized that such use of *utilitas* extended beyond civil obligations, allowing for the assassination of a tyrant for the sake of common utility, even if the perpetrator and the victim were friends or relatives[133]. Marcus Fabius Quintilian argued similarly, contending that actions such as murder, even of one's own children, and more serious crimes, could be justified on the grounds of *utilitas communis*[134].

132 Cic., *Off.* 3,25,95 *Ergo et promissa non facienda non numquam, neque semper deposita reddenda. (…) si is, qui apud te pecuniam deposuerit, bellum inferat patriae, reddasne depositum? Non credo; facias enim contra rem publicam, quae debet esse carissima. Sic multa, quae honesta natura videntur esse, temporibus fiunt non honesta; facere promissa, stare conventis, reddere deposita commutata utilitate fiunt non honesta* ('Therefore, promises are not always to be kept, and the object of a deposit is not always to be returned. […] Suppose also that the man who entrusted you with the money proposes to declare war on your country; should you return the deposited property to him? I do not think you should, because you would be acting against the state, which should be the most dearest thing in the world to you. So there are many things that seem morally right in themselves, but with the change of *utilitas* they turn out not to be morally right: keeping a promise, honoring agreements, returning deposited objects may, with a change of *utilitas*, cease to be morally right'). See also Idem, *Off.* 3,6,30. Cf. also G. Jossa, *L''utilitas rei publicae' nel pensiero di Cicerone*, pp. 275–276.

133 Cic., *Off.* 3,4,19 *Saepe enim tempore fit, ut, quod turpe plerumque haberi soleat, inveniatur non esse turpe; exempli causa ponatur aliquid, quod pateat latius: Quod potest maius esse scelus quam non modo hominem, sed etiam familiarem hominem occidere? Num igitur se astrinxit scelere, si qui tyrannum occidit quamvis familiarem? Populo quidem Romano non videtur, qui ex omnibus praeclaris factis illud pulcherrimum existimat. Vicit ergo utilitas honestatem? Immo vero honestas utilitatem secuta est* ('As it often happens, thanks to exceptional circumstances, that what in ordinary circumstances is considered to be morally wrong turns out not to be so. As an illustration, let us take a special case that may have a wider application: what could be a more horrible crime than killing a person, especially a close one? But if someone kills a tyrant – be he even a very close person – then he has not laden his own soul with guilt, has he? The Roman people certainly do not think so, for they consider such a deed to be the noblest of all glorious deeds. So did *utilitas* take precedence over *honestas*? Not at all; *honestas* went hand in hand with *utilitas*'). Cf. also Quint., *Decl. mai.* 274,5.

134 Quint., *Inst.* 12,1,37 *Nam si hominem occidere saepe virtus, liberos necare nonnumquam pulcherrimum est, asperiora quaedam adhuc dictu si communis utilitas exegerit facere conceditur…* ('If it is often a virtuous deed to kill a man, if it is sometimes a very noble deed to kill one's own children, and even if harsher actions are permitted on the basis of *utilitas communis*…').

While such drastic examples are not typically found in jurists' writings, it is easy to notice that they illustrate a similar, if not the same phenomenon, as seen in jurisprudence *utilitatis causa* decisions: the reference to *utilitas* in decisions that constitute exceptions to the rules. Notably, much like *utilitatis causa* decisions, Cicero's references to *utilitas* have led some researchers to conclude that pragmatism was central to his views on justice[135]. The question is whether this conclusion is correct. Fortunately, the meaning of Cicero's or Quintilian's statements is much easier to reconstruct, and this is the reason why non-legal sources are extremely valuable for our considerations. Hence, in the following sub-chapter, selected non-legal sources on the subject of the relationship between the law, justice, and utility will be analyzed. This analysis will help determine whether Cicero and Quintilian referred to the pragmatic category or to a concept with a broader scope of meaning.

1.2 *Utilitas* among Values: Meaning of the Term in Non-Legal Sources

1.2.1 *Utilitas* in Cicero's Writings

For Roman philosophy[136] and its contemplation of *utilitas*, a significant turning point can be precisely pinpointed – a rare occurrence in history. This pivotal moment was the visit of three Athenian ambassadors – and at the same time representatives of various philosophical schools – in Rome in 155 BCE. Their task was to represent Athens before the Roman Senate and to try to reduce the financial penalties imposed on the Greek polis[137]. The delegation included Stoic Diogenes, Peripatetic Critolaus, and Carneades of Carnea, the scholarch of the Platonic Academy. Among them, it was the last one whose two controversial speeches resonated deeply within Roman society. Carneades' primary goal was to demonstrate the relativity of all judgments. On the first day, he spoke about the inseparability of justice and wisdom, while on the following day, he presented completely opposite arguments, highlighting the relationship between justice and stupidity[138]. The premise of his second speech asserted that a universal law

135 This way in G. Jossa, *L''utilitas rei publicae' nel pensiero di Cicerone*, p. 272; J. Gaudemet, *Utilitas publica*, pp. 486. See also E. M. Atkins, *'Domina et Regina Virtutum': Justice and Societas in 'De officiis'*, 'Phronesis' 1990, vol. 35, no. 3, p. 289.

136 It should be emphasized, however, that the following considerations focus on Roman philosophy specifically, not just philosophy in Rome. See G. M. Müller, F. M. Zini, *Philosophie in Rom – Römische Philosophie?, Kultur-, literatur- und philosophiegeschichtliche Perspektiven*, Berlin-Boston 2019, pp. 1–40.

137 See J. G. F. Powell, *The Embassy of the Three Philosophers to Rome in 155 BC* [in:] *Hellenistic Oratory: Continuity and Change*, C. Kremmydas, K. Tempest (ed.), Oxford 2013, pp. 219–248. See also Cic., *De orat.* 2,155–160; Plut., *Cat. Mai.* 22–23; Gell., NA 6,14,8–10.

138 According to Plutarch, this sensational rhetorical show frightened Cato the Elder. Fearing that the philosopher's words might have harmful effects and corrupt the youth, the censor ensured that the

of nature, applicable to all beings, did not exist. According to Carneades, every living creature's natural desire was to pursue the most advantageous state for itself. In his view, the pursuit of natural justice, by considering the interests of others, would lead to self-harm. Consequently, the philosopher posited the existence of primordial competition, negating the idea that justice can be universally recognized[139].

Neither Carneades' arguments nor the subsequent discussion on it could leave Cicero indifferent[140]. With his philosophical background rooted in Stoicism[141], Cicero was not only a philosopher but above all a politically active figure, extending his activities beyond the realm of philosophy and pure theory. He recognized that none of the doctrines of the Greek philosophical schools could fully meet the needs of Roman society. Thus, as Giorgio Jossa noted, Cicero sought to adapt these teachings to the Roman reality, aiming to find a theoretical basis for Roman politics in the wisdom of Greek philosophy. The Roman context, in turn, provided practical confirmation of the views of Greek thinkers[142]. In summarizing the Ciceronian vision of philosophy, Walter Miller assumed that its purpose was not just to impart knowledge but, more impor-

guests left the capital as soon as possible. Cf. Plut., *Cat. Mai.* 22,4.

139 Lact., *Div. Inst.* 5,16,2–3. The lost parts of the *De legibus* manuscript relating to these considerations written by Cicero between 54 and 51 BCE, are reconstructed based on the Lactantius' *Divinae Institutiones* from the early 4th century CE. This procedure should be considered credible, as it does not seem Lactantius had access to other sources dealing with the skeptics' philosophy. It is therefore unlikely that he supplemented Cicero's argument in any way. Cf. J.G.F. Powell, *The Embassy…*, pp. 235–236; J.-L. Ferrary, *Le discours de Philus (Cicéron, De re publica, III, 8–31) et la philosophie de Carnéade*, 'Revue des Études Latines' 1977, vol. 55, pp. 153–155; J. Glucker, *Carneades in Rome: Some Unsolved Problems*, 'Bulletin of the Institute of Classical Studies' 2001, vol. 45, no. 76, p. 71.

140 The same way in A. Steinwenter, *'Utilitas publica…*, p. 88 and G. Longo, *Utilitas publica*, p. 11. In the opinion of some researchers Carneades' *oratio in utramque partem*, as not offering any constructive thought to the Romans, could not in fact make such an impression on them. See W.W. Tarn, *La civilisation hellénistique*, Paris 1936, p. 313; R. Scevola, *'Utilitas publica', I. Emersione…*, p. 312, n. 34. Cicero's contributions to understanding Roman law have long been recognized and continue to inspire researchers. We should fully agree with Wilfried Stroh, who argued that although Cicero was not a jurist, he was certainly a legal thinker of great standing, *Cicero: Redner, Staatsmann, Philosoph*, München 2008, p. 24. The legal perspective on Cicero, for example, in E. Costa, *Cicerone giureconsulto*, Bologna 1927; M. Pallasse, *Cicéron et les sources du droit*, Paris 1946, G. La Bua, *Diritto e retorica: Cicerone iure peritus in Seneca retore e Quintiliano*, 'Ciceroniana on line (Atti del XII Colloquium Tullianum, Salamanca, 7–9 ottobre 2004)' 2006, vol. 12, pp. 181–203; *Cicero's Law: Rethinking Roman Law of the Late Republic*, P.J. du Plessis (ed.), Edinburgh 2016 and J. Zajadło, *Cyceron dla prawników*, Gdańsk 2019.

141 Cicero saw himself as a student of the New Academy rather than a pure Stoic. It should be noted, however, that his reflections were eclectic in nature. For a related discussion, see e.g. D. Kleyn, G. van Niekerk, *Ulpian's praecepta iuris and their role in South African law. Part 1: Historical context*, 'Fundamina: A Journal of Legal History' 2014, vol. 20, no. 1, p. 442 along with the literature cited therein.

142 G. Jossa, *L''utilitas rei publicae' nel pensiero di Cicerone*, p. 272.

tantly, to guide specific actions[143]. Cicero thus infused Greek Stoicism with practical features, making it more accessible to the Roman citizen[144].

Cicero's writings mark the first significant manifestation of Roman reflection on *utilitas*[145]. His most representative work in this context is the three books of the philosophical treatise *De officiis* of 44 BCE, which draws heavily from the ideas of Panaetius of Rhodes[146], an influential figure from Middle Stoicism of the 2nd century BCE. The Greek philosopher's influence is unmistakable, even in the title of Cicero's work, which essentially mirrors the Greek title of Panaetius' treatise: Περὶ τοῦ καθήκοντος[147]. Panaetius structured his work around three fundamental questions. First, what is morally right (τὸ καλόν), and what is not? Second: what is useful (τὸ συμφέρον), and what is not? And finally, how should one act when there is a conflict between these two values? Although Panaetius did not finish his last treatise, the questions he asked served as the foundation for Cicero's *De officiis*, where Latin *honestas* and *utilitas* were the counterparts of Greek τὸ καλόν and τὸ συμφέρον[148].

A good starting point for grasping Cicero's conception of *utilitas* is found in the following passage:

Cic., *Off.* 2,3,9–10
Hoc autem, de quo nunc agimus, id ipsum est, quod "utile" appellatur. In quo verbo lapsa consuetudo deflexit de via sensimque eo deducta est, ut honestatem ab utilitate secernens constitueret esse honestum aliquid, quod utile non esset, et utile, quod non honestum, qua nulla

143 *Introduction* [in:] *Cicero. On Duties*, translated by W. Miller, Cambridge 1913, p. XII. Cf. also G. Jossa, *L'utilitas rei publicae' nel pensiero di Cicerone*, pp. 269–288; W. Nicgorski, *Cicero's Paradoxes and His Idea of Utility*, 'Political Theory' 1984, vol. 12, no. 4, pp. 557–578; K. E. Chang, *The Community, the Individual and the Common Good: 'To Idion' and 'To Sympheron' in the Greco-Roman World and Paul*, London 2013, p. 111.

144 W. Nicgorski, *Cicero's…*, pp. 570–573.

145 According to I. Mastino, in his writings, Cicero quoted the term *utilitas* as many as 352 times, *'Utilitas valuit propter honestatem': Cicerone e il principio giuridico dell'utilitas*, 'Diritto@Storia' 2013, no. 11 (available online at: http://www.dirittoestoria.it/11/D&Innovazione/Mastino-Cicerone-Principio-giuridico-utilitas.htm).

146 On the philosopher in G. Reale, *Storia della filosofia antica. I sistemi dell'età ellenistica*, vol. 3, Milano 1997, pp. 435–446.

147 J. Gaudemet, *Utilitas publica*, p. 468. Some researchers claim that Cicero wrote his treatises *De Re Publica* and *De legibus* inspired by the Plato's dialogues Πολιτεία (Lat. *De re publica*) and Νόμοι (Lat. *De legibus*). Cf. K.E. Chang, *The Community…*, p. 110, n. 3 along with the literature cited therein.

148 A. R. Dyck, *A Commentary on Cicero, De officiis*, Ann Arbor 1996, p. 17, 353–355 and P. G. Walsh, *Introduction* [in:] Cicero, *On Obligations (De officiis)*, translated by P. G. Walsh, Oxford-New York 2000, p. XIX. K.E. Chang holds that the *De officiis* treatise was a kind of textbook in which Cicero intended to provide solutions to the problems caused by the abuse of power, emphasizing the ethical aspects of utility. For the pursuit of one's own glory leads to the downplaying of common good (cf. Cic., *Off.* 1,19,62; 1,24,83). Chang claims that the whole work is, in fact, about *utilitas*, *The Community…*, pp. 112–115.

> *pernicies maior hominum vitae potuit afferri.* 10. (…) *Quicquid enim iustum sit, id etiam utile esse censent, itemque quod honestum, idem iustum; ex quo efficitur, ut, quicquid honestum sit, idem sit utile.*
>
> What we are talking about now is precisely what is called the question of 'utility'. As for the meaning of this word, the erroneous way of understanding deviated from the right path, and slowly led to the fact that, by separating morality from utility, it was established morality was something useless, and utility something morally wrong, which could not do more harm to human life. 10. (…) For whatever is just is also useful; likewise, everything that is morally right is also just, from which it follows that everything that is morally right is thereby useful.

In this passage, clear critical references are made to Carneades' ideas. For Cicero, the knowledge of what is morally right (*honestum*), should be closely linked to its practical application. Similarly, any useful action pursued had to be rooted in an understanding of what was morally right. Therefore, it did not matter whether the evaluation of an action was carried out from the point of view of utility or morality because *honestas* and *utilitas* did not serve as separate evaluating criteria. What was *honestum* was always *utile*, and *vice versa*[149]. The concept of inseparability of *utilitas* and *honestas*, forming a unified guide for righteous conduct, was at the core of Cicero's thinking about the concept of utility[150]. He referred to any discrepancy between these two categories as *utilitatis species*[151], indicating a distortion of true *utilitas*.

149 W. Nicgorski, *Cicero's…*, pp. 561–564; E.M. Atkins, *'Domina et Regina Virtutum'…*, p. 284; R. Scevola, *'Utilitas publica', I. Emersione…*, p. 330. Contrary B. Łapicki, *Etyczna kultura starożytnego Rzymu a wczesne chrześcijaństwo*, Wrocław 1956, pp. 59–60.

150 Due to the multitude of sources, only a few representative examples from the *De officiis* will be given here: Cic., *Off.* 3,3,11 *dubitandum non est quin numquam possit utilitas cum honestate contendere;* 3,4,17 *Quocirca nec id, quod vere honestum est, fas est cum utilis repugnantia comparari;* 3,8,35 *…necesse est, quod honestum sit, id esse aut solum aut summum bonum, quod autem bonum, id certe utile, ita, quicquid honestum, id utile;* 3,10,40 *Itaque utilitas valuit propter honestatem, sine qua ne utilitas quidem esse potuisset;* 3,15,64 *Numquam igitur est utile peccare, quia semper est turpe, et, quia semper est honestum virum bonum esse, semper est utile;* 3,19,77 *nullo modo videri potest quicquam esse utile, quod non honestum sit;* 3,21,83 *Honestate igitur dirigenda utilitas est, et quidem sic, ut haec duo verbo inter se discrepare, re unum sonare videantur;* 3,21,85 *nihil esse utile, quod non honestum sit;* 3,22,87 *Quousque audebunt dicere quicquam utile, quod non honestum?*

151 Cic., *Off.* 3,11,46–47 *Cum igitur id, quod utile videtur in amicitia, cum eo, quod honestum est, comparatur, iaceat utilitatis species, valeat honestas (…) Sed utilitatis specie in republica saepissime peccatur (…) Sed nihil, quod crudele, utile (…) Illa praeclara, in quibus publicae utilitatis species prae honestate contemnitur;* 3,8,35 *Cum igitur aliqua species utilitatis obiecta est, commoveri necesse est. Sed si, cum animum attenderis, turpitudinem videas adiunctam ei rei, quae speciem utilitatis attulerit, tum non utilitas relinquenda est, sed intellegendum, ubi turpitudo sit, ibi utilitatem esse non posse…* Cf. also Cic., *Leg.* 1,15,42 and Liv., AUC 28,42,25 See also J. Gaudemet, *Utilitas publica*, p. 470.

Cicero credited Socrates with establishing this close connection[152]. Importantly, this idea remained relevant even in the 4th century CE, as evidenced by a fragment from a commentary on Cicero's rhetorical treatise *De inventione*[153] by Gaius Marius Victorinus[154], a Latin grammarian and rhetorician. Victorinus explained the passage in which Cicero wrote about the beginnings of human societies, wherein people, previously scattered in fields and forests, were gathered by a wise man, and then introduced by him to the secrets of everything that was useful and morally right (*et eos in unam quamque rem inducens utilem atque honestam*)[155]:

> Mar. Victorin., *Expositio in rhetorica Ciceronis*, GL 5, p. 10, l. 10–12
> *Quod quidem honestum utilitati semper adiunctum est et utilitas honestati. Hoc etiam Socrates ait, nihil esse utile quod non honestum sit, nihil honestum quod non utile sit.*
> For what is morally right is always combined with what is useful, and what is useful with what is morally right. And this is what Socrates claims too: nothing is useful if it is not morally right, and nothing is morally right that is not useful.

Explaining the words of young Cicero, Victorinus affirmed that the inseparability of *utilitas* and *honestas*, had been established in the time of Socrates[156]. Importantly, this fragment demonstrates that this thought persisted across centuries, remaining relevant in the period under study.

152 Cic., *Off.* 3,11,9–10 *dubitandum non est quin numquam possit utilitas cum honestate contendere. Itaque accepimus Socratem exsecrari solitum eos, qui primum haec natura cohaerentia opinione distraxissent* ('there is no doubt that *utilitas* can never be contrary to *honestas*. And as we have heard, Socrates used to curse those who first made the conceptual distinction between things naturally inseparable'). In *De legibus*, the relation *utilitas–honestas* was replaced by the link *utilitas–ius*: Cic., *Leg.* 1,33,10–15 *recteque Socrates exsecrari eum solebat qui primus utilitatem a iure seiunxisset; id enim querebatur caput esse exitiorum omnium* ('Consequently, Socrates was right to curse, as he often did, the man who first separated *utilitas* from the law, because this separation, he claimed, was the root of all evil').

153 *De inventione* is a youth treatise, dated back to 84 or the beginning of 83 BCE. See Cicéron, *De l'invention*, texte établi et trad. par G. Achard, Paris 2002, pp. 5–10; B. Awianowicz, *Wprowadzenie* [in:] *O Inwencji Retorycznej. De inventione*, przekład z języka łacińskiego K. Ekes. Wstęp i przypisy B. Awianowicz, Warszawa 2013, pp. 7–14.

154 On the philosopher in, e. g., P. Hadot, *Marius Victorinus: recherches sur sa vie et ses œuvres*, Paris 1971.

155 Cic., *Inv.* 1,2,2.

156 Cf. again Cic., *Off.* 3,11,9–10.

What also draws attention is that the Ciceronian idea of *utilitas* appears to be rooted in a legal perspective[157]. In the previously cited excerpt from *Off.* 2,3,9–10, Cicero writes not only about the inseparability of *honestum* and *utile* but also about their close connection with what is just, *iustum*. Hence, all useful things assumed the status of morally right and just[158], and it was impossible to juxtapose or separate these values[159]. Cicero emphasized the connection between utility and justice in several other passages[160]:

Cic., *Inv.* 2,53,160
Iustitia est habitus animi communi utilitate conservata suam cuique tribuens dignitatem[161].
Justice is the state of the mind, which, for the sake of safeguarding the common utility, gives everyone their due.

Cic., *Off.* 1,31,7–9
Referri enim decet ad ea, quae posui principio fundamenta iustitiae, primum ut ne cui noceatur, deinde ut communi utilitati serviatur[162].
One should refer to those that I laid down at the beginning as the fundamental principles of justice. Firstly, that no harm was done to anyone. Secondly, that common utility was taken care of.

157 Thomas Honsell similarly writes about *utilitas communis, Gemeinwohl…*, p. 97. Cf. also T. Mayer-Maly, *Gemeinwohl…*, pp. 195–206. See also Cic., *Leg.* 1,33,10–15.

158 Cic., *Phil.* 11,12,28 *Iuppiter ipse sanxit, ut omnia quae rei publicae salutaria essent legitima et iusta haberentur*; Idem, *Off.* 3,22,88 *Potius doceret non esse aequam, quia non esset utilis rei publicae, quam cum utilem diceret non esse, aequam fateretur.*

159 W. Nicgorski, *Cicero's Paradoxes…*, p. 570.

160 He derived this synthesis from the dictates of divine and natural law. Cf. Cic., *Inv* 2,22,65 *Utrisque aut etiam omnibus, si plures ambigent, ius ex quibus rebus constet, considerandum est. Initium ergo eius ab natura ductum videtur; quaedam autem ex utilitatis ratione aut perspicua nobis aut obscura in consuetudinem venisse; post autem approbata quaedam a consuetudine aut vero utilia visa legibus esse firmata;* 2,53,160 *Iustitia est habitus animi communi utilitate conservata suam cuique tribuens dignitatem. Eius initium est ab natura profectum; deinde quaedam in consuetudinem ex utilitatis ratione venerunt; postea res et ab natura profectas, et ab consuetudine probatas legum metus et religio sanxit;* Idem, *Off.* 3,6,30–31 *Communis utilitatis derelictio contra naturam est; est enim iniusta. Itaque lex ipsa naturae, quae utilitatem hominum conservat et continet (…) semper officio fungetur utilitati consulens hominum et ei, quam saepe commemoro, humanae societati*; Idem, *Phil.* 11,12,28 *Iuppiter ipse sanxit, ut omnia quae rei publicae salutaria essent legitima et iusta haberentur.*

161 Cf. also *Rhet. ad Heren.* 3,2,3 *Iustitia est aequitas ius unicuique rei tribuens pro dignitate cuiusque.* At this point, it should be recalled that both textbooks, namely *De inventione* and *Rhetorica ad Herennium*, were long attributed to Cicero as they show numerous similarities. His authorship of the latter was not questioned until the 15th century. Currently, it is assumed that their similarity is due to the dependence on one Latin textbook based on a Greek source. This topic is discussed in M. Tullius Ciceron, *De inventione. Über die Auffindung des Stoffes. De optimo genere oratorum. Über die beste Gattung von Rednern.* Herausgegeben und übersetzt von Th. Nüßlein, Darmstadt 1998, pp. 384–386.

162 Cf. Cic., *Off.* 1,7,20 *Sed iustitiae primum munus est, ut ne cui quis noceat, nisi lacessitus iniuria, deinde ut communibus pro communibus utatur, privatis ut suis.*

Cic., *Off.* 1,43,155
Quibus rebus intellegitur, studiis officiisque scientiae praeponenda esse officia iustitiae, quae pertinent ad hominum utilitatem, qua nihil homini esse debet antiquius.
What follows is that at the forefront of activities and duties aimed at acquiring knowledge must be the duties of justice, which serve human utility, which should be the dearest for men.

In Cicero's doctrine, *iustitia* and *utilitas* emerge as intertwined[163] although the precise nature of their relationship is somewhat elusive. In the passage from *De inventione* (*Inv.* 2,53,160), Cicero writes that justice, described through the present active participle *tribuens*[164], is not only a state of mind (*habitus animi*) but, above all, an efficient being, granting each their due[165]. Simultaneously, the actions of justice are carried out *communi utilitate conservata*. The *ablativus absolutus* can be interpreted in this case in two ways: either as a clause of result ('for the sake of safeguarding the common utility'), or as an adverbial of time ('having safeguarded the common utility'). In the former interpretation, *utilitas* appears to be the driving force behind justice. In the latter, since the perfect passive participle *conservata* suggests that the activity precedes, acting in accordance with *utilitas* can be treated as a requirement of *iustitia*. Importantly, what follows from the grammatical structure of the sentence is that it is impossible to grant everyone what is their due without first taking the common utility into account.

It appears that the second interpretation aligns more closely with the content of *Off.* 1,31,7–9, where Cicero, pondering under what circumstances it is justified to break one's word, outlines the fundamental principles of justice (*fundamenta iustitiae*), including not causing harm to others and caring for the common utility. At the same time, he points out that these ideas were previously presented by him, referring to the following passage:

163 Some claim that Cicero considered justice to be the highest moral norm. See G. Jossa, *L''utilitas rei publicae' nel pensiero di Cicerone*, pp. 277, 286–288; 398–399. Roberto Scevola even describes *utilitas* in Cicero's thought as a synonym of justice, *'Utilitas publica', I. Emersione...*, p. 355. See also H. Kupiszewski, *Pojęcie państwa w de re publica Cycerona*, 'PK' 1991, vol. 34, no. 1–2, p. 169.

164 This *participium* can refer to both the noun *iustitia* and *habitus*. Interpretatively, it does not matter much, because according to Cicero, *iustitia* is a *habitus animi*.

165 See G. Falcone, *Ius suum cuique tribuere*, 'AUPA' 2008, vol. 52, pp. 133–176, where the author convincingly argues that the categories of *dignitatem tribuere* or *ius suum tribuere* refer not only to granting benefits but also to giving reprimands. Cf. also A. Corbino, *Ius suum cuique tribuere. Osservazioni minime sulla definizione ulpianea di iustitia (D. 1.1.10 pr.-2 e Rhet. ad Her. 3.2.3)* [in:] *Homenaje al Profesor Armando Torrent*, A. Murillo Villar, A. Calzada González, S. Castán Pérez-Gómez (ed.), Madrid 2016, pp. 155–165.

Cic., *Off.* 1,7,20
Sed iustitiae primum munus est, ut ne cui quis noceat, nisi lacessitus iniuria, deinde ut communibus pro communibus utatur, privatis ut suis.
The first duty of justice is that no one harms anyone unless provoked by injustice, and then that everyone uses public things for common utility, and private things as their own.

In this instance, Cicero defines not causing harm to others, and caring for the common utility (specified in its content) not as the *fundamenta iustitiae*, but as the duties of justice – *munera iustitiae*[166]. *Utilitas*, therefore, did not have to be a criterion to be fulfilled but could also be the very purpose of actions. A similar connection between utility and justice is evident in another above-cited passage, *Off.* 1,43,155, where he concludes that the duties of justice serve the utility of people (*pertinent ad hominum utilitatem*). On the other hand, this phrase can be easily interpreted as inspiration to act, aligning with one of the previously suggested readings of the phrase *communi utilitate conservata* (*Inv.* 2,53,160).

Cicero's writings do not show a clear-cut relationship between the categories of *utilitas* and *iustitia*. In relation to the latter, utility could assume three forms: its cause, its foundation, or its goal. There is no doubt, however, that the criterion of utility significantly influenced the measure of justice, whose paramount task was to care for the *utilitas communis*, a concept of supreme importance for Cicero. The close amalgamation of these two values is an embodiment of the fusion of pragmatism and morality[167], and any potential conflict between them was regarded as an aberration resulting from a misunderstanding of *utilitas*[168].

166 Establishing the full content link between the two fragments, as rightly pointed out by Atkins, is a difficult task, *'Domina et Regina Virtutum'…*, p. 267, n. 12. It is not entirely clear how *utilitati communi servire* (*Off.* 1,31,7–9) was associated by Cicero with the use of public and private goods (*Off.* 1,20,6–21,1 *communibus pro communibus uti, privatis ut suis*). The general premise seems to be that caring for the common utility is not to use public property for one's own.

167 Félix Senn noted that the definition of justice proposed by Ulpian (D. 1,1,10,pr. *Iustitia est constans et perpetua voluntas ius suum cuique tribuendi*) could be supplemented with a condition *utilitate communi conservata*, *De la justice et du droit: explication de la définition traditionnelle de la justice suivie d'une étude sur la distinction du ius naturale et du ius gentium*, Paris 1927, p. 44. A similar thought was also expressed by Anna Plisecka, who recognized that Ulpian's definition was a simplified version of Cicero's formulation, *Definicja sprawiedliwości w filozofii Cycerona i prawie rzymskim*, 'Studia Iuridica' 2002, vol. 40, p. 139.

168 G. Jossa, *L''utilitas rei publicae' nel pensiero imperiale…*, pp. 389, 393. See also A. R. Dyck, *A Commentary…*, p. 493.

1.2.2 *Utilitas* according to Horace

The Roman understanding of *utilitas* extends beyond Cicero's perspective, which was shaped by the ideas of the Greek Stoics. Although there was no member of the Epicurean school among the representatives of the aforementioned Greek delegation from 155 BCE, the works of Quintus Horatius Flaccus, who openly presented his philosophical preferences[169], reflect Epicurean influences in Roman cultural and legal discourse[170]. It is serendipitous that one of Horace's satires contains a phrase that can be considered a definition of *utilitas*, characterizing it as the mother of what is just and right (Hor., *Sat.* 1,3,98 *iusti prope mater et aequi*[171]). This expression holds particular significance for our considerations because, much like Cicero's vision, it is grounded in a legal perspective[172].

169 The poet described himself as a 'hog from Epicurus' flock' (cf. Hor., *Ep.* 1,4,16). Three books of his *Satires* were written in the years 41–30 BCE, and therefore in a period not easy for the poet. After being granted amnesty announced by Octavian, he moved to Rome. The difficult financial situation forced him to take on other professional duties, which prevented him from fully devoting himself to poetry. It is no wonder, then, that philosophical influences are very clearly visible in Horace's works. For more on this topic, see e.g. H.-C. Günther, *Horace's Life and Work* [in:] *Brill's Companion to Horace*, H.-C. Günther (ed.), Leiden-Boston 2013, pp. 26–34.

170 See e.g. F. B. Cicala, *Il concetto...*, p. 9; E. Dovere, *Le discours juridique et moral de l'utilitas à Rome* [in:] *Histoire raisonnée de la philosophie morale et politique*, A. Caillé, Ch. Lazzeri, M. Senellart (ed.), Paris 2001, pp. 108–115; G. Mousourakis, *A Legal History of Rome*, New York 2007, p. 43.

171 Not grounded in the same philosophy, a similar putting together of terms (though only *aequum* and *utile* are explicitly mentioned) can be seen in two passages from Livy. The first example is from 200 BCE, when the Roman treasury faced bankruptcy and could not repay a war loan to private creditors. To address this, the Senate issued a decree proposing a compromise: creditors were granted the use of public land, subject to a symbolic fee representing public ownership. In the future, if the treasury could repay the loan, creditors had the choice to request repayment or retain the land. Livy describes this solution as a compromise between *aequitas* and *utilitas*: Liv., AUC 31,13,5–6 *Cum et privati aequum postularent nec tamen solvendo aere alieno res publica esset, quod medium inter aequum et utile erat decreverunt* ('As the request of these individuals was right, due to the state's inability to repay the loan the Senate passed a resolution that was a compromise between right and useful'). In another passage, Livy states that the Etruscan war could be effectively managed under the leadership of either of the two consuls was *natura aequum et exemplo utile* ('a thing in its nature right, and useful as an example'; AUC 10,24,17). In both cases, what is *utile* and *aequum* align. The same sources are also referenced by D. Mantovani in his work on Roman economic thought, *Inter aequum et utile. The Law as Economics in the Roman World?*, [in:] *Uomini, istituzioni, mercati. Studi di storia per Elio Lo Cascio*, M. Maiuro, G. D. Merola, M. De Nardis, G. Soricelli (ed.), Bari 2019, pp. 505–506 (being the English translation with some changes of the study *Inter aequum et utile. Il diritto come economia nel mondo romano?*, [in:] *Diritto romano e economia. Due modi di pensare e organizzare il mondo (nei primi tre secoli dell'Impero)*, D. Mantovani, E. Lo Cascio (ed.), Pavia 2018, pp. 785–809).

172 Horace's work offers invaluable insights into Roman law. The poet even served as a quaestor for a time. See Suet., *Hor.* 6–8, as well as L. R. Taylor, *Horace's Equestrian Career*, 'American Journal of Philology' 1925, vol. 46, pp. 161–170; D. Armstrong, *Horatius Eques et Scriba: Satires 1.6 and 2.7*, 'Transactions of the American Philological Association' 1986, vol. 116, pp. 255–288; R. Hassan, *La poesia e il diritto in Orazio. Tra autore e pubblico*, Napoli 2014, pp. 15–21. Horace's works continue to inspire researchers of Roman law. Key studies on this topic include E. Costa, *Il diritto nei poeti di*

The passage appears in the third satire from the first book of *Satires*[173]. The primary theme of the third satire, full of legal allusions, revolves around the mockery of the Stoic postulate attributed to Zeno of Citium, the founder of the Stoic school, who lived at the turn of the 4th and 3rd centuries BCE. He asserted that all noble deeds deserved equal recognition and all wrongdoings were to be viewed as equally reprehensible[174]. The poet critiqued this irrational extremity, advocating for punishments proportionate to the guilt and rank of an offence. To illustrate his argument, Horace drew upon Roman law, arguing that stealing a cabbage could not be equated with sacrilege[175]. Obviously, any reasonable Roman would share his opinion, but, as Oliviero Diliberto pointed out, it takes a trained legal eye to notice Horace's subtle references to *sacrilegium, actio de arboribus succisis, actio arborum furtim caesarum* and *actio ex lege Aquilia*[176]. There should therefore be no doubt that the intended audience of this satire was the community of jurists.

Horace further encouraged the temperate control of anger, asserting that a violent temper lacked justification. He argued that, as rational beings, people had an obligation to manage their emotions. To illustrate this point, he presented scenarios such as someone crucifying their servant for licking the leftovers off the table while cleaning, which Horace found utterly insane[177]. Likewise, harshly judging friends for acciden-

Roma, Bologna 1898; F. Stella Maranca, *Il diritto romano nell'opera di Orazio*, 'Annali della Facoltà di Giurisprudenza dell'Università degli Studi di Bari' 1933, vol. 2, pp. 71–89; Idem, *Per lo studio del diritto romano nell'opera di Orazio*, Modena 1935; Idem, *Orazio e la legislazione Romana* [in:] *Conferenze Oraziane in commemorizacione del bimillenario Oraziano*, Milano 1936; H. Insadowski, *Prawo rzymskie u Horacego*, Lublin 1935; T. Mazurek, *Self-Parody and the Law in Horace's 'Satires' 1.9*, 'The Classical Journal' 1997, vol. 93, no. 1, pp. 1–17; T. A. J. McGinn, *Satire and the law: the case of Horace*, 'The Cambridge Classical Journal' 2001, vol. 47, pp. 81–102; O. Diliberto, *Ut carmen necessarium (Cic., leg. II, 59). Apprendimento e conoscenza della Legge delle XII Tavole nel I sec. a. C.* [in:] *Letteratura e civitas. Transizioni dalla Repubblica all'Impero. In ricordo di E. Narducci*, M. Citroni (ed.), Pisa 2012, pp. 141–162; Idem, *La satira e il diritto: una nuova lettura di Horat., sat. 1.3.115–117*, 'AUPA' 2012, vol. 55, pp. 385–402; R. Hassan, *La poesia*.... More sceptical opinions can be found in J. D. Cloud, *Satirists and the Law* [in:] *Satire and Society in Ancient Rome*, S. H. Braund (ed.), Exeter 1989, p. 64. Cloud argues that, due to its playful nature, satire is not a reliable source of knowledge about Roman reality.

173 R. Hassan, *La poesia...*, pp. 94–95.

174 Cic., *Parad.* 3 Ότι ἴσα τὰ ἁμαρτήματα καὶ τὰ κατορθώματα. *Aequalia esse peccata et recte facta.* This concept is also expressed with another phrase by Cicero: *omnia peccata paria* (*Fin.* 4,19,55). Although Cicero's stoic inclinations are known, he strongly opposed this postulate. See J. Ogórek, *Quae ratio intercedat inter Ciceronis Paradoxis Stoicorum et Horati stoicismum, qui Satiris Epistulisque eius continetur*, Lemberg 1902, pp. 28–29; R. P. Bond, *Stoic influence on selected satires of Horace*, Canterbury 1977 (PhD thesis available online at: https://ir.canterbury.ac.nz/handle/10092/4767).

175 Hor., *Sat.* 1,3,115–117.

176 O. Diliberto, *La satira...*, pp. 385–402, R. Hassan, *La poesia...*, pp. 103–121.

177 Horace precisely wrote that such a person would act more insanely than Labeo himself. It was presumed that at this point Horace mentioned Marcus Antistius Labeo, founder of the Proculeian school. As a staunch Republican, he openly criticized Octavian's rule and is mentioned to have deliberately provoked the princeps at Senate meetings (Tac., *Ann.* 3,75). However, this hypothesis can be ruled out. Not only because it is unlikely for the poet to want to attack the respected ju-

tal mishaps, such as breaking a dish, or, when hungry, reaching for a part of the meal that was not supposed to be theirs, seemed nonsensical to the poet. Horace asked: if these were serious offences, what punishment was due, then, if this friend was guilty of stealing, or violating a contract[178]? Horace succinctly summarized his perspective in the following lines:

> Hor., *Sat.* 1,3,96–98
> *quis paria esse fere placuit peccata*[179], *laborant*
> *cum ventum ad verum est: sensus moresque repugnant*
> *atque ipsa utilitas, iusti prope mater et aequi.*
> He who preaches is that all sins are equal are at a loss when they come to face facts. Feelings and customs rebel, and so does *utilitas* herself, the mother, we may say, of justice and right[180].

Horace argued that equating all offenses faced opposition from *sensus* ('consciousness', 'senses', 'sense', 'sense of what was appropriate'), *mores* ('customs'), and *utilitas*. In his view, the last one mentioned was, so to speak, the mother of what was just and right[181]. Horace's concept can be traced directly to the teachings of Epicurus, whose doctrine of the law, like most of the sources on the philosophy of the Garden, was preserved in the tenth book of Diogenes Laertius' *Lives and Opinions of Eminent Philosophers*. The centre of Epicurus' reflection on the law was precisely *utilitas*, expressed with the Greek noun τὸ συμφέρον:

rist, but primarily because, when Horace was composing his *Satires*, Labeo was about fifteen years old, as noted by F. P. Bremer in *Iurisprudentiae antehadrianae quae supersunt. Pars altera: Primi post principatum constitutum saeculi iuris consulti*, F. P. Bremer (ed.), Lipsiae 1898, p. 10. A more convincing suggestion is that Horace referred to Gaius Atinius Labeo, tribune of the plebs in 131 BCE. According to the accounts, in an act of rage, he was supposed to try to throw Quintus Caecilius Metellus Macedonicus down from the Tarpeian Rock for provoking his removal from the group of the senators. At the last moment, however, he was stopped by another tribune. Cf. Liv., AUC 59; Plin., NH 7,143. Cicero reports a slightly less dramatic version of events, where Labeo deprived Metellus of his fortune and sentenced him to death. The whole story ended well thanks to the intervention of another tribune, but Cicero used the term *furor* to describe Labeo's behaviour (*De domo sua*, 47,122). In his satire, Horace used a similar term (*insanior*). Cf. E. Fraenkel, *Orazio*, Roma 1993, p. 125; P. Fedeli, *Commento e note* [in:] *Orazio. Tutte le poesie*, Torino 2009, p. 125; E. Courtney, *The Two Books of Satires* [in:] *Brill's Companion to Horace*, H.-C. Günther (ed.), Leiden-Boston 2013, p. 84, n. 69.

178 Hor., *Sat.* 1,3,78–95.

179 Cf. Cic., *Fin.* 4,19,55.

180 Transl. Horace, *Satires. Epistles. The Art of Poetry*, transl. by H. Rushton Fairclough, Cambridge 1926, p. 41 with minor change as the author of the translation rendered the term *utilitas* as 'Expediency'.

181 In Horace, the link between the categories *utilitas* and *honestas* is also materialized: Hor., *Sat.* 1,4,124 *an hoc inhonestum et inutile factu.*

Epicur., *RS* 31
Τὸ τῆς φύσεως δίκαιόν ἐστι σύμβολον τοῦ συμφέροντος εἰς τὸ μὴ βλάπτειν ἀλλήλους μηδὲ βλάπτεσθαι.
Natural justice is an expression of utility in regard to not harming one another or being harmed by another[182].

Epicur., *RS* 36
Κατὰ μὲν <τὸ> κοινὸν πᾶσι τὸ δίκαιον τὸ αὐτό, συμφέρον γάρ τι ἦν ἐν τῇ πρὸς ἀλλήλους κοινωνίᾳ· κατὰ δὲ τὸ ἴδιον χώρας καὶ ὅσων δή ποτε αἰτιῶν οὐ πᾶσι συνέπεται τὸ αὐτὸ δίκαιον εἶναι.
Generally speaking, justice is the same for all. For it was a useful thing in mutual relations. However, depending on individual countries and conditions, the same thing may not necessarily be just for everyone.

Epicurus envisioned peace and security as attainable when individuals refrained from harming one another[183], a state he equated with natural justice that formed the foundation of any society. The past imperfect (was [continuing] – ἦν) in the *RS* 36 possibly locates his considerations early stages of social processes[184]. Within the same passage, there is a notable clarification regarding the absence of universal applicability of just rules[185]. According to Marcel Conche, this statement implies that, for Epicurus, there were two distinct qualities associated with justice: one established by individuals and operated within the framework of a particular community's laws, and the other rooted in the law of nature[186]. Both were, however, inherently connected to utility and served

182 When translating all Epicurus' maxims, there were considered comments by M. Conche, *Droit naturel et droit positif selon Épicure*, 'Revue philosophique de la France et de l'étranger' 2013, vol. 138, no. 4, pp. 549–556. With regard to this fragment, following Victor Goldschmidt's thought, the French researcher proposed that the expression τὸ τῆς φύσεως δίκαιόν be translated as 'la justice selon la nature', and not as 'le droit naturel', admitting, however, that in principle, these two categories overlap. Cf. V. Goldschmidt, *La doctrine d'Épicure et le droit*, Paris 1977, p. 19. It is particularly important to avoid translating the expression τὸ σύμβολον as a contract. Although in its plural form (τὰ σύμβολα) this term may carry such a meaning, it implies a law-making activity, which Epicurus seems to express by the term ἡ συνθήκη.

183 Therefore, the perfect situation is when members of a given collective live together and do not desire other people's goods. Agricultural societies seem to be closest to the ideal. This way in M. Conche, *Droit…*, p. 550.

184 See E. Spinelli, *Justice, Law, and Friendship: Ethical and Political Topics in Epicurus* [in:] *Philosophie für die Polis*, C. Riedweg (ed.), Berlin-Boston 2019, p. 391.

185 The thought that the law consists partly of rules recognized as just by all people, and partly of norms created only by a particular community and respected only by it, immediately brings to mind Gaius' reflection. Cf. D. 1,1,9 (= G. 1,1 = I. 1,2,1) *Omnes populi, qui legibus et moribus reguntur, partim suo proprio, partim communi omnium hominum iure utuntur* ('All peoples who are governed by the laws and the customs, use partly their own law, and partly the law common to all nations').

186 M. Conche, *Droit naturel…*, p. 522. It is for this reason that crime is not evil in itself (Epicur., *RS* 34, Ἡ ἀδικία οὐ καθ' ἑαυτὴν κακόν…), but because it is an offense against an agreement made between people. Cf. Epicur., *RS* 35.

the collective community as well as its individual members. Again then, the qualities of justice and utility could not be separated:

> Epicur., *RS* 37
> Τὸ μὲν ἐπιμαρτυρούμενον ὅτι συμφέρει ἐν ταῖς χρείαις τῆς πρὸς ἀλλήλους κοινωνίας τῶν νομισθέντων εἶναι δικαίων, ἔχει τὸν τοῦ δικαίου χαρακτῆρα, ἐάν τε τὸ αὐτὸ πᾶσι γένηται ἐάν τε μὴ τὸ αὐτό. ἐάν δὲ νόμον θῆταί τις, μὴ ἀποβαίνῃ δὲ κατὰ τὸ συμφέρον τῆς πρὸς ἀλλήλους κοινωνίας, οὐκέτι τοῦτο τὴν τοῦ δικαίου φύσιν ἔχει (…).
> Among the things acknowledged to be just, whatever is found to be useful in the needs of mutual relations is labelled as just, whether or not it turns out as such for all. If someone establishes a law that is not useful in mutual relations, that law no longer has the nature of justice (…).

In specific communities, the state of general justice, grounded in the principle of not harming one another, was subject to convention-based clarification[187]. Epicurus affirmed that only norms useful to the community could genuinely be considered just. The fact that they might not be considered just or useful by all members of society did not invalidate their status[188]. Here, utility was not merely a priority but the foundational value, as a law could only be characterised as just once it proved useful to society. A law that would be of no use to the community could not therefore be deemed just. It is this reflection that materialized in Horatian verses, where *utilitas* was described as the mother of justice and righteousness, emphasizing the idea that just legal norms should always be guided by the utility of citizens.

187 M. Conche, *Droit naturel…*, p. 556. Epicurus writes about the contractual justice as follows: Epicur., *RS* 33 Οὐκ ἦν τι καθ᾽ ἑαυτὸ δικαιοσύνη, ἀλλ᾽ ἐν ταῖς μετ᾽ ἀλλήλων συστροφαῖς καθ᾽ ὁπηλίκους δή ποτε ἀεὶ τόπους συνθήκη τις ὑπὲρ τοῦ μὴ βλάπτειν μηδὲ βλάπτεσθαι ('There has never been a justice in itself but rather the agreement over not harming and not being harmed in mutual dealings, in any place whatsoever'). As rightly pointed out by Conche, at this point Epicurus did not use the term τὸ δίκαιόν but used the word ἡ δικαιοσύνη instead, *Droit naturel…*, pp. 551–552. Even if both concepts are defined in essentially the same way, the former refers to the natural state, and the latter is created by agreements (αἱ συνθῆκαι) concluded between living creatures. The latter is not identical to the first one, and at the same time cannot be qualified as an absolute category, because it does not arise by itself (καθ᾽ ἑαυτὸ), as it is, as the French researcher put it, 'conventional justice' (*la justice conventionelle*). It is, therefore, a state shaped in accordance with the needs of a given community. In turn, the fullness of the established principles creates the civil law, which may (but does not have to) coincide with the principles of the law of nature.

188 To describe the problem, Conche gives illustrative examples of norms introduced for the special benefit of the military or individual displacements to build a road, *Droit naturel…*, pp. 554–555. This idea is also present in Roman jurists, as discussed below. Cf. D. 1,1,11 and Fragm. Dosith. 1.

1.3 *Utilitas* as Integral to the *Ius* in Jurists' Thought

1.3.1 *Ars iuris* and *utilitas*

The considerations presented in the previous section lead to an inference that, when arguing for release from the obligation to return money deposit, or even considering extreme actions such as taking a life[189], Cicero and Quintilian invoked *utilitas* in a way that surpassed mere pragmatism and embraced ethical considerations. Building on these insights, it is crucial to examine whether the understanding of *utilitas*, as reconstructed form non-legal sources, is consistent with the perspective of jurists.

In this context, it is instructive to start with Dario Mantovani's perspective as presented in his study on Roman economic thought. Drawing upon the work of Joseph Alois Schumpeter, he concludes that this thought 'was essentially qualitative and moral rather than quantitative, and that it is improper to transfer an elaboration that is only modern to notions such as *utilitas* (even when qualified as *publica*)'. He adds that 'we do not have to ask ourselves to what extent economic motivations influenced legal decisions. The Romans tended to think about economic activities in a non-economic way; they were guided by those criteria that the law partly shared with moral philosophy, which are specifically linked to the sphere of *aequitas*'[190]. Thus, in legal thought as well, it is crucial to avoid reducing *utilitas* to a purely pragmatic and material sense and recognize its multidimensional nature.

To delve deeper into this, we should turn our attention to a passage from Domitius Ulpian's *Institutes*, a legal textbook likely penned between 213 and 214 CE[191]. Its introductory part opens a collage composed of fragments of writings of Roman ju-

189 Cf. already quoted Cic., *Off.* 3,4,19; 3,25,95; Quint., *Inst.* 12,1,37.

190 D. Mantovani, *Inter aequum et utile. The Law…*, pp. 519–520. Cf. also D. Mantovani *Giuristi romani…* p. 208, where Mantovani describes *utilitas* and *aequitas* the 'due principali fondamenti del diritto, nella loro funzione di vincolo sociale garante delle posizioni dei singoli e della collettività' and 'termini normativi' (pp. 188–189, esp. with the sources quoted in n. 106). Cf. e.g. Cic., *Caec.* 49 *An tu qui tam diligenter et tam callide verbis controversiam non aequitate diiudicas, et iura non utilitate communi sed litteris exprimis…* ('You, then, showing such care and skill in resolving disputes according to the letter, and not according to *aequitas*, and interpreting the laws by faithfully repeating their wording rather than by using the common utility…'); Idem, *Inv.* 2,47,138 *Demonstrabit nullam esse legem, quae aliquam rem inutilem aut iniquam fieri velit* ('He will demonstrate that no law is intended to promote something that is useless or not right'); 2,48,143 *Leges in consilio scriptoris et utilitate communi, non in verbis consistere; quam indignum sit aequitatem litteris urgeri, quae voluntate eius, qui scripserit, defendatur* ('The meaning of laws is given by the intention of their author and common utility, not wording. How shameful it would be if *aequitas* that the author was trying to defend were thwarted by words'). In Chapter Three, the further context of these phrases will be explained.

191 This dating was proposed by T. Honoré, *Ulpian…*, p. 171.

rists – the *Digest of Justinian*, constituting the foundation of Roman legal reflection[192]. Ulpian commences by providing the etymology of the term of 'law', and, to define it, cites Publius Juventius Celsus, a representative of the Proculeian school from the 2nd century CE:

> D. 1,1,1,pr. (*Ulpianus libro primo institutionum*)
> *Iuri operam daturum prius nosse oportet, unde nomen iuris descendat. Est autem a iustitia appellatum: nam, ut eleganter Celsus definit, ius est ars boni et aequi.*
> Anyone intending to dedicate themselves to the law should initially explore the origin of the term 'law', as it derives its meaning from justice. For, as Celsus aptly put it: 'the law is an art of good and right'.

Celsus' definition[193], framing law as the art[194] of what is good and right (*ars boni et aequi*), was long seen as rhetorical[195] and metaphorical[196]. Scholars often misinterpreted its poetic nature, perceiving the law as an idealistic and timeless art[197]. However, given Celsus' commitment to linguistic precision[198], it is unlikely that he would forsake the rational and realistic perspective typical of Roman jurists. What he meant by describing *ius* as *ars* is still under discussion today, as the term *ars* encompasses various meanings.

192 Similarly M. Bretone, *Tecniche e ideologie dei giuristi romani*, Napoli 1984, p. 101, sees the principle that governs all legal reflection in Celsus' definition of law quoted below.

193 Ulpian praised Celsus' concise phrase as *elegans*. It should be noted that *elegantia* as an evaluation criterion referred to both the content and form. For more on this subject, see H. Ankum, *Elegantia iuris*, 'Annales de la Faculté de Droit d'Istanbul' 2011, vol. 21, no. 37, pp. 45–58. Doubts as to whether Celsus himself could consider the quoted phrase as a *definitio* were expressed in A. Schiavone, *Giuristi e principe nelle Istituzioni di Ulpiano. Un'esegesi*, 'SDHI' 2003, vol. 69, pp. 53–54.

194 Cicero included *ius* in the category of *ars* (*Brut.* 152–153), but in his speech *Pro Murena*, he emphasized the inferiority of the law to rhetoric and the art of war (*Mur.* 22–29). Tacitus (*Ann.* 3,75) and the encyclopaedist Aulus Gellius (NA 13,10,1) included *ius* among *artes* as well. Also, physician Galen of Pergamon listed jurisprudence among the τέχναι λογικαί (ἡ τέχνη νομική; *Op.* 1,39; 5,103 [ed. Kühn]). Cf. V. Scarano Ussani, *L'utilità e la certezza: compiti e modelli del sapere giuridico in Salvio Giuliano*, Milano 1987, pp. 148–149, Idem, *L'ars dei giuristi. Considerazioni sullo statuto epistemologico della giurisprudenza romana*, Torino 1997, p. 54; G. Falcone, *La 'vera philosophia' dei 'sacerdotes iuris'. Sulla raffigurazione ulpianea dei giuristi (D.1.1.1)*, 'AUPA' 2004, vol. 49, pp. 79–83, including n. 80. See also comments presented in T. Viehweg, *Topica e giurisprudenza*, transl. G. Crifò, Milano 1962, pp. 61–63. Roman *artes* also included music, geometry, astronomy, grammar and rhetoric. Cf. Cic., *De orat.* 1,187; Idem, *Off.* 1,6,19.

195 See esp. F. Pringsheim, *Bonum et aequum*, 'ZSS RA' 1932, vol. 52, no. 1, p. 84 and F. Schulz, *Storia della giurisprudenza romana*, Firenze 1968, p. 242.

196 R. Martini, *Le definizioni dei giuristi romani*, Milano 1966, p. 84, who, however, does not negate the technical aspect of the definition.

197 See M. Kuryłowicz, *Sacerdotes iustitiae*, p. 705.

198 Cf. e.g. Cels. D. 33,10,7,pr.–2. See also F. Gallo, *Sulla definizione celsina del diritto*, 'SDHI' 1987, vol. 53, p. 21.

For instance, the concept of *ars* as a system is derived from the Stoic tradition. Consequently, Celsus' phrase was often interpreted as a reference to a systematized set of laws – an idea also found in Cicero[199]. On the other hand, *ius* as *ars* could also denote the craft of skilful application and creation of the law, thus encompassing the broadly understood activity of learned jurists. In this context, Celsus' definition can also be perceived as, to quote Paulina Święcicka, knowledge on 'how to act'[200]. Although the latter interpretation seems closer to the jurist's general declarations regarding the application of the law[201], in the light of the available sources, an unambiguous recon-

199 Cic., *De orat.* 1,186 …*deinde, postea quam est editum, expositis a Cn. Flavio primum actionibus, nulli fuerunt, qui illa artificiose digesta generatim componerent; nihil est enim, quod ad artem redigi possit, nisi ille prius, qui illa tenet, quorum artem instituere vult, habet illam scientiam, ut ex eis rebus, quarum ars nondum sit, artem efficere possit.* ('… Secondly, when Gnaeus Flavius first issued the legal formulas, there was no one who would systematize this material and divide it into types. Nothing can be transformed into a system [*ars*], as long as those who have mastered the field on the basis of which they want to build this system cannot create such system from those elements that do not yet form one'). Such understanding of the concept *ars* was adopted by S. Riccobono, *La definizione del 'ius' al tempo di Adriano*, 'BIDR' 1948, vol. 12, no. 53–54, p. 50 and P. Frezza, *Ius gentium*, 'RIDA' 1949, vol. 2, p. 306.

200 P. Święcicka, *Formalność…*, p. 211.

201 In the preserved sources, Celsus emerges as a proponent of a flexible interpretation of the law, one that aligns with contemporary social needs and interprets the law by its spirit rather than its letter. For example, Cels. D. 1,3,17 *Scire leges non hoc est verba earum tenere, sed vim ac potestatem* ('Knowing laws does not mean understanding their wording but their sense and meaning'); Cels. D. 1,3,24 *Incivile est nisi tota lege perspecta una aliqua particula eius proposita iudicare vel respondere* ('It is only lawful to issue judgments or provide legal advice if you know the entire content of the law, and not just a tiny part of it'). Aldo Schiavone, *Giuristi e principe…*, pp. 52–53, suggests that Celsus might have intentionally kept the term *ars* ambiguous. Cf. also his commentary in J.-L. Ferrary, A. Schiavone, V. Marotta, *Cnaeus Domitius Ulpianus. Institutiones. De Censibus*, Roma-Bristol 2021, pp. 197–199. The definition of *ius* coined by Celsus was also examined by P. Cerami, *La concezione celsina del 'ius' : presupposti culturali e implicazioni metodologiche*, 'AUPA' 1985, vol. 37, pp. 10–28; Idem, *"Ius est ars boni et aequi". Un riesame della definizione celsina*, 'AUPA' 2019, vol. 62, pp. 35–82; V. Scarano Ussani, *L'ars…*, pp. 11–41 and idem, *Tra "scientia" e "ars". Il sapere giuridico romano dalla sapienza alla scienza nei giudizi di Cicerone e di Pomponio*, [in:] *Per la storia del pensiero giuridico romano. Dall'età dei pontefici alla scuola di Servio. Atti del seminario di S. Marino 7–9 gennaio 1993*, D. Mantovani (ed.), Torino 1996, pp. 229–262 along with the studies cited therein. See also F. Gallo, *Sulla definizione…*, p. 21, who although, in principle, is highly critical of Cerami's remarks on Celsus' definition, in this respect remains consistent with the opinion of the other researcher. According to Gallo, when defining *ius* as *ars*, Celsus meant the knowledge of theory and practical skills as well as the effect of specific human activity, and thus the entire phenomenon of law. This thesis that Celsus' concept of *ius* should not be treated synonymously with the concept of *scientia iuris*, as well as the term *ars* not being limited only to the law-making aspect of Roman jurisprudence is argued in F. Gallo, *Sulla definizione…*, pp. 23–26 and Idem, *Celso e Kelsen: Per la rifondazione della scienza giuridica*, Torino 2010, pp. 32–33, 68. Cf. also comments by Cerami, limiting the definition of Celsus' to the activity of jurisprudence only, *La concezione…*, pp. 18–19. If Gallo is right, it should be recognized that the analyzed definition is not limited to the Roman law only but needs to be classified in terms of a general theory of the law, in particular because it does not indicate individual elements of a given legal system, such as legal norms, sources of the law, or effects of law-making activity, which by their nature may take various forms, *Celso e Kelsen…*, p. 70. In Roman law, these include not just jurists' interpretations but also *leges, plebiscita, senatus consulta, constitutiones principium*, and

struction of Celsus' thought is currently impossible[202]. What one can do, however, is explore the foundations of the concept of *ars*. The Greek term ἡ τέχνη, being an equivalent of Latin *ars*, was first[203] defined by Zeno of Citium. His thought was conveyed by Neoplatonist Olympiodorus the Younger in a commentary on the Platonic dialogue *Gorgias* from the 6th century CE:

Olymp., *In Grg.* 12,1[204]
Ζήνων δέ φησιν ὅτι τέχνη ἐστὶ σύστημα ἐκ καταλήψεων συγγεγυμνασμένων πρός τι τέλος εὔχρηστον τῶν ἐν τῷ βίῳ.
Zeno says that art is the totality of co-exercised practices aimed at a useful goal for the things in life.

Zeno of Citium's concept of 'art' (ἡ τέχνη) embodying the totality (or the system) of practices undertaken together to achieve a useful goal (τέλος εὔχρηστον), and, as such, inherently tied to the concept of utility, resonates through both Greek and Latin sources across the ages. The first group includes the fragment from the works of the philosopher Philo of Alexandria[205] living at the turn of the epochs, who considered the criterion of utility crucial for the definition of the term ἡ τέχνη as excluding fraudulent

edicta. Cf. e.g. G. 1,2–7. Even if one accepted Gallo's hypothesis and admitted that the main goal of *ars* was to introduce useful solutions, both general and abstract, as well as individual (cf. *Sulla definizione …*, p. 36), one should not forget, however, that Roman legal institutions, whatever their nature, were an immediate response to daily problems. General norms were not adopted in order to implement a long-term legal policy. See F. Wieacker, *Vom romischen Recht: Zehn Versuche*, Stuttgart 1961, p. 59; M. Ducos, *Les romains et la loi: recherches sur les rapports de la philosophie grecque et de la tradition romaine à la fin de la République*, Paris 1984, pp. 31–34; Ž. Bujuklić, *Ancient and Modern Concepts of Lawfulness*, 'RIDA' 1999, vol. 46, pp. 137–138; J. Bleicken, *Lex publica, Gesetz und Recht in der römischen Republik*, Berlin-Boston 2015, p. 186.

202 However, it seems possible within Ulpian's reflections, as discussed below. For the interpretation of Celsus' phrase *ius est ars boni et aequi*, it would be particularly important to know the context in which it was used. Unfortunately, it is not known from which work Ulpian drew this definition. Scarano Ussani hypothesized that it might have been taken from the analysis of a specific legal case, suggesting the *Digest* as a possible source, however, with the reservation that the exact origin of the fragment could not be established, *L'ars …*, p. 111.

203 However, a similar idea is found in chronologically earlier Aristotle's *Nicomachean Ethics*. See Arist., EN 1094a1–2 Πᾶσα τέχνη καὶ πᾶσα μέθοδος, ὁμοίως δὲ πρᾶξίς τε καὶ προαίρεσις, ἀγαθοῦ τινὸς ἐφίεσθαι δοκεῖ ('All art and all method, and likewise activity and actions seem to aim at some good'). A similar perspective is also attributed to the Epicureans by the scholiast of Dionysius Thrax, the Greek grammarian who lived between 170–90 BCE. See *Epicurea* 227b (ed. Usener): οἱ μέν Ἐπικούρειοι οὕτως ὁρίζονται τὴν τέχνην· τέχνη ἐστί μέθοδος ἐνεργοῦσα τῷ βίῳ τὸ συμφέρον ('The Epicureans define it as follows: art is a method that brings into existence what is useful for life'). As Clive Chandler rightly points out, it is difficult to ascertain the accuracy of this account, *Philodemus on Rhetoric Books 1 and 2: Translation and Exegetical Essays*, New York-London 2017, p. 93.

204 = *SVF* 1,73.

205 Ph., *De congressu eruditionis gratia* 14 [gr. Περὶ τῆς πρὸς τὰ προπαιδεύματα συνόδου] τέχνης μὲν γὰρ ὅρος οὗτος· σύστημα ἐκ καταλήψεων συγγεγυμνασμένων πρός τι τέλος εὔχρηστον, τοῦ εὐχρήστου διὰ

activities. The perspectives of the philosopher Sextus Empiricus[206] and the physician of Greek origin, Galen of Pergamum[207], both writing at the turn of the 2nd and 3rd century CE, also echoed Zeno's viewpoint.

The fusion of both concepts also became a consistent theme in Latin literature[208]. The earliest known definition of the term *ars* by Marcus Terentius Varro, a prominent expert of the Latin language from the 1st century BCE, is preserved by Cassiodorus in a fragment of *Institutions of Divine and Secular Literature* dating from the 6th century CE:

Cass., *Inst.* 2, *praef.*, 4
Scire autem debemus, sicut Varro dicit, utilitatis alicuius causa omnium artium extitisse principia. Ars vero dicta est, quod nos suis regulis artet atque constringat.
For we must know, as Varro argues, that the foundations of all arts were established for the attainment of some useful cause. Undoubtedly, 'art' takes its name from the fact that it binds us and limits us with its rules.

Thus, just like Greek ἡ τέχνη, each Roman *ars* was made according to agreed-upon rules and with a specific purpose in mind. Varro, and later Cassiodorus, referred to this purpose as *utilitas*. The close connection between 'art' and 'utility' is also underscored by Cicero:

Cic., *Mur.* 23–24
Omnes enim artes, quae nobis populi Romani studia concilient, et admirabilem dignitatem et pergratam utilitatem debent habere. 24. Summa dignitas est in eis qui militari laude antecellunt; omnia enim quae sunt in imperio et in statu civitatis ab his defendi et firmari putantur; summa etiam utilitas, si quidem eorum consilio et periculo cum re publica tum etiam nostris rebus perfrui possumus.
For all activities (*artes*) that are to win the support of the Roman people for us must be of both admirable merit and desirable utility. 24. The highest merit is reserved for those who excel in military glory, as they are perceived to safeguard and strengthen everything

τὰς κακοτεχνίας ὑγιῶς προστιθεμένου ('The definition of art is as follows: all practices coordinated with work for a useful purpose; and "useful" is soundly added to rule out bad practices').

206 *M.* 1,109 Πᾶσα τοίνυν τέχνη σύστημά ἐστιν ἐκ καταλήψεων συγγεγυμνασμένων καὶ ἐπὶ τέλος εὔχρηστον τῷ βίῳ ('Each art is thus a totality of practices undertaken together in order to achieve some useful goal for life').

207 *Op.* 19,350 Τέχνη ἐστὶ σύστημα ἐγκαταλήψεων συγγεγυμνασμένων πρός τι τέλος εὔχρηστον τῶν ἐν τῷ βίῳ ('Art is a totality of practices undertaken together [in order to achieve] some useful goal for life'). More on Greek tradition see M. Isnardi Parente, *Techne: Momenti del pensiero greco da Platone ad Epicuro*, Firenze 1966, esp. pp. 287–307, where the author discusses the practical aspect of ἡ τέχνη.

208 An extensive corpus of Latin sources is presented in H. Merle, *Ars*, 'Bulletin de Philosophie Médiévale' 1986, vol. 28, pp. 95–133. This study is particularly interesting for its perspective on the further reception of the concept in Latin literature.

related to the power and condition of the State. They are also of the utmost utility because it is their counsel and responsibility that enables us to enjoy both public and private goods.

Cic., *Div.* 1,51,116
Sic cum omni utilitate quam di hominibus dederunt, ars aliqua coniuncta est per quam illa utilitas percipi possit.
Hence, the whole utility that the gods have bestowed upon humans is associated with some art by which that utility can be obtained.

The first of the aforementioned fragments comes from a speech, likely delivered in November 63 BCE[209], in defence of Roman commander Lucius Licinius Murena. After winning the consul elections, he was accused of electoral bribery under the *lex Tullia de ambitu*. Cicero's task was to save Murena from losing his position[210]. Despite the successful outcome, the speech still evokes discomfort among jurists. The reason for this is the fact that the tactic involved comparing Murena's activities with those of his opponent, jurist Servius Sulpicius Rufus, who also sought the consulship. While praising Murena and his military activities[211], Cicero resorted to attacks directed against the jurist, and above all against jurisprudence. Drawing a comparison between the art of war (*ars bellica*) and jurisprudence (*ars iuris*), he highlighted the distinguishing features of all Roman *artes*: *dignitas* and *utilitas*. Obviously, he pointed to the art of war as an artistry that fully met both required criteria. *Dignitas artis bellicae*, according to Cicero, ensured the security of the state, and its *utilitas* granted the possibility to benefit from both public and private goods[212]. In this juxtaposition, the jurisprudence appeared as *ars imperfecta*, which, as lacking similar benefits, could not lead to gaining the position of consul[213], since only a diligently cultivated art could provide access to real utility, gaining the recognition of the Roman people.

209 D. M. Ayers, *Cato's Speech against Murena*, 'The Classical Journal' 1954, vol. 49, no. 6, p. 247.

210 The speech and the legal act are discussed e. g. in G. Rotondi, *Leges publicae populi Romani*, Milano 1912; F. X. Ryan, *Rank and participation in the republican senate*, Stuttgart 1998, p. 130; C. Rosillo-López, *La corruption à la fin de la république romaine (IIe-Ier s. av. J.-C.): aspects politiques et financiers*, Stuttgart 2010, pp. 42, 61–62; H. Appel, *Strategia Cycerona w procesie karnym 'de ambitu' Lucjusza Mureny* [in:] *Prawo karne i polityka w państwie rzymskim*, K. Amielańczyk, A. Dębiński, D. Słapek (ed.), 2015, pp. 35–46.

211 See M. P. Schittko, *Analogien als Argumentationstyp*, Göttingen 2003, p. 184.

212 A similar juxtaposition of terms, as discussed later, can be found in D. 1,1,1,2.

213 Cic., *Mur.* 23 *quod quidem ius civile didicisti, non dicam operam perdidisti, sed illud dicam, nullam esse in ista disciplina munitam ad consulatum viam* ('I will not say that you have wasted your time learning the civil law, but I will say that there is no clear way to the consulate in your profession'). See also G. Falcone, *La 'vera philosophia'…*, pp. 79–80.

To some extent this oratorical performance might have reflected Cicero's private opinion about jurists, or at least about some of them[214]. However, it is crucial to note that he treated Servius Sulpicius Rufus as a friend, and held him in great respect[215]. The delivered speech was primarily ironic and parody-like[216]. Nevertheless, the criteria characterizing the category of 'art' were not oratorical. They were a manifestation of a general sense of what *ars* was and the features it needed to possess[217]. Furthermore, as evident from the fragment of *De divinatione*, the fusion of the concepts of *ars* and *utilitas* had a divine origin, at least in Cicero's view[218].

The connection between *utilitas* and *ars* is also evident in the works of later authors[219], such as Marcus Fabius Quintilian, a rhetorician and one of the most famous educators of ancient times, who lived in the 1st century CE, and Lucian of Samosata, a Roman satirist and rhetorician of the 2nd century CE:

214 Cicero later presented similar allegations in his treaty *De officiis* (Cic., *Off.* 2,19,65). However, Cicero's doctrine does not lack praise on the discipline of the law. Cf. e.g. Cic., *Top.* 2,9 *Ius civile est aequitas constituta eis qui eiusdem civitatis sunt ad res suas obtinendas; eius autem aequitatis utilis cognitio est; utilis ergo est iuris civilis scientia* ('The civil law is the righteousness [*aequitas*] established for those with a shared citizenship to claim what is theirs. It is therefore useful to know this righteousness. So it is useful to know the civil law').

215 Cic., *Mur.* 7.

216 See G. Falcone, *Difesa del dominium e stabilità della res publica nell'orazione ciceroniana Pro Murena*, [in:] *Fides Humanitas Ius. Scritti in onore di Luigi Labruna*, C. Cascione, C. Masi Doria (ed.), Napoli 2007, pp. 1683–1710; G. La Bua, *Cicero and Roman Education: The Reception of the Speeches and Ancient Scholarship*, New York 2019, pp. 242–244 along with the studies cited therein.

217 The ideas of *dignitas* and *utilitas* are also juxtaposed in other fragments of Cicero's works (cf. e.g. already quoted Cic., *Inv.* 2,53,160; *Rhet. ad Heren.* 2,13,20) and fragments of the *Digest of Justinian* (e.g. Ulp. D. 1,14,3; 5,1,18,1). See also T. Piscitelli, *Dignitas in Cicerone. Tra semantica e semiologia*, 'Bollettino di Studi Latini' 1979, vol. 9, pp. 253–267; G. Falcone, *Ius suum...*, pp. 133–167.

218 Diomedes Grammaticus of the 4th century attributes the following definition to Cicero: GL 1, p. 421, l. 5–7 *Tullius hoc modo eam definit: ars est perceptionum [praeceptionum?] exercitatarum constructio ad unum exitum utilem vitae pertinentium* ('Tullius defines it as follows: art is a juxtaposition of perceptions [principles?] and exercises aimed at one result that will be useful for life'). Whether or not this definition was truly Cicero's, it must have been modelled on Stoic doctrine. A similar explanation is also preserved in Quintilian (Quint., *Inst.* 2,17,41).

219 This connection is seemingly denied by Publius Ovidius Naso in his *Epistulae ex Ponto*. See Ov., *Pont.* 1,53–54 *magis utile nil est/ artibus his, quae nil utilitatis habent* ('Nothing is more useful than the arts that are of no use'). However, it should be remembered that the *Epistulae ex Ponto* were written at a very difficult time for Ovid, specifically during his exile. Consequently, the poet's letters are filled with hyperbolic complaints. In this context, it is not surprising that Ovid separated the two concepts. Legal aspects of Ovid's exile are discussed in M. Dyjakowska, *Prawne aspekty relegacji Owidiusza*, 'Folia Societatis Scientiarum Lublinensis: Humanistyka' 1993, vol. 34, no. 1, pp. 61–72 and A. Łuka, *Inque meo nullum carmine crimen erit. Owidiusza konflikt z prawem*, 'Studia Prawnicze KUL' 2014, vol. 1, no. 57, pp. 85–118.

Quint., *Inst.* 2,17,41
... ille ab omnibus fere probatus finis observatur, artem constare ex perceptionibus consentientibus et coexercitatis ad finem utilem vitae ...
... almost everyone has approved the definition of 'art' as consisting of cognitions agreeing and exercised together in order to achieve a useful goal for life ...

Luc., *Par.* 4
Τέχνη ἐστίν, ὡς ἐγὼ διαμνημονεύω σοφοῦ τινος ἀκούσας, σύστημα ἐκ καταλήψεων συγγεγυμνασμένων πρός τι τέλος εὔχρηστον τῷ βίῳ.
Art, as I remember hearing a learned man speak, is the totality of practices undertaken together in order to achieve some useful goal for life.

Both passages are rooted in the previously quoted Zeno of Citium's definition affirming that *artes* were practised for a useful purpose. Notably, both of them indicate common knowledge of the analyzed definition of the concept of *ars*, and Quintilian even explicitly mentions the general acclaim of this explanation. This fact seems to be indicated by the circle of both authors' audience. The *Institutio oratoria* was addressed primarily to rhetoric teachers and, indirectly, to young apprentices of this discipline, being one of the most crucial in Roman education. Lucian, on the other hand, makes a reference to the Stoic thought by humorously exploring whether parasitism could be considered an art, and, in addition, more perfect than rhetoric or philosophy. Although the recipient of Lucian's refined satire must have been a representative of the intellectual elite[220], and not an average Roman citizen, we can assume that, at least in some circles, at the end of the 2nd century CE the quoted definition was still not only fully understood but also widespread.

What is more, this definition continued to resonate in later times and was reiterated by grammarians. Gaius Marius Victorinus and Pseudo-Asper, from the middle of the 5th century CE, quoted the definitions of the term *ars* analogous to those mentioned earlier, also emphasizing the element of *utilitas* in their content:

Mar. Victorin., *Ars*, GL 6, p. 3, l. 2–5
Ars, ut Aristoni placet, collectio est ex perceptionibus et exercitationibus ad aliquem vitae finem pertinens, id est generaliter omne quicquid certis praeceptis ad utilitatem nostram format animos.
Art, as Ariston argues, is a set of perceptions and exercises relating to a purpose in life. In general, it is all that, by means of specific precepts, shapes the minds for our own utility.

220 D. Marsh, *Lucian and the Latins: Humor and Humanism in the Early Renaissance*, Ann Arbor 1998, p. 2.

Pseudo-Asper, *Ars maior*, GL 5, p. 547, l. 5
Ars est comprehensio praeceptorum ad utilitatem usui accommodata per artificis sui exercitationem.
Art is a set of rules for the utility of practice applied through the exercise of its practitioner.

The interplay between the concepts of *ars* and *utilitas* has been a persistent thread in intellectual discourse, stretching from the time of Varro in the 1st century BCE to the writings and endeavors of figures like Cicero, Quintilian, Lucian, and grammarians in the 4th and 5th centuries CE. Eventually, Cassiodorus, quoting Varro's opinion, further confirmed the enduring stability of the term's meaning. It is highly likely that this connection between *ars* and *utilitas* also permeated the realm of law. Jurists such as Celsus in the 2nd century CE, as well as later figures like Ulpian and possibly the compilers of Justinian's era, likely recognized the inherent link between these concepts. Therefore, to understand Celsus' definition of *ius*, we should place it within this consistent tradition. The nexus between *ars* and *utilitas* illuminates his concept of *ius*, showcasing the integration of the categories *utilitas* and *ius*. In this context, *ius* embodies a pragmatically grounded quality that serves a practical and useful goal within a specific human society, for which the law was created.

1.3.2 *Aequum, bonum, utile*

The category of a useful goal, which the practice of specific art aims to achieve, receives a unique interpretation on the basis of Celsus' definition. Given that *ius* was the art of good and right, the notions of *bonum et aequum* emerge here as the *finis utilis vitae*[221]. This implies that in this context, according to both Celsus and Ulpian quoting him, the

221 The juxtaposition of both terms can be found in the literature from the 3rd and 2nd centuries BCE in Plautus and Terentius (e.g. Plaut., *Capt.* 333; *Curc.* 128–130; *Men.* 580; *Most.* 682; *Pseud.* 389; *Rud.* 1029 and Ter., *Haut.* 642; *Phorm.* 450). The understanding of the ambiguous pair of concepts *bonum et aequum* is widely discussed by Roman law researchers. Key works include: F. Pringsheim, *Bonum et aequum*, pp. 78–155; A. Biscardi, *On aequitas and epieikeia* [in:] *Aequitas and Equity: Equity in Civil Law and Mixed Jurisdictions*, A. M. Rabello (ed.), Jerusalem 1997, pp. 1–11; P. Voci, *Ars boni et aequi*, 'Index' 1999, no. 27, pp. 1–22; P. Cerami, *La concezione...*, pp. 5–250; F. Gallo, *Sulla definizione...*, pp. 7–52; F. Gallo, *'Ars boni et aequi' e ' ius naturale'*, 'SDHI' 2009, vol. 75, pp. 15–42; M. Humbert, *Equité et raison naturelle dans les oeuvres de Celse et de Julien* [in:] *Testi e problemi del giusnaturalismo romano*, D. Mantovani, A. Schiavone (ed.), Pavia 2007, pp. 419–473; W. Waldstein, *"Aequitas" e "summum ius"*, [in:] *Saggi sul diritto non scritto*, Milano 2002, pp. 131–163; Idem, *Equità e ragione naturale nel pensiero giuridico del I secolo d. C.* [in:] *Testi e problemi del giusnaturalismo romano*, D. Mantovani, A. Schiavone (ed.), Pavia 2007, pp. 249–269; M. Kuryłowicz, *Wokół pojęcia aequitas w prawie rzymskim*, 'Studia Iuridica Lublinensia' 2011, vol. 15, pp. 15–27; P. Thomas, *Ars aequi et boni, legal argumentation and the correct legal solution*, 'ZSS RA' 2014, vol. 131, no. 1, pp. 41–59; D. Mantovani, *L'aequitas romana: una nozione in cerca di equilibrio* [in:] *Quante equità?*, D. Mantovani, S. Veca (ed.), Milano 2017, pp. 15–60.

attributes of *utile, bonum* and *aequum* are inherently linked. Thus, the interconnection between *bonum* and *aequum*, should be extended over the category of *utilitas*, at least in this context.

Interestingly, this idea resonates within the scholarly discourse exploring the interplay between *bonum* and *aequum* within Celsus' definition[222]. While the primary aim of this discussion is not to define these concepts, it is worth noting that researchers often, sometimes implicitly, connect the concept of *utilitas* with *bonum* and *aequum*. For instance, Pasquale Voci openly aligns with such a connection, interpreting Celsus' *bonum* in line with Egidio Forcellini's perspective, who characterizes *bonum* as something 'fair, useful, pleasant, or in its class perfect and in harmony with the natural order'[223]. According to Voci, everything that is socially useful and advantageous for the community can be categorized as *bonum*[224].

Additionally, Pietro Cerami views the quality of *bonum* in Celsus' definition as the good and benefit of individuals in terms of their mutual relations[225]. Although this interpretation holds merit, it might not fully encompass the concept's breadth. As Filippo Gallo points out, this perspective confines the legal space strictly to explicitly indicated and specific legal relationships. Gallo offers a broader understanding of the term *bonum*, describing it as a specific outcome resulting from acting in accordance with common sense, encapsulating every good, namely the best possible solution to a legal problem that a person can propose and apply as a result of the reasoning process[226]. Consequently, *bonum* implies a particular benefit arising from legal reflection. As for the concept of *aequum*[227], Cerami explains it as an equilibrium of competing interests within mutual relations[228].

222 Gallo made a very convincing argument, emphasizing that *bonum* and *aequum* were not separate, autonomous elements but formed a hendiadys, in which both concepts complemented each other. The Italian researcher also claimed that the *bonum et aequum* clause was used by Celsus to indicate the relationship between law and justice. These terms together could be understood as synonymous with *iustitia*, *Celso…*, pp. 30–36.

223 LTL, s. v. *bonus*: *Id quod est honestum, aut utile, aut jucundum, perfectum in suo genere et naturae consentiens.* Under the same entry, Forcellini also gives the following explanations: *Generatim ponitur pro utili, opportuno, commodo, salutari et aliquando etiam felici* ('In general, [the term *bonus*] is given as a synonym for useful, convenient, beneficial, profitable and sometimes also fortunate') and *Relative bonum est felicitas, fortuna, utilitas, commodum* ('*Bonum* can relatively mean good fortune, good luck, utility, benefit').

224 P. Voci, *Ars…*, pp. 1–22. F. Gallo, *Celso…*, p. 74, in turn, adds such discriminants to *bonum* only when it is treated as an isolated criterion. According to him, in correlation with *aequum*, it takes the form of a real requirement and has a concrete character.

225 P. Cerami, *La concezione…*, p. 19.

226 F. Gallo, *Celso…*, p. 34.

227 Metaphorically, the term could also be synonymous with *iustum*, LTL, s. v. *aequus*. However, it should be remembered that, in the light of legal sources, the term *aequum* obtained its own technical meaning. Cf. F. Gallo, *Sulla definizione…*, p. 31.

228 P. Cerami, *La concezione…*, p. 19. This opinion is not shared by Gallo, who recognizes *aequum* as a symbol of binding proportional equality within any juridical activity. The Italian researcher un-

The ethical foundation of *utilitas* in Ulpian's thought is further emphasized by his reference to the concept of *iustitia* right before he presents Celsus' definition of law. This connection, as we recall, was also crucial on the basis of Cicero's doctrine[229]. Ulpian states that the term *ius* is derived from *iustitia* (D. 1,1,1,pr.: *est autem a iustitia appellatum*). This assertion goes beyond mere etymology[230], as Giuseppe Falcone insightfully points out, focusing on the transmission of values that the law should embody[231]. Therefore, both the existing norms and those to be enacted in the future should align with the primary idea of justice. Falcone contends that Ulpian's text not only emphasizes the strong link between *ius, bonum,* and *aequum,* but also introduces an additional element of *iustitia* to Celsus' perspective[232]. Following this logic, it should be acknowledged that, since law, as an art, seeks to realize a useful goal for individuals by upholding the ideals of good and righteousness, the intentions of justice itself align with these objectives. Consequently, since the *bonum et aequum* syntagma is inextricably linked to the category of *utilitas* through the concept of *ars,* Ulpian's framework encompasses not three but four interwoven categories: *iustitia, ius, bonum et aequum,* and *utilitas*[233].

The connection between *ius, bonum et aequum* and *utilitas* is consistently reinforced by other jurists, as evident in almost every fragment where they make an attempt to define the concept of the 'law'. As will be further analyzed in Chapter Two, Ulpian explicitly references *utilitas* in the continuation of the above-quoted fragment when describing *ius publicum* and *ius privatum* (D. 1,1,1,2). Another notable example is found in Paulus' *Libri ad Sabinum,* where the jurist explains the multiple meanings of the term *ius*:

derstands this category more broadly, encompassing the creation, interpretation, and application of the law, *Celso...,* p. 35. Voci proposed an even broader understanding, considering it to indicate any activity based on and consistent with justice, *Ars...,* p. 1.

229 Cf. previous remarks and in particular Cic., *Inv.* 2,53,160; *Off.* 1,31,7–9 and 1,43,155.

230 The origin of the words is exactly the opposite. See *Dictionnaire étymologique...,* pp. 329–330, s. v. *ius*. Falcone offers fascinating insights into the correlation of this paragraph with Cicero's thought, (esp. Cic., *Leg.* 1,6,18), *La 'vera philosophia'...,* pp. 89–90. Additionally, Schiavone's remarks on this matter in J.-L. Ferrary, A. Schiavone, V. Marotta, *Cnaeus Domitius Ulpianus...,* pp. 188–189, are worth considering.

231 See G. Falcone, *La 'vera philosophia'...,* pp. 45–46; P. Fabry, *Nomen iuris est autem a iustitia appellatum: Ulpien, l'étymologie, l'idée de justice dans la pensée juridique et politique de Rome,* 'RHD' 2014, vol. 92, no. 4, pp. 489–515. Ulpian often refers to the technique of explaining etymology in order to clarify the importance or genesis of a specific institution or concept. Cf. also A. Schiavone, *Giuristi e principe...,* p. 7, n. 9.

232 G. Falcone, *La 'vera philosophia'...,* pp. 44–47.

233 The link between these categories also pointed out in *Rhet. ad Heren.* 2,13,20.

D. 1,1,11 (*Paulus libro quarto decimo ad Sabinum*):
Ius pluribus modis dicitur: uno modo, cum id quod semper aequum ac bonum est ius dicitur, ut est ius naturale. Altero modo, quod omnibus aut pluribus in quaque civitate utile est, ut est ius civile (...).
The law can be defined in many ways. Firstly, when what is always right and good is called the law, as in the case of the natural law. Secondly, when it is useful to all, or most of people in a given society, such as in the case of the civil law (...).

As Remo Martini[234] and Mario Talamanca[235] noted, the classification carried out by Paulus fits the concept of the division made in order to clarify the content of an ambiguous term (*vox multa significans*)[236]. In this passage, Paulus offers as many as four meanings of the term 'law'[237], two of which holding particular importance in course of our considerations. Describing the category of the natural law[238], the jurist refers to *bonum et aequum* as its constant distinguishing feature(s). Paulus further highlights the primary feature of *ius civile*[239]: its utility to all, or at least the majority of people, within a society. It seems that Paulus does not reduce this concept to the law of Roman citizens

234 R. Martini, *Le definizioni...*, p. 277.

235 M. Talamanca, *Per la storia della giurisprudenza romana*, 'BIDR' 1977, vol. 80, pp. 231–235.

236 This classification is also mentioned by Boethius: Boeth., *De divisione 6 Divisio namque multis dicitur modis. (...) est alia cum vox multa significans in significationes proprias recipit sectionem.* ('The division is made in many ways [...]. There is another one when an ambiguous term is broken down according to its own meanings'). On this also in A. Mantello, *Il sogno, la parola, il diritto. Appunti sulle concezioni giuridiche di Paolo*, 'BIDR' 1991, vol. 94–95, pp. 357–358.

237 Apart from the *ius naturale* and *ius civile*, Paulus also mentioned the *ius honorarium* and the place where justice is done (*locus in quo ius redditur*). Cf. Paul. D. 1,1,11 *in fine*.

238 For more on *ius naturale* see e.g. E. Levy, *Natural Law in the Roman Period*, 'Natural Law Institute Proceedings' 1949, vol. 2, pp. 43–72; A. Burdese, *Il concetto di ius naturale nel pensiero della giurisprudenza classica*, 'Rivista Italiana per le Scienze Giuridiche' 1954, vol. 7, pp. 407–431; G. Nocera, *Ius naturale nella esperienza giuridica romana*, Milano 1962; W. Waldstein, *Bemerkungen zum ius naturale bei den klassischen Juristen*, 'ZSS RA' 1988, vol. 105, no.1, pp. 702–711; Idem, *Ius naturale im nachklassischen römischen Recht und bei Justinian*, 'ZSS RA' 1994, vol. 111, no. 1, pp. 1–65; T. Honoré, *Ulpian, Natural law and Stoic influence*, 'TR' 2010, vol 78, no 1–2, pp. 199–208. Important contributions on this topic also in the recent volume *Testi e problemi del giusnaturalismo romano*, D. Mantovani, A. Schiavone (ed.), Pavia 2007.

239 The researchers' considerations on the meanings of the concept of *ius civile* were collected and summarized by A.A. Schiller, *Roman Law: Mechanisms of Development*, Hauge-Paris-New York 1978, pp. 367–369, along with the studies cited therein. Schiller emphasized that the meaning of this word changes depending on its juxtaposition with another term. The understanding of the *ius civile* compared with the *ius sacrum* differs from the one contrasted with the *ius honorarium*, the *ius gentium*, or the *ius naturale*. See also F. Gallo, *Celso...*, p. 54, n. 69.

(*ius civile Romanorum*)[240], but suggests a universal dimension, encompassing all legal norms established by a given community[241] for the utility of its members[242].

A similar thought is also conveyed by an earlier source not included in the Justinian compilation, referred to as *Fragmentum Dositheanum de manumissionibus* and attributed to (Pseudo-)Dositheus, who was roughly contemporaneous with Gaius[243], that is the 2nd century CE. Originally written in Latin, *Fragmentum Dositheanum* was later translated into Greek, and then re-translated back into Latin already in ancient times. Although it primarily addresses the subject of manumission, the opening section of this source aligns with Paulus' thought:

240 As a rule, when a community in which a given civil law was to apply was not specified, the term *ius civile* was understood as the law of Roman citizens. Cf. I. 1,2,2 (…) *sed quotiens non addimus, cuius sit civitatis, nostrum ius significamus* ('but whenever we do not say which community it belongs to, we talk about our law').

241 The same meaning of *ius civile* can be found in Gaius' *Institutes* and Justinian's *Institutes*. Cf. G. 1,1 (= D. 1,1,9 = I. 1,2,1) (…) *nam quod quisque populus ipse sibi ius constituit, id ipsius proprium est vocaturque ius civile, quasi ius proprium civitatis* ('This law, which each people has made for themselves, is their own law and is called the *ius civile*, as if society's own law.') and I. 1,2,2 *Sed ius quidem civile ex unaquaque civitate appellatur, veluti Atheniensium: nam si quis velit Solonis vel Draconis leges appellare ius civile Atheniensium, non erraverit. sic enim et ius, quo populus Romanus utitur, ius civile Romanorum appellamus: vel ius Quiritium, quo Quirites utuntur. Romani enim a Quirino Quirites appellantur* ('However, the civil law is named after a particular society, for instance, the Athenians: for if one wanted to call the laws of Solon and Draco the civil law of the Athenians, he would not make a mistake. Thus, the law used by the Roman people is also called the civil law of the Romans, or the law of the Quirites used by the Quirites, because the Romans are called the Quirites from Quirinus'). Somewhat similar understanding of this term is also proposed by Cicero, *Top.* 2,9 *Ius civile est aequitas constituta eis qui eiusdem civitatis sunt ad res suas obtinendas* ('The civil law is the righteousness [*aequitas*] established for those with a shared citizenship to claim what is theirs'). Isidore of Seville later constructed a similar definition with regard to the religious element: *Etym.* 5,5 *Ius civile est quod quisque populus vel civitas sibi proprium humana divinaque causa constituit* ('The civil law is the one that each community or state has established for themselves as their own for human and divine reasons'). Egon Weiss proposed this meaning of the term *ius civile* alongside two others: common practices and the effect of jurists' activity taken together, and the law of jurists, understood as norms whose source is not the activity of any public authority, and thus opposed to the law-making activity of emperors and officials. See RE, vol. X.19, coll. 1206–1208, s. v. *ius civile.*

242 Cicero also speaks in this spirit, *Leg.* 2,5,11 …*Constare profecto ad salutem civium civitatumque incolumitatem vitamque hominum quietam et beatam inventas esse leges…* ('Indeed, it is known that laws were drawn up in the name of the good of citizens, the security of societies, and the peaceful and happy life of people').

243 A convincing argument for such dating was presented in H. L. W. Nelson, *Überlieferung, Aufbau und Stil von Gai Institutiones*, Leiden 1981, pp. 361–370, who argues that the textbook used by (Pseudo-)Dositheus could not be later than the very beginning of the 3rd century. See also M. Wibier, *Transmitting Legal Knowledge: From Question-and-Answer Format to Handbook in Gaius' Institutes* [in:] *Between Orality and Literacy: Communication and Adaptation in Antiquity: Orality and Literacy in the Ancient World*, R. Scodel (ed.), Leiden-Boston 2014, vol. 10, pp. 364–365 and G. Falcone, *Sul c. d. Fragmentum Dositheanum*, 'Specula iuris' 2021, vol. 1, no 1, pp. 203–227, who does not exclude that *Fragmentum* could be an excerpt from Gaius' *Res cottidianae.* On the source also in T. Honoré, *The 'Fragmentum Dositheanum'*, 'RIDA' 1965, vol. 12, pp. 301–323.

Fragm. Dosith. 1
Πᾶν γὰρ δίκαιον ἢ πολιτικὸν προσαγορεύεται ἢ φυσικὸν λέγεται ἢ ἐθνικὸν δίκαιον· ἀπὸ τούτου γὰρ ὠνομάσθη, καὶ πάντα τὰ ἔθνη ὁμοίως τούτῳ εἰσὶν κεχρημένα· ὃ γὰρ καλὸν καὶ δίκαιόν ἐστι, πάντων εὐχρηστίᾳ συμφωνεῖ. Τὸ δὲ δίκαιον πολιτικὸν κύριόν ἐστι Ῥωμαίων, καὶ ἀπὸ τούτων εἰρημένον, ἐπειδὴ ἡμετέρα πόλις ταύτῃ τῇ ἀληθείᾳ χρᾶται, ἀλλ'ἔνιοι προλέγουσιν τοῦτο εἶναι, ὃ πᾶσι πολίταις ἰδίοις ἢ μείζονι μέρει συμφέρει[244] (…).
Omne ius aut civile appellatur aut naturale. Naturale dicitur etiam ius gentium: ab eo enim nominatum quod omnes nationes similiter eo sunt usae: quod enim bonum et aequum est, omnium utilitati convenit. Ius civile autem proprium est civium Romanorum, ab eo dictum, quod nostra civitas ea veritate utitur. Sed quidam praedicent hoc esse, quod omnibus civibus suis aut maiori parti expedit[245] (…).
For every law is called either civil or natural. The natural law is also called the law of nations. It is called this way precisely because all nations have used it similarly: for what is good and just is useful to all. On the other hand, the civil law is specific to Roman citizens, and takes its name from the fact that our community uses it according to its own rules. Nevertheless, some would say that it is the law especially useful to all citizens, or to most of them (…).

(Pseudo-)Dositheus appears to equate the category of *ius naturale* with the law of nations (*ius gentium*[246]) and, much like Paulus, asserts that, as it is good and right[247], it is useful to all people (πάντων εὐχρηστίᾳ συμφωνεῖ; *omnium utilitati convenit*). In doing so, he combines the categories of *bonum, aequum* and *utile*. (Pseudo-)Dositheus goes on to clarify that the term *ius civile* – in this case, understood as *ius civile Romanorum* – tends to be described in two ways. Firstly, while the *ius gentium* received its name due to its similar application across all nations[248], a distinctive feature of the law of Roman citizens was that they applied it according to their principles[249]. The jurist made it clear, however, that some describe *ius civile* as useful to all citizens, or, at the very least,

244 Pseudo-Dositheus, *Hermeneumata Pseudodositheana Leidensia*, G. Flammini (ed.), Monachii-Lipsiae 2004, p. 93. See also *Corpus iuris Romani anteiustiniani*, E. Böcking, E. Puggé, A. M. Bethmann-Hollweg (ed.), Bonnae 1841, pp. 214–215.

245 The text is quoted according to P. Krüger, *Ulpiani Liber singularis regularum. Pauli Libri quinque sententiarum. Fragmenta minora saeculorum p. Chr. n. secundi et tertii*, Berolini 1878, p. 151. See also FIRA II, p. 618. In terms of reconstructing the fragment, there are interesting remarks by K. Lachmann, *Kleinere Schriften zur classischen Philologie*, vol. 2, Berlin 1876 rep. 2018, esp. pp. 196–206, as well as *Versuch über Dositheus*, Berlin 1837. See also *Corpus iuris Romani…*, pp. 214–215.

246 Cf. I. 1,2,11.

247 Paul. D. 1,1,11.

248 Cf. also remarks in G. Aricò Anselmo, *'Ius publicum'…*, pp. 597–598, on the understanding of the term *ius gentium* in the context of the analyzed source. The researcher also notes the correlation of the *Fragmentum Dositheanum* with Gaius' *Institiutes*, recognizing that the author is referring to 'modello definitorio gaiano'. Cf. also G. 1,1. = D. 1,1,9.

249 Cf. I. 1,2,2.

the majority of them. This last mention clearly resonates with Paulus' thought. Further in the source, (Pseudo-)Dositheus seems to lean towards the first description of the *ius civile*. Nevertheless, he distinguishes two sets of legal norms, and the scope of each of them may be, explicitly in the case of *ius naturale* and implicitly in the case of *ius civile*, defined by *utilitas*. In this context, the *ius naturale* is deemed useful for all people[250], whereas the *ius civile* – to a particular community. Consequently, each legal norm is guided by a particular utility.

Such a perspective may shed new light on Paulus' account in D. 1,1,11, as the correspondence between the *ius naturale* and *ius civile*, becomes more apparent. Analyzing this fragment through the lens of *Fragmentum Dositheanum*, implies that the criteria of *bonum, aequum* and *utile*[251] were applicable jointly to both categories of natural and

250 Linking the categories of the *ius naturale* and *utilitas* is also perfectly visible in Cicero's doctrine: Cic., *Inv.* 2,22,65 *Utrisque aut etiam omnibus, si plures ambigent, ius ex quibus rebus constet, considerandum est. Initium ergo eius ab natura ductum videtur; quaedam autem ex utilitatis ratione aut perspicua nobis aut obscura in consuetudinem venisse; post autem approbata quaedam a consuetudine aut vero utilia visa legibus esse firmata* ('Both opponents, or all of them, if there is more than one person involved in the dispute, should consider which elements make up the law. The law, it seems, comes from nature. Some laws have been accepted as customary for their utility: either obvious or hidden to us; only later were they recognized as right through habit, or, having turned out to be useful, were confirmed by the laws'). Cicero does not explicitly mention here *ius civile*, but the nameless *ius* her refers to is undoubtedly the civil law, as these considerations are a continuation of the description of the *constitutio generalis*, namely a dispute in which the parties argue as to the facts. According to Cicero this circumstance could have a twofold character: *negotialis* (substantiative) or *iuridicialis* (concerning the legality of proceedings). The orator began his considerations as follows: *Inv.* 2,21,62: *Negotialis est quae in ipso negotio iuris civilis habet implicatam controversiam* ('The substantive variation is one in which the disagreement goes to the very heart of the matter in proceedings based on the civil law'). Thus, in an earlier paragraph, he indicated that his considerations pertain to the *ius civile*. Furtheremore, at the end of this paragraph, Cicero made a separate clarification regarding the understanding of the *ius naturale* (*Inv.* 2,22,65 *Ac naturae quidem ius esse, quod nobis non opinio, sed quaedam innata vis adferat, ut religionem, pietatem, gratiam, vindicationem, observantiam, veritatem* – 'It is the law of nature that is dictated, not by judgment, but by some innate strength, such as godliness, devotion, gratitude, just retaliation, respect, truthfulness'). Hence, the quoted fragment of *De inventione* certainly refers to the *ius civile*. The same opinion was also expresses by G. Aricò Anselmo, *'Ius publicum'*..., pp. 689–690, n. 149. Cf. also Cic., *Inv.* 2,53,160 *Iustitia est habitus animi communi utilitate conservata suam cuique tribuens dignitatem. Eius initium est ab natura profectum; deinde quaedam in consuetudinem ex utilitatis ratione venerunt: postea res et ab natura profectas et ab consuetudine probatas legum metus et religio sanxit* ('Justice is the state of the mind, which, for the sake of safeguarding the common utility, gives everyone their due. Its beginning comes from nature. Then, some rules have become customary because of their usefulness. Later on, what became of nature and what became customary was ratified by the fear of laws and the reverence of the gods'). See also Cic., *Off.* 3,6,31 *Itaque lex ipsa naturae, quae utilitatem hominum conservat et continent...* ('The very law of nature, which is guided by what is useful for people and protects it ...'). The echoes of this concept, which is based on the discovery of the law and not on its creation, are obvious foundation of the school of the natural law.

251 C.A. Maschi, *La conclusione della giurisprudenza classica all'età dei Severi: Iulius Paulus* [in:] ANRW, vol. 2.15, Berlin-New York 1976, p. 699.

civil law even if their content was to be clarified depending on the type of set of norms[252].

Lastly, when attempting to connect the criterion of *utilitas* to the other values, we should not overlook the statement of Aemilius Papinian, a jurist active at the turn of the 2nd and 3rd century CE:

> D. 1,1,7,1 (*Papinianus libro secundo definitionum*)
> *Ius praetorium est, quod praetores introduxerunt adiuvandi vel supplendi vel corrigendi iuris civilis gratia propter utilitatem publicam* (…)
> The praetorian law is what the praetors introduced to support, supplement, or rectify civil law for the public utility.

As Papinian noted, the role of the praetorian law was to support, supplement, or rec tify *ius civile*[253]. Numerous sources clearly indicate that these objectives were often achieved by invoking the concept of *aequitas*[254], especially in cases where the strict ap-

252 On Paulus seeing the *ius naturale* and *ius civile* as related categories in A. Mantello, *Il sogno…*, p. 359. Similarly T. Honsell, *Gemeinwohl…*, p. 132.

253 Pap. D. 1,1,7,pr. *Ius autem civile est, quod ex legibus, plebis scitis, senatus consultis, decretis principum, auctoritate prudentium venit* ('The *ius civile* is the law that comes from statutes, plebiscites, the Senate resolutions, emperors' decrees, and jurists' authority'). Cf. also V. Scarano Ussani, *L'utilità…*, pp. 96–97 and F. Gallo, *L'officium del pretore nella produzione e applicazione del diritto: Corso di diritto romano*, Torino 1997, p. 88, n. 73. The *ius civile* and the *ius praetorium* did not thus constitute two separate systems but rather two main sources of norms that made a varied yet one and unified legal order. Cf. Marcian. D. 1,1,8 *Nam et ipsum ius honorarium viva vox est iuris civilis* ('For the *ius honorarium* itself is a living voice of the *ius civile*') and Paul. D. 1,1,11. This thesis, promoted especially by Gallo (*L'officium…*, p. 53 and *La riflessione di Papiniano sul ius honorarium* [in:] *Règle et pratique du droit: dans les réalités juridiques de la antiquité: Atti della 51a Sessione della SIHDA – Société Internationale Fernand De Visscher pour l'Histoire des Droits de l'Antiquité [Crotone-Messina, 16–20 settembre 1997]*, I. Piro [ed.], Catanzaro 1999, pp. 31–53), was a response to the concept proposed by Emilio Betti, who recognized the *ius praetorium* and *ius civile* as two separate orders, *La creazione del diritto nella 'iurisdictio' del pretore romano* [in:] *Studi di diritto processuale in onore di Giuseppe Chiovenda nel venticinquesimo anno del suo insegnamento.*, A. Castellari et al. (ed.), Padova 1927, pp. 65–129, as well as *'Iurisdictio praetoris' e potere normativo*, 'Labeo' 1968, vol. 14, pp. 7–23.

254 To give some examples: Marcell. D. 4,1,7,1…*et boni praetoris est potius restituere litem, ut et ratio et aequitas postulabit, quam actionem famosam constituere…*; Ulp. D. 4,6,26,9 ITEM, *inquit praetor,* SI QVA ALIA MIHI IVSTA CAVSA VIDEBITVR, IN INTEGRVM RESTITVAM. *haec clausula edicto inserta est necessario: multi enim casus evenire potuerunt, qui deferrent restitutionis auxilium, nec singillatim enumerari potuerunt, ut, quotiens aequitas restitutionem suggerit, ad hanc clausulam erit descendendum…*; Paul. D. 37,1,6,1…*quamvis enim iure civili deficiant liberi, qui propter capitis deminutionem desierunt sui heredes esse, propter aequitatem tamen rescindit eorum capitis deminutionem praetor…*; G. 3,25 *Sed hae iuris iniquitates edicto praetoris emendatae sunt.*; G. 3,41 *Qua de causa postea praetoris edicto haec iuris iniquitas emendata est…* Moreover, just like *utilitas*, the jurists frequently invoke the concept of *aequitas* (often referred to as *naturalis*) in their *laudationes edicti*: Ulp. D. 2,2,1,pr. *Hoc edictum summam habet aequitatem…*; Ulp. D. 2,10,1,pr. *Aequissimum putavit praetor…*; Ulp. D. 2,13,4,1 *Huius edicti ratio aequissima est…*; Ulp. D. 2,14,1,pr. *Huius edicti aequitas naturalis est…*; Ulp. D. 3,3,33,4 *Aequum praetori visum est…*; Ulp. D. 4,4,1,pr. *Hoc edictum praetor naturalem aequitatem secutus proposuit…*; Ulp. D. 13,5,1,pr. *Hoc edicto praetor favet naturali aequitati…*;

plication of the *ius civile* could lead to unjust outcomes. Therefore, it can be reasonably argued that *aequitas,* while not explicitly articulated, is at the core of *ius praetorium*[255], as it implicitly informs its principles. Notably, when Papinian defines[256] the concept of praetorian law, he refers to the criterion of *utilitas,* stating that *ius praetorium* was introduced for the sake of *utilitas publica.* Thus, even though the direct link between *aequitas* and *utilitas* is not explicitly addressed in this passage, it is justified to conclude that the concepts of *aequum* and *utile* were closely interwoven within the realm of praetorian law[257].

In this context, it is also relevant to mention a passage from the *Rhetorica ad Herennium* that combines the reversed syntagma *bonum et aequum* (and not *aequitas*[258]) with *utilitas.* Although the law described in that passage is not explicitly referred to as *ius praetorium,* the example provided clearly relates to the praetorian law[259]:

Ulp. D. 14,3,1 *Aequum praetori visum est…;* Ulp. D. 27,6,1 *Huius edicti aequitas non est ambigua…* A very comprehensive analysis of this topic with regard to Ulp. D. 2,14,1,pr. has been presented by G. Falcone, *L'esordio del commento ulpianeo all'editto sui patti (D. 2, 14, 1 pr.) tra critica testuale e studio dei percorsi concettuali,* 'AUPA' 2009, vol. 53, pp. 226–254, along with the studies cited thereinin. We should also note that there is even one passage where Ulpian explicitly refers to both of these concepts: D. 14,1,1,pr. *Utilitatem huius edicti patere nemo est qui ignoret. nam cum interdum ignari, cuius sint condicionis vel quales, cum magistris propter navigandi necessitatem contrahamus, aequum fuit eum, qui magistrum navi imposuit, teneri…* For a more extensive recent lists of sources illustrating the connection between *aequitas* and *ius praetorium* and a commentary to them refer to, e. g. U. Babusiaux, *Zur Funktion…,* pp. 603–644; D. Mantovani, *Giuristi romani…,* pp. 141–215.

255 L. Capuano describes it as *l'elemento principale, Dottrina e storia del diritto romano,* Napoli 1878, p. 77.

256 Since one of the goals of Chapter One is to embed the *utilitas* criterion in a broader cultural and literary context, it is essential to quote M. A. Messana here, who states that the definition proposed by Papinian bears traces of Ciceronian rhetoric, *Sui 'libri definitionum' di Emilio Papiniano. 'Definitio' e 'definire' nell'esperienza giuridica romana,* 'AUPA' 1998, vol. 45, no. 2, p. 252.

257 Similarly, while commenting on the same source, S. Riccobono identifies *utilitas* as one of the key aspects of *ius praetorium,* built upon the foundation of *bonum et aequum, La definizione…,* p. 49. F. Longchamps de Bérier connects these values by stating that the praetor promoted *bonum et aequum* while adhering to the principle of *utilitas, The praetor as a promoter of "bonum commune",* 'Legal Roots' 2014, vol. 3, p. 225.

258 My thanks to Professor Giuseppe Falcone for highlighting the need to distinguish between these concepts.

259 As for the syntagma *bonum et aequum* with a direct reference to the praetor's activity in jurisprudential sources, see e. g. Ulp. D. 30,71,2 *In pecunia legata confitenti heredi modicum tempus ad solutionem dandum est nec urguendum ad suscipiendum iudicium: quod quidem tempus ex bono et aequo praetorem observare oportebit.*

> *Rhet. ad Heren.* 2,13,20
> *Ex aequo et bono ius constat, quod*[260] *ad veritatem et utilitatem communem videtur pertinere. Quod genus, ut maior annis LX et cui morbus causa est cognitorem det. Ex eo vel novum ius constitui convenit ex tempore et ex hominis dignitate.*
> The law is based on what is right and good because it is known to serve fairness and common utility. For instance, when the praetor gives a legal representative to a man who is over sixty years of age and has health problems. Accordingly, it is appropriate to establish a new law according to the circumstances and position of the person concerned.

The author of the source believed that the law should serve fairness and common utility. *Veritas*[261] and *utilitas communis* therefore present themselves as the goal of the law[262], which is derived from the *aequum et bonum*. It is particularly noteworthy that the author highlighted the aspect of modifying and adapting the law to the current needs, giving the praetor's appointment of a legal representative for an elderly or sick person as an example of this type of activity[263]. Taking the above into account, it appears justified to claim that the praetorian law also integrated the categories of *aequum* (or even *bonum et aequum*) and *utile*.

260 Here, *quod* can be both a relative pronoun and a conjunction. The choice of any of the variants does not affect the interpretation of the source, because in both cases the *ius* acts as the subject in the subordinate clause.

261 On the topic of *veritas* extensively in T. Giaro, *Dogmatische Wahrheit und Zeitlosigkeit in der römischen Jurisprudenz*, 'BIDR' 1987, vol. 29, pp. 1–104; Idem, *Prawda dogmatyczna i "ponadczasowość" jurysprudencji rzymskiej*, 'CPH' 1988, vol 40, no. 1, pp. 1–31; Idem, *Römische Rechtswahrheiten. Ein Gedankenexperiment*, Frankfurt am Main 2007 as well as in C. Cascione, C. Masi Doria, *Veritas e ius: per una storia della verità giuridica*, Napoli 2013 and the multi-authored volume *Quid est veritas? Un seminario su verità e forme giuridiche*, C. Cascione, C. Masi Doria (ed.), Napoli 2013. Particularly noteworthy are the papers by Masi Doria providing a specific focus on embedding the concept of *veritas* in classical law, *Dalle basi culturali al diritto classico*, [in:] *Veritas e ius: per una storia della verità giuridica*, C. Cascione, C. Masi Doria (ed.), Napoli 2013, pp. 2–62; *Eadem, Linee per una storia della "veritas" nell'esperienza giuridica romana. I. Dalle basi culturali al diritto classico*, [in:] *Quid est veritas? Un seminario su verità e forme giuridiche*, C. Cascione, C. Masi Doria (ed.), Napoli 2013, pp. 1–64.

262 *Utilitas* as a purpose of the law (*das Ziel des Rechts*) was specified in the context of this source also in H. Lausberg, *Handbuch der literarischen Rhetorik. Eine Grundlegung der Literaturwissenschaft*. 3. Auflage mit einem Vorwort von Arnold Arens, Stuttgart 1990, p. 834.

263 Jean-Louis Ferrary also suggests that the source refers to the Pretorian institution, *Le droit naturel dans les exposés sur les parties du droit des traités de rhétorique*, [in:] *Testi e problemi del giusnaturalismo romano*, D. Mantovani, A. Schiavone (ed.), Pavia 2007, p. 79, n. 8. This appears to be one of the oldest sources explicitly mentioning this type of substitution. See D. Mantovani, *L'aequitas...*, p. 34.

1.4 Summary

The concept of *utilitas* held a central place within the Roman legal framework, yet its meaning was not static and varied depending on its contextual usage. *Utilitas* encompassed both economic and ethical dimensions. As such, determining its potential semantic fields is crucial in the context of research on legal interpretation.

This chapter was a first step to answer the question whether *utilitas* in the *utilitatis causa* decisions corresponds solely to pragmatic categories or if its meaning spans a broader spectrum. Given that references to *utilitas,* serving as a tool for jurists to introduce exceptions to the legal norms, are found in the writings of Cicero and Quintilian, our exploration began by seeking to reconstruct the concept's content within a more extensive intellectual context. To this end, we examined the works of Cicero and the phrase defining the term *utilitas* preserved in one of Horace's satires, rooted in Epicurean philosophy.

These sources reveal a passionate debate within the Roman intellectual elite concerning the interplay of justice and utility – a discourse originating from Greek thought. Despite the differences between the views of Cicero and the Epicurean school, cherished by Horace, within the triad of *ius, iustitia* and *utilitas,* their perspectives find compatibility. In both traditions, these ideas are incomprehensible in isolation. In the context of legal philosophy, these concepts harmonize in any action. The assessment of a legal norm's justice depended on its simultaneous perception as useful. The relationship between *utilitas* and *iustitia* was therefore equal, not hierarchical. The former, as the source of the latter, was also a goal to be pursued. Therefore, it can be stated that *utilitas* determined what was just. However, it was not an expression of a utilitarian understanding of justice but of the awareness that the law should serve a community it was established for. In this way, *utilitas* gained a strong ethical foundation in legal philosophy. Cicero expressed this phenomenon through the unification of the categories of *utilitas* and *honestas;* Epicurus – as a natural obligation not to harm one another, symbolizing common utility; and Horace – through the tight connection of *utilitas, iustitia* and *aequitas.*

The ethical dimension of *utilitas* is confirmed not only in non-legal sources but also in jurists' writings. Based on their thought, the analyzed category is presented primarily as a postulate to be implemented yet always linked to the categories of *bonum* and *aequum.* This is evident in the famous definition of the law by Celsus, later recalled by Ulpian, where *ius* was defined as *ars boni et aequi.* The category of *ars* was closely related to *utilitas,* as all ancient *artes* pursued a purpose useful for life (*finis utilis vitae*) and, therefore, for people. This requirement must therefore apply to *ars iuris* too. Thus, the *bonum et aequum* categories should be understood as an object of useful aspirations. In addition, the ethical correlation of *utilitas* is also confirmed by other jurists, including Paulus, who provided the categories of *bonum, aequum* and *utile* as distinguishing features of the law, as well as Papinian, who indicated the pursuit of public utility (*uti-*

litas publica) as the goal of *ius praetorium*, built on the idea of *aequitas*. Thus, *utilitas* as a value therefore meant utility but only one inseparable from the measures of justice, goodness, and righteousness.

The ethical aspect of *utilitas* is evident not only in the philosophical and legal thought reconstructed from literary sources but also in the reflections of Roman jurists. Therefore, this aspect of the analyzed category transcends the type of sources or research area. Consequently, the significance of the category of *utilitas* in the declarations of Cicero and Quintilian, advocating exceptions to legal norms, cannot be narrowly confined to pragmatic categories alone. Hence, at this stage of the considerations, we can hypothesize that such confinement should not apply to the jurisprudence *utilitatis causa* decisions either.

2
Utilitas as a Guideline for Legal Interpretation

2.1 *Utilitas* from the Orator's Perspective

As outlined in Introduction, some scholars have justified the *utilitatis causa* decisions by highlighting the objectives these decisions aimed to fulfil. Leptien referred to these decisions as purpose-driven (*die Zweckmäßigkeitsentscheidungen*), highlighting their teleological nature[264]. He interpreted *utilitas* broadly – as including the needs of practice, economy, society, and the world of values. However, this perspective may not fully capture the unique nature of the *utilitatis causa* decisions, as even the rhetorical model of education aimed to guide thinking and argumentation towards *utilitas*. Cicero, in his treatise *De inventione*, notes that already Aristotle referenced this criterion while characterising different types of matters (*genera*)[265] through the prism of the objectives of the speeches delivered:

> Cic., *Inv.* 2,51,156
>
> *Nam placet in iudiciali genere finem esse aequitatem, hoc est partem quandam honestatis. In deliberativo autem Aristoteli placet utilitatem, nobis et honestatem, et utilitatem, in demonstrativo honestatem. Quare in hoc quoque genere causae quaedam argumentationes communiter ac similiter tractabuntur, quaedam separatius ad finem, quo referri omnem orationem oportet, adiungentur.*
>
> For it is agreed that in the forensic genre, the aim of a speech is righteousness, that is, a certain facet of moral integrity. Aristotle argues that in the deliberative genre, the goal of a speech is utility, but in my opinion it is both moral integrity and utility. The aim in the demonstrative genre is moral integrity. In each type of context certain common and similar arguments therefore apply, and are accompanied by others, tailored to the particular purpose of a given type of speech.

264 This term was used in the titles of both the author's works on the *utilitatis causa* decisions by jurists.

265 The terminology in this regard is not entirely clear. Some sources refer to types of speeches or their topics (*genera rerum/causarum*), while others mention rhetorical types (*genera rhetorices*). See H. Lausberg, *Handbuch…*, p. 53, n. 2.

Cicero differentiated between three types of oratory: demonstrative (*genus demonstrativum*), forensic (*genus iudiciale*) and deliberative (*genus deliberativum*)[266]. The first was used in delivering praise or rebuke, and was typical for ceremonial oratory commemorating individuals or events. The *genus iudiciale* was employed in courts for defence or prosecution, while the *genus deliberativum*, aimed at advising for or against actions in political oratory[267]. The primary goal of every type of speech was always *honestas*. Additionally, deliberative speeches also aimed at *utilitas*[268], understood as the utility of those being advised[269]. Thus, this criterion was each time subject to appropriate clarification[270].

It is also pertinent to mention that the argumentation schemes of what was morally right and useful were used equally willingly within the *genus iudiciale*[271]. Thus, since

266 Cf. Cic., *Inv.* 2,4,12; Idem, *De orat.* 1,141.

267 Cf. Cic., *Inv.* 1,5,7. See also H. Lausberg, *Handbuch…*, pp. 54–56.

268 The same way in Quint., *Inst.* 3,8,1–2. On the other hand, Aristotle claimed that the goal of a deliberative speech was utility itself: *Rhet.* 1,1358b20–29. The same concept can also be found in Cicero. Cf. Cic., *Part.* 83; Idem, *De orat.* 1,141.

269 Cf. Cic., *De orat.* 1,141 *(…) alios in deliberationibus quae omnes ad utilitatem dirigentur eorum quibus consilium daremus* ('other in deliberative speeches, all of which are for the utility of those to whom we advise'). See also Quint., *Inst.* 3,8,42 *Suasoris enim finis est utilitas eius cui quisque suadet* ('The advisor's goal is the utility of the person whom he advises').

270 From the point of view of the state, these were, for instance, its security and power. Cf. Cic., *Inv.* 2,56,169 *Quare utilitatis duae partes videntur esse: incolumitas et potentia. Incolumitas est salutis rata atque integra conservatio; potentia est ad sua conservanda et alterius attenuanda idonearum rerum facultas* ('Therefore, there seem to be two parts of utility: security and power. Security is a stable and intact maintenance of a good condition. Power is the ability to keep one's own goods and weaken other people's goods'). See also H. Lausberg, *Handbuch…*, pp. 127–128.

271 Cf. e.g. Cic., *Inv.* 2,17,54 *id autem ex honestatis et ex utilitatis partibus sumetur* ('a scheme drawn from what is morally right and useful will be used here'); 2,18,55 *Deinde locus communis, per quem facti utilitas aut honestas adaugetur* ('Then a common scheme is used, which highlights the utility or moral integrity of the [accused person's] deed.'); 2,26,75 *Ipsa autem comparatio separata a ceteris generibus controversiarum sic ex sua vi considerabitur, si illud, quod comparabitur, aut non honestum aut non utile aut non necessarium fuisse aut non tantopere utile aut non tantopere honestum aut non tantopere necessarium fuisse demonstrabitur* ('On the other hand, the comparison itself will be considered independently of other kinds of controversy, considering only its significance in such a way that what will be compared was not morally right, useful or necessary, or was not so morally right, so very useful or as much as necessary as the other party insists'); 2,30,94 *In hac ab utroque ex omnibus partibus honestatis et ex omnibus utilitatis partibus…* ('In this case, both parties in dispute, using the arguments of moral integrity and utility…'); 2,41,119 *Ac diligenter illud quoque adtendere oportebit, num illo probato, quod adversarius intellegat, res utilior aut honestior aut magis necessaria ab scriptore neglecta videatur. Id fiet, si id, quod nos demonstrabimus, honestum aut utile aut necessarium demonstrabimus, et si id, quod ab adversariis dicetur, minime eiusmodi esse dicemus. Deinde si in lege erit ex ambiguo controversia, dare operam oportebit, ut de eo, quod adversarius intellegat, alia in re lege cautum esse doceatur* ('It will also be necessary to pay close attention to whether, in the event that our opponent's interpretation was correct, it would appear that the author of the document might have neglected something more useful, more morally right, or more necessary. This will happen if we show what we show as morally right, useful or necessary, and what our opponents are proposing we do not name it as such in any way. Then, if the disagreement is related to the ambiguity of the law, efforts will have to be made to show that this was taken care of by some other law.');

the orator's activity in the field of argumentation and interpretation, which, after all, also included the interpretation of the law, expressed the co-existence of *honestas* and *utilitas*[272], it is obvious that not only in the sphere of philosophy but also of rhetoric *utilitas* was not purely pragmatic.

Rhetoric's discursive nature is especially evident in *genus iudiciale*, where the same situation is analyzed from opposing perspectives – prosecution and defense – each representing conflicting interests. What was useful to one of the parties is here commonly referred to as *utilitas causae*[273]. Under this category, a construction of the speech, presentation of arguments and interpretation of the circumstances were designed to maximize the chances of winning the trial[274]. In this aspect, however, there existed

2,41,121 *Deinde quo tempore scriptum sit, quaerendum est, ut, quid eum voluisse in eiusmodi tempore veri simili sit, intellegatur. Post ex deliberationis partibus, quid utilius et quid honestius et illi ad scribendum et his ad conprobandum sit, demonstrandum* ('Next, one need to consider when the letter was written to determine what the will of the author of the document was likely to be at that point in time. Later, using the means appropriate to an advisory speech, it is necessary to say what would be more useful and more morally right for the author to write and for the judges to recognize'); 2,46,135 *Secunda pars est, in qua est ostendendum, si in ceteris legibus oporteat, in hac non oportere. Hoc demonstrabitur, si lex aut ad res maximas, utilissimas, honestissimas, religiosissimas videbitur pertinere; aut inutile aut turpe aut nefas esse tali in re non diligentissime legi optemperare* ('In the second point, it must be shown that, even in the case of other acts a departure from the literal meaning should be taken into account, it is unacceptable in this case. This will be done either by claiming that a given law relates to the most important, most useful, most morally right and most pious matters, or by pointing out that failure to obey the law completely is highly harmful, disgraceful or wicked.'); 2,48,141 *deinde ex utilitatis et honestatis partibus ostendere, quam inutile aut quam turpe sit id, quod adversarii dicant fieri oportuisse aut oportere, et id, quod nos fecerimus aut postulemus, quam utile aut quam honestum sit* ('Then, by referring to utility and moral integrity, one must show how disadvantageous or shameful it would be what our opponents say should have been done or should be done, and how beneficial and morally right it is what we have done or stand for').

272 See Cic., *Inv.* 2,52,158 *Ex his illud conficitur, ut petendarum rerum partes sint honestas et utilitas* ('From the given definitions it follows that moral integrity and utility are two kinds of what one should strive for'). See also Sen., *Contr.* 1,5,8,7 *utra optio honestior sit, utra iustior, utra utilior…*; Quint., *Inst.* 2,4,38 *Maxime vero commune est quaerere an sit honesta, an utilis*; 3,8,13 *Nam et prudentissimus esse haberique et optimus debet qui sententiae suae de utilibus atque honestis credere omnes velit*; 3,8,22 *Partes suadendi quidam putaverunt honestum utile necessarium*; 3,8,32 *Nam et utilitas ipsa expugnatur ab iis qui dicunt non solum potiora esse honesta quam utilia, sed ne utilia quidem esse quae non sint honesta*; 6,2,11 *Nam quidquid de honestis et utilibus, iustis et iniustis, denique faciendis ac non faciendis dicitur, ἦθος vocari potest.*

273 H. Lausberg translates this term in this context as *das Parteiinteresse, Handbuch…*, pp. 56, 834. This expression is clearly distinct from the jurisprudential expression *utilitatis causa*. In the first instance, the noun *causae* denotes the benefit of one of the two disputing parties and is expressed in the genitive, indicating 'the utility of the party'. In the second instance, *causa*, expressed in the ablative, refers to the cause and motive of an action, which is placed in the genitive. The expression *utilitatis causa* therefore means, as previously mentioned, 'for the sake of utility'. The terminological convergence is perhaps interesting yet coincidental.

274 See e.g. Quint., *Inst.* 4,3,14 *Παρέκβασις est, ut mea quidem fert opinio, alicuius rei, sed ad utilitatem causae pertinentis, extra ordinem excurrens tractatio* ('In my view, a digression is dealing with a topic that, while relevant to the utility of the case, branches from the basic structure [of the speech]'); 5,11,16 *quaedam significare satis erit, ut idem* [*sc. Cicero*] *ac pro eodem* [*sc. pro Milone*]: *'neque enim*

some important limits, because the overriding aim of the *genus iudiciale* was after all *aequitas* – as Cicero describes it – a certain facet of *honestas*. Additionally, appealing to what was useful for the cause did not always align with ethical standards.[275]. Quintilian, drawing from Aristotle,[276] explained that an orator (in rhetoric, the archetype of an honest man, *vir bonus*[277]) could substitute a word with an inappropriate synonym – such as calling a wasteful person generous or a stingy one thrifty – only if it served the *utilitas communis*[278]. Therefore, while *utilitas causae* was a significant objective for the orator, it was not their sole consideration, as the utility of the community remained the paramount value.

posset Ahala ille Servilius aut P. Nasica aut L. Opimius aut me consule senatus non nefarius haberi, si sceleratos interfici nefas esset.' Haec ita dicentur prout nota erunt vel utilitas causae aut decor postulabit ('In some cases, an allusion may suffice. So Cicero again, in the same *Pro Milone* speech: "Neither the famous Servilius Ahala, nor Publius Nasica, nor Lucius Opimius, nor the Senate under my consulship, could be considered not guilty of crimes if it was a crime to kill the wicked". How these things will be mentioned will depend on how well they are known and what the utility or relevance of the case requires'). Cf. Cic., *Mil.* 8. See also Cic., *De orat.* 2,257 *Nam in Caelio sane etiam ad causam utile fuit tuum illud, Antoni* ('Surely your famous saying, Antonius, was also useful in Celius' case').

275 Cf. e.g. Cic., *Flac.* 13 *Quae quamquam utilia sunt causae, timide tamen dico, quod vereor ne Laelius ex his rebus quas sibi suscepit gloriae causa putet aliquid oratione mea sermonis in sese aut invidiae esse quaesitum* ('While it is useful to my case, I say it hesitantly because I am afraid that Laelius may think that some rumor or odium has built up against him in my speech because of the actions he has taken in his thirst for glory').

276 *Rhet.* 1,1367a32.

277 There is an extensive body of literature on this subject. In the context of Quintilian's writings see e.g. M. Winterbottom, *Quintilian and the Vir Bonus*, 'The Journal of Roman Studies' 1964, vol. 54, no. 1–2, pp. 90–97; P.A. Meador, *Quintilian's "vir bonus'*, 'Western Speech' 1970, vol. 34, no. 3, pp. 162–169; I.R. McDonald, *The 'Vir Bonus' and Quintilian VI.3*, 'Studies in Philology' 1975, vol. 72, no. 3, pp. 237–245; A. Brinton, *Quintilian, Plato, and the 'Vir Bonus'*, 'Philosophy & Rhetoric' 1983, vol. 16, no. 3, pp. 167–184; A.E. Walzer, *Quintilian's "Vir Bonus' and the stoic wise man*, 'Rhetoric Society Quarterly' 2003, vol. 33, no. 4, pp. 25–41. Legal issues pertaining to this subject have been recently examined by Giuseppe Falcone and Roberto Fiori. Cf. G. Falcone, *L'attribuzione della qualifica 'vir bonus' nella prassi giudiziaria d'età repubblicana (a proposito di Cato, or. frg. 186 Sbelnd. = 206 Malc.). Con un'Appendice su 'optimus' 'probus' 'fortis* [in:] *Vir bonus. Un modello ermeneutico della riflessione giuridica antica*, A. Lovato (ed.), Bari 2013, pp. 39–90; Idem, *La formula 'ut inter bonos bene agier oportet et sine fraudatione' e la nozione di 'vir bonus'*, 'Fundamina: A Journal of Legal History' 2014, vol. 20, pp. 258–274 and R. Fiori, *Bonus vir: Politica filosofia retorica e diritto nel de officiis di Cicerone*, Napoli 2011; Idem, *Il vir bonus fra tradizioni romane e filosofia greca nel de officiis di Cicerone* [in:] *Vir bonus. Un modello ermeneutico della riflessione giuridica antica*, Andrea Lovato (ed.), Bari 2013, pp. 19–38; Idem, *The vir bonus in Cicero's de officiis: Greek philosophy and Roman legal science* [in:] *Aequum ius. От друзей и коллег к 50-летию профессора Д.В. Дождева*, Moscow 2014, pp. 187–202.

278 Quint., *Inst.* 3,7,25 *Idem praecipit illud quoque, quod mox Cornelius Celsus prope supra modum invasit, quia sit quaedam virtutibus ac vitiis vicinitas, utendum proxima derivatione verborum, ut pro temerario fortem, prodigo liberalem, avaro parcum vocemus: quae eadem etiam contra valent. Quod quidem orator, id est vir bonus, numquam faciet, nisi forte communi utilitate ducetur* ('The same [Aristotle] makes another point, which Cornelius Celsus later emphasized almost too much, namely that because virtues and vices somehow exist next to each other, we should be ready to replace words with their closest synonyms, calling the fool brave, the spender generous, the skinflint thrifty. But a real orator, an honest man, will never do that unless *utilitas publica* induces him to do so').

2.2 *Utilitas* from the Jurist's Perspective

2.2.1 Characteristics of Jurists' Activity (D.1,1,1,pr.–1)

For scholars of Roman law, one of the most important accounts on *utilitas* is a fragment of Ulpian's *Institutes*[279], opening the *Digest*. Its importance for our considerations lies not only in the exposition of the concept of *ars*[280] but above all in the fact that the passage D. 1,1,1,2 explicitly mentions the category under scrutiny. Yet, to grasp the essence of these references, understanding the context in which the jurist framed his discussion is essential:

> D. 1,1,1,pr.–1 (*Ulpianus libro primo institutionum*)
> pr. … *nam, ut eleganter Celsus definit, ius est ars boni et aequi.* 1. *Cuius merito quis nos sacerdotes appellet: iustitiam namque colimus et boni et aequi notitiam profitemur, aequum ab iniquo separantes, licitum ab illicito discernentes, bonos non solum metu poenarum, verum etiam praemiorum quoque exhortatione efficere cupientes, veram nisi fallor philosophiam, non simulatam affectantes.*
> pr. … As Celsus aptly put it: the law is an art of what is good and right. 1. Because of that[281], someone could rightly call us priests. For we honour justice, and preach knowledge of the good and the right, separating what is right from what is wrong, drawing a line between what is allowed and what is not allowed, making people good not only because of the fear of punishment but also because of the incentive of reward, striving for, if I am not mistaken, true and not seeming philosophy.

The quoted fragment, especially the depiction of jurists as priests (*sacerdotes*), and the use of the term 'true philosophy' (*vera philosophia*), has sparked extensive debate among Roman law scholars. Among the various interpretations, Giuseppe Falcone's stands out for its strong textual support and convincing resolution of this interpretative puzzle. Falcone clarifies that Ulpian did not equate jurists with philosophers[282].

279 For further insights on this work, see the recent study by D. Kremer, *Les Institutiones d'Ulpien. Premier manuel de droit romain*, 'Index' 2021, vol. 49, pp. 64–87 and remarks cowritten by A. Schiavone and V. Marotta in J.-L. Ferrary, A. Schiavone, V. Marotta, *Cnaeus Domitius Ulpianus…*, pp. 53–105.

280 Cf. Chapter One.

281 G. Falcone claims that the pronoun *cuius* refers to the term *ius*. As he writes, it is *ius* that is an object of *dare operam*, of *appellatum*, and finally of *ars boni et aequi*, *La 'vera philosophia'…*, pp. 46–47.

282 Ibid., pp. 41–147. Other significant works, which often present differing interpretations, include: C.N. Smiley, *Ulpian ὁ Κειτούκειτος. The Influence of the Stoic Theory of Style in Athenaeus*, 'The American Journal of Philology' 1908, vol. 29, no. 3, pp. 322–328; P. Frezza, *La cultura di Ulpiano*, 'SDHI' 1968, vol. 34, pp. 363–375; Idem, *La persona di Ulpiano (a proposito del volume di Tony Honoré)*, 'SDHI' 1983, vol. 49, pp. 412–422; D. Nörr, *Ethik von Jurisprudenz in Sachen Schatzfund*, 'BIDR' 1972, no. 14, pp. 11–40; Idem, *Iurisperitus sacerdos* [in:] *Xenion: Festschrift für Pan. J. Zepos anlässlich seines 65. Geburtstages am 1. Dezember 1973*, vol. 2, E. von Caemmerer (ed.), Athens-Frei-

In fact, the notion of *vera philosophia*, functioning in the intellectual milieu of the 1st and 2nd centuries CE, referred to moral philosophy[283], rooted in Platonic thought[284]. Stemming from morality[285], *philosophia moralis*, essentially a synonym for ethics[286], was positioned as antithetical to sophistic reasoning[287], which was viewed not as genu-

burg-Köln 1973, pp. 555–572; G. Crifò, *Ulpiano. Esperienze e responsabilità del giurista*, [in:] ANRW, vol. 2.15, Berlin-New York 1976, pp. 708–789; W. Waldstein, *Zur Ulpians Definition der Gerechtigkeit (D. 1,1,1pr.)* [in:] *Festschrift für Werner Flume zum 70. Geburtstag, 12. September 1978*, vol. 1, K. Ballerstedt, F.A. Mann, H.H. Jakobs, B. Knobbe-Keuk, J. Wilhelm (ed.), Cologne 1978, pp. 213–232; Idem, *Römische Rechtswissenschaft und wahre Philosophie*, 'Index' 1994, vol. 22, pp. 31–35; Idem, *Zum Problem der 'vera philosophia' bei Ulpian* [in:] *Collatio Iuris Romani. Études dédiées á Hans Ankum à l'occasion de son 65e anniversaire*, R. Feenstra, A.S. Hartkamp, J.E. Spruit, R.J. Sijpesteijn, L.C. Winkel (ed.), Amsterdam 1995, pp. 607–617; T. Honoré, *Ulpian: Pioneer of Human Rights*, New York 1982; Idem, *Ulpian, Natural law…*, pp. 199–208; L. Winkel, *Die stoische οἰκείωσις-Lehre und Ulpians Definition der Gerechtigkeit*, 'ZSS RA' 1988, vol. 105, no. 1, pp. 669–679; M. Schermaier, *Ulpian als 'wahrer Philosoph'. Notizien zum selbstverständnis eines Römischen Juristen* [in:] *Ars boni et aequi. Festschrift für Wolfgang Waldstein zum 65. Geburtstag*, M. Schermaier, Z. Vegh (ed.), Stuttgart 1993, pp. 303–322; A. Schiavone, *Giuristi e principe…*, pp. 4–56 (esp. p. 23) as well as Schiavone's commentary, in J.-L. Ferrary, A. Schiavone, V. Marotta, *Cnaeus Domitius Ulpianus…*, esp. pp. 191–193; V. Marotta, *Ulpiano e l'impero*, vol. 1, Napoli 2000; Idem, *Iustitia, vera philosophia e natura: una nota sulle institutiones di Ulpiano*, 'Seminarios Complutenses de Derecho Romano. Revista Complutense de Derecho Romano y Tradición Romanistica' 2006, vol. 19, pp. 285–334 (=*Iustitia, vera philosophia e natura: una nota sulle institutiones di Ulpiano*, [in:] *Testi e problemi del giusnaturalismo romano*, D. Mantovani, A. Schiavone (ed.), Pavia 2007, pp. 563–601); M. Kuryłowicz, *Sacerdotes iustitiae*, pp. 699–713; P. Sadowski, *Filozofia prawa w życiu i nauczaniu Ulpiana*, 'ZP' 2008, vol. 8, no. 1, pp. 81–108.

283 This collocation is particularly common in Seneca the Younger. Cf. Sen., *Epist.* 88,24,1–3; 89,9,1–2; 89,9,11,1–3; 106,2,1; 108,1,4; 109,17,2.

284 G. Falcone, *La 'vera philosophia'…*, pp. 57–61. See e.g. Pl., *R.* 473d–536a.; Gell., NA 10,22,1–2,24.

285 Cf. Cic., *Fat.* 1,2–4 *quia pertinet ad mores, quod ἦθος illi vocant, nos eam partem philosophiae de moribus appellare solemus, sed decet augentem linguam Latinam nominare moralem*; Quint., *Inst.* 6,2,8 *mores appellantur, atque inde pars quoque illa philosophiae ἠθική moralis est dicta.*

286 J. Gorczyca SJ, *Zarys etyki fundamentalnej*, Kraków 2014, p. 16.

287 The following sources are quoted after G. Falcone, *La 'vera philosophia'…*, pp. 49–75: Sen., *Epist.* 111,1–4 1. *Quid vocentur Latine sophismata, quaesisti a me. Multi temptaverunt illis nomen inponere, nullum haesit.* (…) 2. *Aptissimum tamen videtur mihi, quo Cicero usus est: cavillationes vocat. Quibus quisquis se tradidit, quaestiunculas quidem vafras nectit, ceterum ad vitam nihil proficit, neque fortior fit neque temperantior neque elatior.* (…) 3. *Talis est, mi Lucili, verus et rebus, non artificiis philosophus. In edito stat admirabilis, celsus, magnitudinis verae.* (…) 4. *hanc constantiam cavillationes istae, de quibus paulo ante loquebar, praestare non possunt. Ludit istis animus, non proficit, et philosophiam a fastigio suo deducit in planum.* ('1. You asked me what sophisms are called in Latin. Many have tried to name them, but none of the names have caught on. (…) 2. However, to me, the most appropriate name seems to be the one used by Cicero; and he calls them cavillations. Whoever has dealt with them is making tricky questions but does not make life any easier and becomes neither bolder, nor more restrained, nor more sublime. (…) 3. Such is, my Lucilius, the true philosopher who is in fact such a man, and is not deceived by some tricks. He admirably stands tall, generous and truly magnificent. (…) 4. This constancy cannot be ensured by distortions I have just talked about. The mind plays with them but makes no progress, and brings philosophy from its destined peak to the lowlands'); Sen., *De brev. vitae* 10,1 *Solebat dicere Fabianus, non ex his cathedrariis philosophis, sed ex veris et antiquis,* CONTRA AFFECTV IMPETV, NON SVBTILITATE PVGNANDVM, NEC MINVTIS VVLNERIBVS SED INCVRSV AVERTENDAM ACIEM. *Non probabat cavillationes:* ENIM CONTVNDI

ine knowledge but merely its semblance[288]. Consequently, the Romans often criticized sophistry as deceitful and unethical. The concept of sophisms, denoted by the term *cavillationes* (also found in legal sources[289]), stand in stark contrast to the esteemed art of law:

DEBERE, NON VELLICARI. ('Fabianus, a philosopher not like today's school lecturers but coming from true and ancient philosophers, used to say: "Passions must not be fought with the subtlety of thinking but with the force of attack, and not by throwing light missiles but by storming their battle arrays". He does not recommend subtle and evasive persuasion, but: "they ned to be – he says – splinter, not lightly tease"'). Seneca writes about was a respected rhetorician and philosopher who lived in the times of Tiberius. Unfortunately, his writings did not survive. Gell., NA 10,22,1–2,24 1. *Plato, veritatis homo amicissimus eiusque omnibus exhibendae promptissimus, quae omnino dici possint in desides istos ignavosque, qui obtentu philosophiae nominis inutile otium et 2. linguae vitaeque tenebras secuntur, ex persona quidem non gravi neque idonea, vere tamen ingenueque dixit. Nam etsi Callicles, quem dicere haec facit, verae philosophiae ignarus, inhonesta indignaque in philosophos confert, proinde tamen accipienda sunt quae dicuntur, ut nos sensim moneri intellegamus, ne ipsi quoque culpationes huiuscemodi mereamur neve inerti inanique desidia cultum et studium philosophiae mentiamur.* (...) 24. *Haec Plato sub persona quidem, sicuti dixi, non proba, set cum sensus tamen intellegentiaeque communis fide et cum quadam indissimulabili veritate disseruit, non de illa scilicet philosophia, quae virtutum omnium disciplina est quaeque in publicis simul et privatis officiis excellit civitatesque et rempublicam, si nihil prohibeat, constanter, fortiter et perite administrat, sed de ista futtili atque puerili meditatione argutiarum, nihil ad vitam neque tuendam neque ordinandam promovente, in qua id genus homines consenescunt male feriati, quos philosophos esse et vulgus putat et is putabat, ex cuius persona haec dicta sunt.* ('1. Plato, a man most devoted to the truth and most willing to reveal it to all of us, spoke truthfully and with dignity, though not through the mouth of a worthy or proper person, all that could be said against these idle and worthless individuals who hiding behind the banner of philosophy, cultivate useless emptiness and obscurity of speech and life. 2. For although Callicles, who speaks on his behalf, unaware of true philosophy, offends philosophers with his piles of wicked and undeserved calumnies, we should treat his statements in such a way that we gradually accept them as a warning to ourselves that we do not deserve such accusations, and that we do not pretend to study and practice philosophy in our empty and stupid indolence (...) 24. These remarks, as I mentioned, Plato put in the mouth of a man of little value but at the same time having a reputation for being guided by common sense, willingness to understand and express himself with unwavering honesty. Obviously, he does not talk about philosophy, which is the teacher of all virtues and excels in the fulfilment of both public and private functions and which, if nothing stands in the way, governs cities and countries with consistency, courage and wisdom. Rather, it speaks of that empty and childish interest in nonsense that adds nothing to the conduct and management of life. By living like this, these people grow old and enjoy "aged joys", and the plebs consider them as philosophers, and so does the one whose mouth the words I quoted come from'). Cf. also Sen. *Epist.* 108,23; Gell., NA 1,2,7; Plut. *Mor.* 78E–F; 79A–B; 81B; 81C. And last one quoted after V. Marotta, *Iustitia...*, p. 289, n. 20: (Pseudo-)Apul., *Asclepius*, 14 *Qui ergo homines post nos erunt, sophistarum calliditate decepti, a vera, pura sanctaque philosophia avertentur* ('The future generations will be then deceived by the cunning of sophists and will deviate from true, pure, and holy philosophy'). Despite this source perfectly fitting Falcone's view, Marotta still does not agree with his interpretation

288 W. Waldstein, *Zum Problem...*, p. 614; G. Falcone, *La 'vera philosophia'...*, pp. 64–68.

289 Ulp. D. 50,16,177 *Natura cavillationis, quam Graeci σωρίτην appellaverunt, haec est, ut ab evidenter veris per brevissimas mutationes disputatio ad ea, quae evidenter falsa sunt, perducatur* ('The nature of a sophism, which the Greeks called a syllogism, is that the considerations lead through small changes from what is evidently true to what is clearly false'). This passage is most likely quoted by Ulpian after Julian. Cf. Iul. D. 50,17,65 *Ea est natura cavillationis, quam Graeci σωρίτην appellant, ut ab evidenter veris per brevissimas mutationes disputatio ad ea, quae evidenter falsa sunt, perducatur.*

Quint., *Inst.* 2,15,24–25
(…) creduntque eum [sc. Platonem] in hac esse opinione, ut rhetoricen non artem sed 'peritiam quandam gratiae ac voluptatis' existimet, et alio loco 'civilitatis particulae simulacrum et quartam partem adulationis', quod duas partes civilitatis corpori adsignet, medicinam et quam interpretantur exercitatricem, duas animo, legalem atque iustitiam, adulationem autem medicinae vocet cocorum artificium, exercitatricis mangonum, qui colorem fuco et verum robur inani sagina mentiantur, legalis cavillatricem, iustitiae rhetoricen.
They believe that Plato is of the opinion rhetoric is not art but 'a certain knowledge of grace and pleasure', and also, as can be read in another passage, 'faking politics' and 'the quarter part of hypocrisy', and since Plato assigns two parts of politics to the body, namely medicine and gymnastics, and two parts to the mind, that is the law and rhetoric, he calls the occupation of cooks 'pseudo-medicine', the occupation of slave traders 'pseudo-gymnastics', as they use paint to imitate color, and fat to imitate real strength; similarly, he calls sophistry (*cavillatrix*) 'pseudo-law', and rhetoric 'pseudo-justice'.

According to Quintilian referring to the Platonic dialogue *Gorgias* sophistry (*cavillatrix*[290]) constituted a mere semblance of the law[291]. The last category, here referred to as *pars legalis* (and by Plato as ἡ νομοθετική[292]), should likely be associated with the legislative context. Interestingly, this idea was further elaborated in the subsequent century by Lucius Apuleius Madaurensis in his work *De Platone et eius dogmate* wherein he posited that sophistry mimicked the *pars iuridicialis*, which he most probably understood as issuing fair judgments. However, in contrast to the views of Plato and Quintilian, Apuleius depicted legal craftsmanship (*professio iuris*) to be ineptly imitating *pars legalis*, synonymous with the knowledge of the law (*scientia iuris*)[293].

Cf. also Cels. D. 34,7,1,1; Scaev. D. 35,1,85; Ulp. 38,17,2,44; Gai. D. 50,16,233. See also G. Falcone, *La 'vera philosophia'…*, pp. 72–73, n. 54 and Ž. Bujuklić, *Ancient and Modern Concepts of Lawfulness*, 'RIDA' 1999, vol. 46, pp. 143–144.

290 The problem of sophistic argumentation appears many times in Quintilian's work. Cf. e.g. *Inst.* 1,5,38; 1,7,33; 2,14,5; 2,17,7; 2,17,30, where the author contrasts *cavillationes* with rhetoric; 7,3,14; 7,4,37, where Quintilian writes about *cavillationes iuris* and *Inst.* 7,9,4; 8,6,2; 9,1,16; 10,7,14; 12,2,14.

291 The wording *pars legalis*, as noted by Serena Querzoli, does not limit the meaning of this term only to statutes, *Materia and officia of rhetorical teaching in Book II of the Institutio oratoria* [in:] *Quintilian and the Law: The Art of Persuasion in Law and Politics*, O. E. Tellegen-Couperus (ed.), Leuven 2003, p. 48.

292 Cf. Plat., *Gorg.* 465 C (…) τοῦτο σοφιστικὴ πρὸς νομοθετικήν (…) τοῦτο ῥητορικὴ πρὸς δικαιοσύνην.

293 Apul., *De Plat.* 2,9,231–234 *Hinc rhetoricae duae sunt (…) partes, quarum una est disciplina contemplatrix bonorum, iusti tenax, apta et conveniens cum secta eius qui politicus vult videri; alia vero adulandi scientia est, captatrix verisimilium (…) Haec [sc. civilitas] eadem utilitati animae procurat duobus modis; altera namque legalis est, iuridicialis altera. Sed prior consimilis est exercitationi, per quam pulchritudo animae et robur adquiritur, sicut exercitatione valitudo corporis gratiaque retinetur; iuridicialis illa medicinae pars est, nam morbis animae medetur sicut illa corporis. Has disciplinas vocat plurimumque earum curationem commoditatis adferre profitetur. Harum imitatrices esse coquinam et unguentariam et artem sophisticam professionemque iuris blandas et adsentationum inlecebris turpes profitentibus, inutiles cunctis. (…) sic sophistice imitata iuridicialem statum dat opinionem stultis, quasi iustitiae studeat, quam iniquitati favere constat. Unguentariam vero professionem iuris imitatur (…) sic*

What stands out is that Quintilian's statement is based on a juxtaposition of the professions recognized as *artes*, such as *pars legalis*, with activities of lesser esteem, referred to as *artificia*. This category includes sophistry and rhetoric, cooking, or slave trading. The disparaging label of *artificium* was also used by Cicero describing the activity of jurists as 'talkative appearances of wisdom' (*verbosa simulatio prudentiae*) in the speech *Pro Murena*[294], mentioned previously in Chapter One. Dieter Nörr posits that by weaving the phrase *nisi fallor*[295] into the fragment of his *Institutes*, Ulpian addressed Cicero's critique. As emphasized, although Cicero's speech carried elements of parody and irony, his critique closely aligns with his perspective on the strict adherence to the literal interpretation of legal texts, which, in his view, often resulted in the distortion of regulations' intended meanings, leading to harm and injustice[296].

haec scientiam imitata iuris simulat quidem virtutem se animis augere, cenervat autem, quod in illis nativae fuerit industriae ('Hence, there are two parts of rhetoric. The first one is the art of contemplating good, adhering to justice, and is appropriate and adequate to the way of life of those who are interested in the affairs of the state. The other one is the expertise of flattery, temptress of appearances [...]. The virtue of politics is useful to the soul in two ways: one is legislative [*legalis*], the other juridical [*iuridicialis*]. The first way is similar to physical exercise by which one acquires the beauty and strength of the soul, just as by exercise the health and fitness of the body are preserved. The juridical [*iuridicialis*] one is an integral part of medicine in that it heals the diseases of the soul as the latter heals the diseases of the body. He calls these 'disciplines' and declares that taking care of them is generally very beneficial. Their imitators are cooking and cosmetics, and sophistic and legal arts, charming advances of flatterers, shameful to those who use them, and useless to everyone [...]. And sophistic art, imitating a juridical status, offers an opinion to the foolish as if it were a devoted believer of justice, although it is known to promote injustice. Legal art thus imitates cosmetics [...]. In this way it mimics the knowledge of the law; pretends to be a virtue that adds value to souls but in fact only weakens the spark of innate diligence in them'). See also M. O'Brien, *Apuleius and the Concept of a Philosophical Rhetoric*, 'Hermathena' 1991, no. 151, pp. 39–50; S. Querzoli, *Materia and officia...*, pp. 49–50; G. Falcone, *La 'vera philosophia'...*, pp. 69–71.

294 The reference to the speech *Pro Murena* suggested by Nörr is also substantiated by the numerous references that Cicero made to the terms *ars* and *studium*, which are the key concepts in the opening paragraphs of Ulpian's *Institutiones*. This connection was already noted by G. Falcone, *La 'vera philosophia'...*, p. 86.

295 This formulation seems to give the statement a sarcastic-polemical tone. See D. Nörr, *Iurisperitus sacerdos*, p. 557; Idem, *Rechtskritik...*, p. 59; G. Crifò, *Ulpiano...*, p. 784, n. 478; G. Falcone, *La 'vera philosophia'...*, *passim*; T. Honoré, *Ulpian...*, p. 79; A. Mantello, *Un illustre sconosciuto tra filisofia e prassi giuridica, Eufrate d'Epifania* [in:] *Sodalitas. Scritti in onore di Antonio Guarino*, vol. 2, V. Giuffrè (ed.), Napoli 1984, p. 978; A. Schiavone, *Giuristi e principe...*, p. 26. V. Scarano Ussani stated that such a polemic would have been more than 250 years old and therefore considered the concept unlikely, *L'ars...*, p. 141. However, these concerns do not seem justified. Firstly, because echoes of identical allegations can be easily found in authors writing closer to Ulpian's time. Secondly, in his commentary *Ad edictum* Ulpian openly engaged in a discussion with Cicero, recalling his opinion not preserved anywhere else, and stating that the definition of the verb *latitare* ('to remain hidden', 'to hide') proposed by him was not precise enough Cf. D. 42,4,7,4. Extensively on the relationship between Cicero's reflection and Ulpian's writing in G. Aricò Anselmo, *'Ius publicum'...*, pp. 447–787 and G. Falcone, *La 'vera philosophia'...*, pp. 41–147.

296 Cf. Cic., *Off.* 1,10,33 *Exsistunt etiam saepe iniuriae calumnia quadam et nimis callida, sed malitiosa iuris interpretatione. Ex quo illud "Summum ius summa iniuria" factum est iam tritum sermone proverbium* ('Harm often results from a distortion or an overly insightful but malicious translation of the law.

In this context, Falcone's interpretation is very convincing, as he stated that the expression *veram et non simulatam philosophiam affectare* referred to interpreting the law according to ideal ethical values[297], and not, following Cicero's words, 'distortion, or an overly astute yet malicious interpretation of the law'[298], bearing comparison with the use of sophisms. Moreover, considering the other activities enumerated in D. 1,1,1,1 – particularly distinguishing between right and wrong (*aequum ab iniquo separantes*), and demarcating the permissible from the impermissible (*licitum ab illicito discernentes*[299]) – it is plausible to argue that Ulpian invoked the expression *ius est ars boni et aequi* not to refer to the systematization of the legal order but the interpretation of the law[300]. As already explained, the term *ars* also teleologically determined the nature of this interpretative effort, pointing to *bonum et aequum* as the object and useful aim of the law[301]. According to Ulpian jurists, as befits priests (*sacerdotes*), concentrated their efforts on interpretation. However, they analyzed not the will of the gods but the law itself.

2.2.2 *Duae positiones: publicum et privatum* (D. 1,1,1,2)

The fragment following D. 1,1,1,pr.–1 contains nominal references to the *utilitas* criterion. The famous D. 1,1,1,2, for it is the one in question, became a source of considerations on the systematization and division of the law into the public and the private; Ulpian

Hence, the words "the greatest law is the greatest injustice" became a common proverb'). Cicero speaks in a similar vein in many places. For discussions on this famous phrase in the context of legal interpretation, see J. Stroux, *Summum ius summa iniuria. Ein Kapitel aus der Geschichte der interpretatio iuris*, Leipzig 1926 (=*Summum ius summa iniuria. Un capitolo concernente la storia della interpretatio iuris [versione dal tedesco di G. Funaioli con prefazione di S. Riccobono]*, 'AUPA' 1929, vol. 12, pp. 639–691) and W. Waldstein, *"Aequitas" e "summum ius"*, [in:] *Saggi sul diritto non scritto*, Milano 2002, pp. 131–163. Cf. e.g. Cic., *Mur.* 25–29; Idem, *Off.* 3,17,71; 3,25,95.

297 G. Falcone, *La 'vera philosophia'…*, *passim*. Cf. also A. Mantello, *Il sogno…*, p. 60. It is also worth noting that the second book of *De Platone et eius dogmate*, the fragment of which was quoted earlier, opens with the theme of moral philosophy. Cf. Apul., *De Plat.* 2,1,19 *Moralis philosophiae caput est, Faustine filii, ut scias quibus ad beatam vitam perveniri rationibus possit* ('An essential part of moral philosophy is that you should know, son Faustinus, by what means one can achieve a happy life').

298 Cic., *Off.* 1,10,33.

299 G. Falcone, *La 'vera philosophia'…*, p. 85, rightly notes that the use of *participia praesentis* underlines the continuity and durability of these aspirations.

300 Therefore, Bretone and Marotta may be right, interpreting *ius* in Ulpian's definition as a synonym of jurisprudence. See M. Bretone, *Tecniche e ideologie dei giuristi romani*, Napoli 1984, p. 262; V. Marotta, *Ulpiano…*, p. 154.

301 Also in P. Cerami, *La concezione…*, p. 19; F. Gallo, *Sulla definizione…* p. 30, n. 87; p. 35, 46. These were not the instruments that the jurist was supposed to use, as suggested by F. P. Casavola, *Giuristi adrianei*, Napoli 1980, p. 38.

did indeed provide a detailed account of both of them, beginning, however, by illustrating the occupation of jurists through the prism of the two mysterious *positiones*:

> D. 1,1,1,2 (*Ulpianus libro primo institutionum*)
> *Huius studii duae sunt positiones: publicum et privatum. publicum ius est quod ad statum rei Romanae spectat, privatum quod ad singulorum utilitatem: sunt enim quaedam publice utilia, quaedam privatim. publicum ius in sacris, in sacerdotibus, in magistratibus consistit. privatum ius tripertitum est: collectum etenim est ex naturalibus praeceptis aut gentium aut civilibus.*
> This occupation is distinguished by two subjects: the public and the private [utility]. Public law is one that concerns the welfare of the Roman state, and the private law is what refers to the utility of individuals. For some matters are useful to the public, and some to private persons. The public law is based on worship, priests, and officials. The private law has three parts, as it is formed by the principles of the natural law, the law of nations, and the civil law.

The opening phrase *huius studii* determines the understanding of the first part of the source. The demonstrative adjective[302] *huius* refers to the previously mentioned circumstances in the text. Thus, this phrase relates to the activity of jurists described in D. 1,1,1,1. and therefore to their interpretative efforts. The concept of *studium* should not be then linked to the context of law studies[303], but understood as a unique type of

302 G. Falcone, *La 'vera philosophia'*..., p. 84.

303 The opening paragraph of the *Institutes of Justinian*, which is a slightly modified version of the passages opening Ulpian's textbook, might be interpreted in this way. See I. 1,1,2–4 2. *His generaliter cognitis et incipientibus nobis exponere iura populi Romani ita maxime videntur posse tradi commodissime, si primo levi ac simplici, post deinde diligentissima atque exactissima interpretatione singula tradantur. alioquin si statim ab initio rudem adhuc et infirmum animum studiosi multitudine ac varietate rerum oneraverimus, duorum alterum aut desertorem studiorum efficiemus aut cum magno labore eius, saepe etiam cum diffidentia, quae plerumque iuvenes avertit, serius ad id perducamus, ad quod leniore via ductus sine magno labore et sine ulla diffidentia maturius perduci potuisset.* 3. *Iuris praecepta sunt haec: honeste vivere, alterum non laedere, suum cuique tribuere.* 4. *Huius studii duae sunt positiones, publicum et privatum. Publicum ius est...* ('When, after generally considering these points, we proceed to the lecture, it seems to us that it is most convenient to interpret the laws of the Roman people if, first, with an easy and simple interpretation, and then with the most careful and accurate interpretation, the individual elements are laid out. For if, at the very beginning, we burden the pupil's still uneducated and weak mind with the multitude and variety of issues, we will do one of the two: he will either give up his studies, or, with great effort and often even self-doubt, which usually turns young men in a different direction, we will finally lead him to what he could have previously been led to by a smoother manner, without much toil and without any self-distrust. 3. The dictates of the law are: to live honestly, not to harm others, to give everyone what is due to him. 4. There are two aspects to this study: public and private. It is the public law to...'). Here, the noun *studium* actually seems to refer to the field of law studies, which was, after all, given a much attention at the beginning of the textbook.

activity involving intense intellectual effort, as Cicero describes it: 'being occupied by some subject persistently and passionately with a feeling of great pleasure'[304].

The rather unusual use of the term *positiones* that comes after has raised objections regarding the authenticity of the source[305]. Interpreting the first part is indeed challenging, as it depends on understanding the relationship between the concept of *positiones* and the terms *publicum* and *privatum*.

One interpretation treats *publicum et privatum* as adjectives related to the noun *studium*. According to this understanding, there would be two attitudes (*positiones*)[306] towards the occupation of interpreting and explaining the law: one concerning public affairs (*studium publicum*), and the other referring to individuals (*studium privatum*). This division would not have to be dichotomous[307]. Jurists could therefore be active in both state and private matters. This perspective on the social role of a citizen, and even a jurist, is also confirmed in other sources[308]. For instance, the activity referred

304 Cic., *Inv.* 1,25,36 *Studium est autem animi assidua et vehementer ad aliquam rem applicata magna cum voluptate occupatio, ut philosophiae, poëticae, geometricae, litterarum*. Cf. also Cic., *Inv.* 2,9,31 *Studium autem, quod est assidua et vehementer aliquam ad rem applicata magna cum voluptate occupatio…* Such an interpretation was earlier opted for by G. Aricò Anselmo, *'Ius publicum'…*, pp. 454, 477, and G. Falcone, *La 'vera philosophia'…*, pp. 84–85.

305 See e.g. S. Perozzi, *Istituzioni di diritto romano*, Roma 1928, p. 86; G. Dulckeit, *Öffentliches und Privatrecht im römischen Recht*, 'Zeitschrift der Akademie für Deutsches Recht' 1935, no. 2, p. 277; A. Steinwenter, *Utilitas publica…*, p. 85; E. Molitor, *Über öffentliches Recht und Privatrecht. Eine rechtssystematische Studie*, Karlsruhe 1949, pp. 8–9; H. Müllejans, *Publicus und privatus im römischen Recht und im alteren kanonischen Recht: unter besonderer Berücksichtigung der Unterscheidung Ius publicum und Ius privatum*, München 1961, p. 17.

306 In terms of this and subsequent meanings of the term *positio* cf. e.g. LTL, OLD, and *A Latin Dictionary*, s. v. *positio*.

307 *Publicum* and *privatum* never constituted separate spheres, as discussed below.

308 See e.g. Cic., *Off.* 2,19,65 *Quae autem opera, non largitione beneficia dantur, haec tum in universam rem publicam tum in singulos cives conferuntur. Nam in iure cavere, consilio iuvare atque hoc scientiae genere prodesse quam plurimis vehementer et ad opes augendas pertinet et ad gratiam. Itaque cum multa praeclara maiorum, tum quod optime constituti iuris civilis summo semper in honore fuit cognitio atque interpretatio; quam quidem ante hanc confusionem temporum in possessione sua principes retinuerunt, nunc, ut honores, ut omnes dignitatis gradus, sic huius scientiae splendor deletus est.* ('Benefits rendered not by monetary gifts but by personal service sometimes apply to the entire community, and sometimes to individual citizens. To protect the man in his rights, to help him with advice and to serve as many people as possible of this sort of knowledge greatly increases the influence and popularity. Thus, among the admirable deeds of our ancestors, we include, among many others, also the fact that they always had great respect for the knowledge and interpretation of our excellent civil law. Before the time of confusion, this teaching had been of interest to the greatest statesmen. Currently, its splendor, like that of other honors and dignities, has faded'). Moreover, this fragment corresponds thematically to the allegations made in the speech *Pro Murena*. If the present interpretation was therefore to be considered correct, describing *positiones* as *studium publicum* and *studium privatum* could be another attempt to counter the accusations made against jurisprudence.

to as *studium publicum* particularly interested Cicero[309]. However, this interpretation seems unlikely, as Ulpian uses the singular form *studium* (*huius studii*) in the text. Additionally, this perspective diminishes the significance of the term *positiones* within the sentence. Its meaning is basically 'adjusted' to the rest of the elements, whereas this concept seems to be the focal point of the fragment, remaining in a special semantic relation to the word *studium*. It is determined by the genitive used here, which, as it is accompanied by the auxiliary verb *esse*, can be considered *genetivus proprietatis*. An expression of this kind translates as 'to have a quality, a sign, a manifestation' and the like[310]. The *positiones* not only exist (*sunt*) but above all constitute a special distinguishing feature of *studium*, which Ulpian writes about.

An alternative reading, which, nevertheless, requires considering the sentence following the phrase *huius studii duae sunt positiones, publicum et privatum*, namely *publicum ius est quod ad statum rei Romanae spectat, privatum quod ad singulorum utilitatem*, seems to indicate this discriminant. According to this interpretation which is the most recognized among researchers of the Roman law, *publicum et privatum* are adjectives referring to the term *ius*. Furthermore, this understanding aligns with the natural sequence of the argument as Ulpian transitions to a discussion on public law in the following sentence. The concept of *positiones* would therefore indicate two 'fields' of law[311], the private and the public law 'approaches', 'areas', or 'branches' distinguished within the activity of legal interpretation. However, in this case, the sentence is supplemented with the notion that does not appear in it, and the meaning of the term *positiones* is again 'tuned' to fit the analyzed sentence.

It is thus worth applying the opposite approach, and starting the exegesis with the word *positiones* rather than with *publicum et privatum*. This shift in perspective opens up new interpretative possibilities. The noun *positiones* is derived from the verb *ponere* meaning 'to put, to place, to lay'[312]. In its first sense, the term *positio* therefore means

309 See e.g. Cic., *Flac.* 105 *tantum in rem publicam studium*; Idem, *P. red. in sen.* 21 *studio in rem publicam fuit*; Idem, *Balb.* 39 *studio rei publicae;* Idem, *Phil.* 13,50 *animo studioque in rem publicam;* Idem, *Epist.* 10,16,1 *studiis beneficiisque in rem publicam*; Idem, *Att.* 8,11,1 *perpetuoque studio in rem publicam;* Idem, *Ad Brut.* 23(1,15),1 *studio rei publicae.*

310 J. Wikarjak, *Gramatyka opisowa języka łacińskiego*, Warszawa 1978, p. 107; H. Menge, *Lehrbuch der lateinischen Syntax und Semantik, Völlig neu bearbeitet von T. Burkard und M. Schauer*, Darmstadt 2000, p. 383; M. Górska, *Łaciński genetivus possessivus (proprietatis) a modalność*, 'Linguistica Copernicana' 2011, vol. 1, no. 5, p. 63; H. Pinkster, *The Oxford Latin Syntax. Volume 1. The Simple Clause*, Oxford 2015, p. 774. For instance: Sen., *Suas.* 1,3 *Magni pectoris est inter secunda moderatio* ('It is the quality of a great spirit to be moderate in prosperity'); Cic., *Sen.* 20 *Temeritas est videlicet florentis aetatis, prudentia senescentis* ('Hastiness is undoubtedly the hallmark of youth, and prudence the hallmark of maturity').

311 Such an interpretation would correspond particularly well with the previously excluded proposal to understand the concept of *studium* in Ulpian's argument as studying or a discipline of law. Forcellini also suggests translating *positiones* as *membra, partes* ('parts') in this context. *Cf.* LTL, s.v. *positio*.

312 *Dictionnaire étymologique...*, p. 520 s.v. *pono*; *Etymological Dictionary...*, p. 479, s.v. *pono*.

'putting, placing, setting', and alike. In the context of a diligently performed activity (*studium*), the *positiones* will then symbolize something that is *put* forward for consideration. Kaser, drawing inspiration from Honsell's work[313], brilliantly describes this notion as *Themen geistiger Bearbeitung*[314], which can be freely translated as the 'subjects of intellectual processing'. Interestingly, this term was probably coined by the German researcher purely intuitively, for he does not give reasons of why he proposes this, and not different understanding. However, he emphasized that Ulpian's *positiones* should be separated from the field of rhetoric, denying the possibility of linking this term with Greek θέσεις[315].

Meanwhile, it is worth taking a closer look at this trace. Forcellini explains the concept of *positio* as follows: *apud Rhetores est fundamentum, quo argumenta innituntur,* θέσις, *thema*[316] ('in the writings of rhetoricians, this is the basis of arguments'). Both θέσις (*thesis*) and *thema*, which Forcellini presents as equivalents of the *positio*, derive from the field of rhetoric. Although not semantically identical, the content of these terms seems contextually very convergent.

The first concept is derived from introductory preparatory exercises known as *progymnasmata*,[317] and addressed to young men preparing for further rhetoric studies. The achievement of the Greek school in the form of the *progymnasmata* scheme included a number of simple forms and rhetorical genres, including the thesis[318]. There is no doubt that *progymnasmata* also became a permanent fixture in Roman education. There are as many as five *progymnasmata* exercises in the *Rhetorica ad Herennium*, and Quintilian's *Intitutio Oratoria* covers their entire sequence[319]. The thesis began to draw

313 T. Honsell, *Gemeinwohl...*, p. 101.

314 M. Kaser, *'Ius publicum'...*, p. 7. This idea aligns well with Schiavone's proposition to interpret the term *positiones* as *temi, posture di studio, prospettive* ('themes, study approaches, perspectives'), see J.-L. Ferrary, Aldo Schiavone, Valerio Marotta, *Cnaeus Domitius Ulpianus...*, p. 201. In the translation within the same book, the noun *positiones* is rendered as *declinazioni*, that imply such terms as 'declinations', 'forms', 'facets', or 'shades', p. 107.

315 M. Kaser, *'Ius publicum'...*, p. 8, n. 18.

316 LTL, s.v. *positio*.

317 On the definition of the term exhaustively in B. Awianowicz, *Progymnasmata w teorii i praktyce szkoły humanistycznej od końca XV do połowy XVIII wieku: dzieje nowożytnej recepcji Aftoniosa od Rudolfa Agricoli do Johanna Christopha Gottscheda*, Toruń 2008, pp. 11–16.

318 The set of progymnasmata exercises also includes rhetorical forms such as a fable (μῦθος, *fabula*), narrative (διήγημα, *narratio*), anecdote (χρεία, *chria, usus*), maxim (γνώμη, *sententia*), refutation and confirmation of arguments (ἀνασκευή, *destructio* and κατασκευή, *confirmatio*), commonplace (κοινὸς τόπος, *locus communis*), encomium (ἐγκώμιον, *encomium, laus*), invective (ψόγος, *vituperatio*), comparison (σύγκρισις, *comparatio*), personification (ἠθοποιία, *ethopoeia*), description (ἔκφρασις, *descriptio*), and proposing a law (εἰσφορὰ τοῦ νόμου, *legislatio*). Textbooks following this model, with some minor exceptions, were composed by Theon of Alexandria, Hermogenes, Aphthonius of Antioch, and Nicholas of Myra. Libanius also wrote his exercises according to this pattern.

319 B. Awianowicz, *Progymnasmata...*, pp. 31–38.

attention of Roman rhetoricians as early as the 1st century BCE[320]. The term θέσις used by the Greek *progymnasmata* followers is sometimes translated into Latin in several ways. Cicero uses the term *propositum*[321] to describe the thesis, but sometimes he also resorts to the expressions like *consultatio,* or *quaestio infinita*[322]. Quintilian usually sticks to the Greek term, sometimes preferring its transcription[323]. The *progymnasmata* theses were also replaced by the lexeme *positiones*[324], the most spectacular of which (as it contains a definition of the concept) being an excerpt from the *Praeexercitamina* by Priscianus Caesariensis. Although this work may seem relatively late in the context of our discussion, dating to the turn of the 5th and 6th centuries, it is a translation[325] of a rhetoric manual written exactly at the height of Roman classical jurisprudence by Hermogenes of Tarsus, one of the most important Greek authors at the turn of the 2nd and 3rd centuries CE.[326] Priscianus then defines the concept of *positio* as follows[327]:

320 Ibidem, pp. 32–34, where numerous sources testify to the presence of progymnasmata exercises in Rome at the turn of the century. For a contrary point of view, see M. L. Clarke, *The Thesis in the Roman Rhetorical Schools of the Republic*, 'The Classical Quarterly' 1951, vol. 1, no. 3–4, pp. 159–166.

321 See e. g. Cic., *Top.* 21,79. Notably, the terms *propositum* and *positio* both derive from the same verb. See *Dictionnaire étymologique…*, p. 520 s. v. *pono*. Moreover, according to the online databases 'Classical Latin Texts' and '*Corpus Corporum – repositorium operum Latinorum apud universitatem Turicensem*' the term *positio* never appears in Cicero's works. Furthermore, Cicero does not seem to distinguish between *thesis* and *thema*, as discussed below. In his writings, both concepts, namely *propositum* and *positio*, appear closely related in meaning.

322 Cf. Cic., *De orat.* 2,41–42 *Infinitum mihi videbatur id dicere, in quo aliquid generatim quaereretur, hoc modo: expetendane esset eloquentia? Expetendine honores?*; 3,28,109 *haec autem altera quaestio infinita et quasi proposita consultatio nominatur*. Quintilian also uses the term *quaestio infinita*: Quint., *Inst.* 10,5,11 *In hoc optime facient infinitae quaestiones, quas vocari theseis diximus, quibus Cicero iam princeps in re publica exerceri solebat.*

323 Cf. e.g. Quint., *Inst.* 2,4,24 *Theseis autem quae sumuntur ex rerum comparatione*; 3,4,11 *Quidam putant etiam eas* θέσεις *posse aliquando nominari quae personis causisque contineantur*. Quintilian also gives a slightly more extensive catalogue of concepts. Cf. Quint., *Inst.*, 3,5,5 *Infinitae sunt quae remotis personis et temporibus et locis ceterisque similibus in utramque partem tractantur, quod Graeci* θέσιν *dicunt, Cicero propositum, alii quaestiones universales civiles, alii quaestiones philosopho convenientis, Athenaeus partem causae appellat.*

324 In that sense, it seems, in Quint., *Inst.* 7,4,40 *Sed mihi nec omnes persequi materias in animo est (fingi enim adhuc possunt), nec omnis earum quaestiones, quia positionibus mutantur.*

325 However, this is not a literal translation. Awianowicz describes *Praeexercitamina* as a 'Latin paraphrase of Hermogenes' textbook' (see *Progymnasmata…*, p. 23) or as a 'loose translation of *Progymnasmata*' (ibidem, p. 82).

326 Hermogenes' lectures were most likely listened to by emperor Marcus Aurelius. See Cass. Dio, 71,1. See also G. A. Kennedy, *A New History of Classical Rhetoric. An Extensive Revision and Abridgement of The Art of Persuasion in Greece, The Art of Rhetoric in the Roman World and Greek Rhetoric under Christian Emperors with Additional Discussion of Late Latin Rhetoric*, Princeton, New Jersey 1994, p. 208; B. Awianowicz, *Progymnasmata…*, p. 42; *Sofiści i retorzy greccy w Cesarstwie Rzymskim (I–VII w.). Słownik biograficzny*, P. Janiszewski, K. Stebnicka, E. Szabat (ed.), Warszawa 2011, pp. 236–237 s. v. *Hermogenes*.

327 Cf. also H. Lausberg, *Handbuch…*, pp. 544–546.

Prisc., *Praeex.* 11,31
Positio est deliberatio alicuius rei generalis ad nullam personam certam pertinens vel aliam partem circumstantiae, ut si tractemus an navigandum, an ducendam uxorem, an philosophandum, non addentes cui, sed ipsam rem per se et per accidentia ei requirentes.
A thesis is to consider some general problem that does not pertain to any particular person, or to some aspect of a specific situation, such as when discussing whether to sail, or marry, or deal with philosophy, without adding who would have to perform this activity but asking about the very essence of the matter and its circumstances.

A *positio* was therefore a general issue put forward for discussion[328], which was the starting point for considering all the 'for and against' arguments of a problem raised[329], and for presenting arguments in favor of adopting a given view.

On the other hand, the *positiones* as explained by Forcellini can also be equivalent to the concept of *themata*. This expression belongs not to *progymnasmata* but to declamations, which constitute the next level of initiation in the exploration of rhetoric. These were exercises that required a young adept to analyze a (fictitious) legal dispute, and then prepare a speech supporting the position of one of the parties. A *thema* is an introductory and elementary part of a *controversia*, in which the factual and legal status is briefly presented, serving as the starting point for further considerations[330]. For illustration – the subject of the fifth *controversia* in the first book of Seneca the Elder's *Oratorum et rhetorum sententiae, divisiones, colores*[331] is as follows: 'a kidnapped woman has the right to choose between the death of her kidnapper, and marrying him without bringing in her dowry. Overnight, a man seduced two women. One demands

328 The nature of the thesis is the easiest to understand by comparing it with a hypothesis. For instance, Hermogenes' *Progymnasmata* 24–25 illustrates a thesis using the thesis school example 'should we get married?'. Hermogenes explains that in considering marriage, one should not refer to specific individuals or circumstances, but rather analyze the question in general terms. If the argument focuses on a specific person or situation, it becomes a hypothesis, not a thesis. Identical or very similar definitions of these categories can be found in numerous sources.

329 Cf. Cic., *Att.* 9,4,1 *In his ego me consultationibus exercens et disserens in utramque partem tum Graece tum Latine et abduco parumper animum a molestiis* et τῶν προὔργον τι *delibero.* ('Practicing these questions and putting forward arguments on both sides, sometimes in Greek, sometimes in Latin, I take my mind off my trouble for a moment, and at the same time reflect on important matters').

330 Quint., *Inst.* 7,1,4 *nam in schola certa sunt et pauca et ante declamationem exponuntur, quae themata Graeci vocant, Cicero proposita* ('in schools, before declamation, some given elements are briefly presented, which the Greeks call *themata*, and Cicero *proposita*'); 4,2,28. *Sed nos ducit scholarum consuetudo, in quibus certa quaedam ponuntur (quae themata dicimus)* ('Our guide, however, is school practice in which specific circumstances are put before us, and we call them '*themata*'). More on the category of *thema*, in particular from the perspective of literary theory, in E. Betti, *Seneca il Vecchio e la cultura retorica e letteraria della prima età imperiale*, Pisa 2007, pp. 46–51.

331 More information about the author and his work are provided in L.A. Sussman, *The Elder Seneca*, Leiden 1978; J. Fairweather, *Seneca the Elder*, Cambridge 1981; E. Betti, *Seneca il Vecchio…*, B. Huelsenbeck, *The rhetorical collection of the Elder Seneca: Textual tradition and traditional text*, 'Harvard Studies in Classical Philology' 2011, no. 106, pp. 229–299.

his death, the other to marry him'[332]. The rhetorician's task was to present the motives for defending the rights of each woman. Importantly, the aim of the exercize is not to win the dispute but to practice the art of argumentation[333]. However, a *thema* was not only the subject of discussion; it also set its limits. Although an orator was free to use all his oratory talents, he had no right to go beyond the circumstances specified in the subject (*thema evertere*)[334]. This meant that a rhetorician had to focus solely on the problem presented.

The above paragraphs clearly show that the content of the terms *thesis* and *thema* does not coincide semantically[335]. *Publicum et privatum* is not a perfect counterpart to any of the above categories either. These concepts are far from even the most concise description of the factual and legal situation (*thema*), or the general issue submitted for discussion, in which all 'for and against' arguments (*thesis*) could be distinguished. However, both *thesis* and *thema* indicate the category that is the sole basis for the presented considerations. It seems that this was the meaning of the term *positio* that Ulpian wanted to propose. It is therefore likely that the jurist used the term *positiones* in relation to the notions of *publicum et privatum* to some extent metaphorically.

The proposed understanding of the term *positio* opposes the traditional approach of Roman law researchers, who typically diligently separate the fields of law and rhetoric[336]. However, adhering to a contrary approach is fully justified, not only because it clarifies the understanding of the analyzed fragment. First, it is important to remember who the target audience of Ulpian's textbook was, described by the jurist himself as

332 Sen., *Contr.* 1,5 *Rapta raptoris aut mortem aut indotatas nuptias optet. Una nocte quidam duas rapuit; altera mortem optat, altera nuptias.* On this legal question in J. Kulawiak-Cyrankowska, *The Death Penalty, the "Marriage Penalty' and Some Remarks on the Utility of Senecan Research in the Study of Roman Law*, 'Studia Iuridica' 2019, vol. 80, pp. 197–214 along with the literature cited therein.

333 G.A. Kennedy, *A New History…*, p. 168.

334 Sen., *Contr.* 9,5,10–11 and Quint., *Inst.* 4,2,90.

335 On the other hand, Cicero likely did not see much difference between these terms, as he used the word *propositum* to describe each of them. Cf. already quoted Cic., *Top.* 21,79 and Quint., *Inst.* 7,1,4.

336 The discussion on separating the areas of law and rhetoric was likely stimulated by J. Stroux's publication *Summum ius…*, pp. 5–46. Olga E. Tellegen-Couperus, in turn, attributes the origins of this debate to the Historical School, which categorized the works of Cicero and Quintilian as non-legal sources, *Quintilian and Roman Law*, 'RIDA' 2000, vol. 47, pp. 169–171. Although scholars of Roman law remain divided on this issue, more and more works argue that the law and rhetoric were correlated and complementary disciplines, sharing methods of reasoning and argumentation. Many works on specific aspects of rhetoric crucial for understanding legal interpretation will be quoted in Chapter Three. For more general works on the topic, see e.g.: F. Franchani, *Il diritto nei retori Romani: contributo alla storia dello sviluppo del diritto romano*, Milano 1938; T. Viehweg, *Topica…*, *passim*; F. Horak, *Rationes decidendi: Entscheidungsbegründungen bei den älteren römischen Juristen bis Labeo*, vol. 1, Insbruck 1969; J.A. Crook, *Once again the Controversiae and Roman Law* [in:] *Multarum artium scientia. Festschrift for R. Godfrey Tanner*, Auckland 1993, pp. 68–76; P. Kubiak, *Kilka uwag na temat znajomości prawa u mówców sądowych republikańskiego Rzymu*, 'Krakowskie Studia z Historii Państwa i Prawa' 2015, vol. 8, no. 1, pp. 1–24. A discussion on this topic recently reported in P. Thomas, *Ars aequi et boni, legal argumentation and the correct legal solution*, 'ZSS RA' 2014, vol. 131, no. 1, pp. 41–59.

iuri operam daturus. His path of intellectual formation, which began at home under the care of his father or a slave, took on a real shape when he started his education at a rhetorical school. This boy, whose head was still full of *progymnasmata* and declamations, who started reading Ulpian's *Institutions*[337]. After all, we must not forget that the analyzed fragments are not yet a professional analysis of the law but belong to a category that could be defined as 'preliminary issues'. It therefore seems more than likely that the jurist used a terminology the young apprentice of the law was already well acquainted with[338]. Consequently, the notions of *ars* and *studium*, which, if Mario Bretone and

337 On the model of education in ancient Rome in, among others, G. Boissier, *Les Écoles de déclamation à Rome*, 'Revue des deux mondes' 1902, no. 11, pp. 481–508; A. Gwynn, *Roman Education from Cicero to Quintilian*, Oxford 1926; E.P. Parks, *The Roman Rhetorical Schools as a Preparation for the Courts under the Early Empire*, Baltimore 1945; K. Kolańczyk, *O pochodzeniu i stanowisku społecznym prawników rzymskich*, 'CPH' 1955, vol. 7, no. 1, pp. 227–284; H. Marrou, *A History of Education in Antiquity*, London 1956; D.L. Clark, *Rhetoric in Greco-Roman Education*, New York 1957; I. Lana, *Il primo approccio degli studenti romani con la legge alla scuola del retore*, 'Klio' 1979, vol. 61, no. 1–2, pp. 89–96; W. Rozwadowski, *Nauczanie prawa w państwie rzymskim*, 'CPH' 2003, vol. 55, no. 1, pp. 9–28; K. Wyrwińska, *Grecka myśl filozoficzna i jej wpływ na kształtowanie się rzymskiego kanonu wykształcenia prawniczego. Przyczynek do studium* [in:] *Vetera novis augere: Studia i prace dedykowane Profesorowi Wacławowi Uruszczakowi*, S. Grodziński, D. Malec, A. Karabowicz (ed.), Kraków 2010, pp. 1179–1187; P. Święcicka, *Iurisconsultus et Auditores. Dialektyczna formuła poznania i rozwoju prawa w Rzymie republikańskim*, 'Krakowskie Studia z Historii Państwa i Prawa' 2013, vol. 6, no. 3, pp. 193–227; P. Kubiak, *Kilka uwag...*, pp. 1–24; and in an excellent monograph by G. La Bua, *Cicero and Roman Education, passim*.

338 The style of writing of a jurist from the Severan era also seems to indicate the field of rhetoric. The fragment Ulp. D. 1,1,1,1 is not only the *pompa per enumerationem* of activity of jurists but also an excellent example of the periodic style that Quintilian teaches as follows: Quint., *Inst.* 9,4,128 *Perihodos apta prohoemiis maiorum causarum, ubi sollicitudine commendatione miseratione res eget, item communibus locis et in omni amplificatione* ('The period is well suited to introductions on more important matters, where the topic is worrying and requires recommendation or pity. It is also suitable for commonplaces and any type of amplification'); 9,4,125 *Habet perihodos membra minime duo; medius numerus videtur quattuor, sed recipit frequenter et plura. Modus eius a Cicerone aut quattuor senariis versibus aut ipsius spiritus modo terminatur. Praestare debet ut sensum concludat: sit aperta, ut intellegi possit, non inmodica, ut memoria contineri* ('The period includes at least two clauses, the average number of which appears to be four but often allows for more. Cicero describes its length as length of four senars, or as the length of one breath. The period must contain a complete thought, it must be clear to understand and not too long so that it stays in your memory'); 9,4,123 *Membrum autem est sensus numeris conclusus, sed a toto corpore abruptus et per se nihil efficiens. 'O callidos homines' perfectum est, sed remotum a ceteris vim non habet, ut per se manus et pes et caput* ('A clause, on the other hand, is a thought that is rhythmically complete but separate from its parent body and ineffective in itself. The expression "oh learned men!" is complete but has no force of itself. It is like a hand, foot or head in itself'). The periodic style emphasizes the subject appropriately and, as Quintilian notes, is perfect for introductions. It also fits well with amplification, a rhetorical device involving detailed and comprehensive descriptions, often through enumeration. In Ulpian's text, it manifests as follows: *aequum ab iniquo separantes, licitum ab illicito discernentes, bonos non solum metu poenarum, verum etiam praemiorum quoque exhortatione efficere cupientes, veram nisi fallor philosophiam, non simulatam affectantes*. Individual clauses which make up the quoted enumeration, although rhythmic, acquire their full meaning only in the context of the whole sentence. Reading the fragment Ulp. D. 1,1,1,1 out loud clearly shows that each clause corresponds to the length of a single breath. Moreover, no clause exceeds the limit of seventeen syllables. On

Valerio Marotta are right, are almost synonyms[339] in the context of the analyzed fragment of Ulpian's *Institutes,* also played an important role in the field of rhetoric. Suffice to say, one of the previously quoted definitions of the *ars* concept can be found in Quintilian's textbook[340]. And the above-quoted explanation of the meaning of the term *studium* was taken from Cicero's rhetorical treatise *De inventione*[341]. Finally, it is worth recalling that both terms are often referred to in the speech *Pro Murena,* a battlefield of jurisprudence and rhetoric, in which the former (*verbosa simulatio prudentiae*) gets totally defeated[342]. In these circumstances, it seems highly likely that *publicum et privatum* in Ulpian's thought should be considered precisely as two *positiones*-foundations all arguments were subsequently derived from, as Forcellini aptly put it.

The recurring question then is whether it was the *ius publicum* and *ius privatum* that could correspond to the concept of *positiones studii* and form the two categories from which arguments derived. It seems that such an understanding of the fragment could be maintained although, as already mentioned, it requires the procedure of 'supplementing' the jurist's thought with the *ius* category. Additionally, it raises doubts as to whether listing the public law and the private law as the two grounds of argumentation can be considered exhaustive.

From a grammatical point of view, however, not two but three readings of the sentence *huius studii duae sunt positiones, publicum et privatum* are possible, as the expressions *publicum* and *privatum* can be regarded not as adjectives but neuter nouns. In abstract terms, *publicum* would therefore mean 'what is public', and *privatum* – 'what is private'. Although this is the simplest and most straightforward reading of this passage, this interpretation does not seem to have been proposed in other studies on D. 1,1,1,pr.–2.

Still, in the context of the analyzed fragment these ambiguous[343] categories require further clarification, which Ulpian appears to offer. The first part of the fragment D. 1,1,1,2, summed up by the sentence *sunt enim quaedam publice utilia, quaedam pri-*

these issues see J. G. Heineccius, *Fundamenta stili cultoris. Nunc demum omnibus Io. Matthiae Generi animadversionibus, additamentis, et praefatione locupletata accuravit, digessit, suas quoque observationes adiecit Nicolaus Niclas,* Amstelodami 1761, p. 120.

339 As already noted, researchers interpret the *ius* in Ulpian's definition as the term 'jurisprudence'. Cf. M. Bretone, *Tecniche…*, p. 262; V. Marotta, *Ulpiano…*, p. 154.

340 See again Quint., *Inst.* 2,17,41.

341 Cf. again Cic., *Inv.* 1,25,36 and 2,9,31.

342 It is also significant that the author of the *Institutio oratoria* presents a question 'who deserves more recognition; a jurist or a soldier?' as a perfect example of a rhetorical *thesis* (Quint., *Inst.* 2,4,24 *iuris periti an militaris viri laus maior*). This question is formulated precisely based on fragments of Cicero's speech in defense of Lucius Licinius Murena, which are key to the reflections presented here. Cf. Cic., *Mur.* 22–24.

343 The noun *publicum* can mean a public functionary, public slave, public property, public land, funds, state archives, tax leases, or a public place. The noun *privatum* can in turn mean private property or private profit. Cf. LTL, OLD, *A Latin Dictionary* s. v. *privatus, publicus.*

vatim[344], is arranged symmetrically[345]. Thus, two groups of expressions can be distinguished. First: *publicum, status rei Romanae* and *publice utilia*; and second: *privatum, utilitas singulorum* and *privatim utilia*. Uniformity of meaning within the latter set of concepts is clear. The question arises, however, whether the former also groups parallel categories.

Falcone demonstrated that the relationship between *status rei Romanae* and *publice utilia* can be observed already in Cicero's thought[346]. The scholar noted that Cicero linked these categories in his treatise *De legibus*[347], writing about the auspices being

344 Similarly in V. Marotta, *Ulpiano…*, p. 159. However, some scholars believe that the phrase *quaedam …, quaedam…* unnecessarily interrupts Ulpian's thought (G. Aricò Anselmo, *'Ius publicum'…*, pp. 459–460 along with the literature cited therein) and that it is an interpolation or a post-classical glossa. This way e. g. F. Stella Maranca, *Le "duae positiones" dello "studium iuris"*, Bari 1936, pp. 55–56; A. Steinwenter, *Utilitas publica–Utilitas singulorum*, p. 86; A. d'Ors, *De la Privata Lex al Derecho Privado y al Derecho Civil*, 'Boletim da Faculdade de Direito da Universidade de Coimbra' 1949, vol. 25, p. 22; G. Nocera, *Il binomio pubblico-privato nella storia del diritto*, Napoli 1989, p. 154. The further literature quoted in M. Kaser, *'Ius publicum'…*, p. 12, n. 35. The authenticity is strongly advocated in T. Honsell, *Gemeinwohl…*, pp. 100–101; A. Guarino, *L'ordinamento giuridico romano*, Napoli 1980, pp. 451–452 and M. Kaser, *'Ius publicum'…*, pp. 11, 13, 107, who defines it as an indispensable element of reasoning. Also, Honsell rightly noticed that the use of the phrase *quidam, … quidam…* is a kind of Ulpian's linguistic manner, which also speaks for the authenticity of the fragment. Cf. e.g. some of numerous examples: Ulp. D. 1,6,4 *Nam civium Romanorum quidam sunt patres familiarum, alii filii familiarum, quaedam matres familiarum, quaedam filiae familiarum* (…); Ulp. D. 2,14,7,pr. *Iuris gentium conventiones quaedam actiones pariunt, quaedam exceptiones;* Ulp. D. 2,14,7,8 *Pactorum quaedam in rem sunt, quaedam in personam* (…); Ulp. D. 3,3,27,pr. (…) *ceterum si velit quaedam transferre, quaedam relinquere* (…), Ulp. D. 25,1,1,pr. *Impensarum quaedam sunt necessariae, quaedam utiles, quaedam vero voluptariae.* It is also worth noting that the jurist uses this phrase when introducing new issues, as in the case of the analyzed fragment.

345 Ulpian's style could be described here as *membratim scribere*, that is, 'to write in parts'. A similar style can be observed, for instance, in Sallustius. Cf. Sall., *Cat.* 2–3 *Sed nostra omnis vis in animo et corpore sita est; animi imperio, corporis servitio magis utimur; alterum nobis cum dis, alterum cum beluis commune est.* The historian refers here parallelly to two categories: sometimes to *corpus*, and sometimes to *animus*. Cf. also E. H. Guggenheimer, *Rhyme Effects and Rhyming Figures: A Comparative Study of Sound Repetitions in the Classics with Emphasis on Latin Poetry*, Berlin-Boston 2018, p. 39.

346 G. Falcone, *Un'ipotesi sulla nozione ulpianea di ius publicum* [in:] *Tradizione romanistica e Costituzione*, vol. 2, L. Labruna, M. P. Baccari, C. Cascione (ed.), Napoli 2006, pp. 1175–1176. Marotta touches on this correlation as well, providing a satisfactory list of sources. However, they are based on further associations of the *status* and *utilitas* categories. Marotta suggests the following correlation: Cic., *Rep.* 1,2,3 *bene constituta civitas publico iure*; 1,26,41 *omnis civitas, quae est constitutio populi*; 1,25,39 *Est igitur, inquit Africanus, res publica res populi, populus autem non omnis hominum coetus quoquo modo congregatus, sed coetus multitudinis iuris consensu et utilitatis communione sociatus.* Thus, Marotta aptly notices that the categories of *populus* and *civitas* are correlated in Cicero's thought both with constancy (*constitutio, constituta*) as well as the community of benefits (*communio utilitatis*), *Ulpiano…*, p. 159. See also the remarks of P. Cerami, *Potere ed ordinamento nella esperienza costituzionale romana*, 3ed, Torino 1987, pp. 22–25.

347 This argument is not without significance, as already indicated above, G. Aricò Anselmo, *'Ius publicum'…*, pp. 740–773, argues that this treaty may have inspired the tripartite *sacra-sacerdotes-magistratus*.

created for the benefit of the Roman state[348]. While searching for reasons for Ulpian's concentration of the public law around the *status* category, and the private law around the *utilitas* criterion[349], he found a convincing justification in the previously quoted fragment of the *Pro Murena* speech, which enumerates the reasons for the superiority of the art of war over jurisprudence (*Mur.* 23–24)[350]. Cicero stated that only those who perfected themselves in the art of war could secure power and stable condition of the state affairs (*status civitatis*)[351]. Their activity also brought the greatest utility (*summa utilitas*), as they guaranteed both a peaceful life in the state, and the use of public institutions (*re publica … perfrui*), as well as the possibility of enjoying private goods (*nostris rebus perfrui*)[352]. All categories crucial for Cicero's argumentation thus find their counterparts in fragment D. 1,1,1,2[353]. It can therefore be assumed that it was the *Pro Murena*[354] speech, where *utilitas* was directly related to the possibility of using what was public (*res publica*), and what was private (*res nostrae*), that inspired Ulpian.

If we can therefore agree that the two triads from the fragment of the *Institutes* group twin terms, it should be stated that the *privatum*, corresponding to the categories *utilitas singulorum* and *privatim utilia*, represented the private utility, while the *publicum*, being correlated with the notions of *status rei Romanae* and *publice utilia*, was an expression of the idea of public utility. According to Ulpian, the *publicum* (*utilitas publica*) and the *privatum* (*utilitas privata*) were the two foundational pillars of jurists' deliberations. Defining them as *positiones* made it clear that it was these two fields that each jurist's attention should be focused on[355].

348 Cf. Cic., *Leg.* 2,12,30–32 *Quod sequitur vero, non solum ad religionem pertinet sed etiam ad civitatis statum… auspicia ista ad utilitatem esse rei publicae composita.* It should also be noted that Falcone advocates linking the concept of *sacerdotes* occurring in D. 1,1,1,1–2. He believes that Ulpian deliberately wrote that jurists 'could be called priests', and then pointed to priests as the foundation of the public law. In this context, the term *sacerdotes* would therefore have a double meaning and include priests of the gods as well as priests-jurists, *La 'vera philosophia'…*, pp. 41–147. Similarly, P. Stein states that Ulpian actually referred to two categories of priests: those who dealt with the state religion and jurists-apologists for justice, guarding the interests of citizens, *Ulpian and the distinction between ius publicum and ius privatum*, in: *Collatio iuris romani, études dediées á Hans Ankum à l'occasion de son 65e anniversaire,* vol. 2, R. Feenstra, A. S. Hartkamp, J. E. Spruit, R. J. Sijpesteijn, L. C. Winkel (ed.), Amsterdam 1995, p. 504.

349 G. Falcone, *Un'ipotesi…*, p. 1184.

350 It is worth recalling that that Quintilian used this passage to compose an example of a thesis. Cf. Quint., *Inst.* 2,4,24 *iuris periti an militaris viri laus maior.*

351 Cic., *Inv.* 2,56,169.

352 G. Falcone, *Un'ipotesi…*, pp. 1189–1193.

353 It also does not seem to be a coincidence that the same passage contains a statement that almost resembles the definition of the concept of *ars*, and that a moment later *ars iuris* was downgraded to the category of *artificium* by Cicero. Cf. Cic., *Mur.* 24 *Quorum in isto vestro artificio, Sulpici, nihil est.*

354 Similarly G. Falcone, *Un'ipotesi…*, p. 1192, who yet is of opinion that *publicum* and *privatum* correspond to the categories of *ius publicum* and *ius privatum*.

355 As previously noted, *thema evertere,* namely going beyond the circumstances specified in the theme, was forbidden. See again Sen., *Contr.* 9,5,10–11 and Quint., *Inst.* 4,2,90.

2.3 *Utilitas publica* and *utilitas singulorum*

2.3.1 *Utilitas publica – utilitas singulorum* Relation in Intellectual Tradition

Recognizing that *utilitas publica* and *utilitas privata* were to constitute the two foundations for jurists' deliberations, we should focus on how these ideas relate to each other in the thought of Roman jurisprudence. First, however, we should note that in the intellectual tradition these two concepts never symbolized contradictory or mutually exclusive values. For the Romans, the *publicum* was common to all citizens and concerned each of them individually[356]. This universality thus implied the existence of a group consisting of given entities[357]. The state was like one organism, with the citizens being its elements[358]. Consequently, both the group and the individual were oriented towards the achievement of essentially similar goals. This is likely why Cicero indicated that the *res publica* stood for a double bond of agreement: both with regard to the common law as well as the community of utility (*communio utilitatis*)[359], and therefore represents the socio-economic affairs and interests of citizens[360]. That is the reason for which the terms *utilitas rei publicae, utilitas publica* and *utilitas communis* should be treated synonymously[361]: as indicating the utility of all Roman citizens, and at the same time each of them individually.

356 As G. Nocera noted, the adjectives *public* and *private* come from the same matrix, *Il binomio publico-privato nella storia del diritto*, Napoli 1989, p. 7. For further insights on this topic, see also the remarks of P. Catalano, *Populus Romanus Quirites*, Torino 1974, pp. 97–159 and P. Cerami, *Potere…*, pp. 26, 29–45.

357 This issue was aptly described by A. Paturet, *Ulpien D. 1.1.1.2…*, p. 126, who wrote that a community cannot exist without its individuals who create it. P. Catalano writes about *una pluralità di individui riuniti o uniti* ('a plurality of individuals gathered or united'), *Populus…*, p. 105. P. Cerami describes *res Romana* as *ente plurimo collettivo* ('multiple collective entity'), *Potere…*, p. 31.

358 Cf. e.g. Cic., *Off.* 1,25,85; 3,5,22; Idem, *Phil.* 8,15–16; Tac., *Ann.* 1,12; Liv., AUC 1,8,16. The concept of *partes corporis* was also present in the arguments of Roman jurists. Cf. Alf. D. 5,1,76,pr.; Pomp. D. 41,3,30,pr. See also P. Catalano, *Populus…*, p. 156; P. Cerami, *Problemi storico-dogmatici in tema di funzionario di fatto*, [in:] *Studi in onore di Gioacchino Scaduto. Diritto civile e diritto romano*, vol. 3, Padova 1970, pp. 404–405; Idem, *Potere…*, pp. 25–26, 171, 197.

359 Cic., *Rep.* 1,25,39 *Est igitur, inquit Africanus, res publica res populi, populus autem non omnis hominum coetus quoquo modo congregatus, sed coetus multitudinis iuris consensu et utilitatis communione sociatus* ('So, as Africanus says, the Republic is the matter of the people. This people, however, is not just any gathering of humans collected in any way but is a gathering of a large group united by lawful consensus and a community of utility'). In this context, P. Cerami aptly emphasized the semantic equivalence between *res publica* and *res populi*, *Potere…*, p. 23. Cf. also G. 1,3 *…populi appellatione universi cives significantur…* ('under the designation of the people, all citizens are indicated').

360 G. Longo, *Utilitas publica*, p. 14; M. Schofield, *Cicero's Definition of Res Publica*, [in:] *Cicero the Philospher. Twelve Papers*, J. G. F. Powell (ed.), Oxford-New York 1995, rep. 2002, pp. 75–76; J. W. Atkins, *Cicero on Politics and the Limits of Reason: The Republic and Laws*, Cambridge 2013, pp. 131–133; R. Scevola, *'Utilitas publica', I. Emersione…*, p. 341.

361 Cic., *Sest.* 91 *Tum res ad communem utilitatem, quas publicas appellamus…* ('Then the things of common utility that we call public'). Cf. G. Jossa, *L''utilitas rei publicae' nel pensiero imperiale…*, p. 400;

As Cicero further explains his political vision, the conflict between the utility of the individual and the community as a whole could not really arise[362], because there was no state in which what would harm the entire community would be at the same time beneficial to individual citizens[363]:

Cic., *Off.* 3,6,26
Ergo unum debet esse omnibus propositum, ut eadem sit utilitas unius cuiusque et universorum; quam si ad se quisque rapiet, dissolvetur omnis humana consortio.
There can only be therefore one assumption that the utility of individuals should be identical to the interests of all. Otherwise, if everyone seeks gain only for themselves, the human community will be destroyed.

The utility of community members, understood both collectively and individually, was a value that needed protection. So, they were not opposing interests but formed a coherent whole. The conflict between these values was only apparent. For every citizen should strive to protect the utility of the entire community as the overriding good[364]. Being guided by the utility of the community did not mean sacrificing one's own[365]. Quoting the Stoic philosopher Chrysippus, Cicero maintained that just as it was legit-

P. Cerami, *Potere…*, p. 171, (esp. n. 150 where the author explains that, in his view, this is essentially the same idea approached from different perspectives), 197; P. G. Walsh, *Introduction…*, p. XXIV. Here we can reference the statistics by I. Mastino, who recorded the frequency of Cicero using the term *utilitas* in this sense. And so the term *utilitas communis* appears in his works 28 times, *utilitas rei publicae* 26 times, and *utilitas omnium* 2 times only, *'Utilitas valuit propter honestatem'….* Similar statistics, based on H. Merguet's *Lexikon zu den philosophischen schriften Cicero's mit angabe sämtlicher stellen* and *Lexikon zu den Reden des Cicero, mit Angabe sämmtlicher Stellen*, vol. 1–4, Jena 1877–1884 was earlier proposed by J. Gaudemet, who further noted that each of the terms *utilitas publica, utilitas populi* and *utilitas civium* appears in Cicero's works twice only, and the term *utilitas civitatis* only once. It should also be mentioned that, based on a fragment of Cicero's treatise *De inventione* (*Inv.*, 1,40,27), Gaudemet concluded that while the terms corresponded with each other, they were not equivalents, because the opposite of the term *utilitas communis* is *propria utilitas*, and of *utilitas publica – utilitas privata*. He also claimed that the term *utilitas publica*, rarely used by Cicero, carried a negative overtone. This quality would make it possible to justify unjust actions in the name of the good of the state (*Off.* 3,11,47), *Utilitas publica*, pp. 467–472. R. Scevola agreed with the proposal of a semantic separation of the two terms, claiming the former refers to the community, while the latter carries political significance. However, he leaned towards the thesis of N. Rampazzo that these terms are, in fact, parallel and their meanings overlap. This thesis seems to be a satisfactory summary of these terminological considerations. Cf. R. Scevola, *'Utilitas publica', I. Emersione…*, p. 340, n. 71 and N. Rampazzo, *Quasi praetor…*, pp. 487–488, 497.

362 Cic., *Off.* 3,6,27. Cf. M. Kaser, *'Ius publicum'…*, p. 21. See also Cic., *Rep.* 1,32,49 … *ex utilitatis varietatibus, cum aliis aliud expediat, nasci discordias* ('discord arises from the variety of *utilitates*, where different measures are useful to different citizens'). Cf. P. Cerami, *Potere…*, pp. 176–177.

363 Cic., *Off.* 3,12,52; 3,27,101.

364 Cf. Cic., *Fin.* 3,19,64; Idem, *Off.* 1,25,85. This is a natural consequence of perceiving the citizens of the state as *partes corporis*. Cf. J. Gaudemet, *Utilitas publica*, p. 470; and G. Longo, *Utilitas publica*, p. 16.

365 The opposite argument was the basis of Carneades' speech against justice. Cf. Lact., *Div. Inst.* 5,16,2–3.

imate for a man participating in a race to try their best to win, individuals could and should strive for what was favourable to them. However, all activities needed to be carried out within the limits of the legal order, and with respect for the rights of other citizens[366]. Understood as a utility of the community of individuals, *utilitas publica* was therefore a prism one should look through when taking any action[367].

An example that interestingly illustrates this perspective is the story of Lucius Pedanius Secundus, the city's prefect of 61 CE, as documented by Tacitus[368]. The official was killed by one of his slaves, and the reasons for this event remained unclear. The historian speculated that Pedanius might have refused to manumit the slave. Nevertheless, he did not rule out that the perpetrator and the victim might have been love rivals. Regardless of the cause of the murder, according to the old custom, all slaves of the official had to be sentenced to death. And there were nearly four hundred of them. There was a disagreement among the public and senators. Some argued it was necessary to abandon the established custom and avoid what could be considered mass murder. Others advocated following the accepted rules, as it was the duty of the slaves to protect their master's life. The opinion of the other group was defended by the jurist and politician Gaius Cassius Longinus, who ended his speech before the Senate in this way:

> Tac., *Ann.* 14,44
> *At quidam insontes peribunt. Nam et ex fuso exercitu cum decumus quisque fusti feritur, etiam strenui sortiuntur. Habet aliquid ex iniquo omne magnum exemplum, quod contra singulos utilitate publica rependitur.*
> But undoubtedly some will die innocently! When one in ten soldiers in the army is killed, the brave ones are not spared either. Every harsh punishment against individuals at the expense of the public utility has something of unrighteousness in it.

Believing that law serves the utility of the entire community, the jurist had no qualms about sacrificing innocent lives, as in the case of decimation, to protect the greater good. He noted, however, that his preferred solution, contrasting the public utility to the good of individuals, was not fully in line with *aequitas*[369]. Thus although some inequality between public and private utility was noticed, they were never contrasted

366 Cic., *Off.* 3,10,42.

367 Cicero therefore condemned the use of a temporary monopoly and the sale of grain at a higher price when the seller was aware of shortages in a given region and knew that the same goods would soon be offered by other sellers (Cic., *Off.* 3,12,50–53). Likewise, it was not appropriate to remain silent about the hidden defects of the object of sale (Cic., *Off.* 3,13,54–57), and even worse to pretend that the goods had qualities they did not actually possess (Cic., *Off.* 3,14,58–60).

368 Tac., *Ann.* 14,42–44. On the case also in V. Scarano Ussani, *L'utilità…*, pp. 23–24.

369 G. Jossa, *L'utilitas rei publicae nel pensiero imperiale…*, p. 401; A. Schiavone, *Ius: L'invenzione del diritto in Occidente*, Torino 2005, pp. 361–362.

with each other. This thesis was also valid in the field of politics[370]. And since the actions of the princeps were formally dependent on the will of the citizens[371], they also had to take their utility into account. This is confirmed by the thought of Marcus Aurelius[372], who ruled in 161–180 CE:

> Marc. Aurel., *Med.* 5,22
> Ὃ τῇ πόλει οὐκ ἔστι βλαβερόν, οὐδὲ τὸν πολίτην βλάπτει. ἐπὶ πάσης τῆς τοῦ βεβλάφθαι φαντασίας τοῦτον ἔπαγε τὸν κανόνα· εἰ ἡ πόλις ὑπὸ τούτου μὴ βλάπτεται, οὐδὲ ἐγὼ βέβλαμμαι.
> What is not harmful to the state does not harm the citizen. Whenever you imagine you have been harmed, stick to the rule: if it did not harm the state, it did not harm me.

The above statements are not merely a simple reminiscence of the Stoic thought[373] but contain a political declaration too. Most probably written as a set of personal notes, the *Meditationes* provide an interesting insight into Marcus Aurelius' views on state authority. According to him (just like in Cicero's thought) what was good for the community was also good for the affairs of all the Roman citizens individually. There was also no discrepancy between the sphere of *utilitas publica* and the interests of the state

370 For instance, this can be seen in the edict of emperor Vespasian of December 27, 74 AD: FIRA 1,73, ll. 5–6 Ἐπειδὴ τὰ τοῖς ἐλευθέροις πρέποντα ἐπιτηδεύματα / ταῖς τε πόλεσι κοινῆι καὶ ἰδίαι χρήσιμα καὶ τῶν θεῶν ἱερὰ νομίζεται ('Because the professions of free people are considered useful to cities publicly and privately and are dedicated to the gods'). It is also worth reading excerpts from the treatise *De officiis*, which seem to convey the same thought. Cf. Cic., *Off.* 2,19,65 *Quae autem opera, non largitione beneficia dantur, haec tum in universam rem publicam tum in singulos cives conferuntur* ('Benefits rendered not by monetary gifts but by personal service sometimes apply to the entire community, and sometimes to individual citizens'); 2,21,72 *Sed quoniam de eo genere beneficiorum dictum est, quae ad singulos spectant, deinceps de iis, quae ad universos quaeque ad rem publicam pertinent, disputandum est. Eorum autem ipsorum partim eius modi sunt, ut ad universos cives pertineant, partim, singulos ut attingant; quae sunt etiam gratiora. Danda opera est omnino, si possit, utrisque, nec minus, ut etiam singulis consulatur, sed ita, ut ea res aut prosit aut certe ne obsit rei publicae* ('Now that we have finished talking about the benefits rendered to an individual, we should now deal with those that affect the general public, as well as the state. Of these, some are of such a nature as to concern all citizens, and some are of such a nature as to concern only each individual citizen. And the latter entails greater gratitude. If possible, we should use all means to do both kinds of benefits, but we must be careful in protecting the interests of individuals, so that what we do for them is beneficial, or at least not harmful to the state').

371 A. Guarino, *Res gestae divi augusti: testo critico, introduzione, traduzione e commento*, Milano 1968, p. 52; G. Longo, *Utilitas publica*, p. 11. Cf. also Ulp. D. 1,4,1,pr. (= I. 1,2,6) *Quod principi placuit, legis habet vigorem: utpote cum lege regia, quae de imperio eius lata est, populus ei et in eum omne suum imperium et potestatem conferat* ('What the emperor has decided has the force of the law. Particularly because by virtue of the *lex regia*, which granted him *imperium*, the people have committed to and onto him all their authority and power').

372 Cf. also Marc. Aurel., *Med.* 6,45; 6,54; 10,6.

373 One can also find reflections similar to the philosophy of the Garden of Epicurus in Marcus Aurelius. In the context of these considerations cf. e.g. Marc. Aurel., *Med.* 2,1 τὸ οὖν ἀντιπράσσειν ἀλλήλοις παρὰ φύσιν ('Thus, it is against nature to harm each other'). See also Marc. Aurel., *Med.* 7,64.

authority. The overriding goal of all activities of the princeps was *utilitas rei publicae*, equated with the category of *utilitas omnium*, the utility of all[374]. This is confirmed by historiographers' testimonies on the reign of Octavian Augustus (27 BCE–14 CE)[375], Tiberius (14–37 CE)[376] and Vespasian (69–79 CE)[377]. Pliny the Younger speaks in the same spirit in *Panegyricus Traiani* (98–17 CE)[378]. This is also evidenced by the accounts on Hadrian's reign (117–138 CE)[379], and numerous fragments of Marcus Aurelius' writings[380].

374 G. Longo, *Utilitas publica*, pp. 11, 13; P. Cerami, *Potere...*, pp. 173–175, 195–198.

375 Dio. Cass., 54,3,6–7 συμφέροντα τῷ δημοσίῳ διέταξεν ('he took these measures in accordance with the public good').

376 Suet., *Tib.* 3,29 *Dixi et nunc et saepe alias, p. c., bonum et salutarem principem, quem vos tanta et tam libera potestate instruxistis, senatui servire debere et universis civibus saepe et plerumque etiam singuli.* ('I have said it now, and I have often said it on other occasions, senators, that a good ruler caring for the benefit of the state, whom you provided with so vast and unlimited power, should serve the Senate and all citizens, often and above all individuals').

377 Tac., *Hist.* 4,7,9 *pertinere ad utilitatem rei publicae, pertinere ad Vespasiani honorem...* ('It was a matter of concern for the utility of the state, and the honour of Vespasian').

378 Plin., *Panegiricus* 67,4 *Si bene rem publicam et ex utilitate omnium rexerit* ('if he managed the state well and for the utility of all'); 67,8 *Ego quidem in me, si omnium utilitas ita posceret, etiam praefecti manum armavi* ('After all, I would put a weapon into a soldier's hand to be used against me if that was what the utility of all would require'). Cf. also Plin., *Panegiricus* 68,1; 94,5 and Plin., *Epist.* 3,20,12.

379 SHA, *Hadr.* 8,3 *Et in contione et in senatu saepe dixit ita se rem publicam gesturum, ut sciret populi rem esse, non propriam.* ('In both assemblies and in the Senate, he often said that he would govern the state in such a way that it was clear that it was a cause for the whole people and not his own') and CIL 8,26416 (*ara legis Hadrianae*) *Quia Caesar noster pro infatigabili cura sua, per quam adsidue pro humanis utilitatibus excubat.* ('Because our emperor, thanks to his constant care, ceaselessly watches over the benefits [*utilitates*] of people'). Similar statements from Hadrian's era can also be found in historians' works. This way e.g. Florus, a historian at the turn of the 1st and 2nd centuries CE, describing the period of the Roman Kingdom: *Epit.* 1,2,8,1 *Haec est prima aetas populi Romani et quasi infantia, quam habuit sub regibus septem, quadam fatorum industria tam variis ingenio, ut rei publicae ratio et utilitas postulabat* ('It is the first period of the Roman nation and at the same time almost [its] childhood, which passed under [the rule of] seven kings, who, by a purposeful fate, possessed as many different qualities as were necessary for the sake of state and utility'). Therefore, there is no doubt that the ideal concept of a good ruler was accompanied by a strong conviction that his actions had to be directly related to the idea of *utilitas publica*. On this subject V. Scarano Ussani, *L'utilità...*, p. 26. More about Florus in the context of Hadrian's reign in A. Garzetti, *Floro e l'età adrianea*, 'Athenaeum. Studi di letteratura e storia dell'antichità' 1964, no. 42, pp. 136–144.

380 See e.g. Marc. Aurel., *Med.* 4,12 Δύο ταύτας ἑτοιμότητας ἔχειν ἀεὶ δεῖ· τὴν μέν, πρὸς τὸ πρᾶξαι μόνον, ὅπερ ἂν ὁ τῆς βασιλικῆς καὶ νομοθετικῆς λόγος ὑποβάλλῃ, ἐπ' ὠφελείᾳ ἀνθρώπων· τὴν δέ, πρὸς τὸ μεταθέσθαι, ἐὰν ἄρα τις παρῇ διορθῶν καὶ μετάγων ἀπό τινος οἰήσεως. τὴν μέντοι μεταγωγὴν ἀεὶ ἀπὸ τινος πιθανότητος ὡς δικαίου ἢ κοινωφελοῦς γίνεσθαι, καὶ τὰ προηγμένα τοιαῦτα μόνον εἶναι δεῖ, οὐχ ὅτι ἡδὺ ἢ ἔνδοξον ἐφάνη. ('One should always have two resolutions ready: one to do only what the governing and legislative reason suggests for the good of people, and the other to change the judgment when someone corrects you and dissuades you from any opinion. However, this change should always result only from a certain belief that it is right or useful for the public – and some such cause should be the only one – and not that it is pleasant or can bring fame') and Idem, *Med.* 7,5 ἢ πράσσω, ὡς δύναμαι, προσπαραλαβὼν τὸν δυνάμενον κατὰ πρόσχρησιν τοῦ ἐμοῦ ἡγεμονικοῦ ποιῆσαι τὸ εἰς τὴν κοινωνίαν νῦν καίριον καὶ χρήσιμον. ὅ τι γὰρ ἂν δι' ἐμαυτοῦ ἢ σὺν ἄλλῳ

Nevertheless, it cannot be ignored that *utilitas* often served emperors only as a pretext for achieving their own goals, and even causing damage to individuals. Public utility was already an argument in the times of Augustus to justify civil wars[381] and political killings[382]. Cicero strongly criticized the interpretation of such behaviour as genuinely undertaken for the common utility. To him, they were merely a semblance of true *utilitas*, a *species utilitatis*[383]. A reflection of the same beliefs can be found in the passage in which Tacitus summed up the persecution of Christians found guilty of starting the fire of Rome in 64 CE:

> Tac., *Ann.* 15,44
> *unde quamquam adversus sontes et novissima exempla meritos miseratio oriebatur, tamquam non utilitate publica, sed in saevitiam unius absumerentur.*
> Even when it therefore concerned offenders who deserved punishment of unprecedented severity, nevertheless, a feeling of pity arose, because they died to satisfy one man's cruelty, and not for the public utility.

While Tacitus offers no final judgment on the legal responsibility of Christians, he bitterly highlights the contradiction between Nero's cruelty and the overarching duty to govern with the public utility in mind. Thus, there is no doubt that the historian believed such a contradiction should never occur.

ποιῶ, ὧδε μόνον χρὴ συντείνειν, εἰς τὸ κοινῇ χρήσιμον καὶ εὐάρμοστον. ('Or I do them as best I can, supported by the one who, with the help of my will, is able to fulfil a task currently appropriate and useful for society. For everything I do alone or with the help from others should have only one purpose in mind: what is useful for the community and harmonious with it'). See also Idem, *Med.* 5,35.

381 Tac., *Ann.* 1,9–10.

382 Tac., *His.* 1,41; Suet., *Oth.* 12,2.

383 Cic., *Off.* 3,11,46. Cf. also Cic., *Leg.* 1,15,42, Idem, *Off.* 3,11,47 and Liv., AUC 28,42,25. See also J. Gaudemet, *Utilitas publica*, p. 470.

2.3.2 *Utilitas publica, utilitas singulorum* and Legal Thinking

In the law, as explained by Honsell[384] and Kaser[385], *utilitas publica* and *utilitas singulorum* were not contradictory or mutually exclusive categories. Instead, they complemented each other[386], or at least harmoniously coexisted[387]. Leptien, Mayer-Maly and

384 T. Honsell, *Gemeinwohl…*, pp. 93–137, esp. pp. 96–104. According to Honsell, the conflict between the two can only be observed in post-classical sources (p. 104). Cf. P.S. 2,19,2 *Eorum qui in potestate patris sunt sine voluntate eius matrimonia iure non contrahuntur, sed contracta non solvuntur: contemplatio enim publicae utilitatis privatorum commodis praefertur* ('The marriages of those who are under the paternal power are not legally valid without his consent. However, a marriage once concluded cannot be dissolved at the will of the father. Thus, the recognition of *utilitas publica* prevails over the privileges of individuals'). However, this example does not fully illustrate the juxtaposition of public and private utility but is further evidence for the special nature of *utilitas* as an interpretative criterion, which will be discussed below. Occasionally, in this context the passage Ulp. D. 1,18,6,6 is quoted: *Ne quid sub nomine militum, quod ad utilitates eorum in commune non pertinet, a quibusdam propria sibi commoda inique vindicantibus committatur, praeses provinciae provideat.* Careful reading, however, allows to avoid the impression of juxtaposing the utility of private entities and community: 'The governor of a province should make sure that individual soldiers do not use their position and demand unfair benefits for themselves that do not serve the common benefit of the army'. See also B. Isaac, *Army and Violence in the Roman World* [in:] *Empire and Ideology in the Graeco-Roman World: Selected Papers*, Cambridge 2017, pp. 78–80.

385 M. Kaser, *'Ius publicum'…*, pp. 4, 12, 19, 91.

386 Cf. Paul. D. 3,3,42,1 *Ad actionem iniuriarum ex lege Cornelia procurator dari potest: nam etsi pro publica utilitate exercetur, privata tamen est* ('A representative may be appointed to bring an *actio iniuriarum* under the *lex Cornelia*. Despite the fact that it is brought because of the public utility, it is nevertheless of a private nature'); Paul. D. 39,4,9,5 = P.S. 5,1a,6 *Quod illicite publice privatimque exactum est, cum altero tanto passis iniuriam exsolvitur. per vim vero extortum cum poena tripli restituitur: amplius extra ordinem plectuntur: alterum enim utilitas privatorum, alterum vigor publicae disciplinae postulat* ('What was unlawfully enforced, either privately or publicly, is repaid to those who suffered injury in double the amount. However, if the extortion was done by force, the reimbursement is tripled. Furthermore, those responsible are subject to extraordinary prosecution. This is because the utility of private persons requires one approach, while the seriousness of public order requires another'); Ulp. D. 43,8,2,2 *Et tam publicis utilitatibus quam privatorum per hoc prospicitur. loca enim publica utique privatorum usibus deserviunt, iure scilicet civitatis, non quasi propria cuiusque, et tantum iuris habemus ad optinendum, quantum quilibet ex populo ad prohibendum habet. propter quod si quod forte opus in publico fiet, quod ad privati damnum redundet, prohibitorio interdicto potest conveniri, propter quam rem hoc interdictum propositum est.* ('This [interdictum] cares for both public and private utility. Public places serve both public and private purposes. They are the property of a community, not everyone individually, and we have the same right to use them as any human to prevent their abuse. Therefore, if any work was undertaken in a public place that would cause private damage, one can apply for a prohibition interdictum, for which reason this interdictum was introduced').

387 Cf. e.g. Paul. D. 9,3,33,pr. …*pretia rerum non ex affectione nec utilitate singulorum, sed communiter fungi…* ('the value of property is not determined by the individual preference or utility but in a general manner'; the same statement is also found in Paul. D. 35,2,63,pr.); Ulp. D. 43,8,2,22 *Viarum quaedam publicae sunt, quaedam privatae, quaedam vicinales. publicas vias dicimus, quas Graeci βασιλικάς, nostri praetorias, alii consulares vias appellant. privatae sunt, quas agrarias quidam dicunt. vicinales sunt viae, quae in vicis sunt vel quae in vicos ducunt: has quoque publicas esse quidam dicunt: quod ita verum est, si non ex collatione privatorum hoc iter constitutum est. aliter atque si ex collatione privatorum reficiatur: nam si ex collatione privatorum reficiatur, non utique privata est: refectio enim*

Honsell also noted that *utilitas publica* is presented in the sources as a value oriented towards the interests of individuals[388]. Therefore, it is unlikely that fragment D. 1,1,1,2 should be seen as a revolutionary political declaration[389] separating the public good from the benefits of individuals. Although Ulpian distinguished between the categories of *utilitas publica* and *utilitas privata,* he did not contrast them. For neither the term *positiones,* nor the expression *quaedam…, quaedam…,* nor the phrase *spectat ad* can be understood as indicating contrasting areas[390]. *Spectare ad* did not imply turning in opposite directions but adopting appropriate ones depending on the needs of a specific situation and also complementary perspectives on the same value with a dual nature. Kaser describes this matter brilliantly, stating that *utilitas publica* and *singulorum* do not collide but converge[391].

Moreover, when Ulpian wrote that *publicum ius est quod ad statum rei Romanae spectat, privatum quod ad singulorum utilitatem*[392], he seemed to specify the nature of jurists'

idcirco de communi fit, quia usum utilitatemque communem habet ('Some roads are public, some private, some local. What we understand as public roads is what the Greeks call royal roads, and what our people call praetorian or consular roads. Private roads are what some call agrarian roads. Local roads are those that are in villages or that lead to villages. This type some call public roads, which is true as long as they were not constituted by the contribution of the land by private individuals. It is different if they are repaired by private contributions; for what is repaired by private contributions is by no means private. For this reason, repairs can be communal, as the road is for use and common utility'). The same is also confirmed by the imperial constitution, which is somewhat later in relation to the period discussed here. However, due to its popularity, it is worth quoting its full content here. See Diocl. et Maxim. C. 12,62,3 *Utilitas publica praeferenda est privatorum contractibus: et ideo si constiterit fisco satisfactum esse ob causam primipili, poteris obligatam tibi possessionem dotis titulo petere, ut satis doti fieri possit* ('*Utilitas publica* should take precedence over contracts of private persons. Hence, if it is established that the claims of the Treasury against the administrator of provision and payments in the legion have been satisfied, you can claim the release of the property owed to you as a dowry to satisfy your claim').

388 U. Leptien, *Utilitatis causa…,* pp. 61, 202–208; T. Mayer-Maly, *Gemeinwohl…,* p. 137; T. Honsell, *Gemeinwohl…,* p. 106, n. 48/49.

389 Such an interpretation is supported in P. Stein, *Ulpian…,* pp. 503–504.

390 T. Honsell, *Gemeinwohl…,* pp. 99–104; M. Kaser, *'Ius publicum'…,* p. 10; A. Paturet, *Ulpien…,* p. 117.

391 M. Kaser, *'Ius publicum'…,* p. 19. Cf. also G. Aricò Anselmo, *'Ius publicum'…,* p. 460.

392 This is not the place to delve into the semantics and scope of the terms *ius publicum* and *ius privatum,* nor to determine the criteria for defining these categories. It should be noted that, according to preserved sources, jurists up to the time of Ulpian did not seem to attach any particular importance to the separation of the public and private law. The term *publicum privatumque ius* (e.g. Liv., AUC 3,34,6 *fons omnis publici privatique iuris*) did not imply the existence of two areas of the law but referred to it as a whole. Also in the context of the quoted source, it is unlikely that the aim of the jurist, who a moment earlier also treated the *ius* as a monolith in the form of *ars boni et aequi,* would constitute a separate division between these two categories. Especially that the above-mentioned values were desirable in every area of the law. So while the distinction between the *ius publicum* and the *ius privatum* is evident in the jurist's statements, he probably intended to specify each area rather than create a division. Even if we were to follow the prevailing view and indicate *utilitas* as the criterion for the distinction, even in this respect it would not be possible to consider *utilitas publica* as a contrast category for *utilitas privata.* The following meanings of the *ius publicum*

interpretative efforts. The phrase *spectare ad* should be understood not only as observing or taking something into account[393], but mostly teleologically, meaning 'striving for something', 'heading in a certain direction', 'aiming achieving something'[394]. In Ulpian's thought, *utilitas*, both private and public, correlated with the term *status*, implying the care for the stability and uniformity of the state[395] – it was therefore a goal that the law should pursue[396]. Furthermore, as rightly stated by Cerami, it was a specific requirement that needed to be determined on a case-by-case basis[397].

Since the object of the aspirations of the law was anything useful for the state and anything useful for individuals, jurists were expected to share these same aspirations. It can therefore be concluded that Ulpian indicated the teleological interpretation[398] as the fundamental method of interpreting the law, where the purpose of legal norms was tied to *utilitas*, be it of an individual, or of the whole community[399]. The drive expressed in the phrase *spectat ad* perfectly corresponded to the concept of art practiced for a specific and useful purpose, and seeing *ius* as *ars* oriented legal thinking into the categories of the good, the fair and the useful.

The teleological element can also be seen in the writings of other jurists:

are distinguished in the literature (usually in relation to *ius privatum*): 1) law created as part of the activity of the authorities in opposition to legal private acts, 2) law that cannot be waived by the will of private persons, 3) law that concerns the interests of the state, also understood as a collective of private entities, 4) mandatory and unchangeable law in opposition to law depending on the will of the parties; 5) general norm, applicable in the absence of a particular norm, 6) substantive law as opposed to the subjective law. Cf. M. Kaser, *'Ius publicum' – 'Ius privatum' (zugleich Besprechung von Nocera, 'Ius publicum')*, 'SDHI' 1951, vol. 17, pp. 267–278; G. Aricò Anselmo, *'Ius publicum'...*, pp. 447–787; M. Kaser, *'Ius publicum'...*, pp. 1–101; V. Marotta, *Ulpiano...*, pp. 154–155; A. Paturet, *Ulpien...*, pp. 115–126; J. Stagl, *Die Funktionen...*, pp. 522–523.

393 M. Kaser, *'Ius publicum'...*, p. 11.

394 LTL, *s. v. specto*. See also T. Honsell, *Gemeinwohl...*, p. 101.

395 The noun *status* should be interpreted in the context of the meaning of the verb *stare*, implying such categories as 'to be stable, firm, in balance', 'to remain stable, firm', 'to persist'. This way in G. Aricò Anselmo, *'Ius publicum'...*, pp. 595–596; V. Marotta, *Ulpiano...*, p. 161; G. Falcone, *Un'ipotesi...*, pp. 1174–1173.

396 The criterion of *utilitas*, both *publica* and *privata*, is interpreted in this way by G. Luraschi, who, however, bases his analysis on the phrase *quid enim si publica utilitas ex hoc emergit?* (Ulp. D. 47,10,5,11 'Why not, since *utilitas publica* results from it?'), *Il 'praemium' nell'esperienza giuridica romana* [in:] *Studi in onore di Arnaldo Biscardi*, F. Pastori (ed.), Milano 1983, vol. 4, p. 250. Nevertheless, it seems that the reference to *utilitas* in this fragment serves one more function, as discussed in Chapter Three. On the other hand, M. Kaser, *'Ius publicum'...*, p. 11, believes that in the light of the analyzed fragment, *utilitas* is only an aim of the private law.

397 P. Cerami, *Potere...*, p. 117.

398 This way A. Mantello, *Il sogno...*, p. 60; G. Falcone, *La 'vera philosophia'...*, p. 74.

399 Obviously, the idea of teleological interpretation remains relevant when considering *publicum* and *privatum* as adjectives to the noun *ius*.

D. 1,3,25 (*Modestinus libro octavo responsorum*)
Nulla iuris ratio [aut aequitatis benignitas] patitur, ut quae [salubriter][400] *pro utilitate hominum introducuntur, ea nos duriore interpretatione contra ipsorum commodum producamus ad severitatem.*
No principle of the law [or the benevolence of righteousness] allows us, on the basis of a rigid interpretation, to lead to a severe understanding of those legal solutions that are [with good effect] introduced for the utility of people.

As Ulpian's student Herennius Modestine emphasized, all laws were introduced for the utility of people (*pro utilitate hominum*[401]). Their interpretation had to therefore take this basic assumption into account, and therefore be teleological[402]. Consequently, the interpretation could neither be unreasonably harsh, nor contradict the public utility – the fundamental idea in the name of which the law was made[403]. For Modestine, *utilitas* was both a general determinant of interpretation[404], and a criterion for assessing the solutions introduced and decisions proposed.

400 The expressions in square brackets are considered interpolations. See G. Beseler, *Beiträge zur Kritik der römischen Rechtsquellen*, vol. 2, Tübingen 1911, p. 32, who acknowledges only the first one, E. Albertario, *L'uso traslato di 'salubris, salubritas, salubriter' nelle fonti giuridiche romane*, 'Rivista di Filologia e di Istruzione Classica' 1929 vol. 57, p. 89 and G. Longo, *Utilitas publica*, pp. 19–20, who argued for the Justinian provenance of the fragment, without excluding, however, that its basis may be a source from the classical period. Indeed, several aspects raise particular doubts regarding this fragment. Firstly, its inflated style is more typical of imperial constitutions than of juristic writings. Similarly, the presence of the term *salubriter*, which is a *hapax legomenon* in the *Digest of Justinian* but frequently appears in imperial constitutions, is noteworthy. The use of the plural form (*nos… producamus*) is not uncommon among jurists, but it could also be an example of the imperial *pluralis maiestatis*. Additionally, *utilitas hominum*, as explained in the next footnote, is not a common expression among jurists. Finally, Modestine does not seem particularly fond of abstract nouns, which this fragment is full of. For example, apart from this fragment, *utilitas* in Modestine's writings appears only in Coll. 10,2,2 and Coll. 10,2,3; *aequitas* only in D. 39,5,22 and D. 42,1,20; *severitas* and *benignitas* only here (although *severitas* appears in other juristic writings, it is far more common in imperial constitutions, and *benignitas* is rarely used in legal sources – apart from this instance, it appears only once more in the *Digest of Justinian* in Marcian. D. 48,19,11,pr.). All these could be potential indicators of interpolations.

401 As the only one of the jurists, he used the expression *utilitas hominum*, and not *utilitas communis*, or *utilitas publica*. Also note that the expression *utilitas hominum* it is not a frequent collocation. We can find a similar one in Cicero (e. g. *Inv.*, 1,3,19 *summis hominum utilitatibus*) and in the *Code of Justinian* (eg. Iust. C. 4,11,1,pr. *nos autem pro communi hominum utilitate*), and in this case the more classical phrase *utilitas communis* was used anyway.

402 Cf. also T. Honsell, *Gemeinwohl…*, p. 125, who in this context writes about rational interpretation.

403 D. Nörr, *Rechtskritik…*, p. 140, who interprets this passage as an appeal to the authorities.

404 This coherence of Ulpian's and Modestine's thought supports recognizing at least some authenticity of the fragment. On the other hand, it is surprising that, while many references to *utilitas* by Ulpian were preserved in the *Digest of Justinian* (cf. Chapter Three), no decision in which Modestine referred to it directly has survived in this corpus. Two examples of *ad utilitatem* references made by Modestine can be found in *Collatio legum Romanarum et Mosaicarum*: Coll. 10,2,2; 10,2,3. On this subject in M. Navarra, *Note in tema di 'utilitas': Modestino e Coll. 10.2*, 'Labeo' 2004, vol. 50, no. 1, pp. 84–134.

Similarly, according to Papinian, as already emphasized in Chapter One, *utilitas publica* set the direction of activities of the magistrates (D. 1,1,7,1[405]). Writing that *ius praetorium* had been introduced *propter utilitatem publicam,* the jurist set its goal, as the preposition *propter* should be understood as indicating a specific purpose. In this context, *utilitas publica* means an intention, a direction of action, something to be achieved, and therefore what the *ius praetorium* was supposed to strive for and serve. Thus, whenever officials introduced a new legal measure to support, supplement, or rectify civil law, it was done in the name of public utility. It is therefore justified to consider that the norms of the praetorian law must have been interpreted in accordance with the same guideline.

It is worth noting, however, that in the minds of jurists *utilitas publica* seems to undergo some clarification. Both previously quoted (Pseudo-)Dositheus (Fragm. Dosith. 1) and Paulus (D. 1,1,11) defined the *ius civile* as that law that was useful to all or most of the members of a given community (*plures,* τὸ μεῖζον μέρος; *pars maior*)[406]. Consequently, jurists were not under the illusion that legal solutions could always serve the

405 *Ius praetorium est, quod praetores introduxerunt adiuvandi vel supplendi vel corrigendi iuris civilis gratia propter utilitatem publicam* ('The praetorian law is what the praetors introduced to support, supplement, or rectify civil law for the public utility').

406 Even if this agreement of the accounts does not indicate a general acceptance of such an opinion, it at least suggests its presence in the reflection of the Romans. The provenance of this concept, however, seems to be Greek. Cf. Arist., *Ethic.* 1129b οἱ δὲ νόμοι ἀγορεύουσι περὶ ἁπάντων στοχαζόμενοι ἢ τοῦ κοινῇ συμφέροντος πᾶσιν [ἢ τοῖς ἀρίστοις] ἢ τοῖς κυρίοις κατ᾽ ἀρετὴν ἢ κατ᾽ ἄλλον τινὰ τρόπον τοιοῦτον· ('For laws regulate everything aiming at what is beneficial to all <either for the best> or for those who wield power, either by their virtue or by something else of that kind'); Epic., *RS* 37 Τὸ μὲν ἐπιμαρτυρούμενον ὅτι συμφέρει ἐν ταῖς χρείαις τῆς πρὸς ἀλλήλους κοινωνίας τῶν νομισθέντων εἶναι δικαίων, ἔχει τὸν τοῦ δικαίου χαρακτῆρα, ἐάν τε τὸ αὐτὸ πᾶσι γένηται ἐάν τε μὴ τὸ αὐτό ('Among the things acknowledged to be just, whatever is found to be useful in the needs of mutual relations is labelled as just, whether or not it turns out as such for all'). See also Cic., *Part.* 62–63 *sitne ius id quod maiori parti sit utile* ('is the law what is useful to the majority?').

general public[407], and they reasonably limited the target group of recipients of legal solutions[408].

Moreover, the thoughts of both jurists, and Paulus in particular, seems to correspond interestingly with Ulpian's account[409]. By pointing to what was *bonum, aequum,* and *utile* as the genesis and foundation of the law[410], Ulpian simultaneously defined the goals of this activity, and the criteria jurists were supposed to apply when making their

407 This common-sense thinking was characteristic not only of jurists. Cf. Liv., AUC 34,3,5 *Nulla lex satis commoda omnibus est: id modo quaeritur, si maiori parti et in summam prodest. si quod cuique privatim officiet ius, id destruet ac demolietur, quid attinebit universos rogare leges quas mox abrogare in quos latae sunt possint?* ('There is no law that would satisfy everyone sufficiently. It is just a question of whether it pleases the majority and is ultimately beneficial. If everyone abolishes and violently removes a law that they personally do not like, then what good is it of all to pass resolutions that could soon be removed by those against whom it would be enacted?'). According to Marcus Porcius Cato, as reported by Titus Livius, it was almost impossible for the effects of the law to be beneficial for everyone. However, this is a statement with a strong rhetorical character. This passage is part of a speech delivered by the consul in 195 BCE in favour of maintaining the famous act of the tribune of Gaius Oppius, known as the *lex Oppia*. The act was introduced during the Second Punic War after the devastating defeat of the Roman army at the Battle of Cannae in 216 BCE. It aimed at curbing luxury practices among women. Under it, it was forbidden to decorate oneself with jewellery weighing more than half an ounce of gold and wear colourful robes, and moving in a horse-drawn carriage was significantly limited. After the end of the war, the issue of the law was discussed again in public (cf. Liv., AUC 34,1). Not surprisingly, it was Marcus Porcius Cato who defended it. The *lex Oppia* and laws limiting the luxuries in ancient Rome were of interest to many researchers. For more on this subject, see, among others: M. Kuryłowicz, *'Leges aleariae' und 'leges sumptuariae' im antiken Rom*, 'Acta Universitatis Szegediensis. Acta Juridica et Politica (=Studia in honorem Velimiri Polay)' 1985, no. 33, pp. 271–279; Idem, *Prawo i obyczaje w starożytnym Rzymie*, Lublin 1994, pp. 43–53; Idem, *'Leges sumptuariae' w państwie i prawie rzymskim* [in:] *Z historii państwa, prawa, miast i Polonii. Prace ofiarowane profesorowi Władysławowi Ćwikowi w czterdziestolecie Jego pracy naukowej*, J. Ciągwa, T. Opas (ed.), Rzeszów 1998, pp. 139–154; Idem, *Prawo rzymskie wobec przejawów luksusu i marnotrawstwa* [in:] *Zbytek i ubóstwo w starożytności i średniowieczu*, L. Kostuch, K. Ryszewska (ed.), Kielce 2010, pp. 131–133; A. Pikulska-Robaszkiewicz, *Ustawowa regulacja obyczajów w prawie rzymskim*, 'Studia Iuridica' 1999, no. 37, pp. 213–219; J. Sondel, *Les 'leges sumptuariae' considérées comme l'expression des conditions sociales et économiques de la Rome antique*, 'Archivum Iuridicum Cracoviense' 1973, no. 6, pp. 101–124; Idem, *Ustawy przeciw luksusowi w starożytnym Rzymie*, 'Sprawozdania z Czynności i Posiedzeń PAU' 1994, no. 58, pp. 25–29.

408 However, this does not appear to be the result of a lack of precision. In this spirit, Cujas made the following remark in relation to the above-analyzed passage by Paulus (D. 1,1,11): *vellem addidisset 'vel ei, qui in civitate imperat, quique in ea rerum est dominus'* ('I regret he did not add: "or [in the interest of] the ruler of the state, whoever acts as the superior"'). See J. Cujas, *Opera ad Parisiensem Fabrotianam editionem diligentissime exacta, auctiora atque emendatiora*, vol. 7, Prati 1839, coll. 9. If we were to look for the reasons for such a coined definition, it would be precisely the political consciousness. Repeating the definition of (Pseudo-)Dositheus after half a century, the jurist probably opted for the stability of the existing order, despite the attempts to consolidate the power undertaken by the Severans (cf. e.g. K. Królczyk, *Polityka dynastyczna cesarza Septymiusza Sewera (193–211 r.)*, 'Klio' 2018, vol. 47, no. 4, pp. 181–201). In the light of Paulus' definition, the purpose of the law still does not raise any doubts. The established norms were to serve citizens who were actually holders of power and the beneficiaries of laws.

409 Contrary in M. Navarra, *Ricerche…*, pp. 190–191, n. 38.

410 M. Bretone, *I fondamenti del diritto romano. Le cose e la natura*, Roma-Bari 1998, pp. 228–229.

interpretation[411]. Hence, as for Ulpian, in Paulus, *utilitas* appears as the starting point and at the same time the guiding principle of legal interpretation.

2.4 Summary

The decisions made *utilitatis causa* are occasionally referred to as decisions adopted for teleological reasons. According to this view, their effects in the form of deviations from the rules of the law were to be motivated by the requirements of practice, economy, society, or the world of values. This chapter aimed to verify whether this perspective could explain the special nature of these decisions. To this end, an attempt was made to locate and present the category of *utilitas* in the context of the general principles governing legal interpretation.

Since the interpretation of the law was not a task reserved solely for jurisprudence, the first brief reference was to the field of rhetoric. It was shown that *utilitas* paved the way for the reflection and argumentation of orators. Moreover, the term was understood in two ways. First, as the benefit of those who were advised. In this sense, the entire interpretative activity of rhetoricians was teleological. Second, *utilitas* is also present in the sphere of rhetoric in the form of common utility (*utilitas communis*) with a clear ethical connotation, and in this understanding it remained the highest value for orators.

As a result of the conducted considerations, it was also shown that the interpretation and demonstration oriented towards *utilitas* were characteristic for jurists too. A particularly valuable source confirming this thesis is the initial fragments of the *Digest of Justinian* taken from Ulpian's *Institutes* (D. 1,1,1,pr.–2), where the categories *utilitas publica* and *utilitas privata* are referred to several times. Importantly, these concepts expressed conflicting or even disharmonious interests neither in non-legal sources nor in the thought of jurisprudence. The utility of community members, understood both collectively and individually, formed a coherent whole. According to Ulpian, *uti-*

411 It is worth mentioning here Blicharz's remark, who claims that legal thought does not end with compliance with the law and customs of ancestors but also requires checking against the *utilitas*, *bonum*, and *aequum* criteria. However, he does not interpret the passage of Paul. D. 1,1,11 as reflecting the legal method, but an attempt to understand what the law is. See G. Blicharz, *Giudicare una decisione del pretore: La relazione tra diritto e fatto nel passo di Paolo (D. 1,1,11) e nel caso di Barbarius Philipus (D. 1,14,3)*, 'Seminarios Complutenses de Derecho Romano. Revista Complutense de Derecho Romano y Tradición Romanistica' 2016, vol. 29, pp. 345, 352. Additionally, it is noteworthy to highlight the interpretation presented by Maschi that the definition of the law proposed by Paulus (D. 1,1,11 *Ius pluribus modis dicitur: uno modo, cum id quod semper aequum ac bonum est ius dicitur, ut est ius naturale…*) was not supposed to correspond to the vision of the legal system but to the method appropriate to Roman jurisprudence. In this context, the adverb *semper* is extremely meaningful, implying the obligation to constantly strive to implement just legal solutions. See C. A. Maschi, *La conclusione…*, pp. 697–701.

litas, both *publica* and *privata*, marks out two foundations (*positiones*) of deliberations and argumentation, and also the goal of the interpretation. For the jurist, *utilitas* was therefore both the starting point and keynote of his interpretation. Ulpian's view is not isolated here, as other jurists share such an opinion. (Pseudo-)Dositheus, Paulus, Papinian and Modestine also pointed to the examined criterion as the subject of the aspirations of the law. Consequently, jurists' thinking and interpretation also had to be directed towards *utilitas* as a core value.

This concept fundamentally shaped the entire practice of Roman legal interpretation. *Utilitas*, indeed, is a sign of teleological interpretation yet not in the way Hans Ankum suggested. This category cannot be reduced to pragmatism only. However, Ankum was correct in identifying a strategic element in it. Reflecting on this category can be classified as a method of reasoning and law interpretation, involving implementation, determination, as well as creative development. Always fused with what was good and right, *utilitas* constituted a certain universal, yet multi-faceted and teleological paradigm driving the activity of Roman jurisprudence. Therefore, the assumption of the teleological interpretation *ex utilitate* should be adopted in relation to absolutely every interpretative activity, not only those resulting in a departure from the rule. Consequently, the explanation of the phrase *utilitatis causa* as adopting a decision for teleological reasons does not fully capture the uniqueness of these decisions. The question about their nature thus still requires separate analyses.

3
Utilitatis causa Interpretation

3.1 *Ex utilitate, non ex scriptione interpretari*

Considering *utilitas* as a determinant and purpose of the interpretation naturally led to its frequent use in argumentation and justification of decisions. Therefore, as discussed in Introduction, scholars rightly argue that *utilitas* served jurists to resolve legal doubts arising from uncertain factual states[412], supported and justified the adoption of decisions[413], as well as guided the interpretation of terms and concepts[414]. These were use-

412 E. g. Ulp. D. 37,9,1,5 *Sed et si sub condicione postumus sit exheredatus, pendente condicione Pedii sententiam admittimus existimantis posse ventrem in possessionem mitti, quia sub incerto utilius est ventrem ali* ('And if, however, a posthumous child was disinherited under the condition while the condition is pending, we accept Pedius' view that an unborn child should possess because, when there is uncertainty, it is more useful to support the unborn child'). A similar argumentation by Ulpian was also preserved in D. 49,4,1,5.

413 E. g. Tryph. D. 27,1,45,4 *Si tanta corporis aut mentis valetudine ab agendis rebus libertus prohibeatur, ut ne suis quidem negotiis sufficiat, necessitati erit subcumbendum, ne inpossibile iniungatur tutelae munus, quod obiri a liberto non potest cum incommodo pupilli et adversus utilitatem eius* ('If a manumitted person is so physically or mentally ill that he would not be able to take care of his own affairs, one should yield to the requirements of these circumstances so as not to impose an impossible duty of tutelage on him, which he might not perform otherwise than to the detriment of the pupil and against his utility'). Similarly also in Ulp. D. 29,2,42,pr.; Paul. D. 35,1,84; Paul. D. 49,14,47,1. Cf. also Paul. D. 17,1,22,pr.; Ulp. D. 47,8,2,24.

414 See e. g. Ner. D. 2,11,14 *(...) eadem et fortius adhuc dici possunt, si procurator ita stipulatus esset* QVANTI EA RES ERIT: *ut hanc conceptionem verborum non ad ipsius, sed ad domini utilitatem relatam interpretemur* ('[...] The same can be said even more emphatically when while promising something in the form of stipulation, a representative used the following words "whatever will be the value of this thing", because we interpret this phrase as referring to the utility of his principal, and not his own'); Ner. D. 43,20,6 *De interdicto de aqua aestiva, item cottidiana quaerentes primum constituendum existimabamus, quae esset aqua aestiva, de qua proprium interdictum ad prioris aestatis tempus relatum reddi solet, hoc est aestiva aqua utrumne ex iure aestivo dumtaxat tempore utendi diceretur, an ex mente propositoque ducentis, quod aestate eam ducendi consilium haberet, an ex natura ipsius aquae, quod aestate tantum duci potest, an ex utilitate locorum, in quae duceretur. placebat igitur aquam ob has duas res, naturam suam utilitatemque locorum in quae deducitur, proprie appellari, ita ut, sive eius natura erit, ut nisi aestate duci non possit, etiamsi hieme quoque desideraretur, sive omni tempore anni duci eam ipsius natura permitteret, si utilitas [personis]<regionis>, in quam ducitur, aestate dumtaxat usum eius exigeret, aestiva recte diceretur* ('Reflecting on the interdictum protecting the actual use

ful solutions in the broadest sense of the word, allowing for the consideration of recognized values, but also of the goals of particular legal institutions. In this sense, *utilitas* was, as Rampazzo aptly describes it: 'a working tool in the hands of legal craftsmen'[415].

Among the decisions where *utilitas* is explicitly mentioned, those usually referred to as the *utilitatis causa* decisions play a special role. As previously indicated, these rulings are unique as they appear to contradict the established rules of law[416]. Previous chapters have shown that neither pragmatism nor a purely teleological approach fully explain their character. Thus, the question of the adversary nature of *utilitas* in this context remains unresolved. Even if it can already be seen in Pap. D. 1,1,7,1[417], which states that the *ius praetorium* corrected the *ius civile*, the actual role of this criterion in the *utilitatis causa* decisions is still a mystery. However, non-legal sources may provide some hints leading to its solution. In *De Inventione*, Cicero highlights a distinctive feature of interpretation guided by and oriented towards *utilitas*:

> Cic., *Inv.* 1,38,68–69
>
> 68. *Quinquepertita argumentatio est huiusmodi: "Omnes leges, iudices, ad commodum rei publicae referre oportet et eas ex utilitate communi, non ex scriptione, quae in litteris est, interpretari. Ea enim virtute et sapientia maiores nostri fuerunt, ut in legibus scribendis nihil sibi aliud, nisi salutem atque utilitatem rei publicae proponerent. Neque enim ipsi, quod obesset, scribere volebant, et, si scripsissent, cum esset intellectum, repudiatum iri legem intellegebant. Nemo enim leges legum causa salvas esse vult, sed rei publicae, quod ex legibus omnes rem publicam optime putant administrari. Quam ob rem igitur leges servari oportet, ad eam causam scripta omnia interpretari convenit: hoc est, quoniam rei publicae servimus, ex rei publicae commodo atque utilitate interpretemur. Nam ut ex medicina nihil oportet putare proficisci, nisi quod ad corporis utilitatem spectet, quoniam eius causa est instituta, sic a legibus nihil convenit arbitrari, nisi*

of the servitude of water consumption in the summer as well as every day, we decided that first it was necessary to determine what the water drawn during the summer period is, for which it was customary to give a separate interdictum referring to the summer before, namely whether on the basis of the user's intention and plan to draw it in summer, or whether as a result of the nature of the water itself, as it can only be drawn in the summer, or for the utility of the places where it is conducted to. So if the nature of the water was such that it could only be drawn in the summer although it would also be demanded in the winter, or whether nature allowed it to be conducted at any time of the year, but for the utility of the place to which it is conducted requires its use only in the summer, in these cases it is rightly referred to as water drawn in the summer').

415 N. Rampazzo, *Quasi praetor…*, p. 516.

416 See again U. Leptien, *Utilitatis causa…*, pp. 237–240; H. Ankum, *'Utilitatis causa receptum'. On the pragmatical methods…*, p. 28; Idem, *'Utilitatis causa receptum': sur la méthode…*, p. 132; Idem, *The functions…*, pp. 6 and 22; Idem, *Utilitatis causa…*, p. 1121; M. Kaser, *Das römische Privatrecht…*, p. 212; A. M. Honore, *Legal Reasoning…*, pp. 61, 66; M. Navarra, *Ricerche…*, pp. 4, 206; B. Spagnolo, J. Sampson, *Principle…*, pp. 5–6. Cf. also E. Seidl, *Moderne…*, pp. 103–112.

417 Pap. D. 1,1,7,1 *Ius praetorium est, quod praetores introduxerunt adiuvandi vel supplendi vel corrigendi iuris civilis gratia propter utilitatem publicam* ('The praetorian law is what the praetors introduced to support, supplement, or rectify civil law for the public utility').

quod rei publicae conducat, proficisci, quoniam eius causa sunt comparatae. 69. Ergo in hoc quoque iudicio desinite litteras legis perscrutari et legem, ut aequum est, ex utilitate rei publicae considerate.

68. The five-part argument is, for instance, as follows: 'Judges! All laws should be considered in terms of the benefit of the state, and should be explained in the light of the common utility, and not in line with the letter of the law. For our ancestors were characterized by such virtue and wisdom that when writing laws, they had nothing else but the good and utility of the state in mind. They did not want to enact laws that would be detrimental to the state, and they knew that, even if they had, these would be rejected the very moment it would be pointed out to. Nobody wants to keep laws for their own sake but for the sake of the state, because everyone is of the opinion that the state is best managed through laws. All written laws must be interpreted with the same reason laws must be upheld: because we serve the state, we should explain laws for its good, and for its utility. For as it must be assumed that the achievement of medicine is only what is associated with the utility of the body, and because this is why medicine was invented, it should be assumed that what laws offer is only what is beneficial for the state, because for the state they were laid down. 69. In the course of this hearing, let us stop seeking the letter of the law, and consider, which is appropriate, the essence of the law, starting from the utility of the state'.

This fragment evokes and contrasts two types of interpretation that any contemporary lawyer would recognize: literal (*ex scriptione*; *ex litteris*), and teleological, aligned with the intention of the law and aimed at the utility of the state and its citizens (*utilitas communis*; *rei publicae commodum atque utilitas*; *commodum rei publicae*). This juxtaposition is rooted in a rich rhetorical tradition, which is crucial to our considerations, and can be exemplified by the case Cicero presents in the following fragment. After contrasting literal (*ex scriptione*) and teleological (*ex utilitate*) interpretations, Cicero cited an example of a speech in defence of the Theban general Epaminondas (c. 418–362 BCE)[418], who exceeded his military command term and kept *imperium* longer than permitted by law[419], leading to victory at the Battle of Leuctra (371 BCE), and saving his homeland. The question arose whether Epaminondas indeed broke the law, or whether exceptional circumstances justified departing from the legal rules.

This and similar problems in legal interpretation were classified by rhetoricians according to the so-called *status* (gr. στάσεις)[420], types of issues determining the matter of the dispute. The Epaminondas case follows the pattern known as *status scripti et*

418 *The Oxford Classical Dictionary*, S. Hornblower, A. Spawforth (ed.), Oxford-New York 1996, s. v. Epaminondas.

419 Cicero claims that Epaminondas kept the *imperium* for just a few days longer (*Inv.* 1,33,55). The historian Cornelius Nepos argues otherwise, writing that this state lasted as long as four months (*Epam.* 7–8).

420 *Status* were also described as *constitutiones*. For terminology, see e.g. Cic., *Inv.* 1,8,10; Quint., *Inst.* 3,6,2–3. See also H. Lausberg, *Handbuch…*, pp. 64–65.

voluntatis[421]. The first category indicates an interpretation that strictly adheres to the content of the (usually written[422]) legal rule[423]. The other term, in turn, refers to an interpretation consistent with the intention of either the law (*sententia legis*), or its author[424].

421 For instance, such a term was preserved in Quint., *Inst.* 3,6,61 and Isid., *Orig.* 2,5,9. Among other names there can be mentioned *status scripti et sententiae* (*Rhet. ad Heren.* 1,19), or *scripti et voluntatis quaestio* (Quint., *Inst.* 7,6,1). This subject has aroused considerable interest among researchers. In the legal context, discussions often focus on the influence of rhetoric on Roman law. For more on this topic, see: F. Lanfranchi, *Il diritto nei retori romani…*, pp. 65–81; J. Santa Cruz Teijeiro, *Notas para un estudio expositivo sobre el influjo de la retórica en el Derecho romano*, "Revista de estudios políticos" 1952, vol. 64, pp. 109–124; Idem, *Influencia de algunas disciplinas no jurídicas en el derecho romano*, "Anuario de historia del derecho español" 1957, vol 27, pp. 343–398; Idem, *Der Einfluß der rhetorischen Theorie des status auf die römische Jurisprudenz, insbesondere auf die Auslegung der Gesetze und Rechtsgeschäfte*, 'ZSS RA' 1958, vol. 75, no. 1, pp. 91–115; G. Gandolfi, *Studi sull'interpretazione degli atti negoziali in diritto romano*, Milano 1966, pp. 243–339; U. Wesel, *Rhetorische Statuslehre und Gesetzesauslegung der römischen Juristen*, Köln–Berlin–Bonn–München 1967; Idem, *Zur Deutung und Bedeutung des Status Scriptum et Sententia*, 'TR' 1970, vol. 38, no. 3, pp. 343–366; B. Vonglis, *La lettre et l'esprit de la loi dans la jurisprudence classique et la réthorique*, Paris 1968; Idem, *Droit romain et rhetorique*, 'TR' 1969, vol. 37, no. 2, pp. 247–256; M. Bretone, *Il giureconsulto interprete della legge*, "Labeo" 1969, vol. 15, no. 3, pp. 289–310; T. Giaro, *Excusatio necessitatis nel diritto romano*, Warszawa 1982, pp. 38–40; L. Calboli Montefusco, *La dottrina degli 'status' nella retorica greca e romana*, Hildesheim 1986, pp. 153–166; M. Hillgruber, *'Scriptum' und 'voluntas' in der Rechtswissenschaft der römischen Republik*, 'Museum Helveticum' 1995, vol. 52, no. 3, pp. 170–180; J.W. Tellegen, *The Reliability of Quintilian for Roman Law: On the Causa Curiana* [in:] *Quintilian and the Law: The Art of Persuasion in Law and Politics*, O.E. Tellegen-Couperus (ed.), Leuven 2003, pp. 194–197; R. Martini, *Antica retorica giudiziaria (gli status causae)*, "Diritto@Storia" 2004, no. 3 (available online at: https://www.dirittoestoria.it/3/TradizioneRomana/Martini-Antica-Retorica-Giudiziaria.htm); G. La Bua, *Diritto e rhetorica…*, pp. 181–203; J. Dingel, *Scholastica materia. Untersuchungen zu den Declamationes minores und der Institutio oratoria Quintilians*, Berlin-New York 1988, rep. 2013, pp. 131–138; E. Berti, *Le controversiae della raccolta di Seneca il Vecchio e la dottrina degli status*, 'Rhetorica: A Journal of the History of Rhetoric' 2014, vol. 32, no. 2, pp. 125–144.

422 This is by no means a universal requirement. For instance, illustrating the potential tensions between *scriptum* and *voluntas*, Cicero referred to the case of a soldier who killed a military tribune who was abusing him sexually. The legal rule forbidding the killing of a man was described by Cicero as *communis lex omnium*. Therefore, it should not be classified within the category of *lex scripta*. Cf. Cic., *Inv.* 2,42,124. The described situation was said to take place in the army of Gaius Marius. See Cic., *Mil.* 9; Quint., *Inst.* 5,11,15.

423 It should be added that the same principles as for the interpretation of *leges* were also applied to the interpretation of contracts, testaments and other declarations of intent, both written and oral ones. See Cic., *Top.* 26,96 *Iam hoc perspicuum est, non magis in legibus quam in testamentis, in stipulationibus, in reliquis rebus quae ex scripto aguntur, posse controversias easdem existere* ('For this is evident that these kinds of disputes are no more incidental to laws than to wills, or stipulations, or to anything else which rests on letters'); Quint., *Inst.* 7,5,6 *Quod de legibus dico, idem accipi volo de testamentis pactis stipulationibus, omni denique scripto: quod de scripto, idem de voce* ('What I say about the laws I want to be adopted also in relation to testaments, pacts, stipulations, and also to all written texts: what applies to written texts also applies to the spoken word').

424 See Cic., *Inv.* 2,47,139 *scriptorem ipsum, si exsistat, factum hoc probaturum et idem ipsum, si ei talis res accidisset, facturum fuisse; ea re legis scriptorem certo ex ordine iudices certa aetate praeditos constituisse, ut essent, non qui scriptum suum recitarent, quod quivis puer facere posset, sed qui cogitatione assequi possent et voluntatem interpretari; deinde illum scriptorem, si scripta sua stultis hominibus et*

This *status* was applicable in two situations. Firstly, in the event of a dispute as to the interpretation of the letter of the law, when each party assigned a different intention to its content, it was the so-called *genus ex iure obscuro* (based on the obscurity of the law)[425]. The other type of *status*, defined by Quintilian as *genus ex iure manifesto*, having its source in the unambiguous legal regulation, is particularly valuable for the our considerations. Quintilian explains that even if the legal rule is clear and does not raise any interpretation doubts, it may not always apply.

Opposing the rule of the law could be accomplished in three ways. Firstly, when the text itself showed that it was not always possible to follow it. As was when the law provided that children who did not fulfil the duty to support their parents were to be imprisoned, but nevertheless no such punishment was imposed on infants[426]. This method was thus expressed in the reflection on whether the legal rule covered every factual state, or whether, based on the general logic and wording used, it could be concluded that there were particular cases in which the norm was not applicable.

Secondly, when the case itself clearly showed that a law could not apply. Here, Quintilian quoted the example of a foreigner who chased the enemy away by climbing the city walls, even though under the law this was punishable by death[427]. In such cases,

barbaris iudicibus committeret, omnia summa diligentia perscripturum fuisse; nunc vero, quod intellegeret, quales viri res iudicaturi essent, idcirco eum, quae perspicua videret esse, non asscripsisse; neque enim vos scripti sui recitatores, sed voluntatis interpretes fore putavit ('He will say that the author of the document, if he had been still alive, he would have praised the action and would have done the same if he had been in a similar situation; that the legislator appointed judges of a certain state and age not to merely read the text of the law, which could be done by any child, but to be able to follow his plan and understand his will. He then finds that if the author of the document had addressed it to foolish people and barbaric judges, he would have described everything in detail; but since he knew what kind of people would be judges, he did not add what he took for granted. "He believed", the orator will say, that "you judges will not recite his writings but explain his thoughts"').

425 Cf. Quint., *Inst.* 7,6,1–4, where as an example, Quintilian quotes the phrase *Bis de eadem re ne sit actio*, explaining that the *obscuritas* of the phrase consists in the fact that it is not known whether it refers to the plaintiff or to the action. For further analysis of the relationship between law and rhetoric in this context refer to T. Wycisk, *Quidquid in foro fieri potest – Studien zum römischen Recht bei Quintilian*, Berlin 2008, pp. 350–352; R. Quadrato, *Retorica e giurisprudenza: da Quintiliano a Gaio*, 'SDHI' 2013, vol. 79, pp. 837–858.

426 Quint., *Inst.* 7,6,5 *Sed contra scriptum tribus generibus occurritur. Unum est in quo ipso patet semper id servari non posse:* LIBERI PARENTES ALANT AVT VINCIANTVR: *non enim alligabitur infans. Hinc erit ad alia transitus et divisio:* NVM QVISQVIS NON ALVERIT? NVM HIC? <NVM> PROPTER HOC? ('There are three ways to question the letter of the law. One of them applies when it is clear from the text itself that it cannot always be followed. [The law states:] "children must provide for their parents, or they will be imprisoned". Yet no infant will ever be chained! At this point, there will be a turn to other questions and a distinction: "Does this apply to anyone who does not provide? Will it apply to this man? Is it also for this reason?"'). Cf. also Fort., *Rhet.* 2,10 (p. 107 H.); Iul. Vict., *Rhet.* 3,14 (p. 384 H.).

427 Quint., *Inst.* 7,6,6–7 *<Ponunt> quidam tale genus controversiarum in quo nullum argumentum sit quod ex lege ipsa peti possit, sed de eo tantum de quo lis est quaerendum sit.* PEREGRINVS SI MVRVM ESCENDERIT CAPITE PVNIATVR. *Cum hostes murum escendissent, peregrinus eos depulit: petitur ad supplicium. 7. Non erunt hic separatae quaestiones:* AN QVISQVIS, AN HIC, *quia nullum potest adferri*

that is, when the exceptional circumstances of the situation justified a departure from the rules of the law, the *contra scriptum* argument was derived from the sense of justice referred to as *aequitas*.

Thirdly, the letter of the law was also opposed when the words used could indicate the intention behind the regulation. Consequently, if the law stated that a man captured (*deprensus*) while carrying some iron objects (*ferrum*) at night had to be imprisoned, the use of the expression *deprensus* clearly implied that the regulation did not apply to everyone who carried any iron object but to those who had iron weapons on them. The restrictive interpretation of *ferrum* led to considering it an abuse to imprison a man who was wearing an iron ring at night[428]. In this case, the norm was not applied, despite a strictly literal interpretation suggested otherwise.

The essence of the *status scripti et voluntatis* was that, despite the rule being clear and its literal interpretation leading to incontestable[429] results, this clarity and unambiguity were broken through the *sententia/voluntas*[430]. The tension between the categories of *scriptum* and *voluntas* was thus expressed in their basic determinants of interpretation.

argumentum contra scriptum vehementius eo quod in lite est, sed hoc tantum, an ne servandae quidem civitatis causa. Ergo aequitate et voluntate pugnandum ('6. Some set a type of dispute in which there is no argument that can be derived from the law itself but the only question is the subject-matter of the dispute. [The law states:] "if a foreigner climbs the wall, he is to be punished with death". When the enemy climbed the wall, the foreigner drove him out. It is demanded to punish him. 7. There are no separate questions here: "Does this apply to everyone?" and "Does this apply to this person?", because no argument can be made stronger against the letter of the law than the very circumstance at issue. So the only question is whether it should be forbidden even for the sake of saving the city. Therefore, one should use the weapon of justice and the intention of the law'. Cf. also Fort., *Rhet.* 1,23 (s. 99 H.); Sulp. Vict., *Rhet.* 61 (p. 351 H.); Iul. Vict., *Rhet.* 3,14 (p. 384 H.).

428 Quint., *Inst.* 7,6,8 *Tertium cum in ipsis verbis legis reperimus aliquid per quod probemus aliud legum latorem voluisse, ut in hac controversia:* QVI NOCTE CVM FERRO DEPRENSVS FVERIT, ALLIGETVR: CVM ANVLO FERREO INVENTVM MAGISTRATVS ALLIGAVIT; *hic, quia est verbum in lege* DEPRENSVS, *satis etiam significatum videtur non contineri lege nisi noxium ferrum* ('The third type is when we find in the wording of the law something that allows us to show that the intention of the legislator was different, as in the case of the following dispute. [The law states:] "Let a man caught carrying iron at night be imprisoned". A judge imprisoned a man who was carrying an iron ring. Since the word "caught" is used in the text of the law, it seems sufficiently clearly communicated that the only "iron" covered by the law is a weapon'). Cf. also Fort., *Rhet.* 2,10 (p. 107 H.); Iul. Vict., *Rhet.* 3,14 (p. 384 H.).

429 For this reason, the issue of ambiguity (*status ambiguitatis*), where a linguistic error makes a literal interpretation impossible to unambiguously determine the content of a legal rule or declaration of intent, will not be analyzed further. See e. g. Quint., *Inst.* 3,6,43; 7,5,6. For instance, such an error could result from homonymy or order of the sentence. Attempts were made to resolve these problems based on the natural use of a language, a sense of justice, or the will of the legislator. It should be noted, however, that in *De oratore* Cicero stated that the disagreement between *scriptum* and *voluntas* already constituted a form of ambiguity. Cf. Cic., *De orat.* 2,110. The boundaries of *status* do not always seem to be categorically defined. See also L. Calboli Montefusco, *La dottrina…*, pp. 153–154.

430 Since the focus will be those *status* in which the *scriptum* conflicts with the *sententia*, the topic of *status legum contrarium* (conflicting laws), where the central issue is the contradiction between two written legal rules, will not be addressed here. In such case, the problem lies in the dual inter-

For the letter of the law, these were logic and common rules for the use of the language, and for the intention – *aequitas,* the principle of a natural sense of justice[431]. Notably, the party advocating *pro scripto* did not deviate from what was right. On the contrary, they identified the category of *aequitas* with a literal interpretation of the law. Conversely, the party defending *sententia/voluntas* did not question the value of the letter of the law but believed that in a given case, special circumstances necessitated departing from the literal interpretation.

The landscape of rhetorical cases analyzed under the *status scripti et sententiae* is extremely vivid[432]. However, it is not that aspect but the settlement of the dispute proposed by the party arguing *ex sententia* that attracts particular attention when examining the *utilitas* category. It should be added at this point that Hermagoras of Temnos, the Greek rhetorician and author of rhetorical textbooks living in the 2nd century BCE, whose classification of *status* was decisive for the further development of this theory[433],

pretation *pro scripto* and, in effect, the double *voluntas,* and the choice of which one should take precedence. See e. g. Quint., *Inst.* 7,7,1. Cf. also ibid., pp. 119–121.

431 See e. g. Cic., *Inv.* 2,46,136 *…is, qui contra scriptum dicet, aequitatis aliquid afferat oportet. Nam summa impudentia sit eum, qui contra quam scriptum sit aliquid probare velit, non aequitatis praesidio id facere conari.* ('Someone who advocates something contrary to the literal wording of the law will inevitably always call for some *aequitas.* For it would be extremely impudent for anyone who proposes to accept as right something that contradicts what is written to attempt it without the support of *aequitas*'); 2,47,138 *Contra scriptum autem qui dicet, primum inducet eum locum, per quem aequitas causae demonstretur…* ('A person who is against the literal understanding of the text will begin by using a pattern that shows that there is *aequitas* on his side…'); Idem, *Caec.* 65 *…ex aequo et bono non ex callido versutoque iure rem iudicari oportere…* ('the matter must be judged on what is right and good, and not on the basis of legal tricks and cunning'); Idem, *De orat.* 1,244 *at in hoc genere pueri apud magistros exercentur omnes, cum in eius modi causis alias scriptum, alias aequitatem defendere docentur* ('And the students practice this kind of speeches with their teachers, learning to defend sometimes the letter of the law, and sometimes *aequitas*'); Quint., *Inst.* 7,3,25 *Quae tamen omnia, sicut in ceteris, confirmat aequitas…* ('All of them, as well as in other matters, are supported by *aequitas*'). See also H. Lausberg, *Handbuch…,* pp. 78, 95 and 109–110; M. Kuryłowicz, *Wokół pojęcia…,* p. 18.

432 Rhetorical sources, including the previously quoted examples from Quintilian's *Institutio oratoria,* are discussed and analyzed in U. Wesel, *Zur Deutung…,* pp. 343–366.

433 On the rhetorician, reconstruction of his work, as well as the value of his writings for his contemporaries e. g. in R. Nadeau, *Classical systems of stases in Greek: Hermagoras to Hermogenes,* 'Greek, Roman, and Byzantine Studies' 1959, vol. 2, no. 1, pp. 51–71; K. Barwick, *Zur Erklärung und Geschichte der Staseislehre des Hermagoras von temnos,* 'Philologus' 1964, vol. 108, no. 1–4, pp. 80–101; Idem, *Zur Rekonstruktion der Rhetorik des Hermagoras von Temnos,* 'Philologus' 1965, vol. 109, no. 1–4, pp. 186–218; A. Braet, *Cicero modifications of the status principles systematized by Hermagoras,* 'Rhetorica: A Journal of the History of Rhetoric' 1989, vol. 7, no. 3, pp. 239–259; M. Heath, *The Substructure of stasis-theory from Hermagoras to Hermogenes,* 'The Classical Quarterly' 1994, vol. 44, no. 1, pp. 114–129; Idem, *Hermagoras: Transmission and Attribution,* 'Philologus' 2002, vol. 146, no. 2, pp. 287–298; L. Calboli Montefusco, *Logica, retorica e giurisprudenza nella dottrina degli status,* [in:] *Per la storia del pensiero giuridico romano. Dall'età dei pontefici alla scuola di Servio. Atti del seminario di S. Marino 7–9 gennaio 1993,* D. Mantovani (ed.), Torino 1996, pp. 209–228; A. G. Gross, *Why Hermagoras Still Matters: The Fourth Stasis and Interdisciplinarity,* 'Rhetoric Review' 2004, vol. 23, no. 2, pp. 141–155; B.S. Bennett, *Hermagoras of Temnos* [in:] *Classical Rhetorics and Rhetoricians: Critical*

described the *status* in question as κατὰ ῥητὸν καὶ ὑπεξαίρεσιν. This information is provided by Quintilian, translating the Greek phrase as *dictum et exceptio* (literal content and exception)[434]; given that the later[435] Greek name usually used in this context took the form of κατὰ ῥητὸν καὶ διάνοιαν[436], being the Latin equivalent of *scriptum et voluntas/sententia*, it is undoubtedly an exceptional term. Hermagoras' phrase perfectly describes the consequences of the interpretations advocated by the party arguing *contra scriptum*. According to this viewpoint the correct resolution of the issue resulted in an exception to the literal wording of a legal rule[437], as in a given case it was impossible to implement what clearly resulted from it[438]. In this context, we speak either about the

Studies and Sources, M. Ballif, M. G. Moran (ed.), Westport 2005, pp. 187–193; F. Woerther, *Hermagoras. Fragments et témoignages*, Paris 2012; G. Thiele, *Hermagoras: Ein Beitrag zur Geschichte der Rhetorik*, Berlin-Boston 2019.

434 Quint., *Inst.* 3,6,61.

435 W. Stroh, *Taxis und Taktik: Die advokatische Dispositionskunst in Ciceros Gerichtsreden*, Stuttgart 1975, p. 86, n. 21.

436 Cf. Quint., *Inst.* 3,6,46; Iul. Vict., *Rhet.* 3,11 (p. 382 H.). The fact that these categories were not alien to Roman jurists is evidenced, for instance, by Ulpian's direct reference to them: D. 1,3,30 *Fraus enim legi fit, ubi quod fieri noluit, fieri autem non vetuit, id fit: et quod distat* ῥητὸν ἀπὸ διανοίας, *hoc distat fraus ab eo, quod contra legem fit* ('The law is circumvented when something occurs that the law did not wish to happen but did not explicitly forbid. And what distinguishes the wording from the intention of the law also distinguishes acting while circumventing the law from acting against the law').

437 This approach to the concept of 'exception' in this context seems to be the most appropriate. I share the prevailing opinion among researchers that, within the framework of *status scripti et voluntatis*, two forms of effects of *contra scriptum* interpretation can be distinguished: restrictive and extensive, as explained in more detail in the following paragraphs. At this point, however, it should be emphasized that it is not certain whether the other category covering the effects of applying a norm even when its literal wording did not allow for it, fitted the Hermagoras' scheme κατὰ ῥητὸν καὶ ὑπεξαίρεσιν. Since this *status* was later referred to as κατὰ ῥητὸν καὶ διάνοιαν, and moreover, it is only in Cicero that the first attestations of the extensive form of *status scripti et voluntatis* are manifested, the term 'exception' from Hermagoras' scheme is usually understood only restrictively. Obviously, it cannot be ruled out that the extensive aspect was developed later on (this way W. Stroh, *Taxis…*, p. 86, n. 21), perhaps even by Cicero (K. Büchner, *Humanitas Romana. Studien über Werke und Wesen der Römer*, Heidelberg 1957, p. 90). Nevertheless, it seems equally plausible to understand it as an exception to what is dictated by the literal interpretation of *scriptum*, encompassing both the non-application of a norm that, according to its literal wording, should be applied, and its application contrary to what the literal interpretation demands.

438 B. Vonglis, *La lettre…*, pp. 119–122, 138–140; U. Wesel, *Rhetorische Statuslehre…*, esp. pp. 30–40; Idem, *Zur Deutung…*, pp. 343–366; L. Calboli Montefusco, *La dottrina…*, pp. 159–160.

omitting (*omittere*) the literal content of the letter of the law[439], the content not standing (*stare*)[440], not being implemented (*fieri*)[441], or even repealing (*tollere*)[442] the law.

Frequently, this meant not applying the rule even though its literal interpretation required it[443]. The Epaminondas case opening this chapter is a good illustration here. The answer to the question of whether the Theban commander had broken the law obviously depended on which camp the orator belonged to. According to the party arguing *ex scriptione* the answer had to be affirmative[444]. According to the opposing party, arguing *contra scriptum*, the legal norm should not apply because one could not care about the common utility (*utilitas communis/publica*) and disobey the law[445] within the very same activity. This argument aligns with the second of the aforementioned patterns of interpretation proposed by Quintilian: the party arguing *a sententia/ex utilitate* believed the case itself made it clear that the rule could not apply.

In the context of the considerations presented here, what stands out is the term *ex utilitate* (*communi/publica*), which is repeatedly emphasized in the content of the quoted fragment of *De inventione*. Specifying the content of the examined criterion is straightforward. *Utilitas* here is the counterpart to the utility of all citizens[446]. Even

439 Cic., *Inv.* 1,38,69 *Scripto videlicet legis omisso scriptoris sententiam considerare debebat* ('Obviously, after omitting the letter of the law, he should consider what the legislator meant').

440 Quint., *Inst.* 7,6,7 *Fieri tamen potest ut ex aliis legibus exempla ducamus, per quae appareat semper stari scripto non posse…* ('However, one can take examples from other laws to show that what the text says cannot always stand').

441 *Rhet. ad Heren.* 1,10,14 *Deinde [dicemus – JKC] id quod scriptum sit aut non posse fieri aut non lege, non more, non natura, non aequo et bono posse fieri, quae omnia noluisse scriptorem quam rectissime fieri nemo dicet* ('Then we will say that what follows from the text either cannot be realized, or at least cannot be realized without violating the law, customs, the law of nature, or what is good and right – and no one will deny that the author wished all of these to be most strictly observed').

442 Cic., *Inv.* 2,45,131.

443 Wesel limited the consequences of this *status* to the restrictive aspect only; according to the vast part of doctrine – quite wrongly. See W. Stroh, *Taxis…*, pp. 83–84, n. 15; B. Vonglis, *Droit romain…*, pp. 247–256; L. Calboli Montefusco, *La dottrina…*, pp. 157–159. This interpretation stemmed from how Wesel perceived the nature of *status scripti et voluntatis*. Contrary to the general opinion, Wesel did not see a conflict between the strict and extended interpretations in this scheme but a complete omission of *scriptum* resulting in its non-application. Consequently, he believed that the *scriptum* was beyond interpretation at all. Cf. U. Wesel, *Rhetorische Statuslehre…*, p. 41; Idem, *Zur Deutung…*, p. 343. These observations are not without merit. The effect of *a sententia* argumentation (in its restrictive aspect) is indeed the *scriptum* being not applicable in a given case. In fact, nonetheless, the *contra scriptum* decision is not a decision against the rule but against what its literal understanding suggests. Indeed, the vast majority of rhetorical and, as it will turn out, legal decisions are examples illustrating the restrictive aspect of this *status*. Yet, the same framework also includes those decisions where the *contra scriptum* decision was based on the application of the norm, even though the literal interpretation clearly indicated that such application was not possible.

444 Cicero gives an example of such argumentation in *Inv.* 1,39,70.

445 See again Cic., *Inv.* 1,38,68–69.

446 *Utilitas civitatis* is invoked in another rhetorical example that illustrates *utilitas* in a similar function (Quint., *Decl. min.* 348). In this scenario, a general, fearing imminent treason, imprisoned several

without familiarity with Cicero's views outlined in Chapter One, it is clear that this category was not just purely pragmatic but also had strong ethical overtones. As stated in the source, *utilitas,* being the idea underlying the legal order, was also the ultimate goal of the law. Therefore, it was intended to be a guiding determinant of interpretation. This category, as corresponding to the highest and most important intention of a law, or a legislator, is thus consistent with the terms *sententia* and *voluntas*. Consequently, the *ex sententia/voluntate/utilitate* perspectives represent the same type of interpretation: the *contra scriptum* one[447]. This pattern also includes the release from civil obligations and taking a man's life, both justified by *utilitas,* as discussed in the previously quoted writings of Cicero and Quintilian[448].

The effect of the *ex sententia/voluntate/utilitate* interpretation could also be quite the opposite, as leading to the application of the rule, even if its literal understanding did not allow it. Cicero presented this spectacularly in his speech in defence of Aulus Caecina, likely in 69 BCE[449]. To briefly recall: Caecina's trial opponent was Sextus

suspects and, based on intelligence suggesting their plans to betray the state, set fire to the prison before their guilt could be formally proven. Although accused of unlawful punishment without trial, the general defended his actions by asserting his supreme wartime authority. He further argued that even if his actions were considered wrongful, they were necessary for the protection of the state, invoking *utilitas civitatis* to justify his departure from the legal prohibition against punishing without trial. This argument is captured this way in the speech: Quint., *Decl. min.* 348,4: *Erraverim sane; sed id satis probationi existimavi, si hoc ad utilitatem civitatis pertinere credidi* ('Suppose I made a mistake: but I thought it enough for approval if I believed this concerned the *utilitas civitatis*').

447 The tension between the categories *utilitas* and *scriptum, scriptio, verba, litterae* and the like is also confirmed by other fragments of *De inventione*. See Cic., *Inv.* 1,40,73 *Quodsi leges omnes ad utilitatem rei publicae referri convenit, hic autem saluti rei publicae profuit, profecto non potest eodem facto et saluti communi consuluisse, et legibus non obtemperasse* ('After all, all laws should refer to the utility of the state, and that man contributed to its saving. In one and the same act, he really could not take care of the common good and disobey laws'); 2,48,141 *deinde leges nobis caras esse non propter litteras, quae tenues et obscurae notae sint voluntatis, sed propter earum rerum, quibus de scriptum est, utilitatem et eorum, qui scripserint, sapientiam et diligentiam* ('then, the laws are valuable to us not because of the wording used in them, which is fragile and indistinct signs of the author's intention, but because of the utility of the things that are written about, and the wisdom and care of the authors'); 2,48,143 *Leges in consilio scriptoris et utilitate communi, non in verbis consistere; quam indignum sit aequitatem litteris urgeri, quae voluntate eius, qui scripserit, defendatur* ('The meaning of laws is given by the intention of their author and common utility, not wording. How shameful it would be if the righteousness that the author sought to defend was thwarted by mere words').

448 Cic., *Off.* 3,4,19, 3,25,95 and Quint., *Inst.* 12,1,37.

449 On this subject e.g. in F. Ruffini, *L'actio spolii. Studio storico-giuridico,* Torino 1889, pp. 8–23; G. Nicosia, *Studi sulla deiectio,* Milano 1963; W. Stroh, *Taxis…,* pp. 80–103; B.W. Frier, *The Rise of the Roman Jurists. Studies in Cicero's pro Caecina,* Princeton 1985; G. Falcone, *Ricerche sull'origine dell'interdetto uti possidetis,* Palermo 1996, pp. 252–288; J.W. Tellegen, *Savigny's System and Cicero's Pro Caecina,* 'OIR' 1996, vol. 2, pp. 91–106; L. Fotheringham, *Repetition and Unity in a Civil Law Speech: The Pro Caecina* [in:] *Cicero the Advocate,* J. Powell, J. Paterson (ed.), Oxford 2004, pp. 253–276; A. Lintott, *Cicero as Evidence: A Historian's Companion,* Oxford-New York 2008, pp. 73–80; O.E. Tellegen-Couperus, *Cicero and Ulpian: Two paragons of legal practice,* 'RIDA' 2009, vol. 56, no. 1, pp. 485–497; J. Zajadło, *Oratio pro Aulo Caecina Cycerona – prawo pomiędzy jurysprudencją a retoryką,* 'Ruch Prawniczy, Ekonomiczny i Socjologiczny' 2019, vol. 2, pp. 35–49.

Aebucius, represented by Calpurnius Piso. The dispute before the court of *recuperatores* concerned the admissibility of Caecina's use of the *de vi armata* interdictum. The petition regarding its granting was submitted to the city praetor, Publius Cornelius Dolabella, after Aebucius ordered a group of the armed men to prevent Caecina (not necessarily peacefully) from entering the property, the rights to which Aebucius and Caecina were arguing over. The praetor granted land possession to Caecina.

However, Aebucius maintained that the magistrate's decision did not apply to him. The line of defence was supported by the literal interpretation of the edict's words: VNDE TV AVT FAMILIA AVT PROCVRATOR TVVS ILLVM AVT FAMILIAM AVT PROCVRATOREM ILLIVS VI HOMINIBVS COACTIS ARMATISVE DEIECISTI EO RESTITVAS[450] ('when you, your household, or your representative drive out this person, their household, or their representative with the help of the gathered and armed people, you will bring them back to this place'), and in particular, the literal understanding of the term *deiecisti*. According to the wording, granting the interdictum required to be 'driven out' from the premises. Piso claimed Aebucius' act against Caecina was not 'driving out' (*deicere*) but 'driving [him] away' (*reicere; eicere*) from the property, since Caecina was not even allowed to enter, and one could be driven out only from where they actually were[451].

Cicero argued that the *interdictum* could still apply in Caecina's case, even if the literal wording of the formula spoke against it[452]. It was therefore the *contra scriptum* argumentation but one solely related to the literal understanding of the term *deiecisti*[453],

450 According to the reconstruction by O. Lenel, *Das Edictum perpetuum: ein Versuch zu seiner Wiederherstellung*, Leipzig 1927, p. 467.

451 Cicero refers to this argument several times. Cf. Cic, *Caec.* 24; 31; 38; 64; 66; 79; 84.

452 This was also the opinion of the jurist, likely Servius Sulpicius Rufus, who advised Piso on the matter. Cf. Cic., *Caec.* 79 *Qui cum istam disputationem mecum ingressus esset, non posse probari quemquam esse deiectum nisi ex eo loco in quo fuisset, rem et sententiam interdicti mecum facere fatebatur, verbo me excludi dicebat, a verbo autem posse recedi non arbitrabatur.* ('When we had a discussion on whether it was true that it could be argued that someone could only be driven out of where they were, he agreed that the sense and character of the edict were favourable to us, but that its content precluded my argument. At the same time, he believed that the letter of the law could not be deviated from').

453 As explained by Cicero in *Orat.* 102: *Tota mihi causa pro Caecina de verbis interdicti fuit: res involutas definiendo explicavimus, ius civile laudavimus, verba ambigua distinximus* ('My speech in defence of Caecina concerned only the wording of the interdictum: I explained complicated issues with definitions, I praised the *ius civile*, I recognized the ambiguities of concepts'). So Marius Victorinus is not wrong to classify this problem as *definitio legalis* (*Rhet.* 1,12 [s. 193 H.]). As Cicero explained in *De inventione* (*Inv.* 2,153,51): *Definitio est, cum in scripto verbum aliquod est positum, cuius de vi quaeritur...* ('The definition should be used when there is a term in text whose meaning is under consideration'). This is how this argument was classified in U. Wesel, *Zur Deutung...*, pp. 355–366. At the same time, the vast majority of authors agree with Quintilian (*Inst.* 7,6,7) and Fortunatianus (*Rhet.* 2,10 [s. 107 H.]), rightly maintaining that the problem to be resolved fits into the scheme of *status scripti et voluntatis*. Cf. e.g. B. Vonglis, *La lettre...*, pp. 119–133; Idem, *Droit romain...*, p. 254; W. Stroh, *Taxis...*, pp. 83–86; B.W. Frier, *The Rise...*, p. 121; L. Calboli Montefusco, *La dottrina...*, pp. 158–159. In turn, La Bua considered both *status* to be applied. See G. La Bua, *Diritto e retorica...*,

and not directed against the entire regulation. When arguing *ex aequitate/voluntate/sententia* (and these terms are repeatedly mentioned throughout the speech), Cicero referred to legislator's intention, explaining that his will was to oppose the unlawful force. Thus, the edict's interpretation should not be limited to the wording but should consider all circumstances[454]. He criticized Piso for basing his defence on the literal interpretation of one word, showing the issue boiled down to a matter as small as a single letter[455]. This is how Cicero contrasted the *ex litteris* interpretation with the *ex utilitate* one[456]:

Cic., *Caec.* 49
An tu qui tam diligenter et tam callide verbis controversiam non aequitate diiudicas, et iura non utilitate communi sed litteris exprimis …
You, then, showing such care and skill in resolving disputes to the letter, and not according to righteousness, and interpreting the laws by faithfully repeating their wording, rather than by applying common utility …

Cic., *Caec.* 50
an cum voluntas et consilium et sententia interdicti intelligatur, impudentiam summam aut stultitiam singularem putabimus in verborum errore versari, rem et causam et utilitatem communem non relinquere solum sed etiam prodere?
… or rather, since the will, assumption, and intent of the interdictum are clear to us, do we consider it a manifestation of perfect insolence and unparalleled stupidity to worry about the doubts that the wording gives rise to, abandoning and even betraying the matter, the cause, and common utility?

p. 186. Obviously, this is fully justified, as Cicero, arguing *contra scriptum*, claims that the regulation provided for in the edict should apply to Caecina's case, even if the literal interpretation argued against it. Therefore, one cannot agree with Wesel that the speech *Pro Caecina* did not fit into the scheme of *status scripti et voluntatis*, at the same time excluding the so-called extensive aspect of this *status*. However, Wesel's arguments should not be dismissed lightly, as he suggested that the analyzed *status* could be an example of *ambiguitas* or *ratiocinatio*. Cf. U. Wesel, *Zur Deutung…*, pp. 355–366. The latter category will be discussed later in this work. For now, it suffices to say that the *status ratiocinationis* consisted in the inclusion of a case not covered by the regulation according to a literal interpretation in the legal order. In fact, from Piso's perspective, arguing *pro scripto*, this may have seem the solution proposed by Cicero.

454 Cic., *Caec.* 63.

455 Cic., *Caec.* 38; 66.

456 In *Pro Caecina,* Cicero also highlights the close relationship between the legal field and *utilitas*. See Cic., *Caec.* 70 *Nam qui ius civile contemnendum putat, is vincula revellit non modo iudiciorum, sed etiam utilitatis vitaeque communis* ('For whoever believes that the law should be scorned breaks the ties that support not only the judicial procedure but also the utility and life of the community'). In Cic., *Caec.* 55, there is also mention of the utility coming from the interdictum (*utilitas interdicti*).

Cicero invoked *utilitas* not only in the same sense, but also in the same function as in the fragment of *De inventione* quoted earlier. It was therefore a determinant of interpretation, supporting *contra scriptum* argumentation.

The solution proposed by the party arguing *ex utilitate* in the *status scripti et voluntatis* always involved breaking the literal wording of a legal norm. It should be noted that this category was treated by rhetoricians in two ways. Sometimes, a 'norm' was understood as a normative entity, as, for instance, in the case of Epaminondas, or in the quoted examples of not fulfilling the duties to support the parents, or of climbing the city walls. Other times, however, it was viewed from a textual-semantic perspective: it was then understood as a linguistic expression[457]. Then the *contra scriptum* interpretation was based on breaking the literal meaning of terms that verbalized a specific norm. This process could be carried out in two ways, and consisted either in departing from the literal understanding of the word, as in *Pro Caecina*, or in modifying the scope of a given term, as in the Quintilian's iron ring example. In this way, an intentional dimension, and therefore in line with *sententia/voluntas/aequitas/utilitas*, was given to the word's meaning, described as *vis*. In the *contra scriptum* interpretation, these four categories seemed to be closely blended. The effect of such an interpretation was always the same: breaking the unequivocal content of the rule. As a result, one either deviated from the norm's application, despite its literal interpretation requiring it, or on the contrary, applied it despite the literal interpretation suggesting otherwise. Influencing the application of the norm, the *ex utilitate* interpretation thus led to the verification of the scope of behaviours prohibited, prescribed and permitted by the law.

3.2 Jurisprudence *contra scriptum* Decisions

3.2.1 *Ex utilitate, non ex (subtili et stricta) ratione interpretari*

Many researchers, including Johannes Stroux[458], Juri Himmelstein[459], José Santa Cruz Teijeiro[460], Giuseppe Gandolfi[461], Bernard Vonglis[462], Uwe Wesel[463], and Jan Willem Tellegen[464], showed that Roman jurists knew and used the *status scripti et voluntatis*

457 On this subject see discussion on *status finitionis* in H. Lausberg, *Handbuch…*, pp. 71–80.
458 J. Stroux, *Summum ius…*, pp. 28–33.
459 J. Himmelschein, *Studien zu der antiken Hermeneutica iuris* [in:] *Symbolae Friburgenses in honorem Ottonis Lenel*, Leipzig 1931, pp. 373–424.
460 J. Santa Cruz Teijeiro, *Influencia…*, pp. 343–398; Idem, *Der Einfluß…*, pp. 91–115.
461 G. Gandolfi, *Studi sull'interpretazione…*, pp. 243–339.
462 B. Vonglis, *La lettre…*, 118–200; Idem, *Droit romain…*, pp. 247–256.
463 U. Wesel, *Rhetorische Statuslehre…*, esp. pp. 133–139; Idem, *Zur Deutung…*, pp. 343–366.
464 J.W. Tellegen, *The Reliability…*, p. 194. The author refers to the fragment of Quintilian's *Institutio oratoria*, which explicitly states that this *status* was known to and applied by jurists. See Quint.,

in interpreting the law. However, it is often believed is that the scheme used by jurists did not correspond exactly to the rhetorical one that falls within the term κατὰ ῥητὸν καὶ ὑπεξαίρεσιν coined by Hermagoras[465]. Researchers argue that jurists applied a modified version of the *status*, aiming to introduce analogical solutions[466], or depart from the literal interpretation, however, in such a way as to limit or extend the scope of application of the norm[467], without breaking its unequivocal content and opposing to its literal interpretation[468].

Inst. 7,6,1 *Scripti et voluntatis frequentissima inter consultos quaestio est, et pars magna controversi iuris pendet* ('Jurists often raise the question of letter and intention; a large proportion of legal disputes are dealt with under this theme').

465 B. Vonglis, *Droit romain…*, p. 253; U. Wesel, *Zur Deutung…*, p. 344. The authors express this thought explicitly on the indicated pages.

466 Bretone offers noteworthy criticism of Wesel's work, suggesting that Wesel's use of legal analogy, as understood in contemporary legal theory, and his proposed transposition of concepts may be overly simplistic. See M. Bretone, *Il giureconsulto…*, pp. 307–310.

467 U. Wesel, *Rhetorische Statuslehre…*, pp. 115–199; Idem, *Zur Deutung…*, p. 344; B. Vonglis, *La lettre…*, pp. 118–200. An example quoted in this regard is in particular the passage of Paul. D. 23,2,44,5, in which a fragment of the first book of Paulus' commentary *ad legem Iuliam et Papiam* is preserved, confirming that the jurist excluded certain persons from the scope of application of the prohibitions to contract marriage provided for in Augustus' matrimonial legislation: D. 23,2,44,pr.;5 pr. *Lege Iulia ita cavetur:* QVI SENATOR EST QVIVE FILIVS NEPOSVE EX FILIO PRONEPOSVE EX FILIO NATO CVIVS EORVM EST ERIT, NE QVIS EORVM SPONSAM VXOREMVE SCIENS DOLO MALO HABETO LIBERTINAM AVT EAM, QVAE IPSA CVIVSVE PATER MATERVE ARTEM LVDICRAM FACIT FECERIT. NEVE SENATORIS FILIA NEPTISVE EX FILIO PRONEPTISVE EX NEPOTE FILIO NATO NATA LIBERTINO EIVE QVI IPSE CVIVSVE PATER MATERVE ARTEM LVDICRAM FACIT FECERIT, SPONSA NVPTAVE SCIENS DOLO MALO ESTO NEVE QVIS EORVM DOLO MALO SCIENS SPONSAM VXOREMVE EAM HABETO. 5. *An et is noceat, qui antequam adoptaret artem ludicram fecerit? atque si naturalis pater antequam filia nasceretur fecerit? et si huius notae homo adoptaverit, deinde emancipaverit, an non possit duci? ac si talis pater naturalis decessisset? sed de hoc casu contrariam legis sententiam esse Pomponius recte putat, ut eis non connumerentur* ('pr. The *lex Iulia* provides as follows: "No senator or his son, his son's grandson, and his grandson's great-grandson born to his son will consciously and intentionally have a manumitted fiancée, or wife, or a woman who practises or practiced acting, or whose father or mother are or were actors. Moreover, a senator's daughter, his son's granddaughter, or his grandson' great-granddaughter born to his son cannot knowingly and intentionally become a fiancée, or wife of a manumitted man, or of a man who is now, or was an actor in the past, or has a father or mother who are or were actors. Likewise, neither of these persons may knowingly and intentionally have them for a fiancée, or wife". 5. Is this also an obstacle that someone was an actor before adopting? Or if a natural father practiced this profession before his daughter was born? And if a man of this kind adopted <a girl>, and then manumitted her from his power, can't she be married? Or if a natural father, who was a man of this sort, died? Pomponius rightly believes that these cases do not follow the intention and spirit of the law, so that they will not be included <among the above-mentioned>'). Indeed, Paulus' considerations can be subsumed under the *status scripti et voluntatis* scheme but, unlike those discussed in the first subsection of Chapter Three, they arise not *ex iure manifesto* but *ex iure obscuro*. A similar example of considerations arising from the ambiguity of the law can be found in Quintilian (*Inst.* 7,6,4).

468 It is quite surprising that Vonglis was so strongly opposed to the presence of the κατὰ ῥητὸν καὶ ὑπεξαίρεσιν scheme in jurists' decisions. Among the examples of jurisprudence interpretation *ex sententia*, he included a fragment Tryph. D. 26,6,4,1 *Sin autem idoneis datis tutoribus pluribus unus eorum vel decessit vel temporalem excusationem accepit, mater, quae propterea in loco illius alium non*

The present considerations aim to challenge this belief. The very fact that Roman law scholars describe decisions taken *utilitatis causa* as 'exceptions to rules or principles' might already suggests the convergence between rhetorical and jurisprudence interpretations. Additionally, Vonglis' observation further supports this perspective, as he argues that the use of rhetorical schemes in the practice of interpretation – rather than merely rhetorical terminology – proves the rhetoric's influence on jurisprudence[469]. Thus, although the content of the *utilitatis causa* decisions does not reference to the terms *scriptum, voluntas* or *sententia* (one of the reasons being the intention of the legislator was not the leitmotif of the jurists' interpretation[470]), understanding the disharmony between these categories helps to clarify the adversative nature of these decisions and present their coherent image[471].

In place of what rhetorical theory of interpretation would call the *scriptum*, jurists sometimes seemed to use the notion of *ratio* in the *utilitatis causa* decisions . One of the oldest direct[472] evidences of invoking *utilitas* in the analyzed context is the famous fragment of the *Digesta* by Salvius Julian, a jurist of the 2nd century CE[473]. The term *ra-*

petit, quia numerus reliquorum administrationi tutelae sufficiebat, incidit quidem in verba constitutionis, sed sententia excusatur ('If, on the other hand, several suitable guardians were appointed, and one of them either died or obtained grounds for being temporarily excused, then the mother who did not request the appointment of another guardian in his place due to the fact that the number of other guardians was sufficient to provide care, although she falls under the terms of the imperial regulation, is excused by its spirit and intention'). See B. Vonglis, *La lettre…*, pp. 122–124. However, it is an excellent example of breaking the unambiguity of the norm, perfectly fitting in with the term coined by Hermagoras.

469 The explicit formulation of this thesis appears in B. Vonglis, *La lettre…*, p. 203; Idem, *Droit romain…*, p. 252. It was also accepted in J. Kodrębski, Rec. *'Sententia legis', Bernard Vonglis, Paris 1967*, 'CPH' 1972, vol. 24, no. 1, p. 243.

470 T. Giaro, *Prawda…*, p. 15.

471 Indeed, this is not the first attempt to utilize rhetoric as a means to provide fresh insights into jurisprudence sources. A noteworthy recent endeavor in this regard was undertaken by Tessa G. Leesen, who intriguingly explained the differences between Sabinians and Proculeians based on this approach, *Gaius meets Cicero: Law and Rhetoric in the School Controversies*, Leiden 2010. Another significant publication in this regard, distinguished by its meticulous collection and citation of literature (including much of it referenced above) and providing a comprehensive view on the topic, is the recent work by G. Cossa, *I giuristi e la retorica*, [in:] *Dogmengeschichte und Historische Individualität Der Römischen Juristen. Storia dei dogmi e individualità storica dei Giuristi romani. Atti del seminario internazionale (Montepulciano 14–17 Giugno 2011)*, C. Baldus, M. Miglietta, G. Santucci, E. Stolfi (ed.), Trento 2012, pp. 299–363.

472 Papinian and Ulpian refer to the decisions that were of the *utilitatis causa* type by jurists active before Julian, that is, by Labeo (1st century BCE) and Pegasus (1st century CE; Pap. D. 46,3,95,7), as well as by Celsus (turn of the 1st and 2nd centuries CE; Ulp. D. 40,9,1). However, since these are not direct accounts, and the reconstruction of the arguments carried out by the jurists quoted above is not possible, it is considered that these references are primarily of argumentative value, which will be discussed below.

473 The problem discussed by Julian has received numerous analyses by Roman law scholars, recently compiled and broadly discussed in W. Ernst, *Justinian's Digest 9.2.51 in the Western Legal Canon: Roman Legal Thought and Mondern Causality Concepts*, Cambridge-Antwerp-Chicago 2019. See, for example, D. Pugsley, *Causation and Confessions in the Lex Aquilia*, 'TR' 1970, vol. 38, no. 2,

tio appears there twice. Julian explored the issue of estimating the value of the damage caused by the death of a slave. The problem he analyzed is so astonishing that in fact it resembles a rhetorical *quaestio* rather than a legal case. First, the slave was mutilated so severely that death was imminent. Shortly after, another person wounded the slave again, causing his immediate death[474].

Julian wondered if the perpetrators were responsible for killing the slave under the first chapter of the *lex Aquilia de damno*[475]. He pointed out that although initially, under the *lex Aquilia de damno,* only those who killed with their own hands were held accountable. However, over time, the wording began to be interpreted more broadly, holding those who inflicted wounds causing not immediate but eventual death responsible[476]. Consequently, Julian decided that each perpetrator should be held accountable for killing the slave under the first chapter of the *lex Aquilia*[477], though the basis for estimating the value of the damage differed for each[478]. He addressed potential doubts arising from this solution:

pp. 167–170; H. Ankum, *Das Problem der überholenden Kausalität bei der Anwendung der lex Aquilia im klassischen römischen Recht,* [in:] *De iustitia et iure. Festgabe für Ulrich von Lübtow zum 80. Geburtstag,* Berlin 1980, pp. 325–358; V. Scarano Ussani, *L'utilità…, passim,* and esp. p. 5, n. 4, where the author extensively quotes the literature on the subject; J.-F. Gerkens, *'Aeque perituris…': Une approche de la causalité dépassante en droit romain classique,* Liège 1997, pp. 166–184; M. Navarra, *Ricerche…,* pp. 21–29.

474 Iul. D. 9,2,51,pr.

475 For more on dating this law, see P. Święcicka, *'Lex Aquilia de damno' – problemy z datacją ustawy,* 'Krakowskie Studia z Historii Państwa i Prawa' 2008, vol. 2, pp. 17–32.

476 Iul. D. 9,2,51,pr. (…) *lege Aquilia is demum teneri visus est, qui adhibita vi et quasi manu causam mortis praebuisset, tracta videlicet interpretatione vocis a caedendo et a caede. rursus Aquilia lege teneri existimati sunt non solum qui ita vulnerassent, ut confestim vita privarent, sed etiam hi, quorum ex vulnere certum esset aliquem vita excessurum* ('It was recognized that under the *lex Aquilia* only the one who caused death by the use of force and, as it were, with his own hands is held liable [for killing]. The interpretation of the word "to kill" [*occidere*] was obviously based on the concepts of "to hit" [*caedere*] and "a blow" [*caedes*]. Subsequently, it was found that under the *lex Aquilia,* not only those who injured in such a way that they immediately killed, but also those who mutilated in such a way as to be sure the wound would cause death are held liable').

477 Iul. D. 9,2,51,pr. …*statuendum est utrumque eorum lege Aquilia teneri* ('Each of them must be considered liable [for killing a slave] under the *lex Aquilia*'). Although Julian uses the phrase *lege Aquilia teneri,* it is clear from the context that this is not about liability in general but specifically for killing a slave, which falls under the first chapter of the *lex Aquilia.* This way also in M. Navarra, *Ricerche…,* p. 22.

478 Iul. D. 9,2,51,2 *Aestimatio autem perempti non eadem in utriusque persona fiet: nam qui prior vulneravit, tantum praestabit, quanto in anno proximo homo plurimi fuerit repetitis ex die vulneris trecentum sexaginta quinque diebus, posterior in id tenebitur, quanti homo plurimi venire poterit in anno proximo, quo vita excessit, in quo pretium quoque hereditatis erit* ('The estimate of a killed slave's value will not be the same for each of the two people. Whoever wounded him earlier will pay the highest value of the slave in the previous year, counting 365 days from the date of the wound. Whoever injured him later will be liable for the highest price the slave could have been sold at in the year preceding the day he lost his life, also taking the value of the inheritance into account').

D. 9,2,51,2 (*Iulianus libro octogesimo sexto digestorum*)
eiusdem ergo servi occisi nomine alius maiorem, alius minorem aestimationem praestabit, nec mirum, cum uterque eorum ex diversa causa et diversis temporibus occidisse hominem intellegatur. quod si quis absurde a nobis haec constitui putaverit, cogitet longe absurdius constitui neutrum lege Aquilia teneri aut alterum potius, cum neque impunita maleficia esse oporteat nec facile constitui possit, uter potius lege teneatur. multa autem iure civili contra rationem disputandi pro utilitate communi recepta esse innumerabilibus rebus probari potest: unum interim posuisse contentus ero. cum plures trabem alienam furandi causa sustulerint, quam singuli ferre non possent, furti actione omnes teneri existimantur, quamvis subtili ratione dici possit neminem eorum teneri, quia neminem verum sit eam sustulisse.
Thus, due to the killing of the same slave, one person will have to compensate for the damage more, and the other less. This is not surprising, since it is understood that each of them caused the death of the person through different acts and at separate times. If someone were to think that we had wrongly dealt with this matter, he should consider that it would be far more ridiculous to assume that none of them would be held liable [for killing the slave] under the *lex Aquilia*, or even better – that only one of the perpetrators would be responsible, since neither the misdemeanours should go unpunished nor can it be easily determined which of the two should be held liable [for killing the slave] under the law. In fact, it can be shown on countless examples that many solutions have been adopted under the civil law contrary to the method of inference due to the category of *utilitas communis*. For now, I will be content to identify only one of them. It is recognized that when several people steal a beam none of them could lift alone, they are all sued for theft although the strict interpretation could suggest that none of them can be sued because it is true that none of them took the beam (alone).

Despite the uncertainty regarding which wound was fatal and the inability to definitively attribute the act of killing to one perpetrator, Julian believed that both individuals should be held accountable for the slave's death under the first chapter of the *lex Aquilia*. His opinion breaks the established unambiguous understanding of the term 'to kill' (*occidere*), both in its literal and broadened over time jurisprudential sense, according to which – as Wolfgang Ernst clearly explains – the individual whose actions undoubtedly caused the death should be held accountable for the act of killing[479].

479 W. Ernst, *Justinian's Digest…*, pp. 111–128.

Julian realized that his view could be rejected[480] but argued it would be much worse (*longe absurdius*[481]) to hold only one or neither accountable[482], since it was unknown whose activity caused the death. He justified his opinion even further by stating that many decisions had already been adopted *contra rationem disputandi* due to the *utilitas communis*. The expression *ratio disputandi* is usually interpreted as a method of reasoning based on strict logic[483], that is, following the rules of correct inference, and opposed to *absurdum*. Thus, *ratio disputandi* brings to mind an interpretation according to the formal-dogmatic method, focusing on linguistic and logical analysis of a legal text[484]. Here, *ratio disputandi* is the opposite of *utilitas communis*, as implied by the prepositions *contra* and *pro* (*contra rationem disputandi pro utilitate communi*). It is therefore clear that both *contra rationem disputandi* and *pro utilitate communi* interpretations lead to the same result.

480 In light of the earlier remark on the fact Celsus had resolved the problem differently, Julian may have been referring to the founder of the Proculeian school himself, or one of the jurists who shared his views. Cf. K.-H. Schindler, *Ein Streit zwischen Julian und Celsus*, 'ZSS RA' 1957, vol. 74, no. 1, pp. 204–207; U. Leptien, *Utilitatis causa…*, p. 199, n. 4; V. Scarano Ussani, *L'utilità…* p. 9; M. Navarra, *Ricerche…*, p. 25.

481 On the *ad absurdum* argumentation e. g. in P. Capone, *Valore ed uso giurisprudenziale di absurdus/e*, 'SDHI' 1997, vol. 63, pp. 197–257; A. Wacke, *Ne occasio sit maioris tumultus faciendi: Absurditätsargument und Folgenberücksichtigung in römischen Rechtsquellen, Teil 2* [in:] *Een Rijk Gerecht, Opstellen aangeboden aan Paul Nève*, B. C. M. Jacobs, E. C. Coppens (ed.), Nijmegen 1998, pp. 585–602; T. Giaro, *Absurditätsargumente in der römischen Jurisprudenz*, 'OIR' 2006, vol. 11, pp. 31–61; Idem, *L'expérience de l'absurde chez les juristes romains* [in:] *Mater familias. Scritti romanistici per Maria Zabłocka*, Z. Benincasa, J. Urbanik (ed.), Varsavia 2016, pp. 243–268.

482 Regarding the statement *cum neque impunita maleficia esse oporteat nec facile constitui possit, uter potius lege teneatur* see comments in V. Scarano Ussani, *L'utilità…*, pp. 30–49. Traces of this thought can also be found in the works of rhetoricians. See e. g. Calp. Flacc., *Declam.* 32 *Publicae utilitatis est omnium reorum iudicari causas, ne aut nocens evadat poenam aut innocens patiatur infamiam* ('It is of public utility that all cases are judged in such a way that neither the perpetrator escapes punishment nor the innocent suffers defamation'). On this declamation in A. Casamento, *Colorem timere peius quam sanguinem. Paintings, family strife and heroism.* [in:] *Reading Roman Declamation – Calpurnius Flaccus*, M. T. Dinter, C. Guérin, M. Martinho (ed.), Berlin–Boston 2017, p. 100.

483 This interpretation of the expression *contra rationem disputandi* gained the acceptance of the doctrine. Cf. translations proposed in F. Schwarz, *Begriffsanwendung…*, p. 203 ('entgegen strengen Logik'). See also M. Talamanca, *Rec. a V. Scarano Ussani*, 'BIDR' 1988, vol. 91, p. 879; M. Navarra, *Ricerche…*, pp. 26–27. It is more difficult to reconstruct the Ankum's view who, although applying this phrase to the process of reasoning (cf. *'Utilitatis causa receptum'. On the pragmatical methods…*, p. 23 ['against the rules of strict logic']; Idem, *the functions of expressions…*, p. 9 ['contrary to the rules of logic']), in the summary of the other article still translates *contra rationem disputandi* as 'contrary to dogmatic rules' (p. 21), which relates not so much to the process of interpretation as the application of the norms themselves, or the lack thereof.

484 In this spirit, Seidl translates this expression as *gegen die Begriffsjurisprudenz*, filling it with the category of legal positivism. See E. Seidl, *Moderne…*, p. 106. It is worth mentioning that today this method is often accused of 'being heartless', as it relies on formalized procedures for the interpretation of norms. However, Ziembiński dismisses this criticism, attributing a teleological aspect to the formal-dogmatic approach. See Z. Ziembiński, *Problemy podstawowe prawoznawstwa*, Warszawa 1980, p. 24. Recently, a very interesting perspective on the method was offered by D. Van Kędzierski, *Metodologia i paradygmat polskich szczegółowych nauk prawnych*, 'Transformacje Prawa Prywatnego' 2018, vol. 3, pp. 5–59.

As an example of a similar decision – and thus also adopted *pro utilitate communi* and *contra rationem disputandi* – Julian recalled a situation in which each of the persons jointly stealing a beam too heavy for one of the accomplices to lift it alone could be held accountable for theft. As noted by the jurist, this decision was contrary to the strict interpretation (*ratio subtilis*), according to which none of the perpetrators could answer individually, since the act was only possible through cooperation. This example is similar to Quintilian's example of a person apprehended while carrying iron objects (*ferrum*) at night (*Inst.* 7,6,6–7). Here, the word *tollere*, at the center of the interpretational problem, can have multiple meanings. Its most common meaning is 'to lift up', or 'raise up', which is the sense Julian has in mind when he writes *quam singuli ferre non possent* or *neminem verum sit eam sustulisse*. According to this interpretation none of them could be considered a thief since none lifted the beam alone. However, the term *tollere* can also mean 'to take unlawfully' or 'to steal', aligning perfectly with the main issue at hand (*cum plures trabem alienam furandi causa sustulerint*)[485]. Indeed, in this case, debating the word's meaning creates a false impression of debating the issue as the same word could at the same time both apply and not apply to each of the perpetrators. Certainly, the second interpretation prevailed, allowing for the application of the norm and the subsequent charges for theft against the perpetrators, even though, as Julian indicates, a meticulous interpretation could have led to different outcomes.

Since the case of stealing the beam was supposed illustrate interpretative actions similar to those proposed by Julian in relation to the perpetrators of the slave's death, within the analyzed fragment, the terms *ratio disputandi* and *ratio subtilis* should be treated as related expressions, whether in terms of content or function[486]. Navarra rightly associates the category of *subtilitas* here with the sophisms (*cavillationes*)[487],

485 See OLD, s. v. *tollo*.

486 Talamanca defined them as dialectical argumentative categories. See M. Talamanca, *Per la storia…*, p. 306, n. 236. The connection of these concepts is also strongly confirmed in the sources. Cf. e.g. Cic., *Sest.* 14, *si non subtilius disputandum*; Idem, *Part.* 139,13 *subtiliter disputandi et copiose dicendi artis est*; Idem, *Brut.* 31 *his opposuit sese Socrates, qui subtilitate quadam disputandi refellere eorum instituta solebat verbis*; Idem, *Leg.* 1,62,6 *Cumque se ad civilem societatem natum senserit, non solum illa subtili disputatione sibi utendum putabit…*; Idem, *Tusc.* 4,33,1–3 *Habes ea quae de perturbationibus enucleate disputant Stoici, quae λογικά appellant, quia disseruntur subtilius*.

487 M. Navarra, *Ricerche…*, p. 27 along with the literature cited therein. The link between the categories is evidenced e. g. in Quint., *Inst.* 7,3,14,2–4 *Quibusdam ne placuit quidem omnino subtilis haec et ad morem dialecticorum formata conclusio, ut in disputationibus potius arguta verborum cavillatrix quam in oratoris officio multum allatura momenti* ('Some indeed reject this subtle form of argumentation modelled on dialectical methods entirely and consider it a harsh verbal sophistry for use in debate rather than a significant contribution to the work of the orator'). The fact that *subtilitas* took on a pejorative meaning in the writings of classical jurists, associated with the strict interpretation, focusing mainly on the literal interpretation of the wording was presented in H. Hausmaninger, *Subtilitas als juristische Wertung in den Codex-Konstitutionen Justinians* [in:] *Festschrift Fritz Schwind zum 65. Geburtstag: Rechtsgeschichte, Rechtsvergleichung, Rechtspolitik*, R. Strasser, M. Schwimann, H. Hoyer (ed.), Wien 1978, pp. 71–77; Idem, *Subtilitas iuris* [in:] *Iuris professio: Festgabe für Max Kaser zum 80. Geburtstag*, H.-P. Benöhr, K. Hackl, R. Knütel, A. Wacke (ed.), Wien-Köln-Graz 1986, pp. 59–72.

already discussed in Chapter Two. There is no doubt that in both cases a literal interpretation could raise considerable ethical objections. And while the concept of *ratio disputandi* does not seem to have similar negative connotations, it is clear that, according to Julian, the *pro ratione disputandi* interpretation would lead to undesirable results.

Here, *utilitas communis* is not so much a new argument[488], nor just, as Wolfgang Ernst suggests, a 'tie-breaker' among the legally viable options[489], but rather complements the presented reasoning, paving the way to go beyond the established interpretation. Falcone rightly notes that here the category under study alludes to the values of *iustitia* and *aequum*[490]. Also, *utilitas* certainly evokes the concept of teleological argument[491], but at the same time suggests more. For all the aforementioned interpretative categories – *ratio disputandi, ratio subtilis* and *utilitas communis* – clearly recall two rhetorical interpretative perspectives: *pro scripto* and *contra scriptum* interpretation. Here, Julian opted for the latter. However, he did not challenge the regulation itself, but rather the established, unambiguous understanding of the term *occidere* in the first chapter of the *lex Aquilia*, under which only the individual whose actions undoubtedly caused the death could be held accountable. Consequently, according to the strict interpretation of the law, the norm should not apply in this case, as it was impossible to determine with certainty whose actions directly caused the slave's death. Julian, however, broke the unambiguous understanding of *occidere*, expanding its scope beyond this literal and established meaning, which allowed the norm to be applied and both perpetrators to be held accountable.

Julian's decision is not the only one where jurists contrasted *ratio* and *utilitas*:

G. 3,160

Item si adhuc integro mandato mors alterutrius alicuius interveniat, id est vel eius, qui mandarit, vel eius, qui mandatum susceperit, solvitur mandatum; sed utilitatis causa receptum est, ut si mortuo eo, qui mihi mandaverit, ignorans eum decessisse exsecutus fuero mandatum, posse me agere mandati actione; alioquin iusta et probabilis ignorantia damnum mihi adferet. et huic simile est, quod plerisque placuit, si debitor meus manumisso dispensatori meo per ignorantiam solverit, liberari eum, cum alioquin stricta iuris ratione non posset liberari eo, quod alii solvisset quam cui solvere deberet.

488 Contrary e.g. in M. Navarra, *Ricerche…*, p. 25, who seems to see this category as a separate, additional argument.

489 W. Ernst, *Justinian's Digest…*, p. 131–133. While the author's argument that Julian proves that the literal interpretation could lead to *impunitas* of both of the attackers should be appreciated, it seems that for the jurist it is not an 'all or nothing' decision, as he himself states that it would be far more ridiculous to assume that only one of the perpetrators would be held liable.

490 G. Falcone, *La 'vera philosophia'…*, pp. 72–73, n. 54.

491 W. Ernst, *Justinian's Digest…*, pp. 141–143. It is certainly worth noting how Ernst analyzed and depicted Julian's interpretation model.

> Similarly, if the death of either party occurs before the commencement of the execution of a mandate, that is either the person who offered the mandate, or the one who accepted it, the mandate is terminated. But for the sake of *utilitas*, it was assumed that if after the death of the person giving the mandate, I carried it out not knowing they had died, I could bring an *actio mandati*. Otherwise, my just and demonstrable ignorance will do me harm. Similar to this solution is what has been adopted by most jurists, that if my debtor, in their ignorance, pays my already manumitted administrator back, he is released, although generally under the strict rule of the law he would not be able to be released, as he had paid another person than he should have.

Gaius certifies that, due to *utilitas*, the rule that the death of any party to the contract resulted in its expiry (*mandatum solvitur morte*) could be broken. The identical solution is found in Paulus (D. 17,1,26,pr.[492]). Both jurists report it was generally accepted[493] that if the mandatarius performed the task, not knowing about the mandator's death, he had the right to sue the deceased person's heirs for reimbursement. Justified ignorance (for Gaius, *iusta et probabilis ignorantia* or, for Paulus, just *ignorantia*) was sufficient to break the rule and verify what seemed to be prescribed by the law.

Supplementing his statement with an example of a similar decision (*et huic simile est*), and therefore also made in the spirit of the *ex utilitate* interpretation, Gaius stated that due to justified ignorance most jurists (*plerisque placuit*[494]) adopted an interpretation favorable to the debtor who had paid an already manumitted administrator, unaware of his changed status. Although, technically, this could not be considered the performance of the obligation – since the payment was made to the wrong individual – the debtor was nevertheless deemed to have performed the obligation effectively and according to the legal rules. As Gaius explained, this decision went against the *stricta iuris ratio*.

Papinian also juxtaposed the terms *utilitas* and *ratio*:

492 Paul. D. 17,1,26,pr. *Inter causas omittendi mandati etiam mors mandatoris est: nam mandatum solvitur morte. Si tamen per ignorantiam impletum est, competere actionem utilitatis causa dicitur. Iulianus quoque scripsit mandatoris morte solvi mandatum, sed obligationem aliquando durare* ('The mandator's death is also included among the causes resulting in the expiry of a contract, because the mandate terminates with death. However, if the contract is continued to be exectuded by a contractor due to his lack of knowledge that the mandator has died, it is held that he is entitled to an action for the sake of *utilitas*. Julian also writes that although a mandate is terminated as a result of the mandator's death, the obligation sometimes continues').

493 The expression *utilitatis causa receptum est* used by Gaius seems to be synonymous with Paulus' *utilitatis causa dicitur*. This way in M. Navarra, *Ricerche…*, p. 177. Even if the latter has a slightly weaker overtone, it is not enough to recognize only the argumentation function of the category in this case. This way in H. Ankum, *The functions…*, p. 22. Both cases therefore speak about the *ius receptum*.

494 The expression used by Paulus in this context has a strong overtone, though weaker than the previously quoted *receptum est*. Cf. T. Giaro, *Geltung…*, p. 79. Thus, the applied phrase speaks against Navarra's thesis that *utilitatis causa* decisions always constituted part of the *ius receptum*.

D. 11,7,43 (*Papinianus libro octavo quaestionum*)
Sunt personae, quae, quamquam religiosum locum facere non possunt, interdicto tamen de mortuo inferendo utiliter agunt, ut puta dominus proprietatis, si in fundum, cuius fructus alienus est, mortuum inferat aut inferre velit: nam si intulerit, non faciet iustum sepulchrum, sed si prohibeatur, utiliter interdicto, qui de iure dominii quaeritur, aget. eademque sunt in socio, qui in fundum communem invito socio mortuum inferre vult. nam propter publicam utilitatem, ne insepulta cadavera iacerent, strictam rationem insuper habemus, quae nonnumquam in ambiguis religionum quaestionibus omitti solet: nam summam esse rationem, quae pro religione facit.
There are people who, although they cannot sanctify a place, are nevertheless entitled to apply for an interdictum against a person who prevents them from burying the body of the deceased in a specific place. Such a person is, for instance, an owner of the land if he buried, or would like to bury the deceased on his land which another person uses. If he buried the deceased, the tomb was not established legally. However, if the burial was to be interrupted, he could successfully apply for an interdictum related to ownership. The same applies to an associate who wants to bury the deceased on jointly owned ground, with the other associate objecting. In this case, to prevent bodies from remaining unburied, in view of *utilitas publica*, we do not take a strict rule into account, which is sometimes used to be omitted in contentious matters concerning the cult of the dead. For the principle that speaks in its favor is superior.

Stricta ratio appears in Papinian's considerations on the protection of the right to bury a body (*ius inferendi*). This right was connected to land ownership[495] but, as the jurist explains, could be limited by others' rights related to the property. For instance, the owner of the land another person was using could not legally bury the deceased there. This is how the expression *iustum sepulchrum facere* should be understood, which defines the scope of *stricta ratio* in Papinian's decision[496]. The right to burial was protect-

495 Cf. G. 2,6 *Religiosum vero nostra voluntate facimus mortuum inferentes in locum nostrum*... ('We make a thing religious by our own will, burying the deceased in our own ground ...') and analogous Marc. D. 1,8,6,4 *Religiosum autem locum unusquisque sua voluntate facit, dum mortuum infert in locum suum*... Cf. I. 2,1,9. See also A. Watson, *The Law of Property in the Later Roman Republic*, 1968, pp. 5–6; M. Kaser, *Zum römischen Grabrecht*, 'ZSS RA' 1978, vol. 95, no. 1, p. 36; M. Jońca, *Przestępstwo znieważenia grobu w rzymskim prawie karnym*, Lublin 2013, pp. 68–69.

496 This meaning of *stricta ratio* is also supported by M. Navarra, *Ricerche*..., p. 87. Paturet and Pölönen also understand this concept as a rule, specifically relating it to the principles of establishing *res religiosa*, linking its meaning with the opening passage of the fragment: *sunt personae, quae, quamquam religiosum locum facere non possunt*. Cf. A. Paturet, *Ulpien D. 1.1.1.2*..., pp. 125–125; J. Pölönen, *Religion in Law's Domain: recourse to supernatural agents in litigation, dispute resolution, and pursuits of justice under the Early Roman Empire*, 'RIDA' 2018, vol. 65, p. 169. However, it seems that these principles remained intact in the case under analysis. This way in M. Navarra, *Ricerche*..., p. 88. Other sources also confirm that the burial did not have to automatically lead to a change of the status of the place to the sanctified one. Cf. e.g. Ulp. D. 11,7,2,7. See also M. Jońca, *Przestępstwo*..., pp. 68–69. The structure of the second part of the fragment also supports the proposed interpretation. All the sentences that provide a theoretical explanation of breaking *stricta ratio* begin with the term *nam*, indicating their related content. However, there appears to be a passage in which *utilitas*

ed by the interdictum on corpse burying (*interdictum de mortuo inferendo*). A fragment of the praetorian edict preserved in Ulp. D. 11,8,1,pr.[497] suggests the interdictum could only apply to those who had the right to bury the deceased on a given land. Papinian states, however, that although the individuals he mentioned were not entitled to this right (the owner of the land another person used, and the associate if the other associate objected), contrary to the rule in force, the interdictum on corpse burying could effectively apply also to them.

Due to the multifaceted nature of the problem, its connection with the sphere of religion, as well as hygiene, *utilitas publica* is usually interpreted here in various manners in this context, considering it either a synonym for 'public order'[498], or linking to the sphere of piety[499]. The aims, or the concrete benefits behind Papinian's interpretation were clearly complex in this case. Nonetheless, it should be emphasized that the reference to *utilitas publica* does not seem to indicate them (or not exclusively), but it primarily breaks the norm's unambiguity.

Finally, *utilitas* and *ratio* appear together also in Ulpian's work:

D. 5,4,1,3 (*Ulpianus libro quinto ad edictum*)
Si ego ex parte me dicam heredem, coheres autem meus possideat hereditatem cum extraneo, cum non plus coheres haberet sua parte, utrum a solo extraneo an vero et a coherede deberem petere hereditatem, quaeritur. et Pegasus fertur existimasse a solo extraneo me petere debere eumque restituturum quidquid possidet, et fortassis hoc officio iudicis debeat fieri: ceterum ratio facit, ut a duobus petam hereditatem, hoc est et a coherede meo, et ille quoque dirigat actionem adversus exterum possessorem: sed Pegasi sententia utilior est.
If I claim that I am an heir to a part of the assets, and the inheritance is owned by my coheir together with a person from the outside of the family, and if my heir does not have more than his share, then should I claim the inheritance only from the person from the outside of the family, or also from my co-heir? Pegasus reportedly thought that I should only bring an action against the person from the outside of the family, and that he is supposed to hand over everything he had inherited, and that it should probably be seen to by the judge *ex officio*. After all, the rule dictates that I bring an action against both, that is also against my co-heir, and so that he also brings an action against the person from the outside of the family, but the opinion of Pegasus is more useful.

was invoked to justify breaking the rules governing the establishment of *res religiosa* – Paul. D. 11,7,3 discussed below.

497 Ulp. D. 11,8,1,pr. *Praetor ait*: QVO QVAVE ILLI MORTVVM INFERRE INVITO TE IVS EST, QVO MINVS ILLI EO EAVE MORTVVM INFERRE ET IBI SEPELIRE LICEAT, VIM FIERI VETO ('The praetor says: "I forbid the use of force to prevent this person from being able to lay a body of the deceased to any place or by any route and bury it there, if they have the right to lay the body of the deceased for burial in this place or access it against your will"').

498 This way in A. Wacke, *Sul concetto di 'dolus' nell''actio de dolo'*, 'Iura' 1977, vol. 28, no. 11–39, p. 30, n. 44. Cf. Also J. Pölönen, *Religion…*, p. 170.

499 U. Leptien, *Utilitatis causa…*, pp. 202–208.

According to Ulpian, the *ratio* required that the co-heir should demand the handover of the part of the estate he was entitled to both from the other co-heir (even if they did not have more than their share in the estate), as well as from a third party. However, he found the opinion of Pegasus more useful, as the latter stated that an heir should bring an action only against the third party. The *sententia utilior* did not only imply a more practical solution, that is, one allowing to avoid unnecessary activities between the three parties involved[500]. The above-mentioned *utilitas* first and foremost authorized to depart from what was dictated by a literal interpretation and modify the scope of prescribed behaviors.

These examples align with the *status scripti et voluntatis* scheme presented earlier. In both jurists' and rhetoricians' writings the subject of interpretation is sometimes a linguistic expression, other times a normative entity. These decisions are not examples of a broad or restrictive interpretation of the rules, but break the literal interpretation's results. Consequently, the rule which should apply according to the literal interpretation does not, as in Gaius and Ulpian, or, does apply, as in Julian or Papinian, although it should not.

These cases in every way correspond to the *a sententia/voluntate/aequitate/utilitate* interpretation scheme. As in the previously quoted rhetorical sources, *utilitas* serves as an instrument to go against the literal interpretation. The *ratio*, in turn, resembles *scriptum*. This is particularly evident in Papinian, who talks about omitting *stricta ratio* (*strictam rationem insuper habemus, quae… omitti solet*) – a phrase also used in rhetorical sources in relation to the *scriptum*[501]. The question then arises about the content of *ratio*, and whether Julian's *ratio disputandi* and *ratio subtilis*, Gaius' *stricta iuris ratio*, Papinian's *stricta ratio* and Ulpian's *ratio* are one another's equivalents. Do they all relate to a process of strict interpretation, or are some of them to be interpreted as the 'rules' of the law? These doubts may not be unequivocally resolved. Only Julian's *ratio disputandi* and *ratio subtilis* do not raise any major doubts, calling an interpretation according to the formal-dogmatic method to mind. However, it is not certain whether everything can be similarly equated. Gaius', Papinian's and Ulpian's *rationes*, can be understood as the strict interpretation, or, respectively, the rules governing the institutions of obligation performance, protection granted under the interdictum *de mortuo inferendo*, or joint-inheritance. It is therefore unclear whether, in this context, the jurists were referring to the 'rule of the law' or the 'rule of the legal interpretation'. Especially since it is also impossible to establish whether the three jurists used this term uniformly. Consequently, it is at least partially understandable why Ankum in his considerations on the *utilitatis causa* decisions does not always distinguish between

500 C.A. Pellat, *Exposé des principes généraux du droit romain sur la propriété et ses principaux démembrements et particulièrement sur l'usufruit: suivi d'une traduction et d'un commentaire du livre VI des Pandectes*, Paris 1853, pp. 141–142.

501 Cf. again Cic., *Inv.* 1,38,69.

these two categories, as was already noted in Introduction. Similarly, Spagnolo and Sampson treat the *ratio*-rule and *ratio*-logic concepts as essentially interchangeable[502]. Fortunately, in the analyzed cases, the specific choice between these meanings does not dictate the course of the analysis. It is clear is that the decisions of Gaius, Ulpian and Papinian concern rules understood as normative entities, not linguistic expressions. Hence, regardless of the meaning of the term *ratio*, both the deviation from the rule and deviation from its strict interpretation would have the same effect.

From the point of view of the considerations presented here, it is particularly important that for jurists the reference to *utilitas* cleared the way for the *contra scriptum* decisions, thus omitting, or even being contrary to the letter of the law. Following the example of the previously quoted passage in Cicero's *De inventione*, this interpretation could be described as *ex utilitate, non ex (subtili et stricta) ratione*. The respectively analyzed decisions were divided into two categories also inspired by the deliberations of the rhetoricians: the next section will discuss those in which the legal rule was treated as a normative entity, as in the fragments of Gaius, Papinian, or Ulpian's writings[503]; in the next part, those in which it was treated as a linguistic expression, as done by Julian.

Before, however, discussing individual decisions adopted *utilitatis causa*, we should still try to explore why Wesel and Vonglis did not notice the pattern of Hermagoras' κατὰ ῥητὸν καὶ ὑπεξαίρεσιν in the interpretation of classical jurists, even though it seems evident already from the four quoted decisions. The reason may lie in their source selection. Both Wesel and Vonglis limited their considerations to the interpretation of *leges*[504] and edicts[505], focusing solely on the so-called written law. Indeed, the rhetorical *status scripti et voluntatis* was usually based on the content of a written norm. However, this was not an absolute rule[506]. It is important to remember that in ancient Roman law, interpretation against the 'letter of the law' – which today could be identified with the text itself – was more complex, given the diversity of legal sources and their origins. Hence, the *ex utilitate, non ex litteris interpretari* approach should be understood more broadly: as an interpretation that departs from its literal and strict understanding of what is prescribed, prohibited and permitted, regardless of the source of the law[507].

502 B. Spagnolo, J. Sampson, *Principle…*, pp. 3, 5–6. In turn, M. Navarra, *Ricerche…*, p. 89 assigns a more abstract level to *stricta ratio* in Pap. D. 11,7,43 than to the term *ratio disputandi* in Iul. D. 9,2,51,2. However, Navarra does not provide justification for this thesis.

503 Hence, when translating these sources, the term *ratio* was rendered as a 'rule'. However, as the explanation indicates, this translation is somewhat arbitrary.

504 This way in U. Wesel, *Rhetorische Statuslehre…*, pp. 9–14.

505 B. Vonglis, *Droit romain…*, p. 252, considered both sources of law in his analysis.

506 Cf. again Cic., *Inv.* 2,42,124.

507 As explained in Introduction, the focus of this work is not on specific interests behind the decisions but on the role of *utilitas* in the interpretation process. Therefore, although many of the decisions cited below have been extensively studied in the literature, they will be referenced only to the extent that they pertain to the perspective adopted here. For a comprehensive review of general studies on many of the decisions quoted below, see e.g. Navarra's recent book (*Ricerche…*).

3.2.2 Breaking the Unambiguity of a Normative Entity

Determining the content of legal rules in the context of the *utilitatis causa* decisions typically does not cause major difficulties. These decisions often break rules deeply rooted in the legal order, which are usually not disputed among jurists. For example, allowing children with no trade knowledge to engage in economic and legal transactions as entities capable of being addressees of stipulation (Gai. D. 46,6,6,pr.[508]), performing disposition activities on their own behalf (G. 3,109[509]), and possess, provided that the possession was obtained with the consent of a legal guardian (Paul. D. 41,2,32,2[510]). In

508 Gai. D. 46,6,6,pr. *Servum pupilli stipulari ita necesse est, si pupillus abest aut fari non potest: nam si praesens sit et fari potest, etiamsi eius aetatis erit, ut non intellegat quid agat, tamen propter utilitatem receptum est recte eum stipulari* ('The stipulation must be taken by the pupil's slave if the latter is absent or unable to speak. If, however, he is present and can speak, even if his age made it impossible for him to understand what he was doing, it was nevertheless assumed due to *utilitas* that he could effectively receive the stipulation').

509 G. 3,107,109. *Pupillus omne negotium recte gerit, ut tamen, sicubi tutoris auctoritas necessaria sit, adhibeatur tutor, velut si ipse obligetur; nam alium sibi obligare etiam sine tutoris auctoritate potest.* (…) 109. *Sed quod diximus de pupillo, utique de eo verum est, qui iam aliquem intellectum habet; nam infans et qui infanti proximus est non multum a furioso differt, quia huius aetatis pupilli nullum intellectum habent. sed in his pupillis propter utilitatem benignior iuris interpretatio facta est* ('107. A pupil performs every legal act correctly, provided that he obtains the consent of the guardian, when it is necessary, for example, if he himself incurs an obligation, because he may oblige others towards himself also without the consent of the guardian. (…) 109. But what we said about the pupil is true only for those who already have some knowledge. Undoubtedly, both the child and the one who is close to the child in age do not differ much from a mentally ill person, because pupils at this age do not have any discernment. But as for such pupils, a milder interpretation of the law was adopted due to *utilitas*'). More on the justification of the decision M. Navarra, *Ricerche…*, pp. 52–61 along with the literature cited therein.

510 Paul. D. 41,2,32,2 *Infans possidere recte potest, si tutore auctore coepit, nam iudicium infantis suppletur auctoritate tutoris: utilitatis enim causa hoc receptum est, nam alioquin nullus sensus est infantis accipiendi possessionem…* ('A child may legally possess, provided that it has obtained the possession with the consent of the guardian, as the will of the child is supplemented with the consent of the guardian. This was adopted because of *utilitas*, as generally speaking the child has no discernment whatsoever regarding the acquisition of possession …'). The process of arriving at this decision is very interestingly presented in M. Navarra, *Ricerche…*, pp. 98–104. It is worth noting that although Paulus quoted the last decision as an example of the *ius receptum*, the wording of the constitution of emperor Decius paints a different picture of the situation. See Decius C. 7,32,3 *Imp. Decius a Rufo. Donatarum rerum a quacumque persona infanti vacua possessio tradita corpore quaeritur. quamvis enim sint auctorum sententiae dissentientes, tamen consultius videtur interim, licet animi plenus non fuisset adfectus, possessionem per traditionem esse quaesitam: alioquin, sicuti viri consultissimi Papiniani responso continetur, ne quidem per tutorem possessio infanti poterit adquiri. Pp. V k. April. Decio A. II et Grato conss.* ('Emperor Decius Augustus to Rufus. The unencumbered possession of things given to a young child by any person is acquired when it is physically transferred. Although jurists' views differ on the matter, it nevertheless seems more prudent that possession should be obtained by physical transfer, even if there was no fully formed will. Otherwise, as the learned Papinian replied, the child could not acquire possession even through their guardian. Posted under the consulship of Decius Augustus for the second time and Gratus [March 28, 250]'). Assuming that in D. 41,2,32,2 the full opinion of Paulus was preserved, one may have some doubts whether to take his word for it and presume that in his time all jurists saw eye to eye as to the ability of a child to acquire possession with the consent of the guardian. Already in 250 CE, emperor Decius wrote about the divergent opinions

another instance, *utilitas* prompted Ulpian (D. 13,5,5,9[511]) to recognize that entities normally participating in trading through their representatives[512] (such as the mentally ill, municipal communes, minors, and persons under the age of 25) were directly granted an action if someone committed to pay off the debts incurred with those entities to their representatives.

In the decisions discussed below, jurists diverged from the application of an unambiguous norm or applied it, always contrary to the literal interpretation. The catalogue of decisions that should be included in this section is extensive. Along with the previously quoted G. 3,160, Pap. D. 11,7,43 and Ulp. D. 5,4,1,3, it lists 56 individual decisions[513]. To verify if jurists referred to *utilitas* close in meaning to the Ciceronian one, or had a specific benefit in mind, all decisions were categorized based on whether they mention *utilitas* (or its derivatives) alone or accompanied by the adjectives *communis* or *publica*, or – and this aspect designates the source as part of the second group – whether the content of the criterion was further specified.

The first group is discussed in the following section. Many of the decisions qualifying here, such as those quoted above, do not raise (major) interpretational difficulties. Since the purpose of this study is to present the function of *utilitas* in legal thinking rather than the full background of these decisions, the following pages focus on more dubious legal issues, illustrating the variety of areas in which the *utilitatis causa* solutions can be found. The remaining decisions are listed and briefly commented in the Appendix.

of jurists on this matter (*sententiae dissentientes*). He referred to Papinian's statement, ascribing the opinion that a child could not acquire possession even *per tutorem* to him. On this basis, it is difficult to establish the actual perspective of the jurist. It is even possible that the phrase *per tutorem* can mean *tutore auctore*. On this possibility e. g. in H. Peters, *Generelle und spezielle Aktionen*, 'ZSS RA' 1911, vol. 32, no. 1, p. 204; P. Lambrini, *L'elemento soggettivo nelle situazioni possessorie del diritto romano classico*, Padova 1998, p. 59. Therefore, the phrase *utilitatis enim causa hoc receptum est* used by Paulus may be an exaggeration in this case. It also raises questions about the universal recognition of other decisions where the phrase *receptum est* and similar expressions appear.

511 Ulp. D. 13,5,5,9 *Si actori municipum vel tutori pupilli vel curatori furiosi vel adulescentis ita constituatur municipibus solvi vel pupillo vel furioso vel adulescenti, utilitatis gratia puto dandam municipibus vel pupillo vel furioso vel adulescenti utilem actionem* ('If an informal promise was given to a representative of a municipality, a minor's guardian, or a curator of a mentally ill person or a person under the age of 25, referring to a payment given to a municipality, or a minor, or a mentally ill person, or a mature person under the age of 25, then I believe that due to *utilitas* a similar action should be granted to a municipality, a minor, a mentally ill person or a person under the age of 25').

512 According to an alternative interpretation, the present case describes a *constitutum* in favour of a third party and, as such, is invalid. Cf. Ulp. D. 13,5,5,5. This way in H. Ankum, *The functions…*, pp. 19–20. However, Ulp. D. 13,5,5,7 explicitly speaks about the admissibility of giving a promise to a minor's guardian, a representative of a municipality, and a curator of a mentally ill (*Item tutori pupilli constitui potest et actori municipum et curatori furiosi*). Therefore, the above-mentioned doubts do not seem justified. More on them in M. Navarra, *Ricerche…*, pp. 163–167.

513 Some of the fragments, e. g. G. 3,160, Iul. D. 9,2,51,2, Ulp. D. 14,1,1,5, Paul. D. 41,4,2,9, contain two examples of *utilitatis causa* decisions each. This aspect was included in the statistics at the end of this work.

In some cases, jurists explicitly referred to the content of the rules from which they subsequently chose to deviate. One such example can be found in an excerpt from Ulpian's *Libri ad edictum*:

D. 44,4,4,23 (*Ulpianus libro septuagesimo sexto ad edictum*)
Illa etiam quaestio ventilata est apud plerosque, an de dolo tutoris exceptio pupillo experienti nocere debeat. et ego puto utilius, etsi per eas personas pupillis favetur, tamen dicendum esse, sive quis emerit a tutore rem pupilli sive contractum sit cum eo in rem pupilli, sive dolo quid tutor fecerit et ex eo pupillus locupletior factus est, pupillo nocere debere, nec illud esse distinguendum, cautum sit ei an non, solvendo sit an non tutor, dummodo rem administret: unde enim divinat is, qui cum tutore contrahit? plane si mihi proponas collusisse aliquem cum tutore, factum suum ei nocebit.
Many jurists also discussed whether an exception of a guardian's deception would be effective against a pupil who asserted his rights. Although pupils should benefit from having guardians, in my opinion, it is more useful to find that exception can be effectively brought both when someone bought an item belonging to the pupil from their guardian, or entered into an agreement with the guardian regarding something belonging to their pupil, as well as when the guardian used deceit, and thanks to him the pupil got richer. And no distinction should be made as to whether security was granted in relation to the pupil's assets being reduced or not, or whether the guardian is solvent or not, as long as he only manages the property. How could a person contracting with him predict something similar? No doubt, if you present me a situation for settlement in which someone colluded with the guardian, I will assume that his own actions turned against him.

As the jurist explains, pupils should benefit from having guardians. Ulpian refers to the rule that a guardian's fraudulent act cannot harm the ward (expressed as *dolus tutoris pupillo non nocet* based on Pap. D. 26,9,3). However, if a third party, as a result of the guardian's fraud[514], carried out a legal action with him that affected the legal situation of the pupil, and the guardian filed an action against that person, the jurist found it more useful (*puto utilius esse*) to grant the third party an exception on the grounds of the guardian's fraud. The *dolus tutoris* resulted therefore in being unfavourable for the pupil from the point of view of their procedural situation[515], as he could not effective-

514 For sources addressing the guardian's deception and its impact on the pupil's situation, see R. Knütel, *Dolus tutoris pupillo non nocet* [in:] *Iuris professio: Festgabe für Max Kaser zum 80. Geburtstag*, H.-P. Benöhr, K. Hackl, R. Knütel, A. Wacke (ed.), Wien 1986, pp. 101–126. Researchers raised numerous objections as to the authenticity of the source, quoting a fragment of the writings of Paulus, according to which a guardian's bad faith in conducting a legal act precluded the effective transfer of ownership. Cf. Paul. D. 26,7,12,1. See Ibid., p. 121, n. 107; S. A. E. Martens, *Durch Dritte verursachte Willensmängel*, Tübingen 2007, p. 75.

515 Javier E. Rodríguez Diez seems mistaken in claiming that the legal act performed by the guardian must have been lucrative for his pupil, *Potestas alienandi. Transfer of ownership by a non-owner from*

ly claim their rights from a third party if that person was not aware of the guardian's fraud[516]. This source highlights the dual role of the guardian: to safeguard the pupil's interests and to ensure transactional certainty. In this case, by invoking *utilitas*, Ulpian prioritized the latter value[517], resulting in a departure from the rule that pupils should not suffer due to their guardian's fraud.

In another significant example, *utilitas* allowed Papinian to break the rule encoded in the *nomina ipso iure divisa* rule ('obligations are divided under the law itself'). Under the Law of the Twelve Tables, heirs were liable for the debts included in the estate proportionally to their shares[518]. However, the jurist argued for exceptions to this rule:

D. 46,1,49,1 (*Papinianus libro vicesimo septimo quaestionum*)
Ex duobus fideiussoris heredibus si per errorem alter solidum exsolvat, quidam putant habere eum condictionem et ideo manere obligatum coheredem: cessante quoque condictione durare obligationem coheredis probant propterea, quod creditor, qui, dum se putat obligatum, partem ei, qui totum dedit, exsolverit, nullam habebit condictionem. quod si duo fideiussores accepti fuerint verbi gratia in viginti et alter ex duobus heredibus alterius fideiussoris totum creditori exsolverit, habebit quidem decem, quae ipso iure non debuit, condictionem: an autem et alia quinque milia repetere possit, si fideiussor alter solvendo est, videndum est: ab initio enim heres fideiussoris sive heredes ut ipse fideiussor audiendi sunt, ut scilicet pro parte singuli fideiussores qui sunt conveniantur. Sed verior et utilior est in utroque casu illa sententia solutionem non indebitae quantitatis non debere revocari, quod etiam epistula divi Pii significatur in persona fideiussoris, qui totum exsolverat.
Some jurists claim that if one of the two heirs of a guarantor mistakenly pays the entire sum, he is entitled to the action for reimbursement (*condictio*), and therefore the co-heir remains liable. Additionally, after the expiration of this action, the jurists hold that the co-heir's obligation continues because the creditor, believing himself to be liable, who pays part of the debt to the one who paid the whole, is not entitled to a reimbursement action at all. Whereas if there were two guarantors for the sum of, say, twenty, and one of the two

Roman law to the DCFR, Oisterwijk 2016, pp. 218–219, 221. Obviously, it could have resulted in the pupil becoming richer, as Ulpian writes. It is worth adding that in such a case, an action could be granted to a third party against the pupil. Cf. Pap. D. 26,9,3. If, however, the jurist had been concerned only about such activities, the remark regarding the fact that in the matter of granting a third party an *exceptio doli* it should not be considered whether the guardian gave the pupil a stipulation about their property not being depleted after the cessation of tutelage (*satisdatio rem pupilli salvam fore*), or whether the guardian is solvent – and therefore whether the pupil will have a legal or actual possibility of seeking redress for the damage caused to their property – would have been completely pointless. Ulpian, therefore, acknowledged that as a result of the guardian's fraud, the pupil could indeed suffer financial harm.

516 Otherwise, the pupil could effectively assert their rights. Cf. Ulp. D. 4,3,5.

517 This way in J. E. Rodríguez Diez, *Potestas alienandi…*, pp. 217–219.

518 Cf. Gordian. C. 3,36,6; Diocl. C. 2,3,26; Paul. D. 10,2,25,13. See also M. and J. Zabłoccy, *Ustawa XII Tablic. Tekst – tłumaczenie – objaśnienia*, Warszawa 2003, pp. 34–35.

> heirs of one of the guarantors would pay the creditor in full, the one who paid will, indeed, be entitled to the action to reclaim ten, that he was not legally obligated to pay. The question then arises whether he will be able to claim five more if the other guarantor is solvent. At the outset, the heir or heirs of the guarantor should be heard in the same manner as the guarantor himself, ensuring that each guarantor is held responsible for their respective share. Thus, in both cases, the more lawful and useful view would be that no reimbursement can be demanded, as also stated in the letter of the divine emperor Antoninus Pius, regarding the guarantor who paid the full amount.

Papinian describes two problems, which, however, concern the same question: can the heir of a guarantor who has paid the entire debt demand the reimbursement of the surplus (from their co-heirs, or co-guarantors) so that the amount paid by them actually corresponds to what they owed by law?[519] The first case discusses one of the two heirs of the guarantor paying off the entire debt as a result of an error. The second presents a more complex picture: here, there are two co-guarantors, one of whom dies, leaving two heirs, and one of them paid off the debt in full. According to the *nomina ipso iure divisa* rule, in the first situation, the co-heir should only be responsible for half of the debt, while in the other one only for the one-quarter of it. According to Papinian, in the other situation, the co-heir could demand that the co-guarantor repay half of the debt. But what about the remaining quarter of the debt, which he did not have to pay according to the principle of proportional liability for inheritance debts? According to Papinian, each co-heir of the guarantor was as responsible as he was himself (*ut ipse fideiussor*). Therefore, the co-heir could claim the surplus reimbursement neither from the other co-heir[520] nor the co-guarantor, even if they were solvent. Similarly in the first case, they could not claim half of the amount paid. This opinion was described by the jurist as *verior et utilior*[521]. The reference to *utilitas* is therefore fully clear: the deci-

519 A different interpretation is proposed by Debayle and Herforth, who argue that the issue at hand concerns the loss of the right to the benefit of surety (*beneficium divisionis*). Cf. G.-A. Debayle, *Moyens de défense et recours des fidéjusseurs en droit romain et en droit français*, Sauveterre 1879, pp. 31–33; R. Herforth, *Begründet die irrtümliche Zahlung einer fremden Schuld die condictio indebiti? Nach römischen und gemeinem Recht*, Zürich 1902, pp. 97–98. In the case, however, it was not about the right of a guarantor or debtor to request a creditor to distribute the debt among everyone but about the demand for the surplus to be returned by a co-heir or co-guarantor. See also comments on the institution of *beneficium* in R. Świrgoń-Skok, *Beneficjum (beneficium) w źródłach prawa rzymskiego*, 'Studia Prawnoustrojowe' 2007, vol. 7, pp. 229–239.

520 Papinian opposed the opinions expressed by some jurists, which he mentioned himself. See again D. 46,1,49,1 … *quidam putant habere eum condictionem et ideo manere obligatum coheredem*.

521 In the edition by Th. Mommsen and P. Krüger the reading *severior et utilior* was accepted, marking the alternative version in the apparatus. Neither version determines the interpretation of the fragment, and the solution proposed by Papinian can also be regarded as severe for obvious reasons. It seems, however, that the *verior et utilior* reading seems closer to the jurist's idiolect. Cf. Pap. D. 17,1,54,pr., where the analogous phrase appears. This reading was also supported in e.g. M. Colamonico, R. Zingarelli, *Le garanzie delle obbligazioni: Lezioni di diritto romano*, Napoli

sions proposed by Papinian repealed the rule governing the proportional distribution of inheritance debts.

Expanding its influence, *utilitas* has also played a significant role in the rules governing acquisition and losing possession. The latter was discussed particularly widely in the context of possession over fugitive slaves, and possession exercised through them. This discussion was partly reported by Paulus:

D. 41,2,1,14 (*Paulus libro quinquagesimo quarto ad edictum*)
Per servum, qui in fuga sit, nihil posse nos possidere Nerva filius ait, licet respondeatur, quamdiu ab alio non possideatur, a nobis eum possideri ideoque interim etiam usucapi. sed utilitatis causa receptum est, ut impleatur usucapio, quamdiu nemo nactus sit eius possessionem. possessionem autem per eum adquiri, sicut per eos, quos in provincia habemus, Cassii et Iuliani sententia est.
Nerva the Son claims that one cannot possess through a fugitive slave although it is expressed that as long as the slave is not in the possession of someone else, he is still in our possession, and for this reason we may even acquire their property by usucaption during this time. But for the sake of *utilitas*, it was accepted that acquiring property by usucaption may be completed [by the slave] until someone takes possession of him. According to Cassius and Julian, we acquire possession not only through slaves but also through those we have in the provinces.

Paulus wrote that Marcus Cocceius Nerva the Son, a jurist of the turn of the eras, was against the possibility of possessing through a fugitive slave[522]. At the same time, this opinion expresses the rule Paulus referred to in the passage. For despite the fact that it was not possible to possess through a fugitive slave, it was nevertheless accepted (*receptum est*) based on *utilitas* that acquiring property by usucaption in relation to objects the slave owner had acquired through him before the slave fled, would continue until someone else took possession of the slave[523]. Although the loss of possession

1897, p. 166. On the connection between *veritas* and *utilitas* in T. Giaro, *Römische Rechtswahrheiten…*, pp. 424–429, though the analyzed source is not considered there.

522 Paulus seems to have doubts about the validity of this opinion, pointing out that there are jurists who believe that the possession of the slave is lost only when someone else takes control of him. Until then, it is even possible to acquire the property of a slave by usucaption (*licet respondeatur, quamdiu ab alio non possideatur, a nobis eum possideri ideoque interim etiam usucapi*). This way in M. Navarra, *Ricerche…*, pp. 92–94. The jurists' discussion in this regard, along with extensive source material, is referred by E. Albertario, *Les problèmes de la possession relatifs au servus fugitivus*, 'TR' 1930, vol. 10, pp. 465–487, who, however, considers the quoted passage to be interpolated (pp. 469–470).

523 The fact that Paulus meant usucapion of things possessed through the slave and not the slave himself is supported by several points. Firstly, it is apparent from the content of the excerpt, as the initial juxtaposition of opinions addresses different issues: Nerva discussed the possession through a fugitive slave (*per servum, qui in fuga sit, nihil posse nos possidere Nerva filius ait*), while other opinions concerned the possession of the slave himself and his acquisition through usucaption (*licet respondeatur, quamdiu ab alio non possideatur, a nobis eum possideri ideoque interim etiam usu-*

should result in the termination of usucaption, in such cases *utilitas* made it possible to break the scope of forbidden behaviors, and allow for the possibility of acquiring property by usucaption.

Turning to another legal area, *utilitas* also emerges in decisions related to inheritance law. In this context, the fragment of the fourth book of Ulpian's *Libri ad Sabinum* is particularly intriguing:

> D. 40,7,2,4 (*Ulpianus libro quarto ad Sabinum*)
> *Quocumque gradu pupillo servus cum libertate substitutus sit, necessarii causam optinet: quae sententia utilitatis causa recepta est et a nobis probatur. Celsus quoque putat libro quinto decimo cum libertate substitutum statuliberi causam optinere.*
> Regardless of the grade at which a slave was substituted for a minor, along with granting him freedom, the slave obtains the status of the necessary heir. This view is adopted for the sake of *utilitas*, and we agree with it. In the fifteenth book of the *Digest*, Celsus additionally believes that a slave who was substituted for another heir along with granting him freedom obtains the status of a conditionally manumitted slave.

Ulpian reports that because of *utilitas*, it was decided that the slave granted freedom in the will, who in whatever grade was substituted as an heir for a minor, gained the status of *heres necessarius*[524], and therefore could not reject the inheritance. This passage sparked numerous discussions among researchers. In particular, it was proposed to change the phrase *necessarii causam* to *statuliberi causam*[525]. The circumstances of

capi). In such circumstances, if the phrase *sed utilitatis… possessionem* concerned the acquisition of a slave, it would appear completely redundant. Additionally, as indicated, the phrase *sed utilitatis… possessionem* refers directly to Nerva's opinion, which expresses the rule which the jurists then spoke against. Finally, it is consistent with Paulus' certain linguistic tendency. In the *Digest of Justinian*, there are two more fragments in which he used the phrase *usucapionem implere*, and in each case, it pertains to the completion of this activity by another person. Cf. Paul. D. 4,6,30,pr. and Paul. D. 5,3,19,1. The fact that in the analyzed case refers to *usucapio per servum*, and not *usucapio servi* is also argued in Ibidem; F. Klinck, *Erwerb durch Übergabe an Dritte nach klassischem römischen Recht*, Berlin 2004, p. 119; H. Ankum, *The functions…*, p. 16. Also, it does not seem that Paulus is discussing the acquisition of new possession here, which he only addresses in the final part of the fragment, citing the opinions of Gaius Cassius Longinus and Salvius Julian.

524 On this subject e. g. in W. W. Buckland, *The Roman Law of Slavery: The Condition of the Slave in Private Law from Augustus to Justinian*, New Jersey 2000, pp. 505–512; B. Kupisch, *Der Sklave als Zwangs-Erbe, Ulpian/Julian 4 ad Sab. (D. 28,5,6,4): Eine Nach-Lese*, 'TR' 2016, vol. 84, no. 3–4, pp. 379–400. See also R. Świrgoń-Skok, *Kategoria spadkobierców koniecznych (heredes necessarii) jako przykład zapewnienia ciągłości w rodzinie rzymskiej w okresie prawa klasycznego*, 'Studia Iuridica Lublinensia' 2010, vol. 14, pp. 135–146.

525 Such a change would remain consistent with Papinian's account from D. 40,7,36, discussed later. The analyzed fragment is considered interpolated e. g. by U. Leptien, *Utilitatis causa…*, p. 184. Ulp. D. 40,7,2,4 and Pap. D. 40,7,36 are treated as an example of the same problem also by H. Ankum, *'Utilitatis causa receptum'. On the pragmatical methods…*, pp. 25–26. Contrary in M. Navarra, *Ricerche…*, pp. 139–140.

taking the decision, and above all the rule, which in this case was possible to be broken due to *utilitas*, can be found in the *Code of Justinian* (C. 6,27,4,pr.–2[526]). According to this account, having drawn up his will, a certain man designated his minor son an heir, and directly manumitted a slave. In the second grade of his will, he substituted the very same slave for his minor son but without manumitting him. This circumstance opened some discussions among jurists (*quaerebatur inter prudentes*), as according to the old rule (*regula vetus*), the slave became the necessary heir of his owner only when both inheritance and freedom were given to him in the same grade. The passage quoted above makes full sense only in relation to this principle. In the case referred to by the jurist, granting freedom was not combined with substitution in a single grade but in different grades. According to the strict interpretation, it was therefore the minor who should have become the necessary heir of the deceased. However, *utilitas* allowed breaking the scope of forbidden behaviors, leading to the recognition that despite a formal error in the will, the slave gained the status of *heres necessarius* of the testator regardless of the grade (*quocumque gradu*) of the will in which the inheritance and his freedom were left to him[527].

526 C. 6,27,4,pr.–2 *Iust. A. Iuliano pp.* pr. *Cum quidam suum pupillum heredem instituit et servo directis verbis libertatem reliquit et in secundo gradu, in quo pupillarem substitutionem faciebat, ipsum servum sine libertate pupillo suo substituit, quaerebatur inter prudentes, si ex huiusmodi substitutione heres necessarius pupillo existat.* 1. *Causa etenim altercationis ex vetere regula orta est, quia omnibus placuerat hunc servum necessarium heredem domino fieri, cui in eodem gradu et hereditas et libertas relinquebatur, in praesenti autem non in unum tam libertas quam substitutio congregata est, sed in alium et alium gradum.* 2. *Nobis itaque eandem altercationem decidentibus mirabile visum est, si quis putet ex huiusmodi scrupulositate impediri testatoris voluntatem, et maxime domini, et existimet non fieri servum heredem necessarium, sed ei licentiam praestet et libertatem consequi et hereditatem respuere et domini voluntati reclamare: qui si hoc differre temptaverit, etiam puniendus est. sit itaque et vivo pupillo liber, quia testator hoc voluit, et mortuo pupillo necessarius heres, quia et hoc testator voluit. D. XV k. Dec. Constantinopoli Lampadio et Oreste vv. cc. conss.* ('Emperor Justinian Augustus to Julian, Praetorian Prefect pr. A man appointed his minor son as heir and manumitted his slave directly, while in the second grade of his testament, where he substituted his heir with another one, he made the same slave's minor son a substitute but without giving him freedom. A question arose among jurists as to whether such substitution made the minor a compulsory heir. 1. The reason for the dispute was an old rule of the law, as they all agreed that a slave becomes his master's compulsory heir if he is left with both his freedom and his inheritance in the same grade. In this case, however, freedom was not linked to substitution in the first grade but in various grades. 2. In settling this dispute, we have found it noteworthy that if anyone considers that the will of the testator, and especially of the owner, may be hindered by too much strictness, and that the slave does not become a compulsory heir but is instead given the opportunity to both gaining freedom and rejecting the inheritance and thus thwarting his master's will. Then if anyone tries to make this argument, he must be punished. And so the slave will be manumitted during the minor's life, as the testator wanted, and after the minor's death, he will acquire the status of the compulsory heir, because that is also what the testator wanted. Given at Constantinople, under the consulship of the *viri clarissimi* Lampadius and Orestes [November 17, 530]').

527 It is also worth noting that Justinian expanded upon the jurisprudence decision by granting the slave not only the status of the compulsory heir but also freedom. See one more time C. 6,27,4,2. However, Ulpian's account, which refers to the opinion of Celsus stating that a slave substituted

Building on these analyses, the famous passage from Paulus' *Sententiae* should be approached in the same spirit:

> P. S. 2,19,2
> *Eorum qui in potestate patris sunt sine voluntate eius matrimonia iure non contrahuntur, sed contracta non solvuntur: contemplatio enim publicae utilitatis privatorum commodis praefertur. Interp. Viventibus patribus inter filiosfamilias sine voluntate patrum matrimonia non legitime copulantur. Sed si coniuncta fuerint, non solvuntur, quia ad publicam utilitatem antiquitas pertinere decrevit, ut procreandorum liberorum causa coniunctio facta non debeat separari.*
> The marriages of those who are under the paternal power are not legally valid without his consent. However, a marriage once concluded cannot be dissolved at the will of the father. Thus, the recognition of *utilitas publica* prevails over the privileges of individuals. *Interp.* Marriages of sons under power are not valid while their fathers are alive, and without their fathers' consent. But if they were concluded, they are not dissolved, since a long time ago it was decreed that it serves *utilitas publica,* so that the relationship entered into for the purpose of producing offspring should not be dissolved.

(Pseudo-)Paulus confirms that the consent of the family head is necessary for children under his power to enter into a valid marriage[528]. However, he implicitly states that marriages already concluded cannot be terminated by the father who refuses to consent to the continuation of the marriage. This interpretation is supplementary, but it follows logically from the course of the passage, and researchers of Roman law generally agree as to its understanding[529]. Yet it remains disputed whether the head of a family ever had the right to dissolve marriage at all.

for another heir along with being manumitted obtains the status of a conditionally freed slave (Ulp. D. 40,7,2,4) clearly shows that *favor libertatis* was no way the motivating factor behind the analyzed decision. Contrary in H. Ankum, *'Utilitatis causa receptum'. On the pragmatical methods…*, pp. 25–26. See also M. Navarra, *Ricerche…*, pp. 139–140.

528 This way e.g. in Paul. D. 23,2,2 *Nuptiae consistere non possunt nisi consentiant omnes, id est qui coeunt quorumque in potestate sunt* ('A marriage is not valid unless everyone agrees to it, that is, the future spouses and those under whose power they are').

529 G. Ceneri, *Lezioni su temi del jus familiae*, Bologna 1881, p. 85; G. Longo, *Sullo scioglimento del matrimonio per volontà del paterfamilias*, 'BIDR' 1932, vol. 40 , p. 210; E. Volterra, *Lezioni di diritto romano. Il matrimonio romano*, Roma 1961, p. 198; O. Robleda, *El matrimonio en derecho romano*, Roma 1970, p. 252; J. Urbanik, *D. 24.2.4: … Pater tamen eius nuntium mittere posse: l'influsso della volontà del padre sul divorzio dei sottoposti* [in:] *Εὐεργεσίας χάριν. Studies Presented to Benedetto Bravo and Ewa Wipszycka by Their Disciples, Warsaw 2002 [= The Journal of Juristic Papyrology. Supplement no. 1]*, T. Derda, J. Urbanik, M. Węcowski (ed.), Warszawa 2002, p. 295; Idem, *Dissolubility and indissolubility of marriage in the Greek and Roman tradition* [in:] *Mater familias. Scritti romanistici per Maria Zabłocka*, J. Urbanik, Z. Benincasa (ed.), Varsavia 2016, p. 1062. Contrary in J. Gaudemet, *Iustum matrimonium*, 'RIDA' 1949, vol. 2, p. 320, according to whom it follows from the passage that marriage could be entered into without the consent of the head of a family, but it was not *matrimonium iure contractum.*

Olis Robleda answered this question affirmatively[530]. He juxtaposed the above source with excerpts from P. S. 5,6,15[531] and Diocl. et Maxim. C. 5,17,5,pr.[532], according to which under the imperial constitutions of Antoninus Pius and Marcus Aurelius, the head of the family was not allowed to dissolve harmonious marriages of the children under their power[533]. If so, the researcher concluded that dissolving such marriages had been previously acceptable. The opposite position is represented by Eduardo Volterra[534] and more recently Jakub Urbanik. According to the latter, imperial constitutions were aimed at unacceptable cases of frequent (as shown by the author in numerous examples) abuse of paternal authority. Urbanik claims that the constitutions were therefore supposed to confirm the general prohibition of breaking harmonious marriage of children under power, and not to limit the rights previously enjoyed by the head of the family[535]. However, *utilitas publica* quoted in the source, clearly in its adversative function, seems to support Robleda's perspective. Even if the general prohibition against fathers dissolving their children's harmonious marriages was not introduced by the imperial constitutions[536], the presence of *utilitas* in the analyzed fragment should be seen as supporting the idea that, for a certain period, *patres familias* did indeed hold such a right.

In those circumstances, it is clear that the famous expression *contemplatio enim publicae utilitatis privatorum commodis praefertur* must not be regarded as a general declaration of putting the public utility before private individuals. As it aligns with the tradition of the interpretation presented in this section, its significance should be considered only in this context. *Utilitas* does not therefore merely outline the general

530 O. Robleda, *El matrimonio…*, pp. 252–254; Idem, *Il divorzio a Roma prima di Costantino* [in:] ANRW, vol. 14.2, Berlin-New York 1982, pp. 369–372.

531 P. S. 5,6,15 *Bene concordans matrimonium separari a patre divus Pius prohibuit…* ('Divine Pius forbade the father to dissolve a harmonious marriage…').

532 C. 5,17,5,pr. *Diocletianus et Maxim. AA. et CC. Scyrioni. Dissentientis patris, qui initio consensit matrimonio, cum marito concordante uxore filia familias ratam non haberi voluntatem divus Marcus pater noster religiosissimus imperator constituit, nisi magna et iusta causa interveniente hoc pater fecerit.* ('Emperors Diocletian and Maximian Augusti to Scyrio. Our predecessor, the divine Marcus, the most pious emperor, established that the will of a father who would not consent to marriage, and who had initially consented to it, had no power over his daughter remaining under his power and living in harmony with her husband unless the father expressed his will for some important and just reason [August 28, 294]').

533 Robleda interprets the term *prohibuit* in P. S. 5,6,15 in this manner, *El matrimonio…*, pp. 253–254.

534 E. Volterra, *Quelques observations sur le mariage des filiifamilias*, 'RIDA' 1948, vol. 1, p. 232.

535 See J. Urbanik, *D. 24.2.4…*, pp. 293–336 along with the literature cited therein, who argues that this right was granted to the father of a family only in special cases. See also C. Kreuzsaler, J. Urbanik, *Humanity and Inhumanity of Law. The Case of Dionysia*, 'The Journal of Juristic Papirology' 2008, vol. 38, p. 129; Idem, *Rozwód w papirusach. Studium przypadków*, 'U schyłku starożytności. Studia źródłoznawcze' 2010, vol. 9, pp. 167–169; Idem, *Dissolubility…*, esp. pp. 1057–1059.

536 However, this hypothesis cannot be ruled out, especially when considering the *interpretatio*, where it is indicated that this old law came into force under the *decretum*.

tendency of the state policy but mainly performs an interpretative and argumentative function, serving to oppose the results of the literal interpretation.

3.2.2.1 Utilitas *or* utilitates?

Building on the previous analysis, it is evident that the sources confirm that the effects of the *ex utilitate* interpretation coincide with what the rhetoricians would describe as a *contra scriptum* one. Therefore, the interpretative role of the analyzed category should not raise any doubts. However, the question returns as to the content of this criterion, and whether it coincides with the Ciceronian, ethically marked *utilitas communis*. The sources quoted so far, as well as those in the Appendix, only mention *utilitas* on its own, or accompanied by adjectives such as *publica* or *communis*. The fragments in which jurists specified the content of the category under study are analyzed below. Thus, the question arises: does *utilitas*, while being an instrument to break the unambiguous results of the literal interpretation, also expresses a specific utility of the decision?

The clarification of the category can be found primarily in Ulpian's writings:

> D. 23,4,6 (*Ulpianus libro quarto ad edictum*)
> *Pomponius ait maritum non posse pacisci, ut dolum solummodo in dotem praestet, videlicet propter utilitatem nubentium …*
> Pomponius states that the husband cannot conclude a contract under which he would be liable for the return of the dowry only in the event of an intentional act, or neglect aimed at infringing his wife's interests. This is obviously because of the utility of those getting married …

Ulpian agreed with Pomponius, stating that the husband's liability could not be limited only to an intentional act or neglect directly aimed at causing damage to his wife's property (*dolus*) in the event of filing an action for the return of the dowry in the situation of marriage dissolution (*actio rei uxoriae*)[537]. In this case, *utilitas nubentium* certainly corresponds to a solution favorable to the institution of marriage[538] (although the wife's economic interest comes forward) but, above all, opposes the scope of per-

537 In other fragment, Pomponius reports that it was *dolus* and *culpa* that determined the husband's minimum scope of liability: Pomp. D. 24,3,18,1. See also E. Stolfi, *Studi sui 'Libri ad edictum' di Pomponio. II. Contesti e pensiero*, Milano 2002, pp. 148–149.

538 J.F. Stagl, *Favor dotis: die Privilegierung der Mitgift im System des römischen Rechts*, Wien 2009, p. 309, explains the use of the term *utilitas nubentium* with the fact that not limiting the scope of a husband's responsibility benefited the dowry, and thus both spouses. However, he stressed that the meaning of the concept is related to the category of *utilitas publica*. This semantic relationship is also supported in D. 24,3,1, where Pomponius stated the public utility required women to retain

mitted behaviors, as the parties usually had the right to agree on the liability of the debtor[539]. In this case, it is difficult to definitely say whether Pomponius justified this decision by referring to *utilitas nubentium*, or whether this element should be attributed to Ulpian[540]. We know, however, that in other instances, Ulpian also used to specify the content of *utilitas* in other ways:

> D. 2,12,7 (*Ulpianus libro primo de officio consulis*)
> *Oratione quidem divi Marci amplius quam semel non esse dandam instrumentorum dilationem expressum est: sed utilitatis litigantium gratia causa cognita et iterum dilatio tam ex eadem quam ex alia provincia secundum moderamen locorum impertiri solet, et maxime si aliquid inopinatum emergat …*
> In a resolution of the Senate, adopted at the request of divine Marcus Aurelius, it was decided that the date of a hearing should not be postponed in order to present documents more than once. But for the utility of the parties, upon examination of the case, it is customary to allow further postponements, regardless of the documents being in the same or different province, according to the regulations in force in the place where they are located, especially when something unexpected happens …

In this fragment, Ulpian followed a familiar practice: he first indicated a clearly defined scope of the norm, and then justified its breach by *utilitas*. This case seems special as the Senate resolution aimed to counteract the excessive length of proceedings. Although it was decided that the hearing should not be postponed more than once in order to present documents, the *utilitas* of the parties allowed for further adjournments, if there were good reasons for doing so[541]. Navarra did not include this fragment in the catalogue of the decisions taken *utilitatis causa*, claiming that it was not an example of jurists' decisions but of procedural practice[542]. Yet, given the frequent presence of the category in the excerpts taken from Ulpian's writings, it seems very possible that the

their dowry property, linking this with procreation reasons. A similar relationship between these categories can be also observed in Clem. D. 35,1,64,1.

539 This way in I. Koschembahr-Łyskowski, *Coventiones contra bonos mores w prawie rzymskim*, Kraków 1925, pp. 246–247. Cf. Ulp. D. 50,17,23 …*sed haec ita, nisi si quid nominatim convenit (vel plus vel minus) in singulis contractibus: nam hoc servabitur, quod initio convenit (legem enim contractus dedit)* … ('this is so as long as the parties have not concluded an agreement extending or reducing their liability for damage in individual contracts. For what was agreed upon must be respected, as the contract established the law').

540 The second option is supported in M. Navarra, *Ricerche…*, p. 157. Indeed, it seems likely, given both the content of the fragment where *videlicet* seems to introduce a commentary on the decision, and Ulpian's tendency to clarify the content of *utilitas*, as evident in the sources analyzed below.

541 On this fragment in F. Arcaria, *Oratio Marci: giurisdizione e processo nella normazione di Marco Aurelio*, Torino 2003, p. 258.

542 M. Navarra, *Ricerche…*, p. 162, n. 343.

justification referred to taking the *utilitas* criterion into account can still be ascribed to the jurist, especially since the role of the category remained unchanged.

Turning to a different case, Ulpian's reflections presented below preserved in the fragment of his commentary *Ad edictum*, refer to the *actio exercitoria*. According to the praetorian edict, the person who appointed the captain of a ship was responsible for actions performed by him within the scope of his duties[543]. In this context, we encounter another example of the jurist's clarification of the category's content:

D. 14,1,1,5 (*Ulpianus libro vicesimo octavo ad edictum*)
Magistrum autem accipimus non solum, quem exercitor praeposuit, sed et eum, quem magister: et hoc consultus Iulianus in ignorante exercitore respondit. Ceterum si scit et passus est eum in nave magisterio fungi, ipse eum imposuisse videtur. quae sententia mihi videtur probabilis: omnia enim facta magistri debeo praestare qui eum praeposui, alioquin contrahentes decipientur: et facilius hoc in magistro quam institore admittendum propter utilitatem. quid tamen si sic magistrum praeposuit, ne alium ei liceret praeponere? an adhuc Iuliani sententiam admittimus, videndum est: finge enim et nominatim eum prohibuisse, ne Titio magistro utaris. dicendum tamen erit eo usque producendam utilitatem navigantium.
We consider as captain not only the person appointed by a shipowner but also the person appointed by the captain himself. This is what Julian replied in a situation in which the shipowner was unaware of the captain's decision. Anyway, if the shipowner is aware of and consented to the fact that a given person performs the function of the ship's captain, it is considered that he appointed this man personally. I find such an opinion commendable. I must be responsible for all the actions of the captain as the one who appointed him. Otherwise, those who enter into a contract with him will be deceived. And for the sake of *utilitas*, this should be admitted the more readily in the case of a captain than in that of other supervisors of enterprises. What if a captain was appointed with a provision that he does not make someone else a captain? It should be considered whether we accept Julian's opinion here as well. Suppose the shipowner expressly forbids you to appoint Titus as captain. However, it must be assumed that utility of people participating in naval transport requires that such cases should also be taken into account.

Ulpian agreed with Julian, who stated that the captain was considered not only the person appointed by the shipowner but also the person appointed by the captain himself. Adopting such a layer structure resulted in the shipowner being responsible for the behavior of the person appointed as captain without his knowledge[544]. Consequently,

543 Ulp. D. 14,1,1,pr. …*qui magistrum navi imposuit, teneri…*

544 See F. De Martino, *Studi sull''actio exercitoria'*, 'Labeo' 1958, vol. 4, p. 281; A. Kirschenbaum, *Sons, Slaves, and Freedmen in Roman Commerce*, Jerusalem 1987, pp. 101–104; M. Navarra, *Ricerche…*, p. 151. Peter Candy, who while interpreting the expression *ceterum si scit et passus est eum in nave magisterio fungi, ipse eum imposuisse videtur* ('anyway, if the shipowner is aware of and consented to a given person acting as the captain of a ship, it is considered that he has appointed this person

contrary to the content of the edict, it was not the person who appointed the captain that was responsible for his performance. Ulpian, however, considered that such a decision should be adopted in view of *utilitas* (*admittendum propter utilitatem*[545]).

The jurist went a step further and stated that due to *utilitas*, which this time he specified as *utilitas navigantium* (the utility of people participating in naval transport) Julian's opinion should also apply in situations when the shipowner generally stipulated that the captain would not be allowed to delegate his competences, or that he was forbidden to appoint a specific person as captain. In this way, *utilitas* allowed not only the introduction of a decision contrary to the content of the edict[546] but also the will of the shipowner[547].

A further example of Ulpian clarifying the concept of *utilitas* is the famous case inspired by the story of Barbarius Philippus[548], a fugitive slave who was appointed praetor:

> D. 1,14,3 (*Ulpianus libro trigesimo octavo ad Sabinum*)
> *Barbarius Philippus cum servus fugitivus esset, Romae praeturam petiit et praetor designatus est. sed nihil ei servitutem obstetisse ait Pomponius, quasi praetor non fuerit: atquin verum est praetura eum functum. et tamen videamus: si servus quamdiu latuit, dignitate praetoria functus sit, quid dicemus? quae edixit, quae decrevit, nullius fore momenti? an fore propter utilitatem eorum, qui apud eum egerunt vel lege vel quo alio iure? et verum puto nihil eorum reprobari: hoc*

personally') stated that it was a situation in which a shipowner was unaware that the function of the captain had been delegated to another person, and that he was liable under the *actio exercitoria* only if he allowed him to continue his activities upon learning of this, *Limits of Juristc Argument in the Exercitorian Edict* [in:] *Principle and Pragmatism in Roman Law*, B. Spagnolo, J. Sampson (ed.), Oxford–New York 2020, pp. 149–151. However, the analyzed phrase seems to be an insertion by Ulpian himself, stating that in the case of the shipowner's knowledge, no interpretation prob lem would arise. Similarly G. Pugliese, *In tema di actio exercitoria*, 'Labeo' 1957, vol. 3, p. 313, n. 17.

545 On this phrase and comparison of liability under the *actio exercitoria* and *institoria* in M. Navarra, *Ricerche…*, pp. 152–153.

546 This decision appears less severe for the shipowner when considering the opinion of Krzynówek, who argued that contractors primarily relied on their trust in the shipowner's person and property rather than the captain. Therefore, the scope of the *praepositio*, indicating the range of entrusted duties, seems to be much more important than the figure of the captain himself. See J. Krzynówek, *Granice praepositio przy actio exercitoria*, 'PK' 1994, 37, no. 3–4, pp. 177–178. However, this does not alter the fact that the decision prioritized the certainty of commercial transactions, and not the interests of the captain. Cf. also Ulp. D. 44,4,4,23 discussed below.

547 It is ironic that while Julian's opinion broke the clear scope of behavior, it simultaneously defined an alternative scope that jurists then interpreted very literally.

548 It is commonly accepted that Ulpian's questions about the validity of acts performed by the praetor-slave refer to Barbarius. However, the case does not mention him concealing his status when applying for the praetorship. Thus, the phrase *et tamen videamus* seems to introduce a new element for the jurist, and the case he is considering takes on a more theoretical character. Recently, extensively on the case itself, along with reporting on the rich literature, in B. Szolc-Nartowski, *Udział osób nieuprawnionych w wydaniu orzeczenia w postępowaniu cywilnym – uwagi na tle D. 1,14.3 i D. 41,3,44 pr.*, 'ZP' 2006, vol. 6, no. 2, pp. 97–116.

enim humanius est: cum etiam potuit populus Romanus servo decernere hanc potestatem, sed et si scisset servum esse, liberum effecisset. quod ius multo magis in imperatore observandum est. Barbarius Philippus, a fugitive slave, sought the praetorship in Rome, and was appointed praetor. Pomponius is of the opinion that his condition as a slave was no obstacle to him holding the office of praetor. And indeed, he performed the duties of that office. Still, let us consider the case of a slave keeping his condition secret while he performed his duty as praetor. Shall we say that all the edicts and decrees he issued will be of no legal force? Or will they be valid on account of utility of those who instituted proceedings before him either under the statutory law, or by virtue of some other legal act? Indeed, it is right not to consider these actions invalid, for such a view is more kind. Because the Roman people could give such power to a slave, and if they had known that he was a slave, they would have granted him his freedom. The right to do so applies even more to the emperor.

The jurist wondered about the validity of the acts performed by the praetor-slave, who was hiding his real status. Certainly, a slave did not have the capacity to issue legal acts. However, due to of utility of those who performed activities before the slave-praetor (*propter utilitatem eorum, qui apud eum egerunt*)[549], the acts performed with the involvement of the slave-praetor were to be considered valid. This approach protected the interests of these persons, ensured certainty of trading[550], and, from an interpretative point of view, also breached the unambiguous scope of legally prohibited behaviors.

549 Some researchers see *utilitas publica* in the criterion mentioned. Cf. M.E. Lucifredi Peterlongo, *Barbarius Philippus servus fugitivus praetor designatus est. Contributo all'esegesi di D. 1.14.3* [in:] *Contributi allo studio dell'esercizio di fatto di pubbliche funzioni*, Milano 1965, pp. 68–75; P. Cerami, *Problemi…*, pp. 399–405; V. Marotta, *Ulpiano…*, p. 95; B. Szolc-Nartowski, *Udział osób…*, p. 108. Taking Ulpian's words literally, Voci strongly opposed this interpretation and instead leaned towards perceiving a trace of *utilitas privata*. See P. Voci, *D.1,14,3. Note in tema di esercizio di fatto di pubbliche funzioni* [in:] *Studi di diritto romano pubblicati a cura della Facoltà di giurisprudenza dell'Università di Padova*, vol. 1, Padova 1985, pp. 633–635 (= *D.1,14,3. Note in tema di esercizio di fatto di pubbliche funzioni* [in:] *Studi in memoria di Enrico Guicciardi*, Padua 1975, pp. 59–80). On the other hand, Navarra concluded that the quoted case is an example of the confluence of both of these categories, *Ricerche…*, p. 146. Rampazzo discusses precisely the tradition of interpretation of this passage, focusing also on the various interpretations of the concept of *utilitas* throughout the centuries, *Quasi praetor…*, pp. 409–485. Considering the discussions proposed earlier, there is nothing else but to say that none of the authors mentioned is wrong. The category referred to by Ulpian remains the same *utilitas* (*publica*), allowing a departure from a literal interpretation, always in line with *utilitas privata*, and in the analyzed context additionally specified as an advantage for individuals acting before the praetor.

550 B. Szolc-Nartowski, *Udział osób…*, p. 108. See also A. Palma, *Humanior interpretatio. 'Humanitas' nell'interpretazione e nella normazione da Adriano ai Severi*, Torino 1992, p. 114. The situation would require a retroactive annulment of the laws. Cf. G.J. Blicharz, *Giudicare…*, p. 348, who noticed the connection between this passage and the previously analyzed Paul. D. 1,1,11, describing *utilitas* as a significant value for the evaluation of the praetorian law (p. 350). This comes evident from Pap. D. 1,1,7,1. However, such a list of sources shows that in the category of *utilitas* from Ulp. D. 1,14,3, Blicharz rightly saw not only a manifestation of pragmatism but a value underlying the legal order.

Another interesting *ad utilitatem* reference, the content of which was clarified, can also be found in fragment Ulp. D. 17,1,6,7[551]. Ulpian described there a rather complicated dispute that arose between Marius Paulus and Daphnis. Daphnis gave a mandate to Marius Paulus to become his guarantor for a fee. At the same time, Marius Paulus made an agreement with a third party that he would receive a payment from them if they won a lawsuit against Daphnis. His manipulation was discovered and, as a result, he was forced to pay the main debt. As he had become the guarantor as a result of an agreement concluded with Daphnis, Marius Paulus then tried to seek reimbursement from him under an *actio mandati*. In the rescript, however, it was decided that due to the two-facedness of Marius Paulus his actions did not deserve protection. At the end of the passage, Ulpian presents Marcellus' views on as to whether, if the payment for acting as guarantor had been made, an action should be granted at all:

D. 17,1,6,7 (*Ulpianus libro trigesimo primo ad edictum*)
... Marcellus autem sic loquitur de eo qui pecunia accepta spopondit, ut, si quidem hoc actum est, ut suo periculo sponderet, nulla actione agat, sin vero non hoc actum est, utilis ei potius actio competat: quae sententia utilitati rerum consentanea est.
On the other hand, Marcellus speaks about the one granting the surety, taking the money for it, that if it was agreed that it would be granted at the risk of the guarantor, he was not entitled to any action. In the absence of such an agreement, the guarantor will be entitled to an analogous [effective][552] action. This view corresponds to the utility of the things.

Marcellus argued that if the surety was granted by payment, and at the guarantor's own risk, regardless of his intentions, the guarantor had to be refused an *actio mandati* against the main debtor. This was due to the fact that the mandate was performed free of charge[553]. The existence of the payment therefore resulted in a different legal qualification of the contract. Marcellus, however, allowed the breach of this rule. According to him, if the parties did not agree that the surety would be issued at the risk of the guarantor (but still for the payment), the guarantor should be entitled to the *actio utilis*, as Marcellus put it. As noted by William M. Gordon, it is difficult to de-

551 Recently analyzed e.g. in A. Watson, *Mandate and the Boundaries of Roman Contract*, 'BIDR' 1991, vol. 33, pp. 41–48; W. M. Gordon, *Translation and Interpretation* [in:] *Critical Studies in Ancient Law, Comparative Law and Legal History: Essays in Honour of Alan Watson*, J. Cairns, O. Robinson (ed.), Oxford-Portland Oregon 2001, pp. 61–72; D. Gergely, *Salus rei publicae als Entscheidungsgrundlage des römischen Privatrechts*, Budapest 2015, pp. 1–37.

552 W. M. Gordon, *Translation...*, p. 72, also solved the problem of translating the concept of *actio utilis* in the same way.

553 Paul. D. 17,1,1,4 *Mandatum nisi gratuitum nullum est...* ('The mandate which is not gratuitous is invalid'); Iav. D. 17,1,36,1.

cide whether the jurist meant an analogous action, or an effective *actio mandati*[554]. Yet there is no doubt that this decision resulted in breaching the scope of legally permitted behaviors. This is also indicated by *utilitas,* further defined as *utilitas rerum.* Even if interpreting the content of the genitive attribute is not easy in this case[555], the role of the category remains unchanged.

Continuing this line of thought, jurists also referred *ad utilitatem* of entities, which were grant special legal protection. Julius Gallus Aquila (D. 26,7,34[556]) writes that, for the utility of pupils (*utilitas pupillorum*), it was allowed to break a ban on testifying by slaves against their owners[557] if the latter were accused of neglect (*accusatio suspecti tutoris*). In turn, according to Gaius (D. 27,10,17[558]) and Paulus (D. 27,10,11[559]), *utilitas furiosum* might legalize the activities of a mentally ill person's curator that would normally be considered invalid. The act of the curator making a donation from the property of a mentally ill person, or pledging that person's property, was therefore considered valid as long as it was in the interest of his pupil[560]. Paulus also believed that, due to the utility of trading (*utilitas promiscui usus*), an action should be brought against a minor in a situation when he became an heir of his father, who during his lifetime appointed people to run a commercial enterprise, and after his death the *institores* continued to

554 W.M. Gordon, *Translation…,* pp. 70–71. The first possibility is supported by A. Watson, *Mandate…,* pp. 47–48. Cf. also the beginning of Chapter One on the meanings of the term of *utilitas* in legal sources.

555 Both A. Watson, *Mandate…,* p. 45, as well as W.M. Gordon, *Translation…,* p. 72 opted not to translate the word *rerum* in this context. It is true that the meaning of *rerum* here is difficult to ascertain (cf., however, Sch. Ca 22 ad B. 14,1,6,7 (BS 712/12) …' Ἥτις τοῦ Μαρκέλλου γνώμη τῷ χρησίμῳ συνᾴδει τῶν δικαστηρίων [This opinion of Marcellus is in line with the practice of courts] and considerations in H. de Jong, *Ἐντολή (mandatum) in den Basiliken,* Leiden-Boston 2020, pp. 149–155). Its ambiguity and (occasionally) abstractness also make the content of the concept of *utilitas* very close to those cases where no genitive attribute accompanies the noun.

556 Aquila D. 26,7,34 *Respondit ad instruendam diligentiam iudicantis et pupillorum utilitatem admittendam servos quoque eorum* (*sc. tutorum* – JKC) *interrogari posse* ('He replied that in order to deliver information to the judges and due to utility of the pupils, their [*sc.* guardians'] slaves could also be questioned').

557 The prohibition of slaves' testimony against their owners attest Ulp. D. 48,18,1,18; Gord. C. 9,41,6. On this topic, see E. Loska, *Kilka uwag na temat zeznań niewolników w procesie karnym,* 'Zeszyty Naukowe KUL' 2017, vol. 60, no. 3, pp. 449–464.

558 Gai. D. 27,10,17 *Curator furiosi nullo modo libertatem praestare potest, quod ea res ex administratione non est: nam in tradendo ita res furiosi alienat, si id ad administrationem negotiorum pertineat: et ideo si donandi causa alienet, neque traditio quicquam valebit, nisi ex magna utilitate furiosi hoc cognitione iudicis faciat* ('Under no circumstances may a curator of a mentally ill person manumit such a person's slave, as it does not fall within the scope of curatorship. He effectively disposes property of the mentally ill by handing it over if this activity is part of his duties. And therefore, if he makes a donation [from the property of the mentally ill], it will not be valid unless the judge finds it made for the utility of the mentally ill [*utilitas furiosi*])'.

559 Paul. D. 27,10,11 *Pignus a curatore furiosi datum valet, si utilitate furiosi exigente id fecit* ('Pledging property by a curator of a mentally ill person is valid if it was done for the utility of that person [*utilitas furiosi*]').

560 The same list of sources was proposed in J.E. Rodríguez Diez, *Potestas alienandi…,* p. 172.

perform legal activities with third parties (Paul. D. 14,3,17,2[561]). As a rule, since the son remained under guardianship after the death of his father, any legal activities should be performed with the consent of the guardian[562]. In all of the above cases, however, *utilitas* allowed breaking the scope of what could seem prohibited behaviors.

Among the numerous *utilitatis causa* decisions in the interpretative scheme based on breaking the unambiguity of the legal rule understood as a normative entity, the above nine examples clarify the content of the *utilitas* category[563]. In all cases, referencing *utilitas* led to the same results: quoting *utilitas*, whether as a term on its own, or with a genitive attribute, always opened the way to proposing solutions different from those which would be based only on the literal interpretation of the letter of the law. This criterion then always performed a uniform function, which is, to some extent, technical in nature. It therefore seems that there is only one *utilitas* present in jurisprudence, only occasionally defined in one way or another in terms of the content.

Specifying the content of the category in comparison to all *ad utilitatem* references in the decisions taken *utilitatis causa* seems then relatively rare. These specifications always take the form of genitive attribute, pointing to the utility of specific entities. In these sources, *utilitas* undoubtedly moves towards the meaning of *utilitas privata*. Additionally, what draws attention is that in all the above-mentioned decisions *utilitas* plays the role of an argument, and (with the exception of Paul. D. 27,10,11 and Gai. D. 27,10,17) none of them belongs to the sphere of the *ius receptum*. The *ad utilitatem* reference could, therefore, result from the circumstances of the case or, simply, be a matter of style[564]. It then seems that if jurists themselves do not specify the content of the examined category, it is not necessary to do so. *Utilitas* of jurists and *utilitas* of rhetoricians appear as parallel categories, not only in effect but also in nature and (mostly) in content. The particular interest of the case did emerge from behind the *utilitatis causa* decisions, as it did from behind any other case. Nevertheless, the analyzed category did not refer to that interest, or at least not exclusively. The occasional

561 Paul. D. 14,3,17,2 *Si impubes patri habenti institores heres exstiterit, deinde cum his contractum fuerit, dicendum est in pupillum dari actionem propter utilitatem promiscui usus, quemadmodum ubi post mortem tutoris, cuius auctoritate institor praepositus est, cum eo contrahitur* ('If a minor son became an heir of his father, who appointed the persons supervising the enterprises, and contracts were still concluded with them, it should be stated that an action is granted against the pupil for the sake of the utility of commercial transactions, as it is done when, after the death of the guardian, with the consent of whom the enterprise supervisor was appointed, contracts are still concluded with him').

562 This way in A. Petrucci, *Protección de quienes contratan con empresas comerciales en la experiencia jurídica romana. Aplicaciones de la acción institoria*, 'Revista de Derecho Privado' 2007, no. 12–13, p. 201.

563 Moreover, the content of the category was clarified in two of Tryphoninus' decisions concerning the interpretation of declarations of intent, as well as in three cases that do not fit into the *status scripti et voluntatis* scheme but into the *status syllogismi*, as discussed below.

564 The genitive attributes accompanying *utilitas* are used by Tryphoninus, Aquila, Gaius, Ulpian and Paulus, and in the *supra scriptum* scheme also by Macer.

clarification of its content might be therefore considered a jurisprudence addition to the well-established interpretative scheme.

As in Cicero, jurisprudence's reference to this criterion indicates the fundamental purpose of the law, serving also as the main determinant of legal interpretation. Under the appearance of contradictions, this practice, in fact, allows to obtain greater inter-system axiological consistency. In the context of *utilitatis causa* decisions, the analyzed criterion is, as excellently described by Paturet, *un concept unifié et unifiant* ('a unified and unifying category')[565], even if its content was occasionally clarified.

3.2.3 Breaking the Unambiguity of a Linguistic Expression

3.2.3.1 *Covering a Wider Context with the Term*

The following sources illustrate the interpretation of the law understood not as a normative entity but as a lexical expression, as seen in the case of Caecina, or the interpretation of the provisions of the *lex Aquilia* carried out by Julian (D. 9,2,51,2). The Ciceronian postulate *ex utilitate, non ex litteris interpretari* is applied more literally here. The analyses focus on instances where the literal meanings of particular terms were broken, despite their apparent clarity. The sources illustrate how jurists went against the lexical scopes of terms to encompass factual states that, by their literal meanings, should not have fallen within their purview. These were the words whose meaning was sufficiently clear, or whose lexical meaning was determined by grammatical categories, such as number or tense. In the decisions discussed below, it was decided to break the literal meaning of terms, which resulted in either the broadening or narrowing of their interpretation. Consequently, the interpretation *ex utilitate* consistently led to the verification of the scope of the norm's application.

The sources quoted below contain examples where a broader context was included within the scope of the expression than would be indicated by the literal meaning of the term, as was the case in the previously analyzed D. 9,2,51,2. This phenomenon is perfectly illustrated by the excerpts from Paulus' writings, who recalled *utilitas* twice in the context of deliberations on the identity of objects:

565 A. Paturet, *Ulpien D. 1.1.1.2…*, p. 122.

D. 8,2,20,2 (*Paulus libro quinto decimo ad Sabinum*)
Si sublatum sit aedificium, ex quo stillicidium cadit, ut eadem specie et qualitate reponatur, utilitas exigit, ut idem intellegatur: nam alioquin si quid strictius interpretetur, aliud est quod sequenti loco ponitur: et ideo sublato aedificio usus fructus interit, quamvis area pars est aedificii.
If a building that rainwater is drained from was demolished in order to rebuild a construction of the same shape and character in its place, as *utilitas* demands, it should be regarded as the same building. Otherwise, if interpreted more strictly, the building that was erected later is something else, and thus, at the time of demolition, the usufruct expires although the area on which the building stands is part of it.

D. 44,2,14,pr. (*Paulus libro septuagesimo ad edictum*)
… idem corpus in hac exceptione non utique omni pristina qualitate vel quantitate servata, nulla adiectione deminutioneve facta, sed pinguius pro communi utilitate accipitur.
… In the case of this exception, however, the thing is not necessarily the same only if all its previous properties and its quantity are retained, without any addition or loss, but for the common utility this issue is treated more broadly.

Paulus speculated whether a building erected on the site of a previously demolished construction should be treated as a different (*aliud*) or the same (*idem*) building. The problem the jurist resolved brings to mind the paradox of the ship of Theseus. As Plutarch reports, after Theseus' return, the Athenians, wishing to preserve his ship, were replacing the old beams with new ones over time. Philosophers wondered whether the ship of Theseus remained the same entity[566]. However, what could become the subject of long philosophical disputes, presented only two opposing paths of interpretation from Paulus' perspective. According to the strict literal interpretation (*strictius*), it was a different building; according to the *ex utilitate* interpretation, it had to be considered the same construction. Since the jurist examined this issue in the context of the right to drain water from the roof to the neighbour's land, the first interpretation would lead to the termination of the limited real rights. As the new building was constructed in the same shape, Paulus found it useful to consider it the same structure, thus allowing the rights to be maintained[567].

The jurist investigated a similar issue by considering the problem of an identity of the object in the case of *exceptio rei iudicatae*. Paulus therefore did not require that

566 Plut., *Thes.* 23.
567 The fragment in question seems to have been largely overlooked by researchers focusing on the *utilitas* category. Cerami interprets it as practical *utility*, while also acknowledging that an implemented interpretation is more commonly associated with *aequitas* or *benignitas*. See P. Cerami, *Plena interpretatio*, [in:] *Studi in onore di Cesare Sanfilippo*, vol. 3, Milano 1983, pp. 152–154. Leptien briefly addressed it, noting a certain mental flexibility of the jurist. Yet, in terms of interpretation process, he limited himself to qualifying it as *interpretatio benigna*. See U. Leptien, *Utilitatis causa…*, p. 142; Idem, *'Utilitatis causa'…*, p. 66.

there should be absolutely no change in the item. Quite the contrary, he considered an object changed to some extent, whether in quality or quantity, to still be the same. The opposite interpretation would allow the resumption of already adjudicated cases in the event of any change in the object of the dispute.

Breaking the literal sense of the word *idem* (*aedificium/corpus*) was motivated each time by *utilitas* (*utilitas exigit*; *pro communi utilitate*) allowing for a broader understanding of the term. In the first fragment, the jurist clearly contrasts *utilitas* with the phrase *strictius interpretari* ('to interpret more strictly'). In the other one, however, it is correlated with the phrase *pinguius accipere* ('to treat more broadly'). In practice, the *ex utilitate* interpretation thus resulted in covering states of affairs which did not fall within the literal meaning of the term *idem*.

Ulpian similarly argued for breaking the lexical meaning of the term 'inheritance' (*bona*). The jurist discussed an action against a slave manumitted in a will who had stolen something from the inheritance before it was accepted by the heir. Due to the status of the slave, it was not possible to bring an *actio furti* in such cases. However, to ensure such behaviors did not to go unpunished[568], under the praetorian edict, *actio furti* were substituted by another action:

D. 47,4,1,10 (*Ulpianus libro trigesimo octavo ad edictum*)
Haec actio locum habet non tantum in rebus, quae in bonis fuerunt testatoris, sed et si heredis interfuit dolum malum admissum non esse, quo minus ad se perveniret. et ideo Scaevola plenius tractat et si eam rem subripuisset servus, quam defunctus pignori acceperat, hanc actionem honorariam locum habere: plenius enim causam bonorum hic accipimus pro utilitate. nam si in locum deficientis furti actionis propter servitutem hanc actionem substituit praetor, verisimile est in omnibus causis eum, in quibus furti agi potuit, substituisse. et in summa probatur hanc actionem et in rebus pigneratis et in rebus alienis bona fide possessis locum habere: idem et de re commodata testatori.
This action applies not only to items that belonged to a testator's property but also to those items that, in the legal interest of the heir, should not have been lost due to fraudulent acts. Hence, Scaevola more broadly recognizes that if a slave stole a thing the testator had received as a pledge, this praetorian action applies, because here, due to *utilitas*, we treat the concept of 'inheritance' more broadly. For if the praetor substituted this action in place of the one for theft, unavailable due to the slave status, it is reasonable to assume that he intended it to be substituted in all cases where an action for theft could be brought. And it is generally accepted that this action is applicable both to pledged items and to items that belong to others and are possessed in good faith. The same principle applies to items lent for use to the testator.

568 Cf. Ulp. D. 47,4,1,1.

Ulpian explained that the action did not only cover situations when a slave appropriated an item belonging to a testator's property, but, in Scaevola's view, it also applied where the subject of a pledge was stolen from a testator. Additionally, Ulpian stated that such an action could also be brought if a theft referred to someone else's property possessed in good faith, as well as those that had been lent to the testator for use. Thus, although it was an action analogous to the one of theft, its scope was shaped differently. This decision was explained by the jurist by extending the meaning of the term 'inheritance' (*bona*)[569]. In such cases, the concept should not be interpreted literally but more broadly (*plenius*)[570]. *Bona*, therefore, included both things belonging to a testator, and those that at the time of their death belonged to another person, but it was in the heir's interest that they should not be lost. As earlier in Paulus, *utilitas* allowed for breaking the lexical meaning of the term *bona*, and adopting a broader scope of it (*plenius accipere*).

An interesting example of breaking the meaning of the expression is also Ulpian's reflections on the *quod vi aut clam factum est* interdictum, which an owner of the land, or a servitude right holder was entitled to[571]. They had a right to demand that the effects of the violation be removed if something was done on the property by force or in secret. The jurist's doubts arise in this case against the background of Latin grammar:

> D. 43,24,11,4 (*Ulpianus libro septuagesimo primo ad edictum*)
> *Quod ait praetor:* QVOD VI AVT CLAM FACTVM EST, *ad quod tempus referatur, videamus, utrum ad praeteritum an ad praesens. quae species apud Iulianum exposita est: ait enim in hoc interdicto praesentis temporis significationem accipi debere. si tamen, inquit, ex opere damnum datum fuerit aut dominus aut is, cuius fundo nocitum erit, sua impensa id sustulerit, utilius probari, quod Iulianus temptat, ut et damnum sarciatur et impendia restituantur.*
> Let us consider what period of time the praetor's words 'what has been done by force or in secret' refer to: the past or the present moment? This point was clarified in Julian's writings. He claims that this interdictum is about the present tense. If, however, he says, as a result of the work, the damage was caused, and either an owner, or a person whose land was damaged, repaired the damage at his own expense, then it is more useful to recognize what Julian assumes, that is, both to compensate for the damage and reimburse the expenses incurred.

569 The term *bona* means 'possessions, property, or estate'. In legal terms, it often relates to the concept of inheritance. See OLD, s. v. *bonum*; J. Sondel, *Słownik…*, s. v. *bona*.

570 On this topic, see P. Cerami, *Plena interpretatio…*, pp. 107–154.

571 More on the interdictum, as well as on the entitlement to this legal instrument in P. Van Warmelo, *Interdictum quod vi aut clam*, 'Acta Juridica' 1962, vol. 15, pp. 15–37; I. Fargnoli, *Studi sulla legittimazione attiva all'interdetto quod vi aut clam*, Milano 1998, and recently M. Sukačić, *Pitanje aktivne legitimacije za primjenu interdikta quod vi aut clam u klasičnom rimskom pravu*, 'Zbornik radova Pravnog fakulteta u Splitu' 2020, vol. 57, no. 4, pp. 1057–1078.

Ulpian tried to decide about the meaning of the expression *factum est,* and wondered whether it should be applied to the past or present moment. Grammatically, *factum est* may constitute the *indicative perfecti passivi* for the third person singular, and is then translated as 'was done', or it may be determined by the form *est* given in the present tense. In the latter case, the concept of *factum* is a past participle and the whole expression is translated as 'is done'. Quoting Julian's opinion, Ulpian agreed with the latter interpretation.

Such a decision had its practical consequences. In this case, the jurist reflected whether the interdictum was to relate to the factual state at the time of its granting (*interdictum in praesens relatum*), or to the one that existed earlier (*interdictum in praeteritum relatum*). Despite the fact that the meaning of the expression was established, and the interdictum defined as the *interdictum in praesens relatum,* following Julian, Ulpian allowed for the possibility of extending its use. If an owner of the land repaired the damage at his own expense, and restored the previous state by himself, he could apply for an interdictum, and demand compensation[572]. In such circumstances, it was necessary to depart from the understanding of the expression *factum est* established by jurists, and to extend the application of the interdictum to pre-existing factual states.

A different interpretation of this fragment was presented by Kaser, who speculated that the compilers replaced the phrase *in praeteriti temporis* with *in praesentis temporis.* The classification of the interdictum as *in praeteritum relatum* seemed more practical to the German researcher, and thus he justified the reference to *utilitas.* Consequently, the expression *si tamen,* introducing a contrasting thought, was considered by him to be an interpolation[573]. It seems, however, that what raised Kaser's doubts as to the authenticity of the fragment actually supports its classical provenance. The introduction of the opposite concept through the phrase *si tamen* perfectly corresponds to the appointment of *utilitas* as the factor breaking the previously established meaning of the expression *factum est.* Then the analyzed concept is not an argument external to the discussed considerations but complements their course.

Another example of breaking the literal meaning of an expression is Julian's opinion on the possibility of applying warranty for damage that was to be caused on the neighbouring land by a defective building (*cautio damni infecti*):

572 Damage was a necessary condition for applying for the *quod vi aut clam* interdictum. Cf. J.-F. Gerkens, *Selbsthilfe bei Brandgefahr. Überlegungen zu den Rechtsmitteln im Prinzipat* [in:] *Liber Amicorum Guido Tsuno,* P. Thomas, F. Sturm, J. Otto, H. Mori (ed.), Frankfurt am Main 2013, p. 116 along with the literature cited therein.

573 M. Kaser, *Restituere als Prozeßgegenstand. Die Wirkungen der litis contestatio auf den Leistungsstand im römischen Recht,* München 1968, pp. 30–31, esp. n. 2.

D. 39,2,9,pr. (*Ulpianus libro quinquagesimo tertio ad edictum*)
Hoc amplius Iulianus posse dici compellendum eum, ut etiam de praeterito damno caveret: quod enim re integra custoditur, hoc non inique etiam post ruinam aedium praestabitur. integra autem re unusquisque cogitur aut de damno infecto cavere, aut aedibus carere quas non defendit. denique, inquit, si quis propter angustias temporis aut quia rei publicae causa aberat non potuerit damni infecti stipulari, non inique praetorem curaturum, ut dominus vitiosarum aedium aut damnum sarciat aut aedibus careat. sententiam Iuliani utilitas comprobat.
According to Julian, it can be broader stated that a person should also be compelled to provide security for the past damages. Since protection is applied while the building is intact, it will not be unjust to provide it also after its collapse. On the other hand, when the building remains intact, anyone can be required to either ensure security for the future damage, or lead to the loss of ownership of the buildings if the person does not defend the case the buildings are the subject of. Additionally, Julian states that if someone was unable to enter into a stipulation for covering future damages due to time constraints or because of an absence related to public affairs, it is not unjust that the praetor should ensure that the owner of the damaged buildings would either repair the damage, or lose their ownership. *Utilitas* confirms Julian's opinion.

According to Ulpian, Julian insisted that in the event of such damage, a distinction should be made between the reasons for failing to ensure warranty. Consequently, despite the damage was no longer being to happen (*infectum*) but already occurred (*iam factum*), the praetor could act as if the *cautio* had been made unless the warranty was not accepted not because of the negligence of the neighbouring land owner but, for instance, their absence resulting from conducting public affairs, or a short time interval between realizing the threat and the occurrence of the damage. Michael Rainer describes Julian's decision as an 'extremely deliberate extension' (*überaus sinnvolle Erweiterung*) of this institution[574]. This is exactly what *utilitas* quoted at the end of Ulpian's fragment seems to indicate, allowing for breaking of the literal meaning of the term *damnum infectum*.

Finally, breaking the literal sense of the expression appears to be the essence of Ulpian's deliberations below:

D. 13,5,3,2 (*Ulpianus libro vicesimo septimo ad edictum*)
Si is, qui et iure civili et praetorio debebat, in diem sit obligatus, an constituendo teneatur? et Labeo ait teneri constitutum, quam sententiam et Pedius probat: et adicit Labeo vel propter has potissimum pecunias, quae nondum peti possunt, constituta inducta: quam sententiam non invitus probarem: habet enim utilitatem, ut ex die obligatus constituendo se eadem die soluturum teneatur.

574 M. Rainer, *Julian und die cautio damni infecti*, 'Fundamina: A Journal of Legal History' 2010, vol. 16, no. 1, p. 360.

> Is a person in debt under both the civil law and praetorian law liable for an informal promise if he is obliged to act on it within a specified period? Labeo says he is, and so does Pedius. Additionally, Labeo states that informal promises were introduced primarily because of those pecuniary obligations that could not yet be claimed. I could fully accept that opinion. It is in line with *utilitas* that a person required to perform on a specific date, for making an informal promise to pay, would be bound on that day.

The problem concerns the admissibility of submitting an informal payment promise (*constitutum debiti*) by a debtor obliged to perform their obligation within a specified period. An excellent analysis of this fragment has been recently presented by Johannes Platschek[575]. According to his findings, the solution proposed by Labeo (and then adopted by Pedius) could raise doubts in the context of the literal interpretation of the praetorian edict[576]. According to its content, the debtor undertook to pay the *pecunia debita*[577]. Platschek showed that some jurists, including Ulpian, seemed to understand the concept of *debitum* in terms of being both due and payable, and not merely due[578]. Since according to the general rules, it was not possible to effectively demand performance before the claim became due and payable[579], the solution proposed by Labeo broke the literal (at least according to some) meaning of the term *pecunia debita*. It is precisely this circumstance that explains Ulpian's reference to the category of *utilitas*[580].

575 J. Platschek, *Das Edikt De pecunia constituta: Die römische Erfüllungszusage und ihre Einbettung in den hellenistischen Kreditverkehr*, München 2013, pp. 111–126. See also P. Costa, *'Pecunia constituta': ipotesi interpretative*, 'SDHI' 2011, vol. 77, pp. 129–256.

576 The doubts as to the admissibility of this solution were mentioned and finally dispelled by Justinian: C. 4,18,2.

577 Ulp. D. 13,5,1,1 *Ait praetor*: QVI PECVNIAM DEBITAM CONSTITVIT… ('The praetor says: "Who unofficially promised to pay the money due [and payable]"'). The proposed translation is explained by the analysis of the fragment.

578 Cf. Ulp. D. 45,1,41,1 *Quotiens autem in obligationibus dies non ponitur, praesenti die pecunia debetur, nisi si locus adiectus spatium temporis inducat, quo illo possit perveniri. verum dies adiectus efficit, ne praesenti die pecunia debeatur…* ('Whenever the time for making the performance is not specified in the content of the obligations, the money is due and payable on the same day, unless an additional factor indicates a longer period of time in which it can be received. However, adding a date guarantees that the money is not due today …'). The excerpt makes it clear that in this context the term *pecunia debita* (or the expression *pecunia debetur*) refers to money that can be effectively claimed from the debtor.

579 Cf. e.g. Paul. D. 12,6,10; I. 3,15,2. See also J. Platschek, *Das Edikt…*, pp. 117–122.

580 Interestingly, although Ulpian recognized the utility of Labeo's decision, it appears that this time he adhered to the literal interpretation of the edict. As Platschek already noted, this is indicated by the use of imperfect subjunctive *probarem*, in in this case expressing an unreal or non-actual scenario (*coniunctivus irrealis*). In other words, Ulpian appears to be saying: 'I could accept it, but I did not'. See ibidem, pp. 113–114, 122, 125.

3.2.3.2 *Verifying Legal Classification*

Breaking the literal meaning could also result in accepting a different legal classification of behavior, as seen in Caecina's case or Julian's interpretation of the *lex Aquilia* (D. 9,2,51,2). A similar effect is evident in Ulpian's interpretation of the provisions of the praetorian edict regarding the *quod vi aut clam* interdictum:

> D. 43,24,5,7 (*Ulpianus libro septuagesimo ad edictum*)
> *Si quis, cum non denuntiasset opus se facturum eique denuntiatum esset ne faceret, fecerit, utilius puto probandum vi eum fecisse.*
> If someone did not inform that he was about to begin works but was himself notified not to undertake it, and, nevertheless, he did so, I believe it is more useful to recognize that he comitted the act by force.

This fragment relates to the omission of the obligation to notify about the intention to carry out works[581]. Jan J. Ram provided an excellent analysis of the decision, noting that the phrase *puto probandum* ('I believe it should be recognized') suggests doubts about the legal classification of the described facts[582]. According to the literal interpretation, the one who failed to inform did it *clam*, namely secretly[583]. However, due to the additional circumstances, that is the independent notification for the person not to conduct the work, their act should be classified as having been committed by force (*vi*)[584]. *Utilitas* does not introduce here, at least not exclusively, a more favorable decision for the person entitled to an interdictum[585]. Above all, it seems to open the way for a different legal classification than what the literal understanding of the expression *non denuntiasset* would suggest.

Similarly, Papinian proposed a different legal classification than that resulting from the literal understanding of the praetorian edict:

> D. 17,1,54,pr. (*Papinianus libro vicesimo septimo quaestionum*)
> *Cum servus extero se mandat emendum, nullum mandatum est. sed si in hoc mandatum intercessit ut servus manumitteretur nec manumiserit, et pretium consequetur dominus ut venditor et affectus ratione mandati agetur: finge filium naturalem vel fratrem esse (placuit enim pru-*

581 Cf. Ulp. D. 43,24,5,2; Ulp. D. 43,24,11,11.
582 J.J. Ram, *Disputatio iuridica inauguralis de interdicto quod vi aut clam*, Traiecti ad Rhenum 1738, pp. 10–11.
583 This way in Ulp. D. 43,24,3,7.
584 Another instance of Ulpian providing similar legal qualification is preserved in a different fragment. In this instance, however, Ulpian cites the opinions of other jurists. Cf. Ulp. D. 43,24,1,7 *Sed et si contra testationem denuntiationemque fecerit, idem* [*sc. vi* – JKC] *esse Cascellius et Trebatius putant: quod verum est.*
585 J.J. Ram, *Disputatio…*, p. 11.

> *dentioribus affectus rationem in bonae fidei iudiciis habendam). quod si de suis nummis emptor pretium dederit (neque enim aliter iudicio venditi liberari potest), quaeri solet, an utiliter de peculio agere possit. et verius et utilius videtur praetorem de huiusmodi contractibus servorum non cogitasse, quo se ipsi mala ratione dominis auferrent.*
> When a slave mandates a third party to purchase him, the contract is void. But if the very same contract was given for the purpose of manumitting the slave, and the purchaser has not done so, the owner as vendor will both claim the selling price as well, on the ground of affection, will file an *actio mandati*. Imagine that the slave is a biological son or brother of the vendor (as jurists felt that the ground of affection should be taken into account in good-faith actions). If, on the other hand, the purchaser paid with his own money – for otherwise he cannot be absolved of liability arising from the sale – it is usual to ask whether he can effectively bring an *actio de peculio*. It seems more lawful and useful that the praetor did not mean such agreements made by slaves, by which they could free themselves from the power of their owners.

Papinian's reflections address a situation where a slave ordered a third party to purchase and manumit him. The jurist's investigations appear to consist of two aspects. First, if the purchaser did not manumit the slave, the slave owner could claim both the selling price and the execution of the agreement. Both contracts were therefore considered validly concluded. Second, there was doubt as to whether the slave's mandatarius-purchaser could claim reimbursement of expenses form the slave's owner, having fulfilled the agreement and manumitted the slave. The doubts concerned the possibility of filing the praetorian *actio de peculio* under the obligation arising as a result of the mandate being given by the (already manumitted) slave who administered a *peculium*.

Papinian answered negatively, referring to the original intent of, as Giaro aptly put it, 'the historical creator of the edict'[586], which is a rarity for jurists. The expression *et verius et utilius videtur praetorem de huiusmodi contractibus servorum non cogitasse* seems to refer to the linguistic analysis of the phrase contained in the praetorian edict, as the text must have been a point of reference for an attempt to reconstruct the assumptions underlying this act. The expression *videtur… non cogitasse* suggests the interpretation rejected by Papinian, although technically possible, was unacceptable as it distorted the legal institution[587]. Thus, it can be assumed that according to the literal understanding of the praetorian edict an *actio de peculio* against a family head was allowed. It is even likely that in this case, Papinian was referring to the passage preserved in the Ulpian's commentary *Ad edictum*[588]:

586 T. Giaro, *Papinian und die reductio ad absurdum* [in:] *Argumenta Papiniani: Studien zur Geschichte und Dogmatik des Privatrechts*, J. D. Harke (ed.), Berlin, Heidelberg 2013, p. 47, along with the fragment analysis on pp. 46–48.

587 U. Babusiaux, *Id quod actum est: zur Ermittlung des Parteiwillens im klassischen römischen Zivilprozess*, München 2006, p. 185.

588 On the formula in O. Lenel, *Das Edictum…*, pp. 220–222.

D. 15,1,1,2 (*Ulpianus libro undetricesimo ad edictum*)
Verba autem edicti talia sunt: QVOD CVM EO, QVI IN ALTERIVS POTESTATE ESSET, NEGOTIVM GESTVM ERIT.
And the wording of the edict is as follows: 'When a legal transaction has been made with the one who remains under the authority of another person'.

According to the literal interpretation, a transaction mandated by a slave to a third party could be classified as *negotium gerere* with one who remains under another's authority (*cum eo, qui in alterius potestate est*). Yet according to Papinian, actions of slaves who cunningly (*mala ratione*) wanted to free themselves from their owners' power could not be considered as administering assigned property. Thus, Papinian's reference to *utilitas*, accompanied by *veritas*, allowed breaking the literal understanding of the expression *negotium gerere*, narrowing its content, and excluding similar behaviors from being considered legal acts under the edict.

3.2.3.3 *Modifying the Group of Addressees of the Legal Norm*

Jurists also referred to *utilitas* to modify the circle of addressees of the regulation in relation to the one based on the literal understanding of the norm. Ulpian did so, specifying the circle of people who were to be affected by infamy as a result of their stage performances. The broader context of the regulation is essential to understand this modification:

D. 3,2,1 (*Iulianus libro primo ad edictum*)
Praetoris verba dicunt: INFAMIA NOTATVR (...) QVI ARTIS LVDICRAE PRONVNTIANDIVE CAVSA IN SCAENAM PRODIERIT.
The praetor's words are: 'Infamy affects the one who (...) appears on stage to present a performance or recitation'.

D. 3,2,2,5 (*Ulpianus libro sexto ad edictum*)
Ait praetor: QVI IN SCAENAM PRODIERIT, INFAMIS EST. *scaena est, ut Labeo definit, quae ludorum faciendorum causa quolibet loco, ubi quis consistat moveaturque spectaculum sui praebiturus, posita sit in publico privatove vel in vico, quo tamen loco passim homines spectaculi causa admittantur. eos enim, qui quaestus causa in certamina descendunt et omnes propter praemium in scaenam prodeuntes famosos esse Pegasus et Nerva filius responderunt.*
The praetor says: 'Whoever performed on stage is infamous'. According to Labeo's definition, a stage is where someone can stand, or move to perform a spectacle, and what is placed anywhere to put up a performance. It does not matter whether it is a public, or a private place, or a place in a village, as long as all people without any exception have access to the performance. Pegasus and Nerva the Son held the opinion that all those who stoop to compete for profit as well as perform on stage to get a prize are considered *famosi*.

D. 3,2,4,pr.–1 (*Ulpianus libro sexto ad edictum*)

pr. *Athletas autem Sabinus et Cassius responderunt omnino artem ludicram non facere: virtutis enim gratia hoc facere. et generaliter ita omnes opinantur et utile videtur, ut neque thymelici neque xystici neque agitatores nec qui aquam equis spargunt ceteraque eorum ministeria, qui certaminibus sacris deserviunt, ignominiosi habeantur.* 1. *Designatores autem, quos Graeci* βραβευτὰς *appellant, artem ludicram non facere Celsus probat, quia ministerium, non artem ludicram exerceant. et sane locus iste hodie a principe non pro modico beneficio datur.*

pr. On the other hand, Sabinus and Cassius claimed that athletes were by no means performers. They fight to show their courage. In fact, everyone says so, and it seems useful that neither musicians, nor wrestlers, nor charioteers, nor those who sprinkle water on horses, nor other servants from among those who help in organizing sacred competitions are considered disgraced. 1. Celsus further confirms that judges at the games, who are called *brabeutai* by the Greeks, do not perform a spectacle, because they serve, and not perform. Currently, this function is granted by the princeps as an important privilege.

These excerpts comment on the praetorian edict that lists acts resulting in the loss of honor, either due to committing a reprehensible act or practising a profession that brings disgrace. Such professions included those related to the so-called *ars ludicra*, namely the art of presenting a show on stage. Labeo, from the Proculeian school, defined the term 'stage' broadly, focusing on its function, rather than its construction. Essentially, it could be situated in any place with free access to it, used to stage performances (*spectacula*). These, according to Pegasus, Nerva the Son, and also the Proculeians, were provided by all who took part in competitions for profit (*quaestus causa*), or performed on stage to obtain a prize (*propter praemium*). Consequently, they were subject to the edict.

However, such generalization of the above categories turned out to be too broad in practice, as evidenced by Ulp. D. 3,2,4,pr.–1, where a fragment of the commentary *Ad edictum* is preserved. The term *ars ludicra* used in the edict must have raised doubts[589]. Although commonly associated with the art of acting, the sources quoted above indicate its broader understanding. It is difficult to otherwise interpret the fact that Ulpian nominally referred to the expression *ars ludicra* not only in the context of athletes' fights but even in the context of refereeing in sports competitions[590]. Rather than recognizing persons performing these functions could be included in the same group as

589 A thorough analysis of this concept, based on extensive source material, is offered in E.J. Jory, *Ars Ludicra and the Ludus Talarius*, 'Bulletin of the Institute of Classical Studies' 1995, vol. 40, no. 66, pp. 140–145.

590 *Designatores* were recognized as experts in their field, holding particular authority. Cf. A. Wacke, *Gloria und virtus als Ziel athletischer Wettkämpfe und die Unbescholtenheit der Athleten sowie die erlaubten Sportwetten nach römischen Rechtsquellen* [in:] *Kultur(en) – Formen des Alltäglichen in der Antike. Festschrift für Ingomar Weiler zum 75. Geburtstag*, P. Mauritsch, C. Ulf (ed.), Graz 2013, p. 54 along with the literature cited therein.

actors[591], this suggests that *ars ludicra* could encompass various stage performances[592]. This thesis is also supported by semantics. Derived from the verb *ludere*, the adjective *ludicer* is associated with activities related to play, the stage but also sports[593]. Often in the noun form, the term was also used precisely in the context of athletic fights[594] and circus games[595], which were referred to as *ludi* too. Considering the above, and bearing in mind that the term *ars* could mean not only 'art' but also 'dexterity', or 'craftsmanship', the expression *ars ludicra* might be given several meanings, including the more 'Olympic' one. If so, the question as to whether *athletae* and *designatores* practiced *ars ludicra*, which in fact touches upon the problem of interpreting the term, is perfectly understandable[596].

However, making athletes, frequently worshiped as demigods by the public opinion[597], subject to the edict, as well as those who had the privilege of refereeing in sports competitions, was counterproductive to regulatory goals. Ulpian, agreeing with his predecessors, stated that neither group was subject to the edict because they did not perform the *ars ludicra* (implicitly: in the edict's sense). Their active participation in a spectacle, even if it entailed receiving financial rewards or other benefits, was not considered immoral if motivated by the desire to show one's bravery (*virtus*), or resulted from performing a special function (*ministerium*[598]) during games, such as in the case of referees.

In the second part of fragment D. 3,2,4,pr., Ulpian enumerated further categories of people not subject to the edict. Referring to *utilitas* (*utile videtur*), he mentioned choral

591 This way e.g. in G. Horsmann, *Die Bescholtenheit der Berufssportler im römischen Recht. Zur Bedeutung von 'artem ludicram facere' und 'in scaenam prodire' in den juristischen Quellen*, 'Nikephoros' 1994, vol. 7, pp. 207–227. A contrary opinion is presented by Wacke, who argues that athletes and actors constituted two independent and distinct categories. See A. Wacke, *Gloria…*, p. 52.

592 It cannot be ruled out that the term 'stage performer' might also be overly restrictive. Cf. Cic., *De orat.* 2,20 *ars ipsa ludicra armorum et gladiatori et militi prodest* ('the ability to wield a weapon is of value to both the gladiator and soldier').

593 *Etymological Dictionary…*, M. de Vaan (ed.), p. 350.

594 Cf. e.g. Vell. 2,123,1,6–7 *interfuturus athletarum certaminis ludicro.*

595 Cf. e.g. Liv., AUC 27,35,3,2–3 *Olympiae ludicrum*; 28,7,14,4 *Olympiorum sollemne ludicrum.*

596 The fact that both athletes and referees performed their roles, at least in part, for profit (and not only for prestige) also worked against them, in terms of interpretation, as competition winners received financial prizes. In practice, they allowed athletes to repay loans which covered the costs of living and training. Occasionally, however, athletes were able to accumulate considerable fortune. A. Wacke, *Gloria…*, pp. 50–52, expressed doubts about the use of the term *quaestus* (profit) to denote a win bonus, as financial prizes were not legally enforceable. Additionally, the general phrase *in scaenam prodire* could apply to both of the aforementioned categories of persons. Although athletes usually competed on a sandy arena, and not on a wooden landing, as emphasized by Wacke (ibid., p. 50), it should be noted that there are sources testifying athletes fought *in scaena*. Cf. Plin., NH 36,120 *diversis duabus per medium scaenis athletas edidit* ('he organized sports performances in the middle [of the amphitheatre] on two different stages').

597 E. Franciosi, *Gloriae et virtutis causa. Status sociale e giuridico degli atleti nel mondo romano* [in:] *Studi per Giovanni Nicosia*, Milano 2007, vol. 3, pp. 437–468.

598 A. Wacke even equated this term with *officium*, *Gloria…*, p. 54.

singers (*thymelici*), charioteers (*agitatores*), and once again athletes, this time describing them with the synonymous Greek term *xystici*[599]. These groups in fact participated in every form of the Roman *spectaculum*: theatre performances (*ludi theatrales*)[600], circus horse races (*ludi circenses*), and amphitheatre fights (*ludi gymnastici*)[601]. Hence, there should be no doubt that they took part in performances easily characterised by the adjective *ludicer*, even if it does not appear explicitly in the quoted passage.

A question arises as to the reason for excluding them from the circle of people affected by infamy. Although *xystici* and *agitatores* presented their bravery during competitions, it is more difficult to relate this value to choral singers[602]. Additionally, in the same breath, Ulpian mentioned those who performed the ritual act of sprinkling horses with water (*qui aquam equis spargunt*)[603], as well as generally other persons performing special duties during the games (*cetera ministeria*; since the jurist listed the entities, the term *ministeria* should be interpreted personally, not materially, and therefore as 'persons providing service, or function', and not 'a service, an assistance'[604]). The expression *ceteraque eorum ministeria* suggests that both groups indicated by Ulpian belong to the same category of people actively participating in the organization of the sacred games (*qui certaminibus sacris deserviunt*). The aforementioned *designatores* were also included here. Excluding them from not being subject to edict was not due to the fact they presented a special *virtus*, or enjoyed the princeps' favour[605] but because of the noble circumstances in which they performed their functions. The *certamina sacra* celebrated every four years, which should be distinguished from ordinary games[606], traditionally included the triad of musical, gymnastic and equestrian agon[607]. What

599 Ibid., p. 53.

600 *Thymelici* performed at the Theatre of Pompey in 17 BCE when the *ludos saeculares* (games of the century) were celebrated. Cf. fragment of the *quindecimviri* edict CIL 6,877 *ludos quos honorarios dierum VII adiecimus ludis sollemnibus committimus Nonis Iun(iis) Latinos in theatro / ligneo quod est ad Tiberim h(ora) II Graecos thymelicos in theatro Pompei h(ora) III* ('We combined the games organized with the officials' money, lasting seven days, with the celebration games. In the June nones, Latin [plays] will be staged in the wooden theatre on the Tiber at two o'clock, Greek choral performances in the Theatre of Pompey at three o'clock').

601 An interesting discussion on these three places of entertainment can be found in K. M. Coleman, *Public Entertainments* [in:] *The Oxford Handbook of Social Relations in the Roman World*, M. Peachin (ed.), Oxford 2011, pp. 335–357.

602 A. Wacke, *Gloria…*, p. 53, n. 69.

603 They should not be confused with ordinary grooms, ibidem.

604 This meaning is also noted by dictionaries. See e. g. OLD, s. v. *ministerium*.

605 A contrary opinion is presented by Wacke, who argues that the fact that *designatores* were not subject to the edict was due to the imperial bestowal of their role. See A. Wacke, *Gloria…*, p. 54.

606 Ibid., p. 49.

607 This tradition dates back to the beginning of the 6th century BCE and comes from Greece but was also preserved within the Roman Empire. On the games in Naples, see Strab., 5,4,7 νυνὶ δὲ πεντετηρικὸς ἱερὸς ἀγὼν συντελεῖται παρ᾽ αὐτοῖς, μουσικός τε καὶ γυμνικὸς ('And at the present time, sacred competitions are celebrated by them every four years, both in music and gymnastics'). It is also worth getting acquainted with the fragmentally preserved inscription IvO 56 of 2 BCE,

stands out here is the fact it corresponded perfectly with the categories of choral singers, athletes and charioteers mentioned by Ulpian. The solemn aspect of sacred competitions seems to determine the overtone of the entire fragment, not just its final part. As the PanHellenic Games were distinguished from the ordinary games, it would be unacceptable to include the participants of the competition from the group addressed in the edict[608], even if a literal interpretation allowed to classify them as going on stage *artis ludicrae causa*. The barely noticeable reference to *utilitas*, reinforced by the unique phrase *ita omnes opinantur*[609], allowed breaking the linguistic understanding of the expression present in the edict. As rightly pointed out by Hartmut Leppin[610] and Andreas Wacke[611], it was not about establishing exceptions to the rule of imposing consequences on those who presented performances but about establishing the limits of the meaning of the phrase *artis ludicrae causa in scaenam prodire* on the basis of the praetorian edict in order to specify the circle of addressees of the norm in a manner consistent with morality.

The identical function explains the use of *utilitas* also in the following passage:

D. 26,4,5,2 (*Ulpianus libro trigesimo quinto ad edictum*)
In legitimis [et in his, qui a magistratibus dantur,] quaesitum est, an uni decerni tutela possit. et ait Labeo et uni recte tutelam decerni: posse enim aliquos vel absentes vel furiosos esse: quae sententia utilitatis gratia admittenda est, ut uni decernatur administratio.
Regarding legal guardians [and those appointed by magistrates], the questions was asked about whether tutelage could be granted to one person only. Labeo says tutelage can be effectively granted to one person only, as the other guardians may be absent, or mentally ill. This opinion should be adopted for the sake of *utilitas*, so that even one person alone can be granted this function.

found in Olympia, which also mentions the games established by Augustus in Naples. It mentions not only the organization of sports, equestrian and music competitions but, what is particularly interesting, also the amount of financial prizes. The famous *Agon Neronianus* in 60 CE also included the three competitions mentioned. See E. Dvorjetski, *Leisure, Pleasure and Healing: Spa Culture and Medicine in Ancient Eastern Mediterranean*, Leiden 2007, p. 380.

608 In other cases, therefore, these individuals could indeed be subjected to the edictal provisions, which in relation to choral singers is for example confirmed by the *interpretatio* of Constantine's constitution of 319. See C.Th. 2,19,1 *interpr. …si turpibus personis, id est infamibus fuerit hereditas derelicta, hoc est (…) certe thymelicis* ('if the inheritance is left to immoral people, that is to the defamed, that is […] certainly to choral singers').

609 As noticed by A. Wacke, *Gloria…*, p. 57, it is the only such statement in the Digest. Jurists used to use more cautious expressions, such as *plerique* ('majority') or, much less frequently, *fere omnes* ('almost everyone').

610 H. Leppin, *Histrionen: Untersuchungen zur sozialen Stellung von Bühnenkünstlern im Westen des Römischen Reiches zur Zeit der Republik und des Principats*, Bonn 1992, pp. 78–82.

611 A. Wacke, *Gloria…*, pp. 52–53.

The reflections focus on who could be granted legal tutelage (*tutela legitima*)[612]. According to Law of the Twelve Tables, in the event of failing to appoint a testamentary guardian, agnate relatives were appointed guardians *ipso iure*. This collective appointment seems to be crucial for understanding the above passage. Although the content of the Law of the Twelve Tables is known only through its reconstruction, what draws one's attention is the fact jurists habitually used the plural forms[613] when writing about appointing legal guardians. It can therefore be said with high probability that the word *tutores* appeared in the act. The problem jurists debated on is therefore a linguistic one[614]. They tried to settle whether tutelage could be granted to *et uni*, namely to one person only, when other agnates were still alive. First Labeo and then Ulpian affirmed this. To further justify his opinion, the former stated that some *tutores* who should be granted their function by the law could be mentally ill, or absent. Each of these circumstances precluded the possibility of reliable supervision over the pupil's interests. Hence, tutelage should be granted to those who could fulfil their duties responsibly, even if it was only one person, and the law referred to a collective appointment. Then, although the proposed solution was certainly in line with the pupil's interests[615], the chief role of referring to *utilitas* remained unchanged. Ulpian referred to this category

612 The fragment also mentions the guardians appointed by officials in the absence of testamentary or statutory guardians (the so-called *tutela dativa*), which was expressed with the phrase *et in his, qui a magistratibus dantur*. However, this part is rightly considered an interpolation. The official had the power to appoint a person who was both present and mentally healthy from the very beginning. This way in S. Solazzi, *La prestazione dell'auctoritas e la pluralità dei tutori*, 'Atti della R. Acc. di scienze morali e politiche di Napoli' 1935, vol. 57, pp. 212–235; H. Ankum, *'Utilitatis causa receptum'. On the pragmatical methods…*, p. 8, n. 4; A. Guzmán Brito, *Caución tutelar en derecho romano*, Pamplona 1974, p. 250; M. Navarra, *Ricerche…*, p. 167, n. 355.

613 G. 1,155 *Quibus testamento quidem tutor datus non sit, iis ex lege XII tabularum agnati sunt tutores, qui vocantur legitimi* ('For those who have not been assigned a testamentary guardian, under the Law of the Twelve Tables, agnates are guardians that are called statutory ones'); G. 1,165 (…) *eo enim ipso quo hereditates libertorum libertarumque, si intestati decessissent, iusserat lex ad patronos liberosque eorum pertinere, crediderunt veteres voluisse legem etiam tutelas ad eos pertinere, quia et agnatos quos ad hereditatem vocavit, eosdem et tutores esse iusserat* ('It was precisely because the Law [of Twelve Tables] had ordered that the inheritance of manumitted men and women, if they died without leaving a testament, belonged to their *patronus* or his descendants, as ancient jurists recognized that the Law had decided they should also exercise tutelage, because the Law had also ordered that agnates themselves appointed to inherit should also be guardians'. There is no doubt that this excerpt refers to the Law of the Twelve Tables, as it is referred to at the beginning of the paragraph.: G. 1,165 *Ex eadem lege duodecim tabularum…*); Ulp. D. 26,4,5,pr. *Legitimos tutores nemo dat, sed lex duodecim tabularum fecit tutores* ('Nobody appoints statutory guardians. It was the Law of the Twelve Tables that appointed these guardians').

614 The entire monograph dedicated to the analysis of jurisprudence regarding grammatical number and gender was published by M. P. Pavese, *Scire leges est verba tenere. Ricerche sulle competenze grammaticali dei giuristi romani*, Torino 2013.

615 Navarra argues that the decision aligned with the general trend toward unifying tutelage institutions. By entrusting tutelage to only one person, it was supposed to make the guardian's competences similar to those of the *pater familias*. See M. Navarra, *Ricerche…*, p. 168.

not to offer an additional argument to Labeo's opinion[616] but, most probably, to indicate the justification for breaking the linguistic meaning of the term *tutores* used in the Law of the Twelve Tables.

The following source, which preserved Ulpian's reflections on the *quod legatorum* interdictum, appears[617] to illustrate the same interpretative phenomenon:

D. 43,3,1,2–3 (*Ulpianus libro sexagesimo septimo ad edictum*)
2. *Est autem et ipsum apiscendae possessionis et continet hanc causam, ut, quod quis legatorum nomine non ex voluntate heredis occupavit, id restituat heredi. etenim aequissimum praetori visum est unumquemque non sibi ipsum ius dicere occupatis legatis, sed ab herede petere: redigit igitur ad heredes per hoc interdictum ea, quae legatorum nomine possidentur, ut perinde legatarii possint eum convenire.* 3. *Hoc interdictum et heredem heredis bonorumque possessoris habere propter utilitatem huius dicendum est, nec non ceteros quoque successores.*
2. This provision concerns the acquisition of possession, and its subject is that the one who came into possession of something under the pretext of legacy but against the will of an heir, must return it to the heir. The praetor deemed it entirely right that no one should decide freely in their own case, appropriating objects of legacy, but should demand them from the heir. With this interdictum, the heirs are therefore restored what they have on behalf of the legatees, so that the legatees can sue the heir. 3. It must be stated that, for the sake of its *utilitas*, this interdictum is also available to the heirs of the heir under the civil law, and the heir under the praetorian law, as well as to other legal successors.

616 Ibidem.

617 Given Ulpian's frequent *laudationes edicti* (as mentioned in Chapter One) and the complex nature of the term *utilitas*, conclusions regarding the reasons for using the *utilitas* criterion in describing praetorian institutions must be drawn with particular care. A good example is Ulpian's passage on the interdictum *quod in via publica itinereve publico*: D. 43,8,2,37 *Hoc interdicto non is tenetur, qui in via publica aliquid fecit, sed is, qui factum habet. proinde si alius fecit, alius factum habet, is tenetur, qui factum habet: et est hoc utilius, quia is potest restituere, qui factum immissum habet* ('This interdictum does not hold liable the person who has done something on public road, but rather the one who has what has been done. Thus, if one person has done something and another has it, the one who has it is held liable. It is more useful as he can restore everything to its original state who has what has been done or placed on a road or public route'). Due to the fact that Ulpian quotes a fragment of the edict a moment earlier (D. 43,8,2,35 *Praetor ait:* QVOD IN VIA PVBLICA ITINEREVE PVBLICO FACTVM IMMISSVM HABES, QVO EA VIA IDVE ITER DETERIVS SIT FIAT, RESTITVAS. ['The praetor says: "You have to restore what you have to the previous state, and what has been done on a public road and public route, as a result of which the road or route has deteriorated"']), according to which the one who has what has been done or placed on a road or public route can restore everything to its original state in this case, the word *utilius* implies nothing more than the recognition of regulation, which in practice was certainly useful, since it was easier for whoever actually had physical control of a thing to restore it to its former state. On the protection of public roads, including the interdictum *quod in via publica itinereve publico* in R. Kamińska, *Udział pretora w zarządzaniu i ochronie dróg rzymskich* [in:] *Prawne aspekty podróży i turystyki – historia i współczesność: prace poświęcone pamięci profesora Janusza Sondla*, P. Cybula (ed.), Kraków 2018, pp. 221–230.

The *quod legatorum* interdictum allowed an heir to reclaim the object of the legacy arbitrarily taken by a legatee[618]. Although Ulpian does not quote the edict's content, and its relevant fragment was not preserved elsewhere, it can be inferred that heirs might have been able to apply for an interdictum. In fact, what appears in Ulpian's deliberations is the term *heredes*, indicating heirs according to *ius civile*. It was commonly assumed that, in accordance with the content of the edict, the *bonorum possessor*[619] also had a right of action in such cases. Ulpian extended this right of action to heirs' successors. Hence, referring to the *utilitas* criterion seems to fulfil a double function here: it emphasizes the usefulness of the legal instrument, as indicated by the pronoun *huius*, but above all, as in the cases described above, it signals the extension of the addressees' circle of the norm beyond the literal understanding of the wording of the edict.

3.2.4 Interpretation of Declarations of Intent

The category of *utilitas* played a significant role in the interpretation of ambiguous declarations of intent, as evidenced by the following excerpt from Ulpian:

> D. 5,1,66 (*Ulpianus libro altero disputationum*)
> *Si quis intentione ambigua vel oratione usus sit, id quod utilius ei est accipiendum est.*
> If someone expressed an ambiguous intention or used unclear language, the sense more useful to that person should be accepted.

The situation described by Ulpian did not involve a conflict between the actual intent (*voluntas*) and the words used (*verba*). Instead, it pertained to formulation of unclear

618 On this topic in P. Lotmar, *Zur Geschichte des interdictum quod legatorum*, 'ZSS RA' 1910, vol. 31, no. 1, pp. 89–158; O. Lenel, *Das interdictum quod legatorum utile*, 'ZSS RA' 1932, vol. 52, no. 1, pp. 282–284.

619 This is probably based on the reconstructions of the content of the edict by Rudorff and Lenel. Rudorff reconstructed the edict as follows: *Quorum bonorum ex edicto meo illi possessio data est, quod de his bonis legatorum nomine, non ex voluntate eius ad quem ea res pertinet, possides, auto dolo desiisti possidere, si satisdatum sit, aut si per bonorum possessorem non stet ut satisdetur, id illi restituas (antequam ex iure exeas)*. Lenel's reconstruction reads: *Quod de his bonis, quorum possessio ex edicto meo illi data est, legatorum nomine non voluntate illius possides quodque dolo malo fecisti quo minus possideres, id, si eo nomine satisdatum est sive per illum non stat ut satisdetur, illi restituas*. See A. F. Rudorff, *De iuris dictione edictum: Edicti perpetui quae reliqua sunt*, Lipsiae 1869, § 223 p. 205; O. Lenel, *Das Edictum perpetuum…*, § 228 p. 453. Cf. also Fragm. Vat. 90 … *libro I de interdictis sub titulo* IN EVM QVI LEGATORVM NOMINE, NON VOLVNTATE EIVS CVI BONORVM POSSESSIO DATA ERIT, POSSIDEBIT ('in the first book on interdicta under the title "on who will possess under the legacy but not by the will of the one who has been granted *bonorum possessio*"'). Quoting extensive source material, Lotmar demonstrated that *interdictum quod legatorum* applied to heirs under both civil and pretorian law. See Ph. Lotmar, *Zur Geschichte…*, pp. 129–158. The same conclusions can also be found in F. Betancourt, *El libro anónimo De interdictis: Codex vaticanus latinus no. 5766*, Salamanca 1997, pp. 527–581.

statements, allowing for multiple interpretations. The jurist explains that in the event of an ambiguous declaration of intent, *utilitas* guides its interpretation, pointing to the preferred meanings of the terms. When anything was expressed ambiguously, it was necessary to follow the interpretation that was most useful (*utilius*) to the declarant. The reference to *utilitas* is not merely practical but also ethically fair, as it aimed to align the interpretation with the declarant's true intentions.

However, the most interesting references to *utilitas* are those where the content of the declaration of intent did not raise any doubts. The rhetorical *status scripti et voluntatis* was used not only in the interpretation of the law but also in declarations of intent[620]. Perhaps the most famous example of this is the *causa Curiana* of 94–92 BCE[621]. In this case, a dispute before the centumviral court concerned the substitution of Manius Curius as heir in place of the expected son, who, however, was never born. The inheritance substitute was established as follows: SI FILIVS ANTE MORITVR, QVAM IN TVTELAM SVAM VENERIT, TVM MIHI HERES ESTO[622] ('If my son dies before reaching the age of majority, then be my heir'). When the son was never born, a dispute ensued as to whether Manius Curius could inherit as a (substituted) testamentary successor, or whether the inheritance should be granted to the intestate heir Mark Coponius. Ultimately, the former won the case, as Licinius Crassus, who represented him, convinced the judges to prioritize the testator's intent over the literal text of the will. Cicero noted that this case was adjudicated *contra scriptum pro aequo et bono* (*Brut.* 145).

In the *status scripti et voluntatis* scheme, when interpreting declarations of intent, *voluntas* referred to an interpretation corresponding to the intent of the declarant, and *scriptum* to an interpretation strictly adhering to content of the declaration. As determinants of the interpretation, both categories lead to conflicting results. Yet this form of the scheme was not applied in the jurisprudence interpretation of declarations of intent. In this context, the jurists treated the *ex utilitate* and *ex litteris* interpretations uniquely:

> D. 50,12,13,1 (*Papirius Iustus libro altero de constitutionibus*)
> *Item rescripserunt condiciones donationibus adpositas, quae in rem publicam fiunt, ita demum ratas esse, si utilitatis publicae interest: quod si damnosae sint, observari non debere. et ideo non*

620 Cf. Quint., *Inst.* 7,5,6, quoted above.

621 See, e.g., F. Wieacker, *The 'Causa Curiana' and Contemporary Roman Jurisprudence*, 'Irish Jurist' 1967, vol. 2, no. 1, pp. 151–164; J.W. Vaughn, *Law and rhetoric in the causa Curiana*, 'Classical Antiquity' 1985, vol. 4, no. 2, pp. 208–222; J.W. Tellegen, *The Reliability…*, pp. 191–200; C. Filippi, *La causa curiana*, 'Anuario de Derecho Civil' 2004, vol. 9, pp. 131–138; M. Könczöl, *Law, fact and narratives in ancient rhetoric: The case of the causa Curiana*, 'International Journal for the Semiotics of Law-Revue internationale de Sémiotique juridique' 2008, vol. 21, no. 1, pp. 21–33.

622 Cic., *Inv.* 2,42,122; Idem, *De orat.* 1,141.

> *observandum, quod defunctus certa summa legata vetuit vectigal exerceri. esse enim tolerabilia, quae vetus consuetudo comprobat.*
> [Marcus Aurelius and Lucius Verus[623]] decided in the rescript that the conditions attached to the donations made to a municipal commune are considered valid only if they serve *utilitas publica*. And if they are harmful, then one should not take them into account. That is why it should not be taken into account that the deceased, having left a certain amount in the legacy, forbade to levy a tax from the property left to his heirs. For it is fitting, which the old custom approves.

> D. 26,3,10 (*Tryphoninus libro quarto decimo disputationum*)
> *utilitatem pupillorum praetor sequitur, non scripturam testamenti vel codicillorum. nam patris voluntatem praetor ita accipere debet, si non fuit ignarus scilicet eorum, quae ipsa praetor de tutore comperta habet (…).*
> The praetor should follow the utility of a pupil, not the content of the will or codicil. He should acknowledge the will of his father only if the father had been ignorant of the facts the praetor learned about the guardian (…).

Papirius Iustus[624], jurist of the 2nd century CE, reported that emperors Marcus Aurelius and Lucius Verus decided in the rescript that only those conditions that complied with *utilitas publica* were valid. Otherwise, they were considered not added, and used to be omitted in the interpretation of the declaration of intent[625].

Tryphoninus, in turn, explained that the praetor, guided by the *utilitas pupillorum*, should disregard the content of the will or codicils if it was not in the pupil's best interest. The situation described by the jurist therefore did not refer to the doubts as to the interpretation of the text. The issue the jurist writes about is that although the content of the testament was linguistically clear, its literal understanding led to unacceptable results.

A similar declaration was also found in the thirteenth book of Ulpian's *Libri ad Sabinum*:

623 The emperors are indicated in the preceding paragraph. Cf. Papir. D. 50,12,13,pr. *Imperatores Antoninus et Verus Augusti…*

624 On his work as well as the quoted passage in E. Volterra, *L'ouvrage de Papirius Justus Constitutionum libri XX* [in:] *Symbolae iuridicae et historicae Martino David dedicatae*, vol. 1, J. A. Ankum, R. Feenstra, W. F. Leemans (ed.), Leiden 1968, pp. 215–223 and in O. Licandro, N. Palazzolo, *Papirius Iustus. Libri XX de constitutionibus*, Roma 2021.

625 Palazzolo writes in this context about the economic and social bonds that prevented the *civitas* from accepting conditions that did not serve the public utility, Ibidem, p. 184. See also T. Honsell, *Gemeinwohl…*, p. 119 as well as P. Lepore, *Rei publicae polliceri: Un'indagine giuridico epigrafica*, Milano 2012, pp. 351–353, n. 1 for further insights on the interpretation of this passage.

D. 38,17,2,44 (*Ulpianus libro tertio decimo ad Sabinum*)
Tractari belle potest, si pupillo amplum legatum sub condicione sit relictum SI TVTORES NON HABVERIT *et propterea ei mater non petierit, ne condicione deficeretur, an constitutio cesset. et puto cessare, si damnum minus sit cumulo legati. quod et in magistratibus municipalibus tractatur apud Tertullianum: et putat dandam in eos actionem, quatenus plus esset in damno quam in legato. nisi forte quis putet condicionem hanc quasi utilitati publicae obpugnantem remittendam ut alias plerasque. aut verba cavillatus imputaverit matri, cur curatores non petierit. finge autem plenius condicionem conscriptam: nonne erit matri ignoscendum? aut hoc imputatur matri, cur non desideravit a principe condicionem remitti? et puto non esse imputandum.*
The following issue can be a good problem to discuss: whether the constitution ceases to apply if a minor is left with a generous legacy provided that he 'will not have any guardians', and for this reason the mother did not request the praetor to appoint guardians for him so as not to prevent the fulfilment of the condition. I believe that the provisions of the constitution do not apply if the loss of property would be less than the value of the legacy. Tertullianus deals with this question in relation to city magistrates. He argues that an action should be brought against them up to an amount which will be the difference between the value of the loss of property and the value of the legacy. In addition, one might consider that a condition of this kind, as contrary to *utilitas publica*, should be repealed, as is often the case in other situations. And if someone strictly adhering to the wording accused the mother of not asking for the appointment of the curators – for it is assumed that the condition was formulated very precisely – will she not be forgiven? Or can the mother be accused of not asking the emperor to repeal the condition? I do not think she should be facing this accusation.

Ulpian pondered whether the constitution of Septimius Severus would refer to a woman who did not apply for the appointment of a guardian for her child to the praetor, due to a substantial provision left for the child in a legacy provided that the child would not be under tutelage[626]. According to the content of the constitution, the mother who did not apply for to the appointment of a guardian for her child did not have the right to claim their property if the child died intestate[627], which she was usually entitled to under the *senatus consultum Tertullianum*[628]. Yet, Ulpian argued that the constitution should not apply. He pointed out that some might claim it was possible to repeal the condition contained in the declaration of intent, because it was contrary to *utilitas pu-*

626 An extensive analysis of the fragment with numerous references to the literature presented in R. Scevola, *Utilitas publica. II. Elaborazione…*, pp. 22–46.
627 Cf. Mod. D. 26,6,2,2; Ulp. D. 38,17,2,23.
628 On the *senatus consultum* and its dating see M. Meinhart, *Die Datierung des SC Tertullianum, mit einem Beitrag zur Gaiusforschung*, 'ZSS RA' 1966, vol. 83, no. 1, pp. 100–141; Eadem, *Die Senatusconsulta Tertullianum und Orfitianum in ihrer Bedeutung für das klassische römische Erbrecht*, Graz 1967.

blica (*quasi*[629] *utilitati publicae obpugnantem remittendam*). He also noted that such a practice was not at all uncommon[630].

Additionally, Ulpian made reference to the concept of *cavillari*, which, as outlined in Chapter Two, is equivalent to sophisms or twisted reasoning based on a strict interpretation of wording, in this case: the wording of the constitution. Here, the *ex utilitate* interpretation appears to be the complete opposite of sophism. As Ulpian asserts, even if the condition is preserved, one should not apply the regulation, thereby implying also a *contra scriptum* interpretation of the constitution[631].

In each of the above cases, *utilitas* thus made it possible to break the unambiguous results of the literal interpretation of a declaration of intent, and propose a solution different from the one that would arise on its grounds. However, the *ex utilitate* interpretation was not synonymous with the rhetorical *ex sententia* interpretation here. It did not lead to the realization of the declarant's intent, as it should happen according to the original rhetorical scheme. On the contrary, the intent expressed in a written formula was completely ignored if it contradicted *utilitas*. This approach is further exemplified by Tryphoninus:

D. 49,15,12,3 (*Tryphoninus libro quarto disputationum*)
Medio tempore filius, quem habuit in potestate captivus, uxorem ducere potest, quamvis consentire nuptiis pater eius non posset: nam utique nec dissentire. susceptus ergo nepos in reversi captivi potestate ut avi erit suusque heres ei quodammodo invito, cum nuptiis non consenserit. non mirum, quia illius temporis condicio necessitasque faciebat et publica nuptiarum utilitas exigebat.
During captivity, a son who was under the authority of his captured father is allowed to get married although his father cannot consent to it, and, in any case, may not disagree with it. A grandson born out of this marriage will therefore remain under the power of the captive,

629 The jurist's use of the term *quasi* makes it is difficult to determine whether he considered the condition contained in the content of the act as inconsistent with *utilitas*, or whether the contradiction mentioned here implied a certain pattern of conduct. Supporting the view that the quoted example does not directly pertain to non-compliance with *utilitas publica* is B. Biondi, *Il diritto…*, p. 258. Contrary view in T. Honsell, *Gemeinwohl…*, p. 127.

630 It is also noteworthy that a fragment from the same part of Ulpian's *Libri ad Sabinum* is interpreted by Vonglis as an example of the application of *status scripti et voluntatis*. See B. Vonglis, *La lettre…*, pp. 97–98 and D. 38,17,2,40 *Quid si decesserint quidam? puto, licet verba deficiant, sententiam constitutionis locum habere* ('What if some individuals have died? I think, even though words may be lacking, the spirit of the constitution holds its place'). Although this phrase rather fits a different status, namely *syllogismus*, which is discussed in this work later on, it would make sense that the jurist remained within the same interpretative framework. See also M. De Filippi, *Subvenire pupillis*, Labeo 1980, t. 26, pp. 67–73.

631 Some conceptual alternative between the fragments *nisi forte quis putet condicionem hanc quasi utilitati publicae obpugnantem remittendam ut alias plerasque* and *aut verba cavillatus imputaverit matri, cur curatores non petierit* was also noticed by R. Scevola, *Utilitas publica. II. Emersione…*, pp. 23, 33–41.

> his grandfather, when the latter returns, and become his necessary heir somewhat against his will, since the family head did not accept the marriage. No wonder, since it was caused by the conditions and compulsion resulting from these circumstances, and also required by public utility of marriage.

Tryphoninus confirmed the son's right to enter into a valid marriage without his father's consent, when the latter was in the enemy's captivity[632]. He further explained that, in the event of the father's return, the *ius postliminii* was applied in a unique way. In addition to regaining all the lost rights, the returning captive acquired new ones too: the power over the grandson born out of the son's marriage. Entering under the grandfather's power as well as acquiring the status of his necessary heir took place regardless of the will of the family head, and in a way even against it, because, as the jurist explained, the grandfather did not consent to the marriage. The expression *quodammodo invito* ('somewhat against [his] will') brings the *contra scriptum* scheme to mind, where the *scriptum*, as in the previous fragments, corresponds to the intent of the person[633]. However, referring to utility, this time described as *publica utilitas nuptiarum*, allowed Tryphoninus to justify the adoption of the decision potentially contrary to, and certainly not expressly in line with the will of the *pater familias*[634].

All of the above sources provide information of considerable importance. They show jurists did not fully adopt the rhetorical *status scripti et voluntatis* but only to the extent that was useful to them (no pun intended); they thus used the category of *utilitas* as an instrument to break the literal interpretation, leading to the identical effects as the *contra scriptum* interpretation. However, they did not take over the whole pattern. This is evidenced by the cases quoted above, in which the *ex voluntate* interpretation is completely opposite to the *ex utilitate* one, while as claimed by the rhetorical *status*, they should produce the very same effects. So unless otherwise stated[635], here jurisprudence *utilitas* did not correspond with the category of intent, be

632 The question of the validity of marriage entered into under such circumstances was a moot point among jurists. As the legal status of the children of a prisoner of war could potentially change – since all rights, including *patria potestas*, were restored if *pater familias* returned from captivity – it was generally presumed that the children had the right to marry validly only three years after the head of the family was captured or after three years of his absence (Iul. D. 23,2,11 and Ulp. D. 23,2,9,1. See also Paul. D. 23,4,8). However, Tryphoninus does not address these additional conditions here.

633 In fact, had it not been for the formulation used by Tryphoninus, this decision could be qualified as a *supra scriptum* one, since the head of the family did not express his intent at all.

634 Doubts have been raised in the literature about the authenticity of the fragment of *Disputationes* by Tryphoninus. Cf. esp. G. Longo, *Utilitas publica*, pp. 33–34, who argued the portion of the text from *quamvis consentire* to its end was interpolated. It seems, however, that the reference to *utilitas* in a manner consistent, both in terms of content and function, with the one that can be observed in other jurists, proves the authenticity of the fragment.

635 Cf. again Pap. D. 17,1,54,pr.

it the legislator[636] or the declarant. Occasionally, it could come close to the sphere of *sententia legis,* but most of all it was *utilitas* in all its glory – an ethical-pragmatic criterion, usually understood as the utility of a community, consistent with the utility of all citizens, and sometimes only specified in its content, such as in Tryph. D. 26,3,10 and Tryph. D. 49,15,12,3.

3.3 Jurisprudence *supra scriptum* Decisions

3.3.1 *Syllogismus*

Despite its meaningful name, the *status scripti et voluntatis* does not exhaust the cases of conflict between the two categories it comprises. According to the rhetorical theory of interpretation, a problem could also arise when an unambiguous legal regulation exists but is drawn too narrowly, not taking specific factual states into account. In such instances, the *pro scripto* interpretation created confusion[637], preventing it from finding an appropriate solution. The applicable *status* in these cases is referred to as *syllogismus,* or *ratiocinatio*[638], under which the *ex aequitate/sententia/voluntate*[639] interpretation proceeds beyond the literal understanding of the wording, thus including a given case in the legal order. Both the *status scripti et voluntatis* and *syllogismus* express the tension between the categories of *scriptum* and *voluntas.* As explained by Quintilian (*Inst.* 7,8,1): *Syllogismus habet aliquid simile scripto et voluntati, quia semper pars in eo altera scripto nititur; sed hoc interest, quod illic dicitur contra scriptum, hic supra scriptum* ('A syllogism shows a certain similarity to the *status scripti et voluntatis,* because one party always follows a literal interpretation; the difference is, however, that in the other situation we argue against the letter of the law, and in the first one we go beyond it'). These decisions thus complete the legal order – not against but despite the lack of regulation (*supra scriptum*).

The answer to the question whether the *syllogismus* can be found in jurists' decisions remains controversial among researchers. In particular, Himmelstein[640], followed by Wesel[641], limited the influence of rhetoric on jurisprudence to the *status scripti et volun-*

636 Vonglis also argues that the term *sententia (legis)* should not be equated with the will of the legislator. According to him, it represents the meaning attributed to the act by an interpreter who applies an *ex aequo et bono* interpretation, taking social needs into account. Interestingly, the French researcher described this concept as *le sense utile.* See B. Vonglis, *La lettre…,* pp. 196–199.

637 Quint., *Inst.* 7,8,3; 7,8,6.

638 Such terms are found e.g. in Quint., *Inst.* 7,8,1; Cic., *Inv.* 2,40,116; 2,50,148. See also H. Lausberg, *Handbuch…,* pp. 121–122.

639 See e.g. Quint., *Inst.* 7,8,7.

640 J. Himmelschein, *Studien…,* pp. 373–424.

641 U. Wesel, *Zur Deutung…,* pp. 343–344.

tatis. A different opinion was expressed by Vonglis[642]. Indeed, it is not only the *contra scriptum* perspective but also the *supra scriptum* that fits into the *utilitatis causa* decision model. Their nature, then, seems to be constituted by all the tensions that may arise between the 'letter' and the 'spirit of the law'.

3.3.2 Interpretation of the Law

The supplementary role of the *ex utilitate* interpretation can be observed in particular in the interpretation of the written law. The jurisprudence *supra scriptum* interpretation, to use rhetorical terminology, can be observed in the fragment of Terentius Clemens', jurist of the 2nd century CE, commentary *ad legem Iuliam et Papiam Poppaeam* preserved in D.35,1,64,pr.–1:

> D. 35,1,64,pr.–1 (*Terentius Clemens libro quinto ad legem Iuliam et Papiam*)
> pr. *Hoc modo legato dato* SI LVCIO TITIO NON NVBSERIT *non esse legi locum Iulianus aiebat.* 1. *Quod si ita scriptum esset* SI ARICIAE NON NVBSERIT, *interesse, an fraus legi facta esset: nam si ea esset, quae aliubi nuptias non facile possit invenire, interpretandum ipso iure rescindi, quod fraudandae legis gratia esset adscriptum: legem enim utilem rei publicae, subolis scilicet procreandae causa latam, adiuvandam interpretatione.*
> pr. Julian argued that the law did not apply to the legate granted on the condition: 'if she does not marry Lucius Titus'. 1. If, on the other hand, it was written: 'if she does not marry in Aricia', was there any circumvention of the law? For if she were one that could not easily find the possibility of getting married elsewhere, then it should be interpreted that the condition was invalidated by the law itself, because it was added to circumvent the law. This is because the interpretation should support a law useful for the state, namely a law issued for procreation.

The reflections refer to the provisions of the *lex Iulia et Papia Poppaea*, according to which men aged 25 to 60 and women aged 20 to 50 were required to be married. In the event of non-compliance with the statutory orders, such persons, with some exceptions[643], could not inherit under a will. According to the account, it was allowed to leave a legacy to a woman, provided that she did not marry a particular man. However, the condition of not marrying at all was considered not included in the content of the

642 B. Vonglis, *La lettre…*, pp. 153–163.

643 This prohibition did not apply to persons belonging to the individuals classified under the *personae exceptae* category, namely relatives of the testator up to the third grade of lineal descent, as well as to those who were granted the *ius trium liberorum*. Cf. Tit. Ulp. 17,2; 18,1. See P. Voci, *Linee storiche del diritto ereditario romano I. Dalle origini ai Severi*, [in:] ANRW, vol. 2.14, Berlin-New York 1982, p. 431.

legal act[644]. In the above-quoted passage, the jurist examined how to deal with the stipulation that the legatee could not be married in a particular place. Terentius Clemens, citing Julian's opinion, considered the validity of this condition within the framework of the problem of *frauds legi(s)*[645], questioning whether it should be treated as circumventing the provisions of the law (*fraudandae legis gratia adscriptum*). Jurists explain the *in fraudem legis* category as follows:

> D. 1,3,29 (*Paulus libro singulari ad legem Cinciam*)
> *Contra legem facit, qui id facit quod lex prohibet, in fraudem vero, qui salvis verbis legis sententiam eius circumvenit.*
> Anyone who does what the law prohibits acts contrary to the law. On the other hand, the act of circumventing a law is done by those who, while following its wording, go against its intentions.

> D. 1,3,30 (*Ulpianus libro quarto ad edictum*)
> *Fraus enim legi fit, ubi quod fieri noluit, fieri autem non vetuit …*
> A law is circumvented when what it did not want but yet did not forbid happens …

From the above passages one can conclude that circumventing a law was related to behaviors not regulated by it but still inconsistent with its general intention. An unambiguous interpretation of the provisions of a legal act in the form of 'if something is not prohibited, it is allowed' could, however, lead to unacceptable results. The interpretation of the written law did not end with the interpretation of the wording itself. For as Ulpian excellently explained (D. 50,16,6,1): *Verbum* EX LEGIBVS *sic accipiendum est: tam ex legum sententia quam ex verbis* ('The phrase "in accordance with the law" should be applied both to the intention of the law as well as to its wording')[646].

644 Cf. P.S. 3,4b,2 *Condiciones contra leges et decreta principum vel bonos mores adscriptae nullius sunt momenti: veluti si uxorem non duxeris, si filios non susceperis, si homicidium feceris, si larvali habitu processeris et his similia* ('Conditions contrary to the laws and decrees of emperors, or to morality are null and void, such as "if you do not marry a woman", "if you do not beget children", "if you kill a man", "if you appear as a ghost" and alike').

645 On this topic e. g. in J. Brejon, *Fraus legis*, Rennes 1941; M. Kaser, H. Krüger, *Fraus*, 'ZSS RA' 1943, vol. 63, no. 1, pp. 117–174; B. Vonglis, *La lettre…*, pp. 153–156; T. Honsell, *In fraudem legis agere*, [in:] *Festschrift für Max Kaser zum 70. Geburtstag*, D. Medicus, H. H. Seiler (ed.), München 1976, pp. 111–126; O. Behrends, *Die fraus legis: zum Gegensatz von Wortlaut- und Sinngeltung in der römischen Gesetzesinterpretation*, Göttingen 1982; L. Fascione, *Fraus legi: indagini sulla concezione della frode alla legge nella lotta politica e nella esperienza giuridica romana*, Milano 1983; M. Ravljen, *Concept of Avoidance of the Law (Fraus Legis) through Roman and German Law History*, 'Russian Law: theory and practice' 2018, no. 2, pp. 78–88.

646 Cf. also Cels. D. 1,3,17 *Scire leges non hoc est verba earum tenere, sed vim ac potestatem* ('Knowing laws does not mean understanding their wording but their sense and meaning').

The case considered here could not be explicitly forbidden in the content of the *lex Iulia et Papia*. The jurist then wondered whether the inclusion of the condition in question in the declaration of intent would be consistent with the *sententia legis*. According to Papinian, the law prohibited completely depriving an individual of marital autonomy[647]. In this case, the condition did not inherently impede the marriage, but it could lead to such outcomes within specific circumstances. Therefore, its validity needed to be evaluated based on the consequences that would arise from its implementation. If it resulted in an undeniable impossibility to get married, the condition was legally considered invalid. However, the same condition could be deemed valid if its inclusion in a legal act could be justified[648].

In Terentius Clemens' account, the *lex Iulia et Papia* is described as *lex utilis rei publicae*, a law useful to the state. *Utilitas* seems to serve a dual interpretative function in this context. First, the reference to this criterion opened the possibility to apply a supplementary interpretation of the legal act, and to classify a given behavior (depending on the factual circumstances) as either permitted or prohibited. It is also worth noting that here, in case of the *supra scriptum* interpretation of the law, the consequence was a *contra scriptum* interpretation of the testator's will.

Although the category of *utilitas rei publicae* was presented in the context of procreation, it does not mean that the *leges* enacted for other purposes could be considered *inutiles*[649]. The jurist thus clarified the content of the concept. However, he still referred to it in the context of the interpretation process as setting its path and leading to the application of an extensive interpretation of the law's provisions[650]. The statement in the passage can then be regarded as a general guideline of the interpretation process,

647 Pap. D. 35,1,72,4 ...*respondendum est eamque legis sententiam videri, ne quod omnino nuptiis impedimentum inferatur* ('It must be also answered that the spirit of the law appears to be that nothing should in any way impede marriage').

648 See also L. Fascione, *Fraus legi...*, pp. 132–133; V. Scarano Ussani, *L'utilità...*, pp. 53–56, R. Astolfi, *La lex Iulia et Papia*, 4 ed., Padova 1996, pp. 159–166.

649 Hence, a valid, though somewhat specific in scope, perspective is presented by Stagl, who argues that referencing *utilitas publica* allows for a teleological interpretation of the laws derived from this principle. See J. F. Stagl, *Die Funktionen...*, p. 519. The term *lex utilis* can also be found in other literary works. Cicero employs this expression in reference to the Agrarian Law. See e. g. Cic., *Agr.* 2,5,12 ...*si lex utilis plebi Romanae mihi videretur*... ('if the law appeared to me to be useful to the Roman plebeians'); 2,6,14 *omni hoc ratione vobis confirmare possum, Quirites, hoc animo me ad legendam legem cognoscendamque venisse ut, si eam vobis accommodatam atque utilem esse intellegerem, auctor eius atque adiutor essem* ('I assure you, Romans, with utmost sincerity, that I dedicated myself to reading and comprehending this law with the intention that if I had believed it to be well-suited to your interests and useful for you, I would have been a strong advocate and supporter of it'). It is also worth noting that a similar phrase (or concept) – *lex utilior* – was employed by the rhetors, particularly in situations where there was a conflict between two provisions of law (*leges contrariae*). See e. g. Quint., *Decl. mai.* 315,14 ...*mea lex utilior est rei publicae*...; Sen., *Contr.* 1,5,8,7 *utra optio honestior sit, utra iustior, utra utilior*...

650 Cf. also J. F. Stagl, *Favor dotis...*, p. 81.

for which the key was to consider the general objectives of the system principles[651] as well as the spirit of the law.

Similarly, *utilitas* allowed for supplementing the provisions of the praetorian edict:

> D. 44,4,4,33 (*Ulpianus libro septuagesimo sexto ad edictum*).
> *Metus causa exceptionem Cassius non proposuerat contentus doli exceptione, quae est generalis: sed utilius visum est etiam de metu opponere exceptionem. Etenim distat aliquid doli exceptione, quod exceptio doli personam complectitur eius, qui dolo fecit: enimvero metus causa exceptio in rem scripta est …*
> Cassius did not introduce an exception on the grounds of fear, as he was content with the general exception of fraud. But it was found that it was more useful to bring an exception on the grounds of fear in this case as well. It is slightly different from an exception on the grounds of fraud because this one refers to a perpetrator, while an exception on the grounds of fear was designed *in rem* …

Ulpian reports that Cassius, city praetor of 27 CE[652], did not introduce an *exceptio metus causa* in his edict because, as the jurist put it, he was content with an *exceptio doli*. It is not for this study to decide on the motives that guided Cassius[653]. It is vital that his (most likely isolated) views limited the catalogue of exceptions provided in the praetorian edict[654]. The category of *utilitas* (*utilius visum est*) referred to in the passage should be considered in these very circumstances. It allowed jurists[655] to breach the scope of regulation and supplement it with the 'missing' exception.

651 I. Koschembahr-Łyskowski, *Coventiones…*, esp. p. 251. See also N. Rampazzo, *Quasi praetor…*, p. 509.

652 This way in S. A. E. Martens, *Durch Dritte…*, p. 37. Doubts about his identity expressed in A. Burdese, *L'eccezione di dolo generale in rapporto alle altre eccezioni*, 'Diritto@Storia' 2006, no. 5 (available online at: https://dirittoestoria.it/5/Tradizione-Romana/Burdese-Eccezione-dolo-generale.htm).

653 On this topic extensively in R. Fiori, *Eccezione di dolo generale ed editto asiatico di Quinto Mucio: il problema delle origini* [in:] *L'eccezione di dolo generale. Diritto romano e tradizione romanistica*, L. Garofalo (ed.), Padova 2006, pp. 67–74. See also A. Burdese, *L'eccezione…*.

654 A. Burdese, *L'eccezione…*; R. Fiori, *Eccezione…*, p. 67 along with the literature cited therein.

655 Kupisch also attributed this opinion to jurists. However, it is difficult to justify why he considered that Ulpian referred to views with which he did not identify. See B. Kupisch, *In integrum restitutio und vindicatio utilis bei Eigentumsübertragungen im klassischen römischen Recht*, Berlin 1974, p. 174. In fact, it is highly likely that *utilitas* in the fragment originates from Ulpian himself. The phrase *utilius visum est* appears in only one other fragment in the Digest, which is also attributed to Ulpian, and analyzed in this study: D. 47,8,2,1. Fiori, on the other hand, argued that the content of the edict had been supplemented by subsequent officials. See R. Fiori, *Eccezione…*, p. 66. Yet, if that were the case, Ulpian would have rather re-used the verb *proponere* (which appears at the beginning of the passage: …*Cassius non proposuerat*), as it seems to function as a technical term in the context of announcing actions or interdicts in the praetorian edict. Cf. A. Burdese, *L'eccezione…*.

According to Ulpian, the praetor had similar powers in relation to the interdictum *ne quid in flumine publico, quo aliter aqua fluat, uti priore aestatae fluxit* forbidding anything to be done on a public river or its banks that would change the water flow:

D. 43,13,1,pr.; 6 (*Ulpianus libro duodeseptuagesimo ad edictum*)
pr. *Ait praetor:* IN FLVMINE PVBLICO INVE RIPA EIVS FACERE AVT IN ID FLVMEN RIPAMVE EIVS IMMITTERE, QVO ALITER AQVA FLVAT, QVAM PRIORE AESTATE FLVXIT, VETO. (…) 6. *Sunt qui putent excipiendum hoc interdicto* QVOD EIVS RIPAE MVNIENDAE CAVSA NON FIET, *scilicet ut, si quid fiat, quo aliter aqua fluat, si tamen muniendae ripae causa fiat, interdicto locus non sit. sed nec hoc quibusdam placet: neque enim ripae cum incommodo accolentium muniendae sunt. hoc tamen iure utimur, ut praetor ex causa aestimet, an hanc exceptionem dare debeat: plerumque enim utilitas suadet exceptionem istam dari.*
pr. The praetor states: 'I forbid to do anything on a public river or its banks, or to bring anything into it or onto its banks that would cause the water to flow differently than last summer'. (…) 6. There are those who believe that a reservation should be made in this interdictum, namely: 'unless it is done to fortify the banks', obviously so that when something is done to make the water flow differently, it will not be possible to apply the interdictum if it was done to fortify the banks. Others, however, disagree, because even the banks should not be fortified at the expense of the inconvenience of those living nearby. Yet we apply the rule saying it is the praetor who decides on the basis of a given case whether he should allow for such an exception; frequently, *utilitas* encourages one to do so.

According to some jurists, the formula of the interdictum forbidding doing anything changing the current of the water on the river or its banks had to be supplemented with a reservation allowing for works to be carried out to fortify the banks of the river. However, not all jurists agreed with this proposal. Ulpian did not consider it necessary to complete the interdictum formula either. Instead, he proposed an intermediate solution. As he claimed, it was the praetor who, having assessed a specific case, could depart from the literal content of the interdictum and decide to allow for an exception, offering a possible *supra scriptum* interpretation, to which *utilitas* often encouraged[656].

The supplementary *ex utilitate* interpretation found application not only in the interpretation of the text. The analyzed category was also located (and this is the most spectacular example from the point of view of contemporary law) at the source of the institution of *negotiorum gestio*[657]:

656 B. Vonglis, *La lettre…*, p. 186, interprets this passage in the same vein. It is also the only *utilitatis causa* decision that the French researcher included in his study.

657 For these considerations, the fragment quoted in the main text is of particular importance. It should not be overlooked, however, that Gaius presented extensive reflections in this regard. Cf. Gai. D. 44,7,5,pr. *Si quis absentis negotia gesserit, si quidem ex mandatu, palam est ex contractu nasci inter eos actiones mandati, quibus invicem experiri possunt de eo, quod alterum alteri ex bona fide praestare oportet: si vero sine mandatu, placuit quidem sane eos invicem obligari eoque nomine proditae sunt*

D. 44,7,5,pr. (*Gaius libro tertio aureorum*)
... sed neque ex contractu neque ex maleficio actiones nascuntur: neque enim is qui gessit cum absente creditur ante contraxisse, neque ullum maleficium est sine mandatu suscipere negotiorum administrationem: longe magis is, cuius negotia gesta sunt, ignorans aut contraxisse aut deliquisse intellegi potest: sed utilitatis causa receptum est invicem eos obligari ...
... But these actions do not arise as a result of contract or wrongdoing. For it is not considered that the person who dealt with other people's affairs had previously concluded an agreement with the absentee, and it is not a wrongdoing to undertake the management of other people's affairs without a mandate. Even more so, it cannot be assumed that the person whose affairs were dealt with, either concluded a contract or committed a delict unknowingly. However, for the sake of *utilitas*, it was assumed that the one whose affairs are conducted and one who conducted them are mutually obligated ...

As Gaius reported, situations in which someone dealt with other people's affairs without a mandate were located in a 'blind spot' of the law. For it could not be considered that in such cases a contract was concluded, and even more so that conducting someone else's affairs without a mandate was a delict. The *negotiorum gestio* was thus introduced into the legal order by jurists *utilitatis causa* and, in a way, *supra scriptum*, as an institution supplementing the scope of legally regulated behaviors[658].

actiones, quas appellamus negotiorum gestorum, quibus aeque invicem experiri possunt de eo, quod ex bona fide alterum alteri praestare oportet (...) *ideo autem id ita receptum est, quia plerumque homines eo animo peregre proficiscuntur quasi statim redituri nec ob id ulli curam negotiorum suorum mandant, deinde novis causis intervenientibus ex necessitate diutius absunt: quorum negotia disperire iniquum erat, quae sane disperirent, si vel is, qui obtulisset se negotiis gerundis, nullam habiturus esset actionem de eo, quod utiliter de suo impendisset, vel is, cuius gesta essent, adversus eum, qui invasisset negotia eius, nullo iure agere posset* ('If someone administered the affairs of an absent person, and if he did so in terms of a mandate, it is obvious that as a result of the conclusion of the contract, mandate actions arise between them, which they may bring against each other as to what one should give to the other in accordance with principles of good faith. And if it was without a mandate, it was accepted that they were obliged to each other, and for this reason actions were introduced, which we call actions for management of affairs without mandate, by means of which they can sue each about what one should give in accordance with principles of good faith [...]. And it was accepted because people often set off overseas with this thought of coming back in a moment, and therefore do not entrust anyone with taking care of their affairs. Then, as a result of new circumstances, they need to be absent longer. It would be wrong to let their affairs suffer, which would undoubtedly be the case if either the one who undertook the conduct of the affairs were not to be granted an action for the expenses incurred for the benefit of whose affairs he had been conducting, or the one whose affairs were handled could in no way bring an action against whoever had handled his affairs').

658 *Utilitas* referred to here has been interpreted in various ways. Cf. M. Navarra, *Ricerche...*, pp. 44–52, and esp. p. 48 along with the literature cited therein. Contrary to prevailing views, *utilitas* does not correspond to the interests of the person handling someone else's affairs without mandate and whose cases are handled. It is also not a source of obligation but rather of an institution. Finally, contrary to what F. Wieacker argues in *Offene Wertungen...*, p. 35, n. 121, *utilitas* is neither shallow nor redundant in nature.

As in the case of the previously analyzed decisions fitting into the *contra scriptum* scheme, jurists sometimes referred to the category of *utilitas* specified in its content in the *supra scriptum* decisions. And so Macer referred to *utilitas pupillorom*[659], commenting on the rescript of emperors Septimius Severus and Antoninus Caracalla, which supplemented the list of entities authorized to examine cases brought against dishonest guardians with the proconsul's legates (D. 1,21,4,pr.[660]). Before that, this right had been reserved only for praetors in Rome and province governors[661].

A clarification of the category can also be found in Ulpian's writings. He informs that there was a doubt among jurists as to whether it was permissible to file an *actio ex stipulatu* against a guardian or his guarantors at a time when a tutelage action could not yet be made (D. 27,3,16,pr.[662]). Quoting the category of *eadem utilitas* suggesting both actions were aimed at protecting the same utility, most jurists were in favour of introducing a new regulation in the form of a similar solution, and postponing the moment when an *ex stipulatu* action could be brought[663].

Moreover, *utilitas* of the parties (*utilitas contrahentium*) convinced Paulus (D. 20,1,12[664]) to follow Pomponius' opinion and allow for establishing a pledge on the

659 The hypothesis put forward by M. Navarra, *Ricerche…*, p. 174, which attributes the *ad utilitatem pupillorum* reference to the jurist rather than the emperors, should be upheld. In the fragment of Book 35 of *Libri ad edictum*, Ulpian reported on the provisions of the same rescript, without, however, referring to *utilitas* (D. 26,10,1,4). This fragment also emphasizes the state of legal uncertainty resulting from the need to supplement the already legally regulated area, which is typical of *status syllogismi*. As the jurist writes: *An autem apud legatum proconsulis suspectus postulari possit, dubium fuit* ('Nevertheless, it was uncertain whether the suspected guardian could be accused before the proconsul legate').

660 Macer D. 1,21,4,pr. *Cognitio de suspectis tutoribus mandari potest. immo etiam ex mandata generali iurisdictione propter <u>utilitatem pupillorum</u> eam contingere constitutum est in haec verba*: IMPERATORES SEVERVS ET ANTONINVS BRADVAE PROCONSVLI AFRICAE. CVM PROPRIAM IVRISDICTIONEM LEGATIS TVIS DEDERIS, CONSEQVENS EST, VT ETIAM DE SVSPECTIS TVTORIBVS POSSINT COGNOSCERE ('The right to hear cases against dishonest guardians may be transferred. In these words it was decided that due to *utilitas* of pupils such a transfer is effective even when it was carried out on the basis of a general transfer of jurisdiction: "Emperors Septimius Severus and Antoninus Caracalla to Braduas, proconsul of Africa. Since you have transferred your jurisdiction to your legates, this means they may also hear cases brought against dishonest guardians"').

661 Ulp. D. 26,10,1,3. The completed catalogue is presented in the *Institutes of Justinian*: I. 1,26,1.

662 Ulp. D. 27,3,16,pr. *Si cum tutore ex stipulatu agatur vel cum his qui pro eo intervenerunt, erit dubitatio, an, quia tutelae agi non potest, nec ex stipulatu agi possit. et plerique putant etiam hanc actionem propter <u>eandem utilitatem</u> differendam* ('If an *actio ex stipulatu* is brought against a guardian or against those who vouched for him, it will be questioned whether, since an *actio tutelae* cannot be brought, an *actio ex stipulatu* may be taken out. Many jurists are of the opinion that the possibility of bringing this action should be postponed because of the very same *utilitas*').

663 It is also worth noting that in other passages addressing this topic, there is no longer any trace of doubt or evidence of the discussion as to the point at which this action could be brought. Cf. Paul. D. 46,6,1; Ulp. D. 46,6,4,4. On this decision see U. Leptien, *Utilitatis causa…*, pp. 152–156; M. Navarra, *Ricerche…*, pp. 157–158.

664 Paul. D. 20,1,12 *Sed an viae itineris actus aquae ductus pignoris conventio locum habeat videndum esse. Pomponius ait, ut talis pactio fiat, ut, quamdiu pecunia soluta non sit, eis servitutibus creditor utatur (sci-*

servitude of rural land. In this case, jurists' doubts as to the resolution of this issue may have resulted from the inadmissibility of pledges on the servitude of urban land[665]. Nevertheless, since a similar fragment regarding the servitude of rural land was not preserved, and furthermore, the phrase *an… pignoris conventio locum habeat videndum esse* ('it should be considered whether there may be a pledge …') indicates a lack of appropriate regulation rather than a deviation from the rule of the law, it should be considered that this decision is in line with the *supra scriptum* interpretation scheme, and not a *contra scriptum one*. It seems, then, that not only did Pomponius propose a new solution but he also departed from *per analogiam* reasoning. Paulus thus decided that Pomponius' decision should be adopted *propter utilitatem contrahentium*[666].

Finally, it should also be mentioned that analyzing the examined category in the context of the *supra scriptum* interpretation brings to mind the law-making activity of the praetor, allowing for similar actions despite the lack of a statutory or edict basis. After all, their purpose was to regulate situations not covered by the original formula, and that is why there exists their obvious connection with *utilitas* in the function discussed in this section[667].

licet si vicinum fundum habeat) et, si intra diem certum pecunia soluta non sit, vendere eas vicino liceat: quae sententia propter utilitatem contrahentium admittenda est ('It should be considered whether there may be a pledge for servitude of a road, a passage, a drive or the use of a water supply. Pomponius states that such a contract should be drawn up in such a way that the creditor could use the servitude [under condition of being the owner of the neighbourly land] until he receives the receivables. And if the debt was not paid on time, he would have the right to sell the servitude to his neighbour. This opinion should be taken due to utility of the parties').

665 Marc. D. 20,1,11,3.

666 H. Ankum, *The functions…*, p. 19 and M. Navarra, *Ricerche…*, p. 133 also attribute the *ad utilitatem* reference to Paulus.

667 The connection between *actiones in factum* and *utilitas* is evidenced by Pomp. D. 19,5,11 *Quia actionum non plenus numerus esset, ideo plerumque actiones in factum desiderantur. sed et eas actiones, quae legibus proditae sunt, si lex iusta ac necessaria sit, supplet praetor in eo quod legi deest: quod facit in lege Aquilia reddendo actiones in factum accommodatas legi Aquiliae, idque utilitas eius legis exigit* ('As the number of actions is infinite, factual actions are often needed. But even those actions which are provided for in statutes, if a statute is just and necessary, the praetor supplements those aspects that the statute omits. It does so in relation to the *lex Aquilia*, granting factual actions adapted to the *lex Aquilia*, as required by the *utilitas* of this law'). See also P. Gröschler, *Actiones in factum. Eine Untersuchung zur Klage-Neuschöpfung im nichtvertraglichen Bereich*, Berlin 2002, pp. 12–13; M. F. Cursi, *Dal danno aquiliano al danno extracontrattuale: le radici romanistiche* [in:] *Itinerari giuridici. Per il quarantennale della Facoltà di Giurisprudenza dell'Abruzzo*, G. Canzio (ed.), Milano 2007, pp. 224–226 along with the literature cited therein.

3.3.3 Interpretation of Declarations of Intent

Similarly to the *contra scriptum* interpretation, the *ex utilitate* interpretation according to the *supra scriptum* scheme also served jurists in interpreting declarations of intent:

D. 45,1,115,2 (*Papinianus libro altero quaestionum*)
Item si quis ita stipuletur: SI PAMPHILVM NON DEDERIS, CENTVM DARI SPONDES? *Pegasus respondit non ante committi stipulationem, quam desisset posse Pamphilus dari. Sabinus autem existimabat ex sententia contrahentium, postquam homo potuit dari, confestim agendum et tamdiu ex stipulatione non posse agi, quamdiu per promissorem non stetit, quo minus hominem daret, idque defendebat exemplo penus legatae. Mucius etenim heredem, si dare potuisset penum nec dedisset, confestim in pecuniam legatam teneri scripsit, idque utilitatis causa receptum est ob defuncti voluntatem et ipsius rei naturam …*
Similarly, if someone stipulates as follows: 'do you promise to give me a hundred if you do not give Pamphilus?', Pegasus replied that the claim under an *actio ex stipulatu* would become due no sooner than when Pamphilus could no longer be handed over. At the same time, Sabinus believed that according to the contracting parties' intent it would be possible to bring an action immediately after the slave could be handed over, and that an *actio ex stipulatu* was admissible only after the promisor had influence on the fact he did not hand over the slave. He defended this position by quoting an example of the food left in the legacy. For Mucius wrote that an heir could be sue immediately for the payment of money if he could give food, and he did not. This was adopted due to *utilitas* because of the will of the deceased and the very essence of things …

As Papinian claims, *utilitas* also determined the moment when it was possible to file for the payment of money in the event of failure to hand over the food being the subject of the legate (*legatum penoris*[668]). According to the Republican jurist Quintus Mucius, the legatee had the right to demand the payment of money in lieu of alimony due to him immediately (*confestim*[669]) after the heir did not hand over the food although he could do so.

The jurist referred to this issue in the context of considering the moment in which the payment could be demanded if the promise to pay a hundred in the event of failing to hand over the slave Pamphilus, and this was done in the following form: SI PAMPHILVM NON DEDERIS, CENTVM DARI SPONDES? ('Do you promise to give a hundred if you do not give Pamphilus?'). A literal understanding of such a structured sentence meant that it was only possible to demand the payment of money, not the

668 See e.g. A. Ormanni, *Penus legata: contributi alla storia dei legati disposti con clausola penale in età repubblicana e classica*, Milano 1962.
669 On this concept, also in the context of the analyzed fragment, in G. Beseler, *Confestim – Continuo*, 'ZSS RA' 1931, vol. 51, no. 1, pp. 188–202.

trading of the slave. Furthermore, the promise to pay the money on a negative condition meant that only the objective impossibility of handing over the slave allowed one to file an action. The solution of this problem was the subject of dispute between the Sabinians and the Proculeians. Pegasus believed that money could only be claimed when the handover of the slave became objectively impossible. On the other hand, referring to the intent of the parties and Quintus Mucius' opinion quoted above, Sabinus concluded the action could be brought immediately after the debtor had not handed over the slave, although he had been able to do so[670].

The emphasis on the linguistic approach to the problem allows one to assume that *utilitas* does not appear here accidentally. The order for the payment of money in the event of failure to deliver the legate's subject was probably subject to a condition too. This is also indicated in the source material, according to which the *legatum penoris* was established in two alternative forms: HERES MEVS PENVM DATO, SI NON DEDERIS TANTVM DATO ('heir, hand over the food; if you do not, pay as much')[671], or SI HERES PENVM NON DEDERIT, TANTVM DATO ('if the heir does not hand over food, he should give as much')[672]. The latter expression is easily comparable to the one analyzed by Sabinus and Pegasus. Furthermore, since Sabinus quoted Quintus Mucius' decision as being analogous (*exemplo*)[673] to the one he proposed, it is possible that the Republican jurist's reflections concerned the other of the statements[674], causing an interpretative problem identical to that related to the handover of Pamphilus. It therefore seems that Quintus Mucius departed from the literal interpretation of the SI PENVM NON DEDERIT condition contained in the testament, categorizing it as a simple negative.

670 In the further part of the fragment Pap. D. 45,1,115,2 not quoted here, the jurist agreed with Sabinus' opinion. His reservations regarding the content of the promise support the correctness of the interpretation presented here. The jurist claimed that the wording of the promise should not stipulate payment of money only under a negative condition (SI PAMPHILVM NON DEDERIS, TANTVM DARE SPONDES?). According to a literal interpretation, payment could only be demanded in the case of the objective impossibility of handing over the slave. The jurist argued that the wording of the stipulation should be formulated to encompass both the handing over of the slave and the payment (PAMPHILVM DARI SPONDES? SI NON DEDERIS, TANTVM DARI SPONDES?). As Babusiaux writes, this allowed for 'accelerating' the entire process and to demand the handing over of Pamphilus. If the debtor still did not hand over the slave, the payment of money could also be requested. This aspect is more broadly analyzed in U. Babusiaux, *Id quod…*, pp. 51–54; Eadem, *Papinians Quaestiones: Zur rhetorischen Methode eines spätklassischen Juristen*, München 2014, pp. 63–137 (available online at: https://books.openedition.org/chbeck/1212).

671 Cf. Paul. D. 35,2,1,8; Iul. D. 36,2,19,pr.

672 Cf. Paul. D. 35,2,1,8; Iul. D. 36,2,19,1; Paul. D. 36,2,24,1.

673 This way also in M. Navarra, *Ricerche…*, p. 74.

674 This way in P. Frezza, *Le garanzie delle obbligazioni. I. Le garanzie personali*, Padova 1962, p. 325. Contrary in O. Forzieri Vannucchi, *Studi sull'interpretazione giurisprudenziale romana*, Milano 1973, p. 50; M. Navarra, *Ricerche…*, p. 77, n. 46. In turn, the first of the quoted phrases is analogous to the one that Papinian constructed, following the opinion of Sabinus (PAMPHILVM DARI SPONDES? SI NON DEDERIS, TANTVM DARI SPONDES?). For this reason, it should not raise any interpretational doubts.

He therefore did not limit the right to demand the payment solely to the situation of the objective impossibility of handing over the subject of the legacy[675], which was suggested by the literal interpretation. He considered it sufficient that the failure to hand over the object of the legacy depended on the will of the conditionally obligated party. Hence the wording SI PENVM NON DEDERIT was understood as: 'if he does not hand over the food although he is able to'. The *ad utilitatem* reference thus opened the way to the *supra scriptum* interpretation and recognition of the condition as potestative although it did not follow from the content of the declaration of intent. As a consequence, proving that despite the possibility of fulfilling the obligation, the heir did not hand over the legacy made it possible to immediately request the payment, which was more in line with the testator's will, as well as the alimony nature of the legacy[676].

In his *Quaestiones*, Papinian also referred to *utilitas* in the context of a broader interpretation of the category of persons authorized by the creditor to accept performance of the obligation:

D. 46,3,95,7 (*Papinianus libro vicesimo octavo quaestionum*)
Nam si furiosi vel pupilli persona adiecta sit, ita tutori vel curatori pecunia recte dabitur, si condicionis quoque implendae causa recte pecunia tutori vel curatori datur. quod quidem Labeo et Pegasus putaverunt utilitatis causa recipiendum: idque ita recipi potest, si pecunia in rem vel pupilli vel furiosi versa est, quomodo si domino iussus dare servo dedisset, ut domino daret. ceterum qui servo dare iussus est, domino dando non aliter implesse condicionem intellegendus est, quam si ex voluntate servi dedit. idem respondendum est in solutione, si stipulato Sempronio sibi aut Sticho Maevii servo decem dari debitor Maevio domino pecuniam solverit.
If a mentally ill person or a pupil is authorized by a creditor to collect the debt, both the guardian as well the curator will effectively collect the payment if the money is handed over to them in order to fulfil the condition. Labeo and Pegasus believed that this should be accepted for the sake of *utilitas*. And this can be affirmed if accepting the payment was in the interest of either the pupil or mentally ill, such as when someone ordered to pay the owner paid the slave so that he gave the money to the owner. After all, the one who was ordered to pay the slave by paying the owner also did not fulfil the condition unless he did so with the slave's consent. The same should be answered in the case of payment, if Sempronius took the stipulation promise that ten would be given to him or Stichus, a slave of Maevius, and the debtor would pay it to his owner.

675 Similarly in U. Leptien, *Utilitatis causa…*, p. 194.
676 Astolfi translated the expression *ipsius rei naturam* as *la particolare natura alimentare della disposizione testamentaria*, while Navarra translated it as *caratteri oggettivi della penus legata*. See R. Astolfi, *Studi sull'oggetto dei legati in diritto Romano*, Padova 1964, p. 94; M. Navarra, *Ricerche…*, pp. 77–78.

Papinian considers here whether it is permissible for the guardian or curator to effectively accept the payment from a third party in a situation where a mentally ill person or a pupil was authorized by a creditor to collect the amount owed. The problem therefore concerns the interpretation of a stipulation declaration of intent, in which the pupil or *furiosus*, and not the guardian or the curator, was appointed as *adiectus solutionis causa*. Then, in line with the literal interpretation, only entities expressly authorized to collect the debt amount could effectively accept the payment from a third party. However, according to the jurist, Labeo and Pegasus decided that due to *utilitas* it should be approved (*recipiendum*) that the guardian and curator could effectively accept the payment too[677]. Papinian agrees with the opinions of his predecessors[678]. However, he analyzes not only the situation of naming a pupil or mentally ill person in the declaration of intent but also once concerning the slave and the slave's owner. According to the interpretation proposed by Papinian, the explicitness of establishing the *solutionis causa adiectus* is broken by assuming that a pupil or a mentally ill person also means the one who exercises legal guardianship over them, and that a slave can also mean their owner and the other way round. In this sense, the *ad utilitatem* reference was an argument for specifying a broader group of entities authorized by a creditor to accept the payment than that which would result from the literal wording of the stipulation.

Ulpian informs about yet another possibility to supplement the content of the declaration of intent:

D. 26,2,10,4 (*Ulpianus libro trigesimo sexto ad Sabinum*)
Servus alienus ita dari tutor potest SI LIBER ERIT, TVTOR ESTO. *quin immo et si pure datus sit, videtur inesse haec condicio* CVM LIBER ERIT. *potest autem quis et extraneo servo defendere ex hac causa fideicommissariam libertatem: quid enim interest, suum servum an alienum tutorem scripserit, cum pupilli favore et publicae utilitatis adsumpta libertas sit in persona eius, qui tutor scriptus est? potest igitur et huic fideicommissaria libertas defendi, si voluntas apertissime non refragetur.*
A slave belonging to somebody else can be appointed a guardian in the following manner: 'Let him be a guardian when he becomes free'. Indeed, even if it were made without adding a condition, the wording of the declaration is deemed to already contain implicitly the condition 'when he becomes free'. One may also defend the position that the testament secured a manumission through a *fideicommissum* of someone else's slave in such a way. Does it matter if in the testament one made his own or someone else's slave a guardian, since the

677 Papinian's reasoning leads to the conclusion that the representatives of the Proculeian school referred to *utilitas*. If so, this would constitute the earliest documented reference by jurists to the category in question. This way in M. Navarra, *Ricerche…*, p. 14.

678 H. Ankum, *The functions…*, p. 8. However, Navarra aptly emphasizes that the opinion of Labeo and Pegasus was accepted with some reservation. The acceptance of the performance had to happen both in the interest of a debtor and, which was a novelty emphasized by Papinian, a pupil or a mentally ill person. See M. Navarra, *Ricerche…*, pp. 14–21.

> person who was appointed guardian had freedom granted for the benefit of the pupil and for the sake of *utilitas publica*? So, if the will of the deceased is not expressly opposed to this, it may be argued that someone else's slave was manumitted through a *fideicommissum*.

The content of the excerpt shows that someone else's slave could be appointed a guardian provided he was given freedom. Ulpian adds, however, that even though an addition CVM LIBER ERIT ('when he becomes free') was not mentioned in the will, the condition was still considered to be added[679]. The jurist further maintains that it was also possible to defend the interpretation based on the fact that making someone else's slave a guardian was a request directed at the heir or legate to (buy out and) manumit someone else's slave (*fideicomissaria libertas/manumissio fideicomissaria*[680]). As Ulpian writes, it should not matter whether one's own slave or someone else's slave was appointed guardian. This remark is not accidental. Regarding one's own slave, it was most likely assumed that making him a guardian implicitly meant at the same time manumitting him through a *fideicommissum*[681]. Ulpian therefore believed that a similar assumption could be made of someone else's slave. Thus, while the testator's will did not expressly oppose it, such an interpretation extending the expression TVTOR ESTO, was justified by the benefit of the pupil (*favor pupilli*) and *utilitas publica*[682]. The combination of these categories with the implied *favor libertatis* posed an interpretative challenge for researchers. Honsell stated that the analyzed category could here represent an effective appointment of a guardian, or liberation of a slave as acting for the public interest. According to him, it might as well be a pleonasm[683]. Stagl took it even

679 This view did not persist in the later law. Cf. I. 1,14,1 … *servus autem alienus pure inutiliter datur testamento tutor. sed ita:* CVM LIBER ERIT *utiliter datur…* ('The absolute handing over a someone else's slave as a testamentary bequest is ineffective. But if it done this way: "when he is free", it is done effectively').

680 See G. 2,263–272.

681 C. 7,4,10,pr. *Impp. Valerianus et Gallienus AA. Daphno.* pr. *Etsi non adscripta libertate testator servum suum tutorem filiis suis dederit, receptum est et libertatis et pupillorum favore, ut per fideicommissum manumisisse eum videatur.* ('Emperors Valerian and Gallienus, Augusti, to Daphnus. pr. Although when a testator appointed his slave as guardian for his sons, he did not manumit him, it is customary to consider, in favour of freedom and minors, that the testator manumitted the slave in the form of fideicommissary manumission' [February 27, 260]).

682 This information was also preserved in the further part of the rescript quoted in the previous footnote but without reference to *utilitas publica.* See C. 7,4,10,1 *Et si non suum proprium, sed alienum servum condicionem eius sciens tutorem adscripserit, aeque fideicommissariam libertatem datam, nisi aliud evidenter defunctum sensisse appareat, prudentibus placuit* ('Even if he had appointed a guardian not his own but someone else's slave, being fully aware of his status, the jurists accepted that he had likewise manumitted the slave in the form of fiduciary emancipation unless the deceased had explicitly opposed it'). It is also worth noting that in Ulpian's statement, the reference to *utilitas publica* is argumentative. In this context, the jurist's opinion should not probably be qualified as *ius receptum*. However, this situation appears to have changed over the course of several decades, as Valerian and Gallienus seemingly took this view as part of *ius receptum*.

683 T. Honsell, *Gemeinwohl…*, pp. 113–114.

further by suggesting that the passage could be interpreted as the gradual abolition of the institution of slavery for the public interest[684]. Here, it is crucial to note that there are numerous passages that position certain aspects of guardianship within the realm of *ius publicum*[685]. Perhaps, it should not come as a surprise, then, that Ulpian combined *favor pupilli* and *utilitas publica,* especially that he employed the latter category in the context of appointing a guardian also in D. 38,17,2,44[686], introducing a *contra scriptum* interpretation of the declaration of intent. Therefore, the presence of *utilitas publica* in the above quoted fragment also appears to be linked to the process of interpretation: its role was to break the wording of the will and supplement its content with provisions not included there.

The following excerpt from the second book of Papinian's *Definitiones* should also be interpreted in a similar vein:

> D. 40,7,36 (*Papinianus libro altero definitionum*)
> *In tabulis secundis filio servum data libertate substitutum iure statuliberi prudentes munierunt: quod utilitas recipit, scilicet ut cum sua causa alienaretur, ne patris testamentum puer filius rescindat. quae iuris auctoritas citra dilectum ordinis ad secundum quoque vel tertium substitutum porrecta est.*
> Jurists secured the position of a slave substituted for a son with his simultaneous manumission by granting him the status of a conditionally freed slave (*statuliber*). Such a decision is allowed by *utilitas,* obviously so that the disposal of such a slave would not change his legal situation, and the son would not go against his father's testament. The authority of jurists extended this principle indiscriminately also to the second and third grade of testamentary substitutions.

Papinian explains that a slave manumitted in a will who was appointed a pupillary substitute for the testator's son was granted the status of *statuliber,* namely a slave manumitted upon a condition. Such a slave was still an object of ownership but was treated a little more leniently. Thus, although he could be disposed of, the *statuliber* retained the right to his conditional freedom. Regardless of the will of its current owner, when the condition was fulfilled, the *statuliber* thus obtained his freedom[687].

684 J.F. Stagl, *Die Funktionen…*, p. 521; Idem, *Camino…*, pp. 92–93.

685 See B. Albanese, *Le persone nel diritto privato romano*, Palermo 1979, p. 62 and more recently G. Viarengo, *Studi sulla tutela dei minori*, Torino 2016, pp. 12–19 along with the literature and sources cited therein. Cf. also Mod. D. 26,6,2,2; Ulp. D. 26,7,5,7.

686 On these two fragments see also R. Scevola, *"Utilitas publica", II. Elaborazione…*, pp. 9–46.

687 W.W. Buckland, *The Roman Law of Slavery…*, pp. 286–291 along with the literature cited therein as well as an extensive list of sources.

The view Papinian writes about was previously expressed by Celsus[688], which is confirmed by the already analyzed fragment of the fourth book of Ulpian's *Libri ad Sabinum* (D. 40,7,2,4)[689]. Although in both sources the jurists referred to the category of *utilitas*[690], contrary to the views presented by Ankum and Finazzi, this does not indicate that in both cases an identical solution was proposed in the form of assigning the substitute slave the position of *statuliber*[691]. As already explained, in Ulp. D. 40,7,2,4, a slave was granted the status of a testator's *heres necessarius* although granting him freedom was not combined with the substitution in the same grade of the will but in different grades. It was thus a decision omitting the rule of the law[692].

Here, *utilitas* quoted by Papinian suggests that the case could have involved a literal interpretation of the will, the content of which did not include the conditional manumission. Nevertheless, it was decided that a slave substituted for a son and manumitted at the same time obtains the status of *statuliber* regardless of the wording of the testament. This decision strengthened the position of substituted slaves[693] but most of all secured a more complete fulfilment of a testator's will. So even if, for whatever reason, a slave was disposed of before an heir's son reached maturity, this did not in any way ruin the testamentary provisions[694]. It is worth noting here that, unlike in the case of the *status scripti et voluntatis* reception, all the above-quoted decisions based on *utilitas* in the *supra scriptum* scheme were consistent with the testator's will.

Then, is Navarra right saying that the *utilitates* from Ulp. D. 40,7,2,4 and Pap. D. 40,7,36 do not overlap?[695] She is and she is not. As noted in Introduction, Navarra always aims at clarifying the content of the category under study. She then rightly notices that the goals of Ulpian's and Papinian's decisions were divergent. It is also easy to notice a certain difference in the effects of applying the *utilitas* criterion.

688 Moreover, another passage Ulp. D. 40,7,2,1 reveals that this view was also shared by Julian but not by Cassius. It seems that in Papinian's times the decision was not yet part of *ius receptum* but was still a matter of debate. Therefore, the jurist's opinion should be interpreted as an expression of support for views of Celsus and Julian.

689 Ulp. D. 40,7,2,4… *Celsus quoque putat libro quinto decimo cum libertate substitutum statuliberi causam optinere* ('… in Book 15 of the *Digest*, Celsus also claims that a slave who was substituted for another heir along with being manumitted obtains the status of a conditionally freed slave').

690 G. Finazzi, *La sostituzione pupillare*, Napoli 1997, p. 421 argues the reference to *utilitas* was already present in Celsus' decision. On the other hand, M. Navarra, *Ricerche…*, p. 139, thinks that it is an element added by Papinian.

691 H. Ankum, *'Utilitatis causa receptum'. On the pragmatical methods…*, pp. 25–26; G. Finazzi, *La sostituzione…*, p. 230.

692 Cf. again C. 6,27,4,pr.–2, as well as previous comments on this topic.

693 For this reason, the present decision used to be interpreted as a manifestation of *favor libertatis*, combined with the category of *utilitas*. Cf. H. Ankum, *'Utilitatis causa receptum': sur la méthode pragmatique…*, p. 131; Idem, *'Utilitatis causa receptum'. On the pragmatical methods…*, p. 25; U. Leptien, *'Utilitatis causa'…*, p. 61. This fragment is interpreted as a manifestation of *favor substitutionis* by G. Finazzi, *La sostituzione…*, p. 409.

694 Similarly in M. Navarra, *Ricerche…*, p. 139.

695 Ibid., pp. 139–140.

To use rhetorical terminology, in Pap. D. 40,7,36, it is referred to in the context of, in a way, the *supra scriptum* interpretation; in Ulp. D. 40,7,2,4, it is an example of the *contra scriptum* interpretation. This does not mean, however, that the quoted decisions mention separate *utilitates*. For in each of them, *utilitas* is an instrument that allows a departure from a literal interpretation, and thus its role in the thought of jurisprudence remained unchanged. Finally, this is confirmed by the last of the decisions discussed in this section:[696]

> D. 13,5,24 (*Marcellus libro singulari responsorum*)
> *Titius Seio epistulam emisit in haec verba:* REMANSERVNT APVD ME QVINQVAGINTA EX CREDITO TVO EX CONTRACTV PVPILLORUM MEORVM, QVOS TIBI REDDERE DEBEBO IDIBVS MAIIS PROBOS: QVOD SI AD DIEM SVPRA SCRIPTVM NON DEDERO, TVNC DARE DEBEBO VSVRAS TOT. *quaero, an Lucius Titius in locum pupillorum hac cautione reus successerit. Marcellus respondit si intercessisset stipulatio, successisse. item quaero, an, si non successisset, de constituta teneatur. Marcellus respondit in sortem teneri: est enim humanior et utilior ista interpretatio.*
> Titius sent a letter to Seius with the following words: 'I have fifty left of your loan which you arranged with my pupils. I will be obliged to return this amount to you on the Ides of May (May 15) in coins of good quality. If I do not do so by the deadline set above, I will owe you this interest'. I am asking whether Lucius Titius became a debtor to Seius in the place of his pupils on the basis of this promise. Marcellus replied that if a stipulation promise was made, he substituted his pupils. I am also asking: if he would have not substituted the pupils, is he responsible for making an informal promise to fulfil an existing obligation? Marcellus replied that he was liable with regard to capital. Such an interpretation is more kind and more useful.

Seius lent money to Titius' pupils. In his letter, the latter promised to return the loan, while promising penalty interest in the event of a delayed repayment. The first question refers to whether there is a novation, meaning whether Titius assumed the debt obligations in place of his pupils. Marcellus replied that the obligation would only be renewed if the stipulation had been made. The second question concerns whether Titius would have been liable for making an informal promise to pay someone else's debt (*constitutum debiti alieni*) if no new obligation was created. Marcellus answered that Titius was indeed responsible for the payment, however only up to the amount of the capital (*in sortem*), that is, without the promised penalty interest, as such interpretation was more kind (*humanior*) and more useful (*utilior*). These terms used to be understood as referring to the 'softening' Titius' responsibility *per se*[697]. It seems, how-

696 This decision predates the ones discussed in this section. However, since the context provided here significantly aids in its interpretation, I have chosen to depart from the usual chronological order.
697 A. Palma, *Humanior…*, p. 38.

ever, this was not the essence of the problem. Interest was promised on a stipulation basis, or it was agreed on the basis of an ordinary *pactum*, for instance, added to a *bonae fidei* contract. Neither of these situations occurs in the present case.

An in-depth analysis of the fragment has been recently carried out by Paolo Costa, who explains that, in fact, the interpretative doubt in the text does not concern interest but whether the declaration of the debt payment submitted by Titius in the letter can be interpreted as *constitutum debiti alieni*[698]. The key issue here is therefore the phrase TIBI REDDERE DEBEBO ('I will be obliged to return to you') and the doubt whether it constitutes a source of an informal obligation under the praetorian law. Indeed, it recognizes the obligation to pay, but it does not explicitly promise debt payment[699]. By way of interpretation breaking the literal meaning of the word REDDERE DEBEBO thanks to the reference to *utilitas*, Marcellus concluded that Titius' declaration could indeed be considered a promise to pay someone else's debt. The interest, however, was not considered due, as it was not part of the loan contract with the pupils. Thus, the *ex utilitate supra scriptum* interpretation allowed the extension of the scope of application of this institution to situations not covered by it[700] according to the literal interpretation of the declaration of intent.

3.4 *Utilitatis causa* Decisions and *ius singulare*

When analyzing the *utilitatis causa* decisions, we should refer to the topic of *ius singulare* (singular law)[701]. Similarly to the decisions quoted, *iura singularia* are seen as exceptions to the rules. This analogy as well as the fact that *utilitas* is one of the categories that make up the definition of *ius singulare* coined by Paulus made some researchers associate these two areas with each other[702].

698 P. Costa, *'Constituta per littera' e riconoscimento del debito: ipotesi esegetiche*, 'Teoria e Storia del Diritto Privato' 2021, no. 14, pp. 16–36 along with the literature cited therein.

699 Costa argues that other declarations of intent that may raise similar doubts are also analyzed in Scaev. D. 13,5,26. See Ibidem, p. 25. Ideally, the wording of an obligation to pay someone else's debt should rather contain a verb *solvere* ('to pay'). Cf. reconstruction by O. Lenel, *Das Edictum perpetuum...*, p. 215.

700 C. Zülch, *Der 'Liber singularis responsorum' des Ulpius Marcellus*, Berlin 2001, p. 58; P. Costa, *'Constituta...*, pp. 30–31.

701 Similar considerations are conducted by M. Navarra, *Ricerche...*, pp. 195–204. Her most important conclusions will be presented in the following subsection.

702 R. Orestano, *Ius singulare e privilegium in diritto romano: Contributo storico-dommatico*, Tolentino 1937, pp. 22–23, who gives Iul. D. 9,2,51,2 as the example of the *ius singulare*. In his analysis of the decisions taken *utilitatis causa*, Ankum also included the definition of the *ius singulare* as formulated by Paulus, which is quoted below. Cf. H. Ankum, *'Utilitatis causa receptum'. On the pragmatical methods...*, p. 28.

Such a perspective seemed to be supported by Papinian's opinion preserved in D. 41,2,44,1. The jurist stated that through their slaves, owners acquired the possession of things that became part of the *peculium* even if they were not aware of this circumstance. This decision was adopted according to Papinian *utilitatis causa iure singulari,* namely for the sake of *utilitas* as the *ius singulare. Utilitas* appeared in this decision in its well-known function: as an instrument of breaching the literal interpretation. On the other hand, the concept of *ius singulare* plays the role of a certain categorization of the decision[703], even not necessarily in a technical sense[704].

It is therefore possible that the *ius singulare* referred to by Papinian and the *ius singulare* defined by Paulus did not coincide in terms of content. If, however, we assumed that both jurists referred to the same category, and equated the effects of the *utilitatis causa* decisions and *iura singularia,* Papinian's expression *utilitatis causa iure singulari* could actually be considered a tautology. Yet it seems that we should be prudent with regard to such conclusions and follow the view of Navarra, who recommends greater caution in formulating theses suggesting the general convergence of the *ius singulare* and decisions taken *utilitatis causa*[705].

Certainly, it is hard to avoid the impression of the twin nature of the *ius singulare* institution and the *utilitatis causa* decisions. This is not the place to analyze individual *iura singularia* but – in order to try to understand to what extent these two sets of norms could overlap – it is worth devoting more attention to theoretical considerations and compare the conclusions that have been formulated so far with Paulus' definition of the singular law:

> D. 1,3,16 (*Paulus libro singulari de iure singulari*)
> *Ius singulare est, quod contra tenorem rationis propter aliquam utilitatem auctoritate constituentium introductum est.*
> The singular law is one introduced against the tenor of a rule and set out for some utility under the authority of lawmakers.

According to Paulus, the basis of *ius singulare* constitute four essential elements: *introductum est, contra tenorem rationis, propter aliquam utilitatem,* and *auctoritas constituentium,* each of which raises questions of interpretation. Here, several alternative hypotheses regarding the correlation of the *ius singulare* institution and the *utilitatis causa* decisions will be therefore presented.

703 Cf. comments on D. 41,2,44,1 in the Appendix.

704 This way in F. Wubbe, *Ius singulare quid sit* [in:] *Ars boni et aequi. Festschrift für Wolfgang Waldstein zum 65. Geburtstag*, M. Schermaier, Z. Vegh (ed.), Stuttgart 1993, p. 469.

705 M. Navarra, *Ricerche…*, p. 200. The researcher also rightly observes that the reference to *ius singulare* did not survived even in a single decision taken *utilitatis causa* by Paulus, which could further challenge the convergence of the two categories. Cf. Ibidem, p. 202.

The jurist thus writes that the singular law is introduced *auctoritate constituentium*, and therefore by virtue of the authority of those making the law. This expression is usually understood by researchers in two ways: either as a circumstance saying that only the emperor[706] was entitled to establish the *ius singulare* (Paulus would then write about the *auctoritas principis*[707]), or that *iura singularia* were also created under the authority of other entities with competence to create the law, jurists in particular[708]. For obvious reasons, agreeing with the first hypothesis would decide about the *iura singularia* and the *utilitatis causa* decisions being two separate fields[709], and conclude the considerations. However, even for a thought experiment, it is worth making a further comparison in the other three aspects.

Paulus explains that the *ius singulare* is part of the law in force. To describe these consequences, he uses the phrase *introductum est*, which, it seems, in terms of the validity, should be equated with the expression *receptum est*[710]. Consequently, only the *utilitatis causa* decisions which were included in the area of *ius receptum* – and therefore not all – could possibly qualify as *iura singularia*[711].

The jurist also noted that the *ius singulare* was established *contra tenorem rationis*. As shown earlier, the concept of *ratio* can be interpreted in many ways, and it is no different in the analyzed case. Some scholars propose a slight supplement here, reading this phrase as *contra tenorem*[712] *rationis iuris*. Consequently, they recognize that the *ius*

706 G. Pugliese, *I principi generali del diritto. L'esperienza romana fino a Diocleziano* [in:] *Atti dei Convegni Lincei 96. Convegno sul tema: I principi generali del diritto (Roma, 27–29 maggio 1991)*, Roma 1992, p. 74, n. 10; A. Guarino, *Il problema dogmatico e storico del diritto singolare* [in:] *Pagine di Diritto Romano*, vol. 6, Napoli 1995, p. 32, n. 107; J. F. Stagl, *Das 'testamentum militare' in seiner Eigenschaft als 'ius singulare'*, 'Revista de estudios histórico-jurídicos' 2014, no. 36, pp. 145–146 along with the list of extensive literature to support his thesis in n. 131. An earlier discussion on this topic in R. Orestano, *Ius singulare...*, pp. 63–67.

707 On the concept of *auctoritas* broadly in R. Domingo, *Auctoritas*, Barcelona 1999.

708 R. Orestano, *Ius singulare...*, pp. 68–73; H. Ankum, *'Utilitatis causa receptum'. On the pragmatical methods...*, p. 28; T. Giaro, *Geltung...*, p. 79, n. 90; A. Wacke, *Das Rechtswort: Tenor*, 'ZSS RA' 2020, vol. 137, no. 1, p. 309, n. 93. Pomponius, for example, writes on the authority of jurists using a similar phrase: D. 50,16,120 ... *auctoritate iura constituentium*.

709 This way in M. Navarra, *Ricerche...*, p. 198.

710 See T. Giaro, *Geltung...*, p. 79, who, while quoting the following sources in n. 90: Pap. D. 40,5,23,3 (the passage discussed in this study); Pap. D. 41,2,44,1; Pap. D. 41,3,44,3 and Ulp. D. 12,1,15, points out that the phrase *iure singulari* is often accompanied by the expression *receptum est*. He also highlights Papinian is the author of most of these accounts.

711 M. Navarra, *Ricerche...*, p. 200, who at this point deviates from her general hypothesis that *utilitas* in the *utilitatis causa* decisions was almost never invoked as an argument.

712 It should be noted that Paulus uses the phrase *contra tenorem rationis*, and not – *contra rationem*, although it is possible that these two terms should be treated synonymously. This way in R. Orestano, *Ius singulare...*, p. 52. In this context, the *tenor rationis* is sometimes interpreted as the 'essence of the content' of the *ratio* (A. Wacke, *Das Rechtswort...*, p. 309 uses the term 'Kerngehalt'), but also as the 'guideline' of the *ratio* and 'logical consequences' resulting from it. Cf. R. Orestano, *Ius singulare...*, p. 52; R. Ambrosino, *Ius singulare*, Milano 1947, pp. 357–358. In the latter sense, Paulus uses the term *tenor* in reference to the *lex Aquilia*. See D. 9,2,56 ...*pro tenore legis Aquiliae*.

singulare is inherently incompatible with the legal order: either with its rules[713], or with the underlying logic[714]. Such interpretation could correspond to a specific category of the decisions taken *utilitatis causa,* namely those classified before as fitting the *contra scriptum* scheme. Certainly, it cannot be ruled out that Paulus used this term in a broader sense that would allow for a multitude of interpretations. However, since the word *contra* clearly indicates a contradiction[715], it seems the potential set of decisions that could be classified as *iura singularia* should also exclude those which, according to rhetorical terminology, jurists accepted *supra scriptum.*

The last element constituting the singular law is introducing it *propter aliquam utilitatem,* namely because of some utility. Although this expression seems to resemble those encountered in the analysis of the *utilitatis causa* decisions, it is in fact most enigmatic. Paulus speaks of a specific utility (*aliqua utilitas*)[716], which – in one form or another – is a distinguishing feature of absolutely every legal norm, regardless of whether it is consistent with the legal order or not[717]. It has been shown, however, that it is not this type of category that appears in the *utilitatis causa* decisions. Although these decisions as well, as explained case-by-case by Ankum, Leptien and Navarra, corresponded to a specific benefit, the criterion of *utilitas* they refer to, in its technical function, is uniform and serves to break the results of a literal interpretation. Jurists' *utilitas* is sometimes clarified in terms of its content. Yet, in such cases it is always someone's or something's utility (*alicuius utilitas*), not a specific one (*aliqua utilitas*). Moreover, the role of the category remains unchanged. Paulus' *aliqua utilitas* is therefore a specific reason for introducing a given norm, yet always having, as Navarra phenomenally described it, an external character to the law-making process[718]. (This fact, however, certainly does not preclude its distinction from *aequitas,* as explained by Falcone[719]). In turn, *utilitas* in the *utilitatis causa* decisions does not indicate the reason for taking them but is an instrument of a legal interpretation, always integral to the law[720].

713 Cf. e.g. Ibid., pp. 51–55 along with the literature cited therein; A. Wacke, *Das Rechtswort…*, p. 309.

714 This way e.g. in R. Ambrosino, *Ius singulare,* pp. 358–361. Both possibilities reported in J. F. Stagl, *Das 'testamentum militare'…*, p. 144, who in n. 116 also presents the literature review.

715 A. Guarino, *Il problema…*, p. 35.

716 R. Orestano, *Ius singulare…*, pp. 56–57. A. Wacke, *Das Rechtswort…*, p. 308 translates this concept even as *Zweckmäßigkeitsgründen,* using the plural form, which indicates that he does not interpret this term as a uniform criterion.

717 Ibid., p. 32; M. Navarra, *Ricerche…*, pp. 197–198 along with the literature cited therein.

718 Ibid., p. 202.

719 G. Falcone, *Beneficia imperiali e 'logica del sistema'. Spunti di metodo tra le righe di Alberto Burdese,* 'BIDR' 2015, vol. 109, pp. 219–223, along with the literature and sources cited therein.

720 While juxtaposing *utilitas* with Paulus' *aliqua utilitas,* Navarra defines the former in the decisions taken *utilitatis causa* as a *criterio autonomo del giurista per la costruzione sistematica,* thus returning to her general hypothesis about the nature of the decisions studied. See M. Navarra, *Ricerche…*, p. 203. Cf. also P. Cerami, *Problemi storico-dogmatici…* p. 402; Idem, *Potere…*, p. 169.

At this point, another fragment should be quoted, in which Ulpian writes that *utilitas*, and additionally the obvious one (*evidens*), needed to support a departure[721] from the law which was long considered to be right:

> D. 1,4,2 (*Ulpianus fideicommissorum libro quarto*)
> *In rebus novis constituendis evidens esse utilitas debet, ut recedatur ab eo iure, quod diu aequum visum est.*
> When introducing novel solutions, the utility must be obvious in order to depart from the law which was long considered to be right.

The 'law' referred to by the jurist should be understood as those norms which Giaro, following Kaser, calls *gewordenes Juristenrecht* (as opposed to *werdendes Juristenrecht*)[722]. Their validity therefore did not raise any doubts among jurists. However, they could be departed from or changed if *utilitas evidens* supported it[723]. Yet, this category also does not coincide with the content of *utilitas* present in the *utilitatis causa* decisions. Due to the reference to *aequitas*, it is perhaps easier to attribute it an ethical tinge to it than to the term *aliqua utilitas* from the excerpt of Paulus' work. Still, *utilitas evidens* symbolizes a specific benefit, an important motive[724] that should stand behind a thoughtful[725] adoption of changes to the law. Obviously, as has been emphasized many times, there had to be the reasons for adopting particular *utilitatis causa* decisions. However, it is not these particular *utilitates*-motives, or at least not exclusively, that were referred to

721 In this context, Ulpian uses the verb *recedere*, which clearly implies the withdrawal or abandonment of the application of the norm, though not necessarily its repeal. In this aspect, Ulpian's account aligns closely with the nature of the *utilitatis causa* decisions. On the other hand, the following fragment was excluded from the analysis: Call. D. 50,9,5 *Quod semel ordo decrevit, non oportere id rescindi divus Hadrianus Nicomedensibus rescripsit nisi ex causa: id est si ad publicam utilitatem respiciat rescissio prioris decreti* ('The divine Hadrian decided in his rescript addressed to the inhabitants of Nicomedia that what had once been decided by the city council should not be overruled, except for a valid reason. That is if the annulment of the earlier decree takes into account the category of *utilitas publica*'). At first glance, the fragment seems similar to Ulp. D. 1,4,2. However, unlike the categories of *evidens utilitas* and *utilitas* in the *utilitatis causa* decisions, *utilitas publica*, as established by Hadrian according to Callistratus, constituted a motive for the repeal (*rescissio*) of the previously binding law.

722 Cf. M. Kaser, *Römische Rechtsquellen und angewandte Juristenmethode: ausgewählte, zum Teil grundlegend erneuerte Abhandlungen*, Wien-Köln 1986, p. 36; T. Giaro, *Geltung…* p. 83. These two categories Schwarz described as *strittiges* and *unstrittiges Recht*. Cf. A.B. Schwarz, *Das strittige Recht der römischen Juristen* [in:] *Festschrift Fritz Schulz*, vol. 2, H. Niedermeyer, W. Flume (ed.), Weimar 1951, pp. 201–225. The most common terms for these categories today are perhaps *ius controversum* and *ius receptum*.

723 M. Navarra grants this power to the emperor, *Ricerche…*, p. 11.

724 T. Giaro, *Geltung…* p. 83; R. Orestano, *Ius singulare…*, pp. 56–57. N. Rampazzo, *Quasi praetor…*, pp. 510–511, highlights that the new solutions should benefit not only for the individual involved but also the community as a whole.

725 M. Zabłocka, *Rzymskie źródła techniki legislacyjnej*, 'Palestra' 2016, vol. 1–2, p. 15.

in the content of the *utilitatis causa* decisions, but the interpretative category allowing for a departure from a literal interpretation.

3.5 Summary

The aim of Chapter Three was to delve into the nature of the *utilitatis causa* decisions and the role of the *utilitas* category within them. The analysis began by examining the function of this criterion in the rhetorical theory of legal interpretation rather than immediately focusing on the works of jurisprudence. It has been shown that, particularly in Cicero's doctrine, *utilitas* played a significant role in the so-called *status* – rhetorical types of issues denoting the matter of the dispute. The analyzed category was used as an interpretation criterion in situations where the letter of the law seemed to contradict its intention. This created a gap between the literal (*ex scripto/litteris*) and teleological interpretation. The latter, made by rhetoricians *ex voluntate/sententia,* that is, according to the will or intention of the law or the legislator, assumed the categories of *aequitas* and *utilitas* as determinants of interpreting legal norms. In the rhetorical theory of legal interpretation, the terms *sententia, voluntas, aequitas* and *utilitas* seem to be intertwined with each other. The last of them pointed out not to pragmatism but the utility of a community, consistent with the utility of all citizens. Both the teleological and ethical aspects of the criterion are therefore evident.

The discrepancy between the letter and spirit of the law was particularly visible when a given case was legally regulated. In such cases the so-called *status scripti et voluntatis/sententiae* could be utilized. The party arguing *ex sententia* reasoned *contra scriptum,* that is, contrary to the literal interpretation. The effects of such an interpretation were not limited to a broader or restrictive understanding of norms but brought about a completely opposite result to that which arose from a literal interpretation. According to the *contra scriptum* interpretation, the correct decision required either the non-application of the norm, even though according to the literal interpretation it should be done, or its application, even though its literal understanding precluded it. The category of the legal rule was understood by rhetoricians in two ways: as a normative entity or as a linguistic expression. The rhetorical *contra scriptum* reasoning was an example of breaking the unambiguous results of their literal interpretation, facilitated by *utilitas.*

The same pattern is easily seen in most jurisprudence *utilitatis causa* decisions. When interpreting *contra scriptum,* jurists referred to *utilitas,* and either departed from the application of the norm, or applied it, always contrary to what was dictated by a literal interpretation. In addition, like rhetoricians, they also perceived the category of rule in two ways, that is, both as a normative entity and a linguistic expression.

Just as the *status scripti et sententiae* did not exhaust the conflict of these two categories based on the rhetorical interpretation of the law, the *contra scriptum* decisions do not express the full essence of the *utilitatis causa* decisions. It also happened that the law was silent on a given issue. Rhetoricians settled such matters under the *status syllogismi*. The *ex sententia* interpretation was then conducted *supra scriptum* and resulted in the inclusion of a given case in the legal order. The unambiguous *ex scripto* interpretation was then broken by creating a new norm. This scheme also corresponds to some of the analyzed decisions of jurisprudence.

Considering both patterns of interpretation, it can be stated that the full nature of the decisions adopted *utilitatis causa* is expressed in the tension between the literal and teleological interpretation, and its content is to break the unambiguous results of the literal interpretation. Although strongly inspired by rhetorical thought, this interpretation was nevertheless the product of jurisprudence. Legal *utilitas*, unlike rhetorical one, was usually not a determinant of an *ex voluntate* interpretation, be it the legislator or the one declaring their intent. Instead, it referred to the highest goal of the law, which was *utilitas*.

Therefore, as a rule, jurisprudence *utilitas* in the analyzed decisions ontologically corresponds to the rhetorical and philosophical *utilitas communis*. Even if jurists sometimes specify its content, the reference always takes place in the same function. Thus, although specific interests stood behind the *utilitatis causa* decisions as for all others, it is not necessary to specify them to recognize the role of the criterion. For *utilitas* does not indicate the individual purposes of a given decision but goes back to the fundamental rule of legal interpretation. The reference in the decision of the analyzed category was thus deeply rooted in intellectual thought. For this reason, the *utilitatis causa* decisions are not, at least not exclusively, a manifestation of jurists' pragmatism. Recognizing them as a typical result of a teleological interpretation does not exhaust their character either. They are not merely examples of a teleological interpretation aimed at resolving ambiguities; instead, they reflect efforts by jurist to correct the unambiguous results of linguistic interpretation and avoid applying what definitely resulted *ex litteris*.

Conclusions

Wherever one looks, they see *utilitas* – this is how the ancient Romans' thinking about the law and in the law could be summarized. The category of 'utility', 'benefit', 'interest' was present in virtually every area of Roman law. And in the so-called *utilitatis causa* decisions, it manifested itself in a particularly distinctive way.

It was the theses expressed in the literature regarding these decisions that guided the reflections aimed at understanding the essence of *utilitas* and its role in legal interpretation. Two trends of inquiries raised questions as to whether the examined criterion was filled only by the pragmatic content, and whether it could be identified as the determinant of the teleological interpretation. Unlike previous research on the *utilitatis causa* decisions, this study was not limited to the achievements of jurisprudence. Instead, it framed legal thought within the broader intellectual tradition of philosophy and rhetoric. In antiquity, the boundaries between these fields were not as rigid as they seem to be today. Since based on the legacy of jurists it is difficult to say whether jurisprudence *utilitas* was closer to Horace's *mater iusti et aequi* or to the mother of pragmatism, exploring these intellectual traditions seemed essential.

The references to *utilitas* in the adversative function are also present in Cicero and Quintilian. Thus, the analysis began with an attempt to reconstruct the content of the concept within a broader intellectual context. It was shown that *utilitas* was not merely an expression of the pursuit of satisfying human needs but also a belief in the solid moral basis of the law. In both philosophical and jurisprudence thought, *utilitas* was inextricably linked with ethical measures such as *aequitas* and *honestas,* as well as justice (*iustitia*). Whether a given legal norm could be assessed as right and just depended on whether it was also perceived as useful. The disintegration of these ideas was practically impossible, not only in philosophy but also in the thought of jurists. A special illustration of the interrelationship between these categories is a definition of the concept of *ius,* described by Celsus as *ars boni et aequi.* Since all ancient *artes* pursued an end useful to life (*finis utilis vitae*), *bonum et aequum* should be interpreted as the object of the useful endeavours of *ars iuris.* Thus, perceiving *utilitas* in legal thought solely through the lens of legal practice needs would be a mistake, although they are undoubtedly part of it. *Utilitas,* however, is a special category, at the same time taking the axiological connotation in the form of moral, ideological-political and economic values into account. These findings were therefore the first step to demonstrate that the references *ad utilitatem* in the *utilitatis causa* decisions were not a mere equivalent of pure pragmatism. Thus, although Ankum is not mistaken in explaining the term *utilitatis causa* as 'meeting the needs of legal practice', this explanation does not fully capture the phenomenon under study.

To determine whether *utilitas* could be understood in teleological terms, and whether it was a manifestation of the legal method, it was shown that this idea determined the entire interpretative activity of Roman jurisprudence. It served as the basis for jurists' considerations, as well as it set the direction of their thought. To put it another way, it contained both the beginning and the end of interpretative actions. Cicero had also earlier indicated a similar relationship between *utilitas* and *iustitia*, presenting the former sometimes as a goal and sometimes as a source of the latter. It was shown that *utilitas publica* and *utilitas privata* were two harmonized perspectives within one category. Always associated with what was good and right, *utilitas* fuelled the activity of Roman jurisprudence. If so, then every interpretative action had to follow the scheme of the teleological *ex utilitate* interpretation. Hence, it is not an exaggeration to say that all the decisions of jurists were in a sense reached in the *utilitatis causa* manner. For this reason, the category of *utilitas* should be seen as a determinant of the method of interpretation and not merely as teleological technique. On the other hand, it weakens the hypothesis that teleological interpretation could suffice to explain the uniqueness of the *utilitatis causa* decisions. Proposing or issuing a decision for a specific benefit could not therefore be their distinctive feature.

Now, Leesen's words come to mind, as she aptly concludes in her study on the intersection of law and rhetoric that 'in some cases, the legal problem could only be reconstructed by using the relevant *formula*'[726]. Here, the source and reasons for the adversative nature of the *utilitatis causa* decisions were found in the rhetorical theory of legal interpretation, specifically in the *status scripti et sententiae/voluntatis* and *status syllogismi*. Within these schemes, the interpretation given *ex voluntate/sententia* (according to the will or intention of the law or the legislator) was opposed to literal interpretation referred to as *ex scripto/litteris*. Under the *status scripti et sententiae*, the party arguing *ex sententia* argumented *contra scriptum*, against literal interpretation. The interpreted law was at times perceived in terms of a normative entity, and at times a linguistic phenomenon. Regardless of whether the focus was on the entire regulation or on specific words, the effects of such an interpretation were not limited to a broader or restrictive interpretation, but, above all, they produced a completely opposite result to that which arose on the basis of a literal interpretation. Consequently, the *contra scriptum* interpretation resulted either in the non-application of the norm (although according to the literal interpretation it should be done) or in its application (although its literal understanding excluded it). On the other hand, under the *status syllogismi*,

726 T. G. Leesen, *Gaius…*, p. 324.

the interpretation *supra scriptum* took place, that is despite the fact that the law did not provide for a proper regulation for a given case. The *ex sententia* interpretation thus allowed rhetoricians to break the unambiguous results of the linguistic interpretation.

For the conducted considerations, the fragments of Cicero's writings are invaluable, certifying that *utilitas* was a determinant of the *ex sententia* interpretation, as the *utilitatis causa* decisions fit perfectly into the aforementioned schemes of rhetorical interpretation, both *contra* and *supra scriptum*. Like rhetoricians, jurists interpreted the law from two perspectives: as a normative entity and as a linguistic expression[727]. Like the rhetorical interpretation, the jurisprudence *utilitatis causa* one invariably led to the breaking of the unambiguous results of literal interpretation. Hence, it resulted either in a departure from the rules of the law, or in breaking the literal meaning of the terms constituting the law as a linguistic phenomenon. So although Wacke is correct when stating that the dominant method of Roman jurists was not based on concepts and definitions[728], these were often the starting point for further considerations. So if it was necessary to decide whether classical jurists represented the *Interessen-* or *Begriffsjurisprudenz* approach, one would have to agree with the former while following Ankum, but with special attention to the linguistic and logical interpretation, the importance of which was emphasized by Seidl.

It is not the tension between the rule and exception, then, but the conflict between the *pro scripto* and *contra scriptum* interpretations that constitutes the starting composition for the decisions taken *utilitatis causa*. For this reason, one should speak of the *utilitatis causa* interpretation rather than just decisions. In consequence, Navarra was correct in sensing traces of controversy and disputes in these sources. However, the preserved fragments of jurists' writings do not indicate that these decisions always transitioned from *ius controversum* to *ius receptum*. It is only the context of the reference that makes it possible to define the role of the criterion. Where jurists write that a decision was *utilitatis causa receptum* or use similar phrases, the analyzed criterion appear to function as a supplementary norm. In other cases, it functions more like an argument. This division is created more or less halfway. However, *utilitas* always remains the benchmark for interpretation to be made. Yet a determinant specific enough to allow for the correction of linguistic interpretation results.

In the rhetorical theory of legal interpretation, *utilitas* was understood as equivalent of the utility of a community, understood not as the interest of the state or some of its institutions but as the utility of all citizens. Hence rhetorical *utilitas* always contains the default attribute *communis* or *rei publicae*. Here, then, the ethical aspect of the criterion is quite obvious. Meanwhile, in jurisprudence sources *utilitas* sometimes appears

727 See Chart 1 illustrating the scale of sources that are examples of the *utilitatis causa* decisions, accounting for both the division into schemes and the subject of interpretation. Additionally, refer to Table 6, which shows the presence of each interpretative scheme across individual jurists.

728 A. Wacke, *Gloria…*, p. 53.

independently, sometimes with the adjective *communis* or *publica,* and at times also with a genitive attribute pointing to the benefit of specific entities[729]. The reference to the criterion, however, always fulfilled a uniform function, corresponding to the one it performed in rhetorical argumentation. *Utilitas* of jurists and *utilitas* of rhetoricians should be therefore considered parallel categories. Thus, in jurisprudence thought there was primarily one *utilitas* – as Kaser wrote, no matter whether it was referred to with or without the adjective *publica,* and as such it always indicated the ethical adequacy of decisions. Then although in each of the quoted cases it is possible to point out to the practical needs behind a given decision, or the intended political and legal goal, they are not, and certainly not exclusively, indicated by the category of *utilitas,* whose role remained unchanged. Therefore, the content of the criterion should be specified only when jurists do so directly.

Although the *ad utilitatem* references in the *utilitatis causa* decisions are uniform in character, they obviously bear the characteristic traces of the style preferred by the jurist. For instance, Ulpian included the category three times in rhetorical questions. He was also the only jurist to use the phrase *utilitatis gratia* along with the expressions *utilitatis causa* and *propter utilitatem.* This reflects not just a linguistic preference but an understanding of the category's true nature. Even if the division of sources according to the given expressions is not particularly helpful in understanding the category of *utilitas,* looking at the content of these expressions is. Ulpian managed to capture the essence of things in the term *utilitatis gratia.* Decisions breaking the unambiguous results of linguistic interpretation were possible not 'because of' but 'thanks to' and 'with the help of' the *utilitas* category.

Leptien noticed that jurists usually additionally explained the adoption of the *utilitatis causa* decisions, which is why he mistakenly considered references *ad utilitatem* as an auxiliary instrument of legal argumentation. Like today, jurists were also bound (at least to some extent) by the principle of inertia, according to which the burden of argumentation rested with those who decided to propose a solution other than the one previously accepted. In the *utilitatis causa* decisions, although welcome, an additional 'legal' justification was not necessary[730], and certainly not for the constitutive nature of the decision. So even if one can find a decision justification in the category of *utilitas,* it primarily constituted its foundation. It is also worth noting that in sources where jurists quoted derivatives of the term *utilitas,* the same pattern of interpretation can be observed. Thus, the result of the analyses is not only supplementing the catalogue of

729 Chart 2 illustrates the various forms of the *utilitas* category as presented in the *utilitatis causa* decisions.

730 For, as Kaser rightly noted, the specific reasons for deeming a particular decision as the most useful (*utilis*) are not explained because the jurist directed his arguments to his 'colleague' (*der juristische Zunftgenosse*), who could intuitively grasp the issues in a similar manner. See M. Kaser, '*Ius publicum*'..., p. 17. See also Table 7 and its accompanying commentary.

the *utilitatis causa* decisions[731] but also showing that the strength of this criterion was not hidden in the word *utilitas* but in the entire category.

While making a reference to the rhetorical tradition, it should be emphasized that *utilitas* of jurists, although it actually embodies the utility of all citizens, did not correspond to the will of the legislator or the intention of the person making the declaration of intent, unless the jurist indicated otherwise. In this sense, the jurisprudence *ex utilitate* interpretation became independent of the rhetorical one. It should also be noted the expression *utilitatis causa* is by no means an argument from the field of judicial rhetoric or a catchphrase but a signal of referring to the value underlying the legal order. It was not thus an extra-systemic criterion; on the contrary – one constituting the foundation of the legal order. For this reason, the *utilitatis causa* decisions cannot be seen as a sign of rejecting the system. It should rather be considered that they prevented intra-system axiological inconsistency. This perspective also sheds new light on the problem of the 'contradiction with the system' and interpretation difficulties (including doubts as to the authenticity of particular passages), which result in the uniqueness of the *utilitatis causa* decisions. Although in concrete cases they appear unacceptable from the point of view of legal dogmatics, at a higher level they comply with the dominating guideline of interpretation. Thus, Paturet is right when he refers to the examined criterion as a unified and unifying category, and Navarra correctly saw an expression of unification and stabilization tendencies in these decisions.

It is also worth bearing the opinion of Giaro in mind, according to whom Roman jurists were guided by an axiological, rather than juridical concept of the validity of the law[732]. Then although the jurist knew the dogmatic starting point for interpretation, the actual validity of the norm depended on its authorization by the jurist. Consequently, the *utilitatis causa* decisions should not be considered as exceptions to the applicable law. On the contrary, they should rather be treated as detailing and refining binding rules, or creating, as Kaser put it, subordinate rules necessary for specific groups of cases. The Roman jurist criticized the law and, by interpreting *utilitatis causa*, created a new legal rule or improved an already existing one. In this sense, the role of the legal interpretation coincides with the tasks of the praetorian law indicated by Papinian, after all introduced *propter utilitatem publicam*, which were *adiuvare, supplere* and *corrigere ius civile*. Thus Seidl rightly noticed that *utilitas* served to fill in loopholes

731 Contrary to M. Navarra, *Ricerche…*, pp. 159–162, I did not include Ulp. D. 19,5,17,2 in this catalogue. In this instance, *utilitas* appears not to be referenced in the specific context discussed in this study, but rather as an expression of the benefit obtained from a contract, which simultaneously determines the extent of a debtor's liability. Similarly, contrary to Navarra, *Ricerche…*, pp. 128–130, Paul. D. 35,1,84 was not included in this group either, where *utilitas* (*filii*) might serve as an instrument of interpretation and a criterion for adopting a specific decision, but it was not employed in an adversative function. Certainly, not every *ad utilitatem* reference is a sign of the *utilitatis causa* decision.

732 T. Giaro, *Geltung…*, p. 82.

in the law. It should be added, however, that it was not only about those loopholes that today could be described as *extra legem* but also those *contra legem*. In the context of the latter category, it is particularly worth mentioning a loophole *contra legem* as seen by Chaïm Parelman: it occurred when referring to some general rule, an interpreter deliberately narrowed the scope of the rule, created a loophole and immediately filled it with a new norm, contradicting the content of the rule prior to limiting its scope[733]. Both in Roman jurists and in Perelman, however, this did not mean repealing the legal norm but only rejecting its application in a given case. The general rule remained in force.

So although the fixed boundaries of what was permitted, prohibited and prescribed did not seem unambiguous, *utilitas* could be an effective tool to overcome them, even before the era of classical jurisprudence – the period of the peak of the *utilitatis causa* decisions, at least in the light of currently available sources. As noted in Introduction, attempts have been made to justify this circumstance in many ways. Watson's hypothesis is convincing, as it justified the lack of references to the criterion in the decisions of Republican jurists with a small number of surviving sources; especially that the adversative function of the analyzed category must have been well known to jurists of that period. As has been shown, Cicero already used it for sure. Thinking in these terms must therefore have functioned in intellectual circles at least from the 1st century BCE. Moreover, analyzing the provisions of the *lex Aquilia*, and writing that 'it can be shown on countless examples that many solutions have been adopted under the civil law contrary to the method of inference due to *utilitas communis* (D. 9,2,51,2 *multa autem iure civili contra rationem disputandi pro utilitate communi recepta esse innumerabilibus rebus probari potest*), Julian certainly meant the solutions of his early-classical, and perhaps even pre-classical predecessors. It cannot be ruled out, however, that the reasons for the popularity of the analyzed category, also in the context of the *utilitatis causa* decisions, can be found elsewhere among the jurists of the late classical period[734]. It seems worth taking a direction already followed by Kaser. Reflecting on the reasons for this phenomenon, he focused on Papinian's definition of the praetorian law preserved in D. 1,1,7,1, and on the so-called *laudationes edicti*, in which references *ad utilitatem* are often found. He stated that jurists may have felt encouraged to interpret the edict through the prism of the aims of the norms he defined as the economic, social, ethical and cultural background, contained in such categories as *aequitas, iusta causa, necessitas* and precisely *utilitas* (*publica*). Such a reference could take the role of a simple eulogy, an argument but also a concrete *ratio*, constituting a justification for those who opted for a decision inconsistent with a literal interpretation[735]. Meanwhile, the fragments

733 Ch. Perelman, *Logika prawnicza: nowa retoryka*, Warszawa 1984, p. 83.
734 This phenomenon is illustrated in more detail in Table 3.
735 M. Kaser, *'Ius publicum'*..., pp. 30–33.

of the *Libri ad edictum* do not constitute even half of the *utilitatis causa* decisions[736]. However, although Kaser limited himself in his deliberations to the interpretation of the praetorian law, he noticed that the justifications of individual decisions could be correlated with the manner of interpreting this law. Yet, as established in Chapter Two, this thought can be extended to the interpretation of any law, regardless of its origin. As has been shown, Ulpian and Paulus also openly focused their juridical reflection on the category of *utilitas*, present in one way or another in the legal field at least since the time of Cicero. In these circumstances, it does not seem to be a coincidence that it is their output that is the most abundant in *ad utilitatem* references, including the *utilitatis causa* decisions[737]. It is therefore possible that this methodological attitude prompted these jurists to refer to this category more often.

Utilitas is a beautiful ancient illustration of what we seem to be rediscovering today. As Bartosz Brożek writes: 'the law is not a coherent story although sometimes we treat it as such; it is full of contradictions, competing points of view and alternative solutions to the same problem. It is a Jackson Pollock painting rather than a still life by Rembrandt'[738]. It is also hard to resist the impression that Roman *utilitas* is an excellent proof that reasonable thinking of those constituting, interpreting and applying the law could free us from regulating all spheres of life, or from perceiving them as bonds, which are impossible to break. Pointing to the utility of the community as the overriding goal of the law, *utilitas* was the basic determinant of interpretation for Roman jurisprudence; and it was strong enough to correct the unambiguous results of linguistic interpretation. By showing that the law could not be reduced to a logical syllogism, *utilitas* simultaneously performed a law-making, corrective but also stabilizing and persuasive function. It was a multifaceted thought tool: a guideline for interpretation, a general clause, and in cases where the decisions taken *utilitatis causa* became part of the *ius receptum*, it also served as a supplementary norm. It directed legal thought, constantly paving the way to what was necessary not only for the needs of practice but above all to what is – to quote Horace – *iustum et aequum*.

736 The division of the *utilitatis causa* decisions according to the type of work they come from is presented in Table 5.

737 Table 4 presents a summary of the number of the *utilitatis causa* decisions according to the works of individual jurists.

738 B. Brożek, *The Legal Mind: A New Introduction to Legal Epistemology*, Cambridge 2019, p. 112.

Appendix

This list includes the fragments being examples of the *utilitatis causa* decisions, whose interpretation does not require extensive commentary. All sources reference *utilitas* appearing on its own – sometimes accompanied by the adjectives *publica* or *communis* – or its derivatives.

1. D. 2,12,3,2 (*Ulpianus libro altero ad edictum*)

Item in eum, qui quid nundinarum nomine adversus communem utilitatem acceperit, omni tempore ius dicitur.

Likewise, proceedings are pending at all times against one who accepted something contrary to *utilitas communis* under trading in marketplaces.

Commentary: This fragment acknowledges that litigation against those accepting bribes in marketplaces can proceed despite Marcus Aurelius's ban on conducting court hearings during harvest and grape harvest times (Ulp. D. 2,12,1,pr.).

2. D. 5,1,18,1 (*Ulpianus libro vicesimo tertio ad edictum*)

Si filius familias ex aliqua noxa, ex qua patri actio competit, velit experiri, ita demum permittimus ei agere, si non sit qui patris nomine agat. nam et Iuliano placet, si filius familias legationis vel studiorum gratia aberit et vel furtum vel damnum iniuria passus sit: posse eum utili iudicio agere, ne dum pater exspectatur impunita sint maleficia, quia pater venturus non est vel dum venit, se subtrahit is qui noxam commisit. unde ego semper probavi, ut, si res non ex maleficio veniat, sed ex contractu, debeat filius agere utili iudicio, forte depositum repetens vel mandati agens vel pecuniam quam credidit petens, si forte pater in provincia sit, ipse autem forte Romae vel studiorum causa vel alia iusta ex causa agat: ne, si ei non dederimus actionem, futurum sit, ut impune fraudem patiatur et egestate Romae laboret viaticulo suo non recepto, quod ad sumptum pater ei destinaverat. et finge senatorem esse filium familias qui patrem habet in provincia, nonne augetur utilitas per dignitatem?

If a son under the power of *pater familias* wants to sue for harm the repair of which is subject to the father's action, and if there is no one to bring an action on behalf of the father, we allow him to file the action. For Julian also believes that if the son under the authority of the father was away from home for legation or educational reasons, and experienced theft or damage, he may then bring an analogous action, so that while waiting for the father the delicts are not left unpunished when the father cannot come, or when the one who caused the damage leaves before the father arrives. For this reason, I have always considered it right that when the case does not result from a delict but from a contract, the son would have the right to bring an analogous action, for instance, when demanding the return of a deposited item, or filing an *actio mandati* or by demanding a reimbursement of the money he had lent if, for instance, his father was in a province, and he himself, for instance, in Rome for educational reasons or for some other legitimate reason, that, if we did not allow for his action, he would not be deceived with impunity, and that he would not suffer poverty in Rome, not having received a small amount of his money which his father had given to support him. And suppose the son who has a provincial father is a senator. Doesn't the dignity of the office support the *utilitas* category?

Commentary: Ulpian referred to *utilitas* to justify granting a son under the authority of the *pater familias* the right to bring an action analogous to the one the *pater familias* was entitled to under his contract, in a situation where passivity related to legal steps could lead to deterioration of the son's situation.

3. D. 5,4,5,1 (*Paulus libro decimo septimo ad Plautium*)

Idem est in extraneo, si ex certa portione heres institutus sit, ex reliqua postumi. quod si forte ita institutio facta est: QVOTCVMQVE MIHI NATI ERVNT ET LVCIUS TITIVS PRO VIRILIBVS PORTIONIBVS HEREDES MIHI SVNTO, *habebit haesitationem, numquid adire non possit, atque qui in testamento portionem suam nescit. sed utilius est posse eum adire qui nescit portionem, si cetera, quae oportet eum scire, non ignoret.*

The same applies to an heir who is not under the power of the testator if he is the heir of a certain share of an estate, and the children born after the death of the testator inherit the remain share. What if he, for instance, was designated heir as follows: 'Let Lucius Titus and all the children born to me be my heirs in equal parts', then he will doubt whether he can accept the inheritance as a person who does not know his share as stated in the will. But it is more useful that a person who does not know his share can accept the inheritance if he knows everything else that he should know.

Commentary: To protect a potential heir, an *aditio hereditatis* was not effective if the one who wanted to acquire an inheritance did not know his share of the estate, and therefore the inheritance debts too[739]. In the analyzed case, Lucius Titus and all the children born after the testator's death were appointed heirs. Hence, the man could not be aware of how much his share in the inheritance would ultimately be. For this reason,

739 On the principle and its interpretation, along with quoting the rich source material and referring also to the presented fragment, see T. Rüfner, *Antritt der Erbschaft unter unsicheren Voraussetzungen: D. 29,2,21,3 (Ulp. 7 ad Sab.)*, 'ZSS RA' 2010, vol. 127, no. 1, pp. 286–295.

according to the literal interpretation, he could not acquire an inheritance. However, Paulus believed that in such circumstances the acceptance of the inheritance was permissible as long as one knew the conditions under which the amount of the share could be changed. In this case, it could both decrease if a posthumous child was born, and increase if, for instance, there was a miscarriage. In this case, *utilitas* allowed for the omission of the rule and breaking the scope of forbidden behaviours.

4. D. 9,2,41,pr. (*Ulpianus libro quadragesimo primo ad Sabinum*)

Si quis testamentum deleverit, an damni iniuriae actio competat, videamus. et Marcellus libro quinto digestorum dubitans negat competere. quemadmodum enim, inquit, aestimatio inibitur? ego apud eum notavi in testatore quidem hoc esse verum, quia quod interest eius aestimari non potest, verum tamen in herede vel legatariis diversum, quibus testamenta paene chirographa sunt. ibidem Marcellus scribit chirographo deleto competere legis Aquiliae actionem. sed et si quis tabulas testamenti apud se depositas deleverit vel pluribus praesentibus legerit, utilius est in factum et iniuriarum agi, si iniuriae faciendae causa secreta iudiciorum publicavit.

Let us see if it is possible to bring an action for wrongful damage if a person destroys the will. In the fifth book of his *Digesta,* Marcellus doubts it and says that such an action cannot be brought. He says: 'How can such damage be measured?'. As for his opinion, I added a comment that from the testator's point of view this is true, since his interest cannot be measured, but it is different for the heir or legatee. For them, testaments are almost like written obligation. At the same point, Marcellus writes that one is entitled to the Aquilian action in the event of the destruction of a debt warrant. Undoubtedly, if someone destroyed the tablets of a testament deposited with him, or read them in the presence of many people, it is more useful to bring an *in factum* action or one for damages if he revealed the secrets of legal matters with the intention of causing damage.

Commentary: According to Marcellus, no action could be brought for unlawful damage in the event of the destruction of a testament. By invoking to *utilitas,* Ulpian justified a partial breach of this rule, stating that in the event of the destruction of the will (as well as disclosure of its contents with the intention of causing damage) the heir or legatee should be granted an action under the Aquilian law.

5. D. 11,7,3 (*Paulus libro vicesimo septimo ad edictum*)

Ex consensu tamen omnium utilius est dicere religiosum posse fieri, idque Pomponius scribit.

By agreement of all, it is more useful to say that the land can be made a place of worship, and so Pomponius writes.

Commentary: The jurist analyzed a situation in which the rights of others were connected with a land on which they wanted to give a burial[740]. The jurist decided that under general consent[741] it was possible to sanctify the ground on which a body was buried[742]. Not much can therefore be said about the factual and legal problem analyzed. However, since Paulus referred to the criterion of *utilitas* (*utilius est dicere*), in the light of the circumstances presented here, it is justified to conclude that the decision adopted by him and Pomponius went beyond the scope of behaviours permitted under the rules governing the establishment of *res religiosa*.

6. D. 12,6,53 (*Proculus libro septimo epistularum*)

Dominus testamento servo suo libertatem dedit, si decem det: servo ignorante id testamentum non valere data sunt mihi decem: quaeritur, quis repetere potest. Proculus respondit: si ipse servus peculiares nummos dedit, cum ei a domino id permissum non esset, manent nummi domini eosque non per condictionem, sed in rem actione petere debet. Si autem alius rogatu servi suos nummos dedit, facti sunt mei eosque dominus servi, cuius nomine dati sunt, per condictionem petere potest: sed tam benignius quam utilius est recta via ipsum qui nummos dedit suum recipere.

An owner manumitted his slave in his will on the condition that he would pay ten. Unaware that the testament was invalid, the slave gave me the ten. The question arises: who can request a reimbursement? Proculus replied that if the slave paid the money out of the *peculium* without the owner's consent, the money remained the property of the owner, and an *actio in rem* should be brought, not a *condictio*. But when, at the slave's request, someone else put out his own money, the money became mine, and the owner of the slave, on whose behalf it was given, may claim it in court by means of the *condictio*. However, it is both more indulgent and more useful for the person who paid to directly recover his money.

Commentary: According to the testator's will, the slave was to be manumitted on the condition that a certain amount of money was paid. This condition was met, but the will turned out to be invalid. The final issue is how to claim reimbursement. If the money came from the slave's *peculium*, the current owner of the slave (and therefore the testator's heir) had the right to file an *actio in rem*. However, if a third party paid the creditor, the creditor became the owner of the money. Then the slave owner should bring a

740 Cf. R. Elvers, *Romanorum de rebus religiosis doctrina*, Gottingae 1851, p. 27.

741 It is unclear, however, whether the consent in question was that of the interested parties or the jurists. The first interpretation is supported by K. Ulrych, *Res extra commercium*, Praga 2014, p. 20 (PhD dissertation available online at: https://dspace.cuni.cz/handle/20.500.11956/53795).

742 As already mentioned in the analysis of Pap. D. 11,7,43, this law was closely related to land ownership. Cf. again G. 2,6; Marc. D. 1,8,6,4; I. 2,1,9. However, a burial did not always result in the creation of *res religiosa*. Cf. e.g. Ulp. D. 10,3,6,6; Ulp. D. 11,7,2,7; Ulp. D. 11,7,8,2; Pap. D. 11,7,43. Sources quoted after M. Jońca, *Przestępstwo…*, pp. 68–69.

condictio against the creditor. Only then could a third party bring a *condictio* against the owner. *Utilitas*, however, allowed Proculus to break the pattern of prescribed behaviors and avoid this storied structure by awarding a third party an action directly against the creditor.

7. D. 16,3,8 (*Papinianus libro nono quaestionum*)

Quod privilegium exercetur non in ea tantum quantitate, quae in bonis argentarii ex pecunia deposita reperta est, sed in omnibus fraudatoris facultatibus: idque propter necessarium usum argentariorum ex utilitate publica receptum est …

This privilege is used not only up to the amount corresponding to the amount of money deposited with the banker, which is still with him, but up to the amount of the entire assets of the fraudster. Such a rule was adopted with regard to *utilitas publica* due to the necessity to use the services of bankers …

Commentary: The banker was usually responsible for up to the amount of money deposited with him. In the event that he committed fraudulent activities concerning his depositors, he was liable to them up to the amount of all his assets (*in omnibus facultatibus*)[743]. In such situations, it was necessary to depart from the literal interpretation of the rule establishing the limits of bankers' liability, and *utilitas publica* paved the way for this solution.

8. D. 23,3,61,pr. (*Clemens libro tertio ad legem Iuliam et Papiam*)

Sive generalis curator sive dotis dandae causa constitutus sit et amplius doti promissum est quam facultates mulieris valent, ipso iure promissio non valet, quia lege rata non habetur auctoritas dolo malo facta. quaerendum tamen est, utrum tota obligatio an quod amplius promissum est, quam promitti oportuit, infirmetur? et utilius est dicere id quod superfluum est tantummodo infirmare.

Regardless of whether a curator with full powers or solely for the establishment of a dowry was appointed, if the dowry promised is more than the value of a woman's property, such a promise is invalid by law itself, because fraudulent approval of the act by the curator cannot be recognized by the law. However, one should consider whether the entire obligation is deprived of legal force, or perhaps only what was promised in excess. It is more useful to say that only what is excessive is deprived of legal force.

Commentary: In the commentary *ad legem Iuliam et Papiam Poppaeam*, Terentius Clemens stated that the pledge of a dowry is invalid by virtue of the law itself, if more

743 This way in R. Scevola, *'Utilitas publica', II. Elaborazione…*, pp. 224–225. The author offers an extremely extensive analysis of the fragment, ibidem, pp. 208–243. Niczyporuk rightly observes that in principle the fragment discusses the unlimited liability of bankers. See P. Niczyporuk, *Bankierzy i operacje bankierskie w starożytnym Rzymie*, Białystok 2013, p. 90.

than the value of a woman's property was promised, and the act was fraudulently approved by her curator. However, applying the *ex utilitate* interpretation[744], the jurist stated that only what was promised in excess should be considered null and void. He therefore described the legal act itself as valid and effective, departing from the literal interpretation and breaking the unambiguous scope of prohibited behaviours.

9. D. 28,2,29,6 (*Scaevola libro sexto quaestionum*)

… nam hic casus ad legem Velleam non pertinet. melius ergo est, ut in eiusmodi utilitate – praesertim post legem Vellaeam, quae et multos casus rumpendi abstulit – interpretatio admittatur, ut instituens nepotem, qui sibi post mortem suus nasceretur, recte instituisse videatur, quibuscumque casibus nepos post mortem natus suus esset rumperetque praeteritus …

… This case does not fall under the *Iunia Vellaea* law. It is therefore better that in matters of this kind, and especially after the *Iunia Vellaea* law (which removed numerous grounds for voiding testaments) coming into force, taking the category of *utilitas* into account, one should adopt the interpretation that who appoints their grandson born after his death as a *heres suus* appoints them correctly, regardless of the circumstances in which a grandson would be born after [the testator's] death as a *heres suus* and void the testament as the one omitted in it …

Commentary: Scaevola's reflections concern the validity of a will in a situation where, after the testator's death, his grandson included in the circle of one's own heirs (*heredes sui*) was born. The problem of interpretation must have been related to whether, although the grandfather included his grandson in his testament, the appointment of heir took a conditional form[745], and as a result of subsequent factual and legal events, it could not be considered that the condition was fulfilled. Consequently, the birth of the grandson should void the will.

This case is particularly interesting from an interpretative perspective. At the same time, there exists a problem with the interpretation of the content of the will, the pro-

744 Terentius appears to support such an interpretation, particularly in matters related to marriages. Cf. also the analysis of Clem. D. 35,1,64,1. J. F. Stagl, *Favor dotis…*, p. 122, explains the use of the term *utilius* by adopting a teleological interpretation in favor of the institution of marriage. See also A. Staffhorst, *Die Teilnichtigkeit von Rechtsgeschäften im klassischen römischen Recht*, Berlin 2006, p. 75. The goal understood in this way was surely behind the solution adopted by Terentius Clemens, but it does fully encompass the role played by *utilitas* in this fragment.

745 As Scaevola's earlier considerations pertain to testaments containing the formula proposed by Aquilius Gallus, it can be assumed that in this instance as well, the jurist is contemplating a situation where the declaration of intent was drawn up according to this formula in the event of death. This way in S. Stepan, *Scaevola noster. Schulgut in den 'libri disputationum' des Claudius Tryphoninus?*, Tübingen 2018, pp. 164–168. According to the formula, grandchildren born after their grandfather's death could inherit if their father died during the testator's lifetime, provided they were born within ten months after their father's death. The formula is preserved in Scaev. D. 28,2,29,pr.

visions of the *lex Iunia Vellaea*[746] and the rule according to which if a grandson who is a *heres suus* is not included in the testament, the act becomes invalid. To secure the validity of the will, Scaevola decided that it was better to admit the interpretation according to which the grandfather who made a grandson his heir did it as if he had done it correctly. Interestingly, *utilitas*[747] seems to point to both interpretation schemes here: both *contra* and *supra scriptum*. The latter would refer to the interpretation of the law, which, quoting the jurist, removed numerous grounds for voiding testaments but did not normalize the situations that Scaevola had in mind. On the other hand, the *contra scriptum* scheme, which seems to be dominant here[748], allows for departing from the rule according to which – due to the literal interpretation of the content of the will and the provisions of the *lex Iunia Vellaea* – the legal act should be considered invalid.

10. D. 29,2,68 (*Paulus libro quinto ad legem Iuliam et Pappiam*)

Cum solus servus heres institutus sit, sicut licet uno tempore omnium dominorum iussu adire hereditatem, ita et separatis temporibus singulorum iussu recte adit: nam quia saepius adit, non ex testamento, sed ex iure dominorum venire utilitatis causa videtur, ne alterius festinatione alterius ius laedatur.

If a slave was appointed a sole heir, just as he is permitted to accept the estate once on the orders of all the owners, he may also lawfully accept it at different times if the individual owners gave the orders independently. For if he accepts the inheritance several times, by virtue of *utilitas*, he is considered to acquire not by virtue of the testament but on the account of the right of the owners, so the right of one is not violated by the haste of the other.

Commentary: According to the rule quoted by Paulus in the passage from the second book of the *Libri ad Sabinum*, the one who had the right to accept the entire inheritance could not accept only a part of it as a result of dividing it (Paul. D. 29,2,1[749]).

746 On this law see F. Lamberti, *Per la datazione della Lex Iunia Vellaea al 26 d. C.*, 'Rivista di diritto romano' 2018, vol. 18, pp. 175–186; S. Stepan, *Scaevola noster…*, pp. 161–164 along with the literature cited therein.

747 The noun *utilitas* seems to be a causative factor in this context. Also H. Ankum, *'Utilitatis causa receptum'. On the pragmatical methods…*, p. 25, interprets it in this manner. However, a more common interpretation, also grammatically permissible, is that the ablative *utilitate* depends on the prefix *in*. Then the fragment should be translated as 'due to the *utilitas* of matters of this kind' or 'due to this kind of *utilitas*'. Cf. e.g. *The Digest of Justinian. vol.* 2 English-language translation edited by A. Watson, Philadelphia 1985, p. 366; S. Stepan, *Scaevola noster…*, p. 157. According to this interpretation, *utilitas* should be considered as specific in its content, which, as has already been shown, also happened. However, this interpretation does not seem applicable here.

748 For this reason, this fragment has been included in the statistics as an example of *contra scriptum* interpretation.

749 Paul. D. 29,2,1 *Qui totam hereditatem adquirere potest, is pro parte eam scindendo adire non potest* ('Anyone who is entitled to the entire inheritance cannot accept only certain shares by dividing the inheritance'). See also Ulp. D. 29,2,10 *Si ex asse heres destinaverit partem habere hereditatis, videtur in*

As can be seen, however, this rule was sometimes ignored. If a jointly-owned slave was appointed heir, he could acquire the inheritance 'at one go' under the order of all co-owners but also at different times under the order of individual co-owners. In the other situation, it was assumed that the inheritance was left to the slave not from the will but under the right of the owners (*iure dominorum*). Accordingly, the acquisition was not whole but partial and *pro quota* and therefore according to the share that the owners had in the ownership of the slave. The alternative breaking the rule[750] was described by Paulus as the *utilitatis causa* acquisition.

11. D. 29,5,3,15 (*Ulpianus libro quinquagesimo ad edictum*)

Hi quoque, qui non potuerunt alias ad libertatem pervenire, ut puta si hac lege distractus erat quis, ne manumitteretur, poterunt propter hoc, quod in commune utile est, ad libertatem perveniri.

Also, those who would not otherwise be able to obtain freedom, such as, for example, when someone was sold with the provision that he cannot be manumitted, will be able to be given freedom on account of what is useful to the community.

Commentary: The reference to *utilitas* allowed freedom to be given to a slave who voluntarily denounced his owner's killer even if he was sold with the provision that he could not be manumitted, or if there were other legal obstacles to it.

12. D. 35,3,3,10 (*Ulpianus libro undeoctogesimo ad edictum*)

Si legatum fuerit praestitum ante interpositam hanc stipulationem, an condici possit, ut cautio ista interponatur? movet quaestionem, quod ea, quae per errorem omissa vel soluta sunt, condici possunt et hic ergo quasi plus solutum videtur ex eo, quod cautio intermissa est. et ait Pomponius condictionem interponendae satisdationis gratia competere et puto hoc probandum quod Pomponius, utilitatis gratia.

If the object of the legacy was given out before granting stipulated security, is it possible to file a *condictio* for the return of the undue debt so that security is granted? This is problematic because one can use this action to claim what was omitted or paid by mistake. Here, however, it is considered that to some extent too much was paid out for the reason that giving the security was omitted. At the same time, Pomponius claims that a *condictio* reimbursement action is due to grant security, and I believe that Pomponius' view should be accepted due to *utilitas*.

assem pro herede gessisse ('If an heir of the entire inheritance has decided to acquire part of it, he is deemed to have acted as an heir for the entire inheritance').

750 U. Leptien, *Utilitatis causa. Zweckmässigkeitsentscheidungen…*, pp. 80–82. See also M. Navarra, *Ricerche…*, pp. 118–120.

Commentary: An heir gave out the object of the legacy by damnation without accepting the security from a legatee, who should have obliged himself to return the surplus over the limit set under the *lex Falcidia* (*cautio ex lege Falcidia*)[751]. As a rule, only the person who provided security or fulfilled the obligation by mistake could file a *condictio*. Yet Ulpian notes that in the present case the heir could give out more than he should have, not for the reasons mentioned but because no security was granted at all. According to the strict interpretation, he should not therefore be able to claim the surplus. Due to *utilitas*, however, Ulpian agreed with Pomponius' opinion, who allowed a *condictio* to be brought in order to grant the missing security.

13. D. 37,3,1 (*Papinianus libro quinto decimo quaestionum*)

Furioso Titius substitutus est: bonorum possessionis tempus, quamdiu furiosus in eadem condicione est, neque instituto neque substituto cedit. nec, si curator furiosi nomine possessionem accipere potest, idcirco spatium temporis, quod scientibus praefinitum est, videbitur cedere: nam et pater infanti filio possessionem accipit, quo tamen cessante infans non excluditur. quid ergo, si curator accipere nolit? nonne iustius atque utilius erit ad eundem modum proximo cuique possessionem dari, ne bona iaceant? quo admisso substitutus cautionem praestare cogitur omnibus his, quibus bona restitui debent, si forte institutus in eodem furore decesserit aut compos mentis effectus ante mortem obierit, quam hereditatem agnosceret. nam et fieri potest, ut vivo furioso substitutus decedat nec tamen furiosus obstet ceteris, si prius et ipse decesserit, quam hereditatem adquireret.

Titius was substituted as the heir of a mentally ill person. The time prescribed for demanding a possession of inheritance does not start to run for the heir or the substitute as long as the mentally ill person's condition remains unchanged. It will also not be considered that the time fixed for making this claim for persons who are conscious begins to run, when a curator of the mentally ill person may acquire a possession of the inheritance on behalf of a mentally ill person. For the father may also acquire possession of the inheritance on behalf of his minor son, but if he fails to do so, the child is not excluded from the inheritance anyway. So what if the curator refuses to accept the inheritance? Would it not be more just and useful to grant possession of an inheritance

751 Such an interpretation is presented in F. Trampedach, *Die condictio incerti*, 'ZSS RA' 1896, vol. 17, no. 1, p. 117; H. Ankum, *'Utilitatis causa receptum'. On the pragmatical methods…*, p. 26. The palingenetic analysis of the source also supports it. In this part of the commentary *Ad edictum*, Ulpian addressed the issue of *cautio ex lege Falcidia* – there is a direct reference to it in the same passage. Cf. Ulp. D. 35,3,3,1 *Haec cautio, quae propter legem Falcidiam interponitur…* The alternative proposal assumes that it was a *cautio evicta hereditate legata reddi*. In such a case, if a successful *hereditatis petitio* was brought against an heir, a legatee could be asked to return the object of the legacy previously granted to them. This interpretation is supported by, e.g., F. Schwarz, *Die Funktion des Irrtums bei Erfüllung gänzlich Oder teilweise nicht geschuldeter Fideikommisse*, 'ZSS RA' 1951, vol. 68, no. 1, pp. 275–276, who, however, questions the authenticity of the part *quasi plus solutum videtur* and assumes that it is a post-classical change of type of *condictio*, and not a simple description of the factual state. M. Navarra, *Ricerche…*, p. 169, also inclines to the second interpretation.

to each next appointed in the same way, lest the estate remains unpossessed? In the event of taking the possession the substitute heir must provide security to all those to whom the estate must be delivered up if, for instance, the appointed heir dies insane, or he dies having regained his mind before death, and death occurs before he accepts the inheritance. It may also happen that the substitute heir dies while the mentally ill person is alive, and the latter will not impede the claims of others, if he dies before acquiring the inheritance.

Commentary: If a mentally ill person was appointed heir, the initial term for demanding the possession of an inheritance (*bonorum possessio*) did not start to run as long as the condition of the insane person remained unchanged. It was also not affected by the fact that the inheritance was given to the management of the curator *furiosi*. If, on the other hand, the curator did not want to take possession of the inheritance, Papinian decided that it was more just and useful (*iustius atque utilius*) to bring the inheritance into possession of the substitute heir. The jurist allowed this solution despite the fact that at that time, it was not yet possible to demand *bonorum possessio*.

14. D. 40,9,1 (*Ulpianus libro primo ad Sabinum*)

Celsus libro duodecimo digestorum utilitatis gratia motus surdum ita natum manumittere posse ait.

Inspired by *utilitas*, Celsus states in the twelfth book of the *Digest* that a person born deaf can manumit.

Commentary: Based on the passage, it is difficult to determine what form of manumission was the subject of Celsus' considerations, and whether in this case it was related to a general prohibition of manumission, or to its particular form. The source shows, however, that *utilitas* allowed to break the scope of forbidden behaviours. It is also possible that the representative of the Proculeian school quoted the analyzed criterion in his considerations himself. Yet, he did not necessarily have to use the term *utilitatis gratia*, which appears only in Ulpian's accounts[752]. It is worth adding that the jurist probably resolved the issue of the admissibility of manumission in the form of *manumissio vindicta*[753] – the problem would then concern the possibility of hearing the formulas spoken by liberty assessor (*assessor libertatis*), especially that in P. S. 4,12,2, there was preserved a rule according to which the mute and the deaf could not manumit in the

752 M. Navarra, *Ricerche…*, p. 162.

753 This way in S. Tondo, *Aspetti simbolici e magici nella struttura giuridica della manumissio vindicta*, Milano 1967, p. 37; H. Ankum, *'Utilitatis causa receptum'. On the pragmatical methods…*, p. 8. Doubts also expressed by M. Navarra, *Ricerche…*, pp. 172–173 due to the fact that performing *manumissio vindicta* by a deaf person (until the times of Justinian) did not gain universal acceptance (P. S. 4,12,2). These doubts likely stem from the author's assumption that decisions taken *utilitatis causa* were to be part of the *ius receptum*.

form of *manumissio vindicta*. However, they were allowed to manumit in front of their friends (*inter amicos*), and in a letter (*per epistulam*)[754].

15. D. 41,2,25,2 (*Pomponius libro vicesimo tertio ad Quintum Mucium*)
Quod autem solo animo possidemus, quaeritur, utrumne usque eo possideamus, donec alius corpore ingressus sit, ut potior sit illius corporalis possessio, an vero (quod quasi magis probatur) usque eo possideamus, donec revertentes nos aliquis repellat aut nos ita animo desinamus possidere, quod suspicemur repelli nos posse ab eo, qui ingressus sit in possessionem: et videtur utilius esse.

With regard to things that we possess by will alone, the question arises whether we will possess them until someone else takes physical possession of them, considering that his possession based on physical control would be more powerful, or, what is somewhat more appreciated, we possess them as long as someone does not forbid us to return, or until we lose our will to possess, suspecting that we may be driven out by whoever gained possession. And that seems more useful.

Commentary: The decision concerns the issue of maintaining possession only by one's own will (*solo animo*). This issue must have raised many doubts among jurists[755]. Pomponius reported that the moment of losing possession of the property was determined for the moment when after returning to the estate, the holder was driven out by the person who had taken charge of the property, or when the will to possess the property was actually lost. Pomponius' reference to *utilitas* probably expresses his own opinion on the matter. This can be seen not only in the phrase *quasi magis*[756] *probatur*, which is

754 P. S. 4,12,2 *Mutus et surdus servum vindicta liberare non possunt. Inter amicos tamen et per epistulam manumittere non prohibentur…* ('A mute and deaf person cannot manumit a slave in a form of a *manumissio vindicta*. However, they are not forbidden to manumit among their friends and in a letter…'). See also M. Wlassak, *Die prätorischen Freilassungen*, 'ZSS RA' 1905, vol. 26, no. 1, p. 426; S. Riccobono, *Stipulatio ed instrumentum nel Diritto giustinianeo*, 'ZSS RA' 1922, vol. 43, no. 1, p. 385; U. Leptien, *Utilitatis causa…*, pp. 178–180.

755 See also G. 4,153 …*quin etiam plerique putant animo quoque retineri possessionem, id est ut quamvis neque ipsi simus in possessione neque nostro nomine alius, tamen si non relinquendae possessionis animo, sed postea reversuri inde discesserimus, retinere possessionem videamur…* ('…Moreover, many believe that possession is also kept by intent, that is, although neither we own possess [physically] nor someone else possesses on our behalf, nevertheless, if we have deviated from it, not with the intention of giving up possession but with the intention of returning to it later, it is believed that we keep possession…'). Using the term *plerique putant* (many believe), Gaius highlights that the issue of possessing *solo animo* was still a topic of debate. On this topic, apart from the studies by G. D'Angelo listed in the footnote below see also the latest study by P. Ferretti, *Possessio, animus e corpus*, *'forum historiae iuris'* 2019 (available online at: https://forhistiur.net/2019-01-ferretti/), along with the literature cited therein.

756 There is an academic discussion regarding the interpretation of the notation *q.m.* present in the source. While the more widely accepted interpretation is *quasi magis*, it would also be possible to consider that this is a reference to Quintus Mucius, as Pomponius' statement is a fragment of a commentary on this jurist's work. On this topic extensively in G. D'Angelo, *La perdita della pos-*

far from a definitive solution to the case, but above all in the statement that the physical control of a third party over a thing, as the jurist described it, was stronger. According to the literal interpretation, the moment of the loss of the property should be therefore determined for the moment when the land was taken over by someone else. *Utilitas,* however, helped Pomponius justify breaking the unambiguous results of the interpretation[757].

16. D. 41,2,40,1 (*Africanus libro septimo quaestionum*)

Si forte colonus, per quem dominus possideret, decessisset, propter utilitatem receptum est, ut per colonum possessio et retineretur et contineretur: quo mortuo non statim dicendum eam interpellari, sed tunc demum, cum dominus possessionem apisci neglexerit …

If, for instance, a tenant through whom a landowner held possession died, it was considered for the sake of *utilitas* that the possession through the tenant of the land would be maintained and continued. Therefore after the death of the tenant, it should not be stated immediately that the possession was interrupted, but only when the owner neglected to take possession of the land …

Commentary: Possession was also maintained when someone possessed on behalf of the owner even if he was not under his power. An example of such a situation was possessing through a tenant[758]. According to Sextus Caecilius Africanus, such possession was not interrupted even by the death of the tenant[759] but only by the owner's neglect to take possession of the land anew. This decision was reached in the *utilitatis causa* manner for obvious reasons: the deceased person could not exercise any control over the thing. *Utilitas* made it possible to break the unambiguous results of a literal interpretation and to extend the scope of permitted behaviours.

17. D. 41,2,44,1 (*Papinianus libro vicesimo tertio quaestionum*)

Quaesitum est, cur ex peculii causa per servum ignorantibus possessio quaereretur. dixi utilitatis causa iure singulari receptum, ne cogerentur domini per momenta species et causas peculiorum inquirere. nec tamen eo pertinere speciem istam, ut animo videatur adquiri pos-

sessio animo retenta nei casi di occupazione, Torino 2007, pp. 18–19, n. 15; Idem, *A proposito di 'animo possidere'*, 'Teoria e storia del diritto privato' 2018, no. 9, pp. 15–16.

757 D'Angelo recognizes the reference to *utilitas* as a general indication of the reasons for the decision. In his view, *utilitas* refers to a specific benefit arising from the decision, and not *utilitas* as an interpretative category. See G. D'Angelo, *La perdita…*, p. 11.

758 See G. 4,153 *Possidere autem videmur non solum, si ipsi possideamus, sed etiam si nostro nomine aliquis in possessione sit, licet is nostro iuri subiectus non sit, qualis est colonus et inquilinus…* ('And it is believed that we possess not only when we possess ourselves, but also if someone is in possession on our behalf even if he is not subject to our law, as is the case of a renter and tenant…').

759 M. Navarra, *Ricerche…*, p. 31, interprets the term *decessisset* not as death but as abandoning property. Further remarks on the passage in G. Nicosia, *Studi…*, pp. 166–170.

sessio: nam si non ex causa peculiari quaeratur aliquid, scientiam quidem domini esse necessariam, sed corpore servi quaeri possessionem.

The question arose as to why persons who are unaware of it acquire possession through the slave by virtue of a *peculium*. I said that because of *utilitas* it was accepted as the *ius singulare* so as not to force the owners to scrutinize the types and the legal basis of the property in the *peculium* at all times. However, it is not the source of the case of the owner appearing to be acquiring by intent alone. For if something is acquired other than by virtue of the *peculium*, the intent of the owner is indeed necessary, but possession is acquired physically through the slave.

Commentary: Papinian explains that a slave owner acquires possession of things that will become part of the *peculium* entrusted to the slave even if he is not aware of it. Thus the owner acquired possession despite the lack of knowledge about a thing belonging to the *peculium*, and therefore the intent to rule it (*animus*)[760]. In this case, *utilitas* allowed for departing from the rule in order to facilitate and stabilize the economic turnover.

18. D. 41,3,44,6 (*Papinianus libro vicesimo tertio quaestionum*)
Eum, qui postea quam usucapere coepit in furorem incidit, utilitate suadente relictum est, ne languor animi damnum etiam in bonis adferat, ex omni causa implere usucapionem.

If a person becomes mentally ill after commencing usucaption, he can complete usucaption on any basis, as *utilitas* suggests, so that the mental illness does not affect substance too.

Commentary: If a healthy person acquired possession that could lead to the acquisition of ownership of things by usucaption, and their disease did not appear until later, due to *utilitas* the course of usucaption was not interrupted although for obvious reasons it could not be concluded that the *furiosus* expressed the intent to possess[761]. Thanks to this, the ill person did not suffer any damage to their property due to their mental condition.

760 Cf. Paul. D. 41,2,1,5 also addresses the acquisition of possession despite the lack of knowledge, as well as the comparative analysis of both fragments conducted by M. Navarra, *Ricerche…*, pp. 64–71 along with the quoted studies. On the fragment in the context of *utilitatis causa* decisions see also H. Ankum, *The functions…*, pp. 14–15.

761 This way in H. Ankum, who argues that the individual retained possession but not intent, *'Utilitatis causa receptum'. On the pragmatical methods…*, pp. 14–15. In contrast, Vallar, contends that in this case, there was no loss of the individual's intent at all (*perseverantia voluntatis*). See S. Vallar, *Perseverantia voluntatis e furor*, 'Quaderni Lupiensi di Storia e Diritto' 2013, vol. 3, p. 158; Eadem, *Folie et droit romain – Quelques observations*, 'Criminocorpus. Revue d'Histoire de la justice, des crimes et des peines' 2016 (available online at : http://journals.openedition.org/criminocorpus/3146). See also P. Lambrini, *Capacità naturale e acquisto del possesso*, Index 1999, vol. 27, pp. 317–332.

19. D. 41,4,2,9 (*Paulus libro quinquagesimo quarto ad edictum*)
Procuratorem quoque, qui ex auctione, quam mandatu domini facit, emerit, plerique putant utilitatis causa pro emptore usucapturum. idem potest dici et si negotia domini gerens ignorantis emerit propter eandem utilitatem.

Most jurists hold that due to *utilitas*, an agent will acquire ownership by usucaption on behalf of a buyer also when the former would purchase something from property he is selling at the auction at the request of his principal. For the sake of the same *utilitas* one can decide accordingly if one would buy something when administering the affairs of a person in the latter's ignorance.

Commentary: The problem of the lack of legal title arose in the situation where an agent purchased property he was selling at an auction at his principal's request[762]. Despite the fact that by the law such a sale and purchase agreement was considered invalid[763], most jurists claimed that, due to *utilitas*, the agent could acquire ownership of property by usucapion as a buyer. In his interpretation, Paulus went a step further and decided that in an analogous situation, also the one conducting others' business without mandate could acquire ownership of the purchased property in the same way[764]. The reference to *utilitas* justified breaking the scope of forbidden behaviors.

20. D. 41,4,2,16 (*Paulus libro quinquagesimo quarto ad edictum*)
Si a furioso, quem putem sanae mentis, emero, constitit usucapere utilitatis causa me posse, quamvis nulla esset emptio et ideo neque de evictione actio nascitur mihi nec Publiciana competit nec accessio possessionis.

If I buy something from a mentally ill person whom I believe is sane, it was decided that I can acquire ownership of property by usucaption for the sake of *utilitas*, though the sale is void. For this reason, I am not entitled an action in the event of eviction, or the *actio Publiciana*, or to add the time of possession of a predecessor.

Commentary: Due to *utilitas*, jurists decided[765] that a person who was not aware of the condition of a mentally ill person who, consequently, was unable to participate in

762 This way the expression *ex auctione, quam mandatu domini facit* is explained by H. Ankum, *The functions…*, p. 17.

763 Paul. D. 18,1,34,7 *Tutor rem pupilli emere non potest: idemque porrigendum est ad similia, id est ad curatores procuratores et qui negotia aliena gerunt* ('The guardian cannot purchase his pupil's belongings. The same principle should also apply to similar cases, namely curators, representatives and those who handle other people's affairs without mandate').

764 Ankum justifies the adoption of this decision by the fact that auctioning property eliminated the risk of an owner suffering some damage to their estate. See H. Ankum, *Quelques problèmes concernant les ventes aux enchères en droit romain classique* [in:] *Studi in onore di Gaetano Scherillo*, vol. 1, Varese-Milano 1972, p. 384.

765 The adoption of this decision is expressed by the term *constitit*, which, while used within the scope of discussion, most likely indicates the final acceptance of the decision by jurists. Hence, the decision can be considered to be part of the *ius receptum*. Cf. T. Giaro, *Geltung…*, pp. 76–79.

legal and economic transactions, bought property from them may acquire ownership of this property by usucapion. This decision was made despite the fact that the sale and purchase agreement was void and therefore there was no legal title to acquire property. In this way, the scope of prohibited behaviours was broken.

21. D. 43,26,6,4 (*Ulpianus libro septuagesimo primo ad edictum*)

Quaesitum est, si quis rem suam pignori mihi dederit et precario rogaverit, an hoc interdictum locum habeat. quaestio in eo est, ut precarium consistere rei suae possit. mihi videtur verius precarium consistere in pignore, cum possessionis rogetur, non proprietatis, et est haec sententia etiam utilissima. cottidie enim precario rogantur creditores ab his, qui pignori dederunt, et debet consistere precarium.

A question arose as to whether the interdictum would apply if someone would give me his thing in pledge and then ask for it to be handed over to him under a precarious tenure. The problem related to the fact that one is also asking that the *precarium* may refer to a thing that is the property of the recipient. I think it is more lawful to think that a *precarium* might refer to a pledge as the request concerns possession, not ownership. This opinion is extremely useful. Every day, creditors meet with requests from people who have given them their things in pledge to hand it back under a precarious tenure, and the *precarium* should be effective.

Commentary: Referring to the analyzed category, Ulpian decided about the possibility of using the *de precario* interdictum in a situation where someone pledged his own things and asked for it to be handed over to them under a precarious tenure, despite the fact that this solution contradicted the rule of inadmissibility of establishing a *precarium* on one's own thing mentioned by the jurist[766].

22. D. 45,1,4,2 (*Paulus libro duodecimo ad Sabinum*)

Si is, qui duplam stipulatus est, decesserit pluribus heredibus relictis, unusquisque ob evictionem suae partis pro portione sua habebit actionem. idemque est in stipulatione quoque fructuaria et damni infecti et ex operis novi nuntiatione: restitui tamen opus ex operis novi nuntiatione pro parte non potest. haec utilitatis causa ex parte stipulatorum recepta sunt: ipsi autem promissori pro parte neque restitutio neque defensio contingere potest.

If a person who took a promise to be paid the double value of thing, died leaving several heirs, each of them will be entitled to an action under eviction in proportion to his share. The same applies also to the stipulation relating to profits and threatened damage and notice of new work, despite the fact that it is not possible to have partial

766 This rule is also confirmed in Iul. D. 16,3,15,pr.; Afr. D. 41,2,40,3; Ulp. D. 43,19,1,11; Ulp. D. 43,26,4,3; Ulp. D. 50,17,45,pr. See also J. Sondel, *Precarium w prawie rzymskim*, Kraków 1971, p. 44; M. Kaser, *Zur Geschichte des precarium*, 'ZSS RA' 1972, vol. 89, no. 1, p. 140. See also study by J. Krzynówek, *Funkcje i stosowanie 'precarium' w rzymskim prawie klasycznym*, PK 1993, vol. 36, no. 3–4, pp. 140–143, who writes about this and other exceptions to the quoted rule.

restitution of the work on notice of new work. This was accepted for the sake of *utilitas* as far as concerns the stipulation recipients. On the other hand, neither partial restoration to the previous state nor partial defence can apply to the promisor.

Commentary: With four types of guarantee security (*duplae stipulatio, stipulatio fructuaria, cautio damni infecti, cautio ex operis novi nuntiatione*), if a promisee died, their heirs were entitled to bring an *actio ex stipulatu* in relation to their share in the inheritance (*pro portione*). Thus although the claim was divided into several separate obligations (also in the case of the indivisibility of the performance, as in the case of restoration to the previous state, and the necessity to demolish an unlawfully erected building[767]), due to *utilitas* it was assumed that the debtor sued by the heir(-creditor with partial claim) was liable in full (as the jurist writes: not *pro parte*). *Utilitas* then made it possible to break the rules governing the divisibility of obligations.

23. D. 47,8,2,1 (*Ulpianus libro quinquagesimo sexto ad edictum*)

Hoc edicto contra ea, quae vi committuntur, consuluit praetor. nam si quis se vim passum docere possit, publico iudicio de vi potest experiri, neque debet publico iudicio privata actione praeiudicari quidam putant: sed utilius visum est, quamvis praeiudicium legi Iuliae de vi privata fiat, nihilo minus tamen non esse denegandam actionem eligentibus privatam persecutionem.

With this edict, the praetor made provisions against the acts committed by force. For if someone is able to prove that he was a victim of force, he can assert their rights in a public criminal trial for force. Some also hold that a private action should not be brought before a public criminal trial. However, what is more useful is the view that although it be prejudicial to the *lex Iulia de vi privata*, an action should not be denied to those who choose to pursue their claims in a private trial.

Commentary: The problem concerns the confluence of a private action (*actio vi bonorum raptorum*) and a public one under the *lex Iulia de vi privata*. According to some jurists, private actions should not be brought ahead public ones. *Utilitas*, however, allowed Ulpian to break this prohibition and to file a private action first, even if it anticipated a criminal court judgment in the same case.

767 It does not seem that the jurist's deliberations are confined to this single case, as interpreted by H. Ankum, *'Utilitatis causa receptum'. On the pragmatical methods…*, pp. 17–18 and M. Navarra, *Ricerche…*, pp. 104–107. This is suggested by the plural form used by Paulus in the key phrase for these considerations: *haec… recepta sunt* (and not – *hoc… receptum est*), relating it to all the cases mentioned.

24. D. 47,10,5,11 (*Ulpianus libro quinquagesimo sexto ad edictum*)
Et ei, qui indicasset, sive liber sive servus sit, pro modo substantiae accusatae personae aestimatione iudicis praemium constituitur, servo forsitan et libertate praestanda. quid enim si publica utilitas ex hoc emergit?

Also, for whoever would expose [such offences], whether he be a slave or a free person, the reward is determined according to the wealth of the accused and is assessed by the judge; and perhaps the slave should be granted freedom. Why not, if *utilitas publica* results from it?

Commentary: *Utilitas* allowed for a departure from the prohibition against slaves participating in criminal trials, permitting them to file reports[768], and even rewarding them with freedom. According to jurists, *utilitas* also appears in a similar function in imperial rescripts, allowing women, soldiers and, again, slaves to file reports. See Marc. D. 48,2,13 and Papir. D. 48,12,3,1. Both sources mention, however, *utilitas annonae*.

25. D. 48,5,27(26),1 (*Ulpianus libro tertio disputationum*)
Derelictam vero a marito accusationem etiam ab alio excitari utile est.

It is useful that the accusation [of adultery] abandoned by the husband may also be brought by another person.

Commentary: Persons authorized to bring accusations of adultery were divided into two categories according to the *lex Iulia de adulteriis coercendis*. The first privileged one, including the woman's kins, could bring the so-called *accusatio iure mariti vel patris* within 60 days from the termination of marriage. As a rule, a third party were entitled to bring accusations only after this period had expired[769]. In the above fragment, the breaking of this principle is accompanied by a reference to *utilitas*. Hence, if the woman's husband or father stated that they would not bring the *accusatio*, a third party could bring accusations immediately. Ulpian confirms this opinion also elsewhere (D. 48,5,16,5) but without reference to the analyzed category.

26. D. 50,10,5,1 (*Ulpianus libro singulari de officio curatoris rei publicae*)
Fines publicos a privatis detineri non oportet. curabit igitur praeses provinciae, si qui publici sunt, a privatis separare et publicos potius reditus augere: si qua loca publica vel aedificia in usus privatorum invenerit, aestimare, utrumne vindicanda in publicum sint an vectigal eis satius sit imponi, et id, quod utilius rei publicae intellexerit, sequi.

768 See M. Kuryłowicz, *Przestępstwa spekulacji contra annonam w prawie rzymskim*, 'Folia Societatis Scientiarum Lublinensis' 1993, vol. 34, no. 1, pp. 11–12; D. Nowicka, *Quid enim si publica utilitas ex hoc emergit? Kilka uwag o informatorach w rzymskim* [in:] *Pro publico bono – idee i działalność*, M. Marszał, J. Przygodzki (ed.), Wrocław 2016, pp. 27–31.

769 See Ulp. D. 48,5,4,1.

Public lands should not be occupied by private persons. The provincial governor will therefore take care of keeping public and private territories separate, and increase public income. If he determines that any public land or buildings would be used by private individuals, he should consider whether to recover the property, or rather make those who use it pay rent, and do what he thinks is more useful to the community.

Commentary: According to Ulpian, despite the prohibition of occupying public lands by private persons, in the event of such a situation, the provincial governor should not immediately demand the return of occupied lands but consider what would be more consistent with his goal, namely increasing public income. So if he found that it would be more useful for the community to impose an obligation on private individuals to pay rent, he should use this tool. Hence, *utilitas* led to reinterpretation of what was legally prohibited.

27. P. S. 5,2,2[770]

Per liberas personas, quae in potestate nostra non sunt, adquiri nobis nihil potest. Sed per procuratorem adquiri nobis possessionem posse utilitatis causa receptum est. Absente autem domino comparata non aliter ei, quam si rata sit, quaeritur.

We cannot acquire anything through free persons who are not under our power. Due to *utilitas*, it was decided, however, that we could acquire possession through an agent. When, however, the principal is absent, he acquires what was obtained only if he ratifies the act.

Commentary: (Pseudo-)Paulus explained that although it was not possible to acquire anything through a free person that was not under the power of the person concerned, due to *utilitas*, acquiring possession through an agent was allowed, thus breaking the scope of the prohibited behaviors.

28. P. S. 5,10,2

De communi pariete utilitatis causa hoc coepit observari, ut aedificet quidem, cuius aedificare interest, cogatur vero socius portionis suae impensas agnoscere.

Due to *utilitas*, regarding a shared wall, it was established that the one in whose interest it was to rebuild it should do so, while the joint owner was forced to pay their share of the costs.

Comment: Despite the use of the verb *aedificare* in the source, which is usually used in the 'building' context, it seems that in this case it is more about rebuilding, or mend-

770 Cf. also Diocl. et Maxim. C. 7,32,8.

ing a shared wall. This interpretation is confirmed by the fragment Pomp. D. 39,2,41[771], which seems to refer to the same factual state. It also mentions the repair of the shared wall, as well as the fact that it should be done by the person who intends to do it properly. Moreover, in this source, both the verbs *reficere* ('rebuild, repair') and *aedificare* are used to describe the act of repairing walls. The above quoted decision (in fact both of them) was a breach of the previous rule, according to which neither of the two neighbours had the right to rebuild the shared wall on their own, because neither of them was its sole owner (Gai. D. 8,2,8).

771 Pomp. D. 39,2,41 *In reficiendo communi pariete ei potius facultas aedificandi praestatur, qui magis idonee reficere parietem velit...* ('In the event of repairing a shared wall, the possibility of carrying out construction work should be given to the person who intends to carry the repair out in the most proper way...').

Tables, Charts, and Graphs

Tab. 1 Occurrence of the root *util** in Roman law sources[772].

Gai Institutiones	46
Pauli Sententiae	19
Digesta Iustiniani	806
Institutiones Iustiniani	50
Codex Iustinianus[773]	64 (210)
Novellae Iustiniani	89
Total	**1080 (1226)**

772 Table 1 reflects the number of fragments in which the root appears. Therefore, the total numbers in Tables differ from each other. It often happens that in one fragment there are two or more concepts that contain the root *util**.

773 The number before the brackets indicates the constitutions issued by Emperor Justinian, while the number after the brackets represents the total number of all imperial constitutions in the *Code of Justinian* that incorporate the discussed terminology. This same approach is applied consistently across all tables.

Tab. 2[774] Frequency of usage of the root *util** across Roman law sources

	G.	P.S.	D.	I.	C.	Nov.
utilitas	1	1	41	1	2 (13)	7
(in)utilitatem	2	1	64	4	6 (22)	34
utilitatis	1	3	25	4	2 (9)	3
utilitati	Ø	Ø	2	Ø	1 (6)	2
utilitate	Ø	Ø	22	Ø	7 (15)	12
utilitates*	Ø	Ø	10	Ø	Ø (13)	11
				269 (329)		
	G.	P.S.	D.	I.	C.	Nov.
utilia	2	Ø	10	1	3 (6)	4
utilis**	18	5	377	20	34 (90)	17
utile	15	3	163	13	8 (14)	7
utilior**	Ø	1	26	Ø	1 (2)	5
utiliter	11	5	151	15	9 (27)	1
utilissimum***	Ø	Ø	4	1	2 (2)	5
	49	19	896	59	75 (230)	108
				1206 (1361)		

The following tables and graphs focus solely on decisions that exemplify the *utilitatis causa* interpretation. In total, 78 fragments and 82 individual decisions were analyzed. The discrepancy arises from the fact that four fragments contain two decisions each that fit this interpretative scheme. These fragments are: Iul. D. 9,2,51,2; Ulp. D. 14,1,1,5; Paul. D. 41,4,2,9; and G. 3,160. For anyone interested in verifying which specific decisions fall into particular categories, the full dataset ('Utilitatis causa decisions – dataset') is available for download on my ORCID profile: https://orcid.org/0000-0001-9498-4845. I found this approach more straightforward and transparent than listing sources in footnotes.

The vast majority (73 %) of *utilitatis causa* decisions originate from the works of jurists from the late classical period. However, in 12 cases, the jurists referring *ad utilitatem* quoted the names of earlier jurists, including Labeo, who was mentioned three times (Ulp. D. 13,5,3,2; Ulp. D. 26,4,5,2; Pap. D. 46,3,95,7). In such instances, it is difficult

774 In the second part of Table 2, both the given terms and their negations are included in the total counts. For example, under the term *utilia*, both *utilia* and *inutilia* are considered. To ensure clarity in the data presented in Table 2, the following simplifications, marked by the symbols below, have been made:
*: includes other cases of the same number, except those listed separately.
**: includes other cases in both singular and plural forms, except those noted separately.
***: includes other cases, genders, and alternations.

to determine whether the use of the *utilitas* category appeared in the original text of the earlier jurist or was a later addition. Therefore, the authorship of the work was used as the decisive criterion. This approach was consistently applied in the preparation of all other tables and graphs.

Tab. 3 *Utilitatis causa* decisions according to periodization of the ancient Roman law.

Period	Number of decisions
early classical	1
mid-classical	18
late classical	60
late classical/postclassical	3
Total	**82**

Tab. 4 Number of *utilitatis causa* decisions according to the works of individual jurists.

Jurist	Number of decisions
Ulpian	34
Paulus	15
Papinian	10
Gaius	6
(Pseudo-)Paulus	3
Tryphoninus	2
Julian	2
Clemens	2
Pomponius	1
Scaevola	1
Proculus	1
Macer	1
Africanus	1
Aquila	1
Papirius Justus	1
Marcellus	1
Total	**82**

Tab. 5 *Utilitatis causa* decisions according to type of work the analyzed fragment comes from.

Literary form	Number of decisions
Edict commentary	35
Case law study	21
Jurist's work commentary	12
Textbook or other introductory work	7
Monographic study	3
Statutory law commentary	3
Imperial constitutions' collection	1
Total	**82**

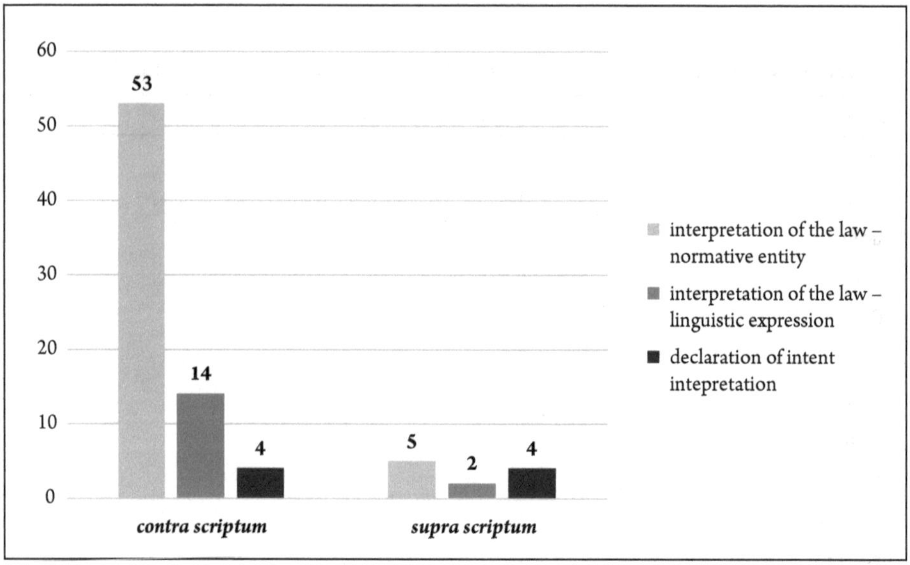

Chart 1 *Utilitatis causa* decisions according to scheme and subject of interpretation.

Chart 1 provides a numerical summary of sources that are examples of the *utilitatis* causa interpretation. This classification also shaped the structure of Chapter Three.

Tab. 6 Representation of *contra* and *supra scriptum* interpretation schemes the in works of jurists.

Interpretation Scheme			
	contra scriptum	*supra scriptum*	Total
Ulpian	30	4	34
Paulus	14	1	15
Papinian	8	2	10
Gaius	5	1	6
(Pseudo-)Paulus	3	Ø	3
Tryphoninus	2	Ø	2
Julian	2	Ø	2
Clemens	2	Ø	2
Pomponius	1	Ø	1
Scaevola	1	Ø	1
Proculus	1	Ø	1
Macer	Ø	1	1
Africanus	1	Ø	1
Aquila	1	Ø	1
Papirius Justus	1	Ø	1
Marcellus	Ø	1	1
Total	**72**	**10**	**82**

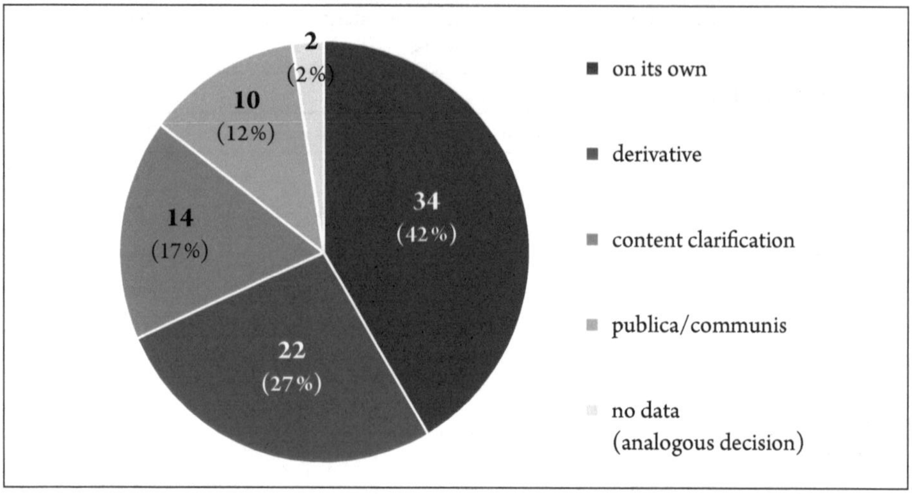

Chart 2 *Utilitatis causa* decisions according to content of the *utilitas* category.

Chart 2 illustrates that jurists more frequently referred to the abstract concept, while explicit clarification of *utilitas* was provided in only 17 % of decisions. In two cases (Iul. D. 9,2,51,2 and G. 3,160), *utilitatis causa* decisions served as model examples for similar rulings, though no direct reference to the criterion was made. Despite the first fragment involving *utilitas communis* and the second simply mentioning *utilitas*, these fragments are categorized separately as 'no data'.

Table 7 illustrates the extent to which other values are referenced in *utilitatis causa* decisions, where they play a supporting role in legal argumentation. In addition to the data below, it should then be noted that jurists made 20 references to the *ex auctoritate* argument. Of the 31 decisions involving an auxiliary argument – whether *auctoritas* or ethical value – only one includes both (Pap. D. 46,1,49,1). In this case, the reference is to the *auctoritas principis* rather than to *iuris peritorum*. Notably, over 60 % of the decisions contain no auxiliary argument, indicating that the inherent strength of the *utilitas* category often made further justification unnecessary.

Tab. 7 References to other values in content of the *utilitatis causa* decisions

	Pap.	Ulp.	Gai.	Proc.	Marcell.	Total
veritas	2	1				3
benignitas			1	1		2
humanitas		1			1	2
dignitas		1				1
religio	1					1
iustitia	1					1
iusta et probabilis ignorantia			1			1
Total	**4**	**3**	**2**	**1**	**1**	**11**

List of Abbreviations

ANRW	Aufstieg und Niedergang der römischen Welt: Geschichte und Kultur Roms im Spiegel der neueren Forschung, H. Temporini, W. Haase (ed.)
AUPA	Annali del seminario giuridico dell'Università di Palermo
BIDR	Bulletino dell'Istituto di Diritto Romano
C.	Codex Iustinianus, [in:] *Corpus Iuris Civilis*, vol. 2, P. Krüger (ed.), Berlin 1963
CIL	Corpus Inscriptionum Latinarum
CPH	Czasopismo Prawno-Historyczne
C.Th.	Codex Theodosianus, Th. Mommsen, P. Krüger (ed.), Berlin 1905
D.	Digesta Iustiniani Augusti, [in:] *Corpus Iuris Civilis*, vol. 1, Th. Mommsen, P. Krüger (ed.), Berlin 1954
Diritto@Storia	Diritto@Storia. Rivista internazionale di Scienze Giuridiche e Tradizione Romana, http://www.dirittoestoria.it/
FIRA	Fontes iuris romani anteiustiniani in usum scholarum, S. Riccobono, J. Baviera, C. Ferrini, J. Furlani, V. Arangio-Ruiz (ed.), I–III Florentiae 1940–1943
G.	Gai institutionum commentarii quattuor, [in:] FIRA, vol. 2, pp. 3–192
GL	Grammatici Latini ex recensione H. Keilii, vol. 1–8, Lipsiae 1855–1880
H.	Rhetores Latini Minores. Ex codicibus maximam partem primum adhibitis emendabat Carolus Halm, Lipsiae 1863
Index	Index. Quaderni camerti di studi romanistici. International Survey of Roman Law
I.	Institutiones, [in:] *Corpus Iuris Civilis*, vol. 1, Th. Mommsen, P. Krüger (ed.), Berlin 1954
Iura	Iura. Rivista internazionale di diritto romano e antico
IvO	Die Inschriften von Olympia, W. Dittenberger, K. Purgold (ed.), Berlin 1896
Klio	Klio – Czasopismo Poświęcone Dziejom Polski i Powszechnym
Labeo	Labeo. Rassegna di diritto romano
LTL	Lexicon Totius Latinitatis J. Facciolati, Aeg. Forcellini et J. Furlanetti seminarii patavini alumnorum cura, opera et studio lucubratum nunc demum juxta opera R. Klotz, G. Freund, L. Doderlein aliorumque recentiorum auctius, emendatius melioremque in formam redactum curante doct. Francisco Corradini ejusdem seminarii alumno, Patavii 1896
OIR	Orbis Iuris Romani
OLD	Oxford Latin Dictionary, P. G. W. Glare (ed.), Oxford 1968.
PK	Prawo Kanoniczne

P. S.	Pauli Sententiae receptae, [in:] FIRA, vol. 2, pp. 317–417.
RE	Paulys Realencyclopädie der classischen Altertumswissenschaft, Stuttgart
RHD	Revue historique de droit français et étranger
RIDA	Revue internationale des droits de l'antiquité
SDHI	Studia et Documenta Historiae et Iuris
SVF	Stoicorum Veterum Fragmenta, vol. 1–4, H. von Arnim (ed.), Leipzig 1906–1924
Tit. Ulp.	Tituli ex corpore Ulpiani, [in:] FIRA, vol. 2, pp. 259–301.
TR	Tijdschrift voor Rechtsgeschiedenis / Revue d'Histoire du Droit / The Legal History Review
ZP	Zeszyty Prawnicze
ZSS RA	Zeitschrift der Savigny-Stiftung für Rechtsgeschichte. Romanistische Abteilung

Index of Sources

Legal Sources

Non-Legal Sources

Epigraphic Sources

References

Editions and Translations of Source Texts Used in Preparation of the Work

Arystoteles, *Etyka Nikomachejska*, transl. D. Gromska, Warszawa 1982.

Cicero M. T., *De inventione. Über die Auffindung des Stoffes. De optimo genere oratorum. Über die beste Gattung von Rednern.* Herausgegeben und übersetzt von Th. Nüßlein, Darmstadt 1998.

Cicero M. T., *O Inwencji Retorycznej. De inventione*, Latin translation by K. Ekes. Introduction and footnotes by B. Awianowicz, Warszawa 2013.

Cicero M. T., *O mówcy*, translation, preface and commentary by B. Awianowicz, Kęty 2010.

Cicero M. T., *Pisma filozoficzne. Tom drugi. O Państwie. O Prawach. O Powinnościach. O Cnotach*, transl. W. Kornatowski. Commentary by K. Leśniak, Warszawa 1960.

Cicéron, *De l'invention*, texte établi et trad. par G. Achard, Paris 2002.

Corpus iuris Romani anteiustiniani, E. Böcking, E. Puggé, A. M. Bethmann-Hollweg (ed.), Bonnae 1841.

Digesta Iustiniani Augusti, vol. 1 and 2, Th. Mommsen, P. Krüger (ed.), Berolini 1870.

Digesta Iustiniani. Digesta Justyniańskie. Tekst i przekład. I. Księgi 1–4, T. Palmirski (ed.), Kraków 2013.

Digesta Iustiniani. Digesta Justyniańskie. Tekst i przekład. IV. Księgi 20–27, T. Palmirski (ed.), Kraków 2014.

Digesta Iustiniani. Digesta Justyniańskie. Tekst i przekład. VI.2 Księgi 41–44, T. Palmirski (ed.), Kraków 2016.

Digesta Justyniańskie. Księga pierwsza, translation by B. Szolc-Nartowski, Warszawa 2007.

Epicurea, H. Usener (ed.), Lipsiae 1887.

Fontes iuris romani anteiustiniani in usum scholarum, vol. 1–3, S. Riccobono, J. Baviera, C. Ferrini, J. Furlani, V. Arangio-Ruiz (ed.), Florentiae 1940–1943.

Gaius, *Instytucje*, Latin translation and preface by C. Kunderewicz, compilation by J. Rezler, Warszawa 1982.

Galenus, *Claudii Galeni Opera Omnia*, ed. C.G. Kühn, vol. I–XIX, Lipsiae 1821–1833.

Gelliusz Aulus, *Noce attyckie (Noctes Atticae)*, vol.1, translation by M. Bielewicz, Wrocław 2017.

Horace, *Satires. Epistles. The Art of Poetry*. Translated by H. Rushton Fairclough. Loeb Classical Library 194. Cambridge 1926.

Instytucje Justyniana, Latin translation and preface by C. Kunderewicz, Warszawa 1986.

Iurisprudentiae antehadrianae quae supersunt. Pars altera: Primi post principatum constitutum saeculi iuris consulti, Bremer F. P. (ed.), Lipsiae 1898.

Marek Aureliusz, *Rozmyślania*, transl. B. Pawlak, M. Reiter, Gliwice 2019.

Pseudo-Dositheus, *Hermeneumata Pseudodositheana Leidensia*, G. Flammini (ed.), Monachii-Lipsiae 2004.

Seneka L. A., *Listy moralne do Lucyliusza*, translation by W. Kornatowicz, preface and footnotes by K. Leśniak, Warszawa 1961.
Seneka L. A., *Pisma filozoficzne I. O krótkości życia. O życiu szczęśliwym. O gniewie. O pocieszeniu do Marcji. O pocieszeniu do matki Helwii. O pocieszeniu do Polibiusza. O niezłomności mędrca. O Opatrzności. O pokoju ducha. O bezczynności*, translation, preface, commentary, layout, index, illustration selection by Leon Joachimowicz, Warszawa 1965.
Swetoniusz Trankwillus G., *Żywoty Cezarów*, translation, introduction, commentary by J. Niemirska-Pliszczyńska. Preface by J. Wolski, Wrocław-Warszawa-Kraków-Gdańsk-Łódź 1987.
Tacyt, *Roczniki, księga XV* [in:] *Dzieła*, vol. 2, transl. S. Hammer, Warszawa 1957.
The Digest of Justinian. Vol. 2 English-language translation edited by A. Watson, Philadelphia 1985.
Trzej satyrycy rzymscy. Horacy, Persjusz, Juwenalis, transl. J. Czubek (Horace) and J. Sękowski (Persius, Iuvenalis), preface and commentary by L. Winniczuk, Warszawa 1958.
Ulpiani Liber singularis regularum. Pauli Libri quinque sententiarum. Fragmenta minora saeculorum p. Chr. n. secundi et tertii, P. Krüger (ed.), Berolini 1878.
Zabłoccy M. i J., *Ustawa XII Tablic. Tekst – tłumaczenie – objaśnienia*, Warszawa 2003.

Dictionaries, Lexicons, and Databases

Berger A., *Encyclopedic Dictionary of Roman Law*, Philadelphia 1968.
Classical Latin Texts. A Resource Prepared by The Packard Humanities Institute (PHI), 2015 (URL: https://latin.packhum.org)
Corpus Corporum – repositorium operum Latinorum apud universitatem Turicensem (URL: https://mlat.uzh.ch/home).
de Vaan M. (ed.), *Etymological Dictionary of Latin and the Other Italic Languages*, Leiden-Boston 2011.
Ernout. A, Meillet. A. (ed.), *Dictionnaire étymologique de la langue latine*, Paris 1951.
Forcellini E. (ed.), *Lexicon Totius Latinitatis*, Patavii 1805.
Glare P. G. W. (ed.), *Oxford Latin Dictionary*, Oxford 1968.
Hederich B., Pinzger G., Passovio G. F. (ed.), *Novum lexicon manuale Graeco-Latinum et Latino-Graecum*, Lipsiae 1827.
Heumann H. G., Seckel E. (ed.), *Handlexikon zu den Quellen des römischen Rechts*, Jena 1926.
Hornblower S., Spawforth A. (ed.), *The Oxford Classical Dictionary*, Oxford-New York 1996.
Janiszewski P., Stebnicka K., Szabat E. (ed.), *Sofiści i retorzy greccy w Cesarstwie Rzymskim (I–VII w.). Słownik biograficzny*, Warszawa 2011.
Korpanty J. (ed.), *Słownik łacińsko-polski: I-Z*, vol. 2, Warszawa 2003.
Kraft F. K. (ed.), *Deutsch-lateinisches Lexikon: aus den römischen Classikern zusammengetragen und nach den besten neuern Hülfsmitteln bearbeitet*, Leipzig-Merseburg 1829.
Lewis C. T., Short C. (ed.), *A Latin Dictionary*, Oxford 1917.
Plezia M. (ed.), *Słownik łacińsko-polski*, vol. 4, Warszawa 1999.
Plezia M. (ed.), *Słownik łacińsko-polski*, vol. 5, Warszawa 2007.
Riedlberger P., Rosenbaum G. , *Amanuensis V5.0.*, München 2020.
Sondel J., *Słownik łacińsko-polski dla prawników i historyków*, Kraków 2006.
Wagner F. (ed.), *Lexicon Latinum*, Brugis 1878.

Monographs, Monographs Chapters, and Articles

Albanese B., *Le persone nel diritto privato romano*, Palermo 1979.

Albertario E., *Les problèmes de la possession relatifs au servus fugitivus*, "TR" 1930, vol. 10, pp. 465–487.

Albertario E., *L'uso traslato di 'salubris, salubritas, salubriter' nelle fonti giuridiche romane*, "Rivista di Filologia e di Istruzione Classica" 1929, vol. 57, pp. 86–96.

Ambrosino R., *Ius singulare*, Milano 1947.

Ankum H., *Das Problem der überholenden Kausalität bei der Anwendung der lex Aquilia im klassischen römischen Recht* [in:] *De iustitia et iure. Festgabe für Ulrich von Lübtow zum 80. Geburtstag*, Berlin 1980, pp. 325–358.

Ankum H., *Elegantia iuris*, "Annales de la Faculté de Droit d'Istanbul" 2011, vol. 21, no. 37, pp. 45–58.

Ankum H., *Navarra, Marialuisa, Ricerche sulla utilitas nel pensiero dei giuristi romani*, "ZSS RA" 2009, vol. 126, no. 1, pp. 524–536.

Ankum H., *Quelques problèmes concernant les ventes aux enchères en droit romain classique* [in:] *Studi in onore di Gaetano Scherillo*, vol. 1, Varese-Milano 1972, pp. 377–394.

Ankum H., *The functions of expressions with utilitatis causa in the works of the Classical Roman lawyers*, "Fundamina: A Journal of Legal History" 2010, vol. 16, no. 1, pp. 5–22.

Ankum H., *Utilitatis causa en los trabajos de los juristas clásicos romanos*, "Revista chilena de derecho" 2016, vol. 43, no. 3, pp. 1121–1132.

Ankum H., *"Utilitatis causa receptum". On the pragmatical methods of the Roman lawyers* [in:] *Symbolae iuridicae et historicae Martino David dedicatae*, vol. 1, J. A. Ankum, R. Feenstra, W. F. Leemans (ed.), Leiden 1968, pp. 1–31.

Ankum H., *"Utilitatis causa receptum": sur la méthode pragmatique des juristes romains classiques*, "RIDA" 1968, vol. 15, pp. 119–133.

Appel H., *Strategia Cycerona w procesie karnym "de ambitu" Lucjusza Mureny* [in:] *Prawo karne i polityka w państwie rzymskim*, K. Amielańczyk, A. Dębiński, D. Słapek (ed.), 2015, pp. 35–46.

Arcaria F., *Oratio Marci: giurisdizione e processo nella normazione di Marco Aurelio*, Torino 2003.

Aricò Anselmo G., *"Ius publicum"-"Ius privatum" in Ulpiano, Gaio e Cicerone*, "AUPA" 1983, vol. 37, pp. 447–787.

Armstrong D., *Horatius Eques et Scriba: Satires 1.6 and 2.7*, "Transactions of the American Philological Association" 1986, vol. 116, pp. 255–288.

Astolfi R., *La lex Iulia et Papia*, 4 ed., Padova 1996.

Astolfi R., *Studi sull'oggetto dei legati in diritto Romano*, Padova 1964.

Atkins E. M., *"Domina et Regina Virtutum": Justice and Societas in "De Officiis"*, "Phronesis" 1990, vol. 35, no. 3, pp. 258–289.

Atkins J. W., *Cicero on Politics and the Limits of Reason: The Republic and Laws*, Cambridge 2013.

Awianowicz B., *Progymnasmata w teorii i praktyce szkoły humanistycznej od końca XV do połowy XVIII wieku: dzieje nowożytnej recepcji Aftoniosa od Rudolfa Agricoli do Johanna Christopha Gottscheda*, Toruń 2008.

Awianowicz B., *Wprowadzenie* [in:] *O Inwencji Retorycznej. De inventione*, przekład z języka łacińskiego K. Ekes. Wstęp i przypisy B. Awianowicz, Warszawa 2013, pp. 7–14.

Ayers D. M., *Cato's Speech against Murena*, "The Classical Journal" 1954, vol. 49, no. 6, pp. 245–253.

Babusiaux U., *Id quod actum est: zur Ermittlung des Parteiwillens im klassischen römischen Zivilprozess*, München 2006.

Babusiaux U., *Papinians Quaestiones: Zur rhetorischen Methode eines spätklassischen Juristen*, München 2014 (available online at: https://books.openedition.org/chbeck/1212).

Babusiaux U., *Zur Funktion der aequitas naturalis in Ulpians Ediktslaudationen* [in:] *Testi e problemi del giusnaturalismo romano*, D. Mantovani, A. Schiavone (ed.), Pavia 2007, pp. 603–644.

Bartošek M., *Utilitas publica? Utilitas communis? Utilitas omnium?*, [in:] *Collectanea opusculorum ad iuris historiam spectantium Venceslao Vaněček septuagenario ab amicis discipulisque oblata: pocta akademiku Václavu Vaněčkovi k 70. narozeninám*, K. Malý (ed.), Praha 1975, pp. 331–352.

Barwick K., *Zur Erklärung und Geschichte der Staseislehre des Hermagoras von temnos*, "Philologus" 1964, vol. 108, no. 1–4, pp. 80–101.

Barwick K., *Zur Rekonstruktion der Rhetorik des Hermagoras von Temnos*, "Philologus" 1965, vol. 109, no. 1–4, pp. 186–218.

Behrends O., *Die fraus legis: zum Gegensatz von Wortlaut- und Sinngeltung in der römischen Gesetzesinterpretation*, Göttingen 1982.

Bennett B. S., *Hermagoras of Temnos* [in:] *Classical Rhetorics and Rhetoricians: Critical Studies and Sources*, M. Ballif, M. G. Moran (ed.), Westport 2005, pp. 187–193.

Berti E., *Le controversiae della raccolta di Seneca il Vecchio e la dottrina degli status*, "Rhetorica: A Journal of the History of Rhetoric" 2014, vol. 32, no. 2, pp. 99–147.

Beseler G., *Beiträge zur Kritik der römischen Rechtsquellen*, vol. 2, Tübingen 1911.

Beseler G., *Confestim – Continuo*, "ZSS RA" 1931, vol. 51, no. 1, pp. 188–202.

Betancourt F., *El libro anónimo De interdictis: Codex vaticanus latinus no. 5766*, Salamanca 1997.

Betti E., *"Iurisdictio praetoris" e potere normativo*, "Labeo" 1968, vol. 14, pp. 7–23.

Betti E., *La creazione del diritto nella "iurisdictio" del pretore romano* [in:] *Studi di diritto processuale in onore di Giuseppe Chiovenda nel venticinquesimo anno del suo insegnamento.*, A. Castellari et al. (ed.), Padova 1927, pp. 65–129.

Betti E., *Seneca il Vecchio e la cultura retorica e letteraria della prima età imperiale*, Pisa 2007.

Biondi B., *Il diritto romano cristiano. Vol. 2. La giustizia, le persone*, Milano 1952.

Biscardi A., *On aequitas and epieikeia* [in:] *Aequitas and Equity: Equity in Civil Law and Mixed Jurisdictions*, A. M. Rabello (ed.), Jerusalem 1997, pp. 1–11.

Bleicken J., *Lex publica, Gesetz und Recht in der römischen Republik*, Berlin-Boston 2015.

Blicharz G.J., *Giudicare una decisione del pretore: La relazione tra diritto e fatto nel passo di Paolo (D. 1,1,11) e nel caso di Barbarius Philipus (D. 1,14,3)*, "Seminarios Complutenses de Derecho Romano. Revista Internacional de Derecho Romano y Tradición Romanística" 2016, vol. 29, pp. 335–352.

Boissier G., *Les Écoles de déclamation à Rome*, "Revue des deux mondes" 1902, vol. 11, pp. 481–508.

Bojarski W., *Remarks on Textual Reconstruction in Roman Law* [in:] *Le droit romain et le monde contemporain. Mélanges à la mémoire de Henryk Kupiszewski*, W. Wołodkiewicz, M. Zabłocka (ed.), Varsovie 1996, pp. 83–89.

Bond R. P., *Stoic influence on selected satires of Horace*, Canterbury 1977 (PhD thesis available online at: https://ir.canterbury.ac.nz/handle/10092/4767).

Braet A., *Cicero modifications of the status principles systematized by Hermagoras*, "Rhetorica: A Journal of the History of Rhetoric" 1989, vol. 7, no. 3, pp. 239–259.

Brejon J., *Fraus legis*, Rennes 1941.

Bretone M., *I fondamenti del diritto romano. Le cose e la natura*, Roma-Bari 1998.

Bretone M., *Ius controversum nella giurisprudenza classica*, "Atti della Accademia Nazionale dei Lincei, Classe di Scienze Morali, Storiche e Filologiche" 2008, ser. 9, vol. 23, fasc. 3, pp. 755–879.

Bretone M., *Il giureconsulto interprete della legge*, "Labeo" 1969, vol. 15, no. 3, pp. 289–310.

Bretone M., *Tecniche e ideologie dei giuristi romani*, Napoli 1984.

Brinton A., *Quintilian, Plato, and the "Vir Bonus"*, "Philosophy & Rhetoric" 1983, vol. 16, no. 3, pp. 167–184.
Brożek B., *The Legal Mind: A New Introduction to Legal Epistemology*, Cambridge 2019.
Büchner K., *Humanitas Romana. Studien über Werke und Wesen der Römer*, Heidelberg 1957.
Buckland W. W., *The Roman Law of Slavery: The Condition of the Slave in Private Law from Augustus to Justinian*, New Jersey 2000.
Bujuklić Ž., *Ancient and Modern Concepts of Lawfulness*, "RIDA" 1999, vol. 46, pp. 123–163.
Burdese A., *Il concetto di ius naturale nel pensiero della giurisprudenza classica*, "Rivista Italiana per le Scienze Giuridiche" 1954, vol. 7, pp. 407–431.
Burdese A., *L'eccezione di dolo generale in rapporto alle altre eccezioni*, "Diritto@Storia" 2006, no. 5 (available online at: https://dirittoestoria.it/5/Tradizione-Romana/Burdese-Eccezione-dolo-generale.htm).
Calboli Montefusco L., *La dottrina degli "status" nella retorica greca e romana*, Hildesheim 1986.
Calboli Montefusco L., *Logica, retorica e giurisprudenza nella dottrina degli status*, [in:] *Per la storia del pensiero giuridico romano. Dall'età dei pontefici alla scuola di Servio. Atti del seminario di S. Marino 7–9 gennaio 1993*, D. Mantovani (ed.), Torino 1996, pp. 209–228.
Candy P., *Limits of Juristc Argument in the Exercitorian Edict* [in:] *Principle and Pragmatism in Roman Law*, B. Spagnolo, J. Sampson (ed.), Oxford-New York 2020, pp. 143–158.
Capone P., *Valore ed uso giurisprudenziale di absurdus/e*, "SDHI" 1997, vol. 63, pp. 197–257.
Capuano L., *Dottrina e storia del diritto romano*, Napoli 1878.
Carrá B. L. C., *Utilitas contrahentium: um princípio de responsabilidade civil romano para uma sociedade globalizada?*, "Revista de Direito Civil Contemporâneo" 2016, vol. 3, no. 8, pp. 139–166.
Casamento A., *Colorem timere peius quam sanguinem. Paintings, family strife and heroism* [in:] *Reading Roman Declamation – Calpurnius Flaccus*, M. T. Dinter, C. Guérin, M. Martinho (ed.), Berlin-Boston 2017, pp. 97–112.
Casavola F. P., *Giuristi adrianei*, Napoli 1980.
Cascione C., Masi Doria C. (ed.), *Quid est veritas? Un seminario su verità e forme giuridiche*, Napoli 2013.
Cascione C., Masi Doria C., *Veritas e ius: per una storia della verità giuridica*, Napoli 2013.
Catalano P., *Populus Romanus Quirites*, Torino 1974.
Ceneri G., *Lezioni su temi del jus familiae*, Bologna 1881.
Cerami P., *"Ius est ars boni et aequi". Un riesame della definizione celsina*, "AUPA" 2019, vol. 62, pp. 35–82.
Cerami P., *La concezione celsina del "ius" : presupposti culturali e implicazioni metodologiche.*, "AUPA" 1985, vol. 37, pp. 5–250.
Cerami P., *Plena interpretatio*, [in:] *Studi in onore di Cesare Sanfilippo*, Milano 1983, pp. 107–154.
Cerami P., *Potere ed ordinamento nella esperienza costituzionale romana*, 3ed, Torino 1987.
Cerami P., *Problemi storico-dogmatici in tema di funzionario di fatto*, [in:] *Studi in onore di Gioacchino Scaduto. Diritto civile e diritto romano*, vol. 3, Padova 1970, pp. 375–423.
Chandler C., *Philodemus on Rhetoric Books 1 and 2: Translation and Exegetical Essays*, New York-London 2017.
Chang K. E., *The Community, the Individual and the Common Good: "To Idion" and "To Sympheron" in the Greco-Roman World and Paul*, London 2013.
Cicala F. B., *Il concetto dell'"utile" e sue applicazioni nel diritto romano*, Milano-Torino-Roma 1910.
Clark D. L., *Rhetoric in Greco-Roman Education*, New York 1957.
Clarke M. L., *The Thesis in the Roman Rhetorical Schools of the Republic*, "The Classical Quarterly" 1951, vol. 1, no. 3–4, pp. 159–166.

Cloud J. D., *Satirists and the Law* [in:] *Satire and Society in Ancient Rome*, S. H. Braund (ed.), Exeter 1989, pp. 49–67.

Colamonico M., Zingarelli R., *Le garanzie delle obbligazioni: Lezioni di diritto romano*, Napoli 1897.

Coleman K. M., *Public Entertainments* [in:] *The Oxford Handbook of Social Relations in the Roman World*, M. Peachin (ed.), Oxford 2011, pp. 335–357.

Collingwood R., *The Idea of History*, New York 1956.

Conche M., *Droit naturel et droit positif selon Épicure*, "Revue philosophique de la France et de l'étranger" 2013, vol. 138, no. 4, pp. 549–556.

Corbino A., *Ius suum cuique tribuere. Osservazioni minime sulla definizione ulpianea di iustitia (D. 1.1.10 pr.-2 e Rhet. ad Her. 3.2.3)* [in:] *Homenaje al Profesor Armando Torrent*, A. Murillo Villar, A. Calzada González, S. Castán Pérez-Gómez (ed.), Madrid 2016, pp. 155–165.

Cossa G., *I giuristi e la retorica*, [in:] *Dogmengeschichte und Historische Individualität Der Römischen Juristen. Storia dei dogmi e individualità storica dei Giuristi romani. Atti del seminario internazionale (Montepulciano 14–17 Giugno 2011)*, C. Baldus, M. Miglietta, G. Santucci, E. Stolfi (ed.), Trento 2012, pp. 299–363.

Costa E., *Cicerone giureconsulto*, Bologna 1927.

Costa E., *Il diritto nei poeti di Roma*, Bologna 1898.

Costa P., *"Constituta per littera" e riconoscimento del debito: ipotesi esegetiche*, "Teoria e Storia del Diritto Privato" 2021, no. 14, pp. 1–56.

Costa P., *"Pecunia constituta": ipotesi interpretative*, "SDHI" 2011, vol. 77, pp. 129–256.

Courtney E., *The Two Books of Satires* [in:] *Brill's Companion to Horace*, H.-C. Günther (ed.), Leiden-Boston 2013, pp. 63–168.

Crifò G., *Ulpiano. Esperienze e responsabilità del giurista*, [in:] ANRW, vol. 2.15, Berlin-New York 1976, pp. 708–789.

Crook J. A., *Once again the Controversiae and Roman Law* [in:] *Multarum artium scientia. Festschrift for R. Godfrey Tanner*, Auckland 1993, pp. 68–76.

Cujas J., *Opera ad Parisiensem Fabrotianam editionem diligentissime exacta, auctiora atque emendatiora*, vol. 7, Prati 1839.

Cursi M. F., *Dal danno aquiliano al danno extracontrattuale: le radici romanistiche* [in:] *Itinerari giuridici. Per il quarantennale della Facoltà di Giurisprudenza dell'Abruzzo*, G. Canzio (ed.), Milano 2007, pp. 215–257.

D'Angelo G., *A proposito di 'animo possidere'*, "Teoria e storia del diritto privato" 2018, no. 9, pp. 1–50.

D'Angelo G., *La perdita della possessio animo retenta nei casi di occupazione*, Torino 2007.

D'Ors A., *De la Privata Lex al Derecho Privado y al Derecho Civil*, "Boletim da Faculdade de Direito da Universidade de Coimbra" 1949, vol. 25, pp. 29–46.

De Filippi M., *Subvenire pupillis*, "Labeo" 1980, vol. 26, pp. 61–73.

De Martino F., *Studi sull'"actio exercitoria"*, "Labeo" 1958, vol. 4, pp. 274–300.

Debayle G.-A., *Moyens de défense et recours des fidéjusseurs en droit romain et en droit français*, Sauveterre 1879.

Diliberto O., *La satira e il diritto: una nuova lettura di Horat., sat. 1.3.115–117*, "AUPA" 2012, vol. 55, pp. 385–402.

Diliberto O., *Ut carmen necessarium (Cic. leg. II, 59). Apprendimento e conoscenza della Legge delle XII Tavole nel I sec. a. C.* [in:] *Transizioni dalla Repubblica all'Impero. In ricordo di E. Narducci*, M. Citroni (ed.), Pisa 2012, pp. 141–162.

Dingel J., *Scholastica materia. Untersuchungen zu den Declamationes minores und der Institutio oratoria Quintilians*, Berlin-New York 1988, rep. 2013.

Domingo R., *Auctoritas*, Barcelona 1999.

Dovere E., *Le discours juridique et moral de l'utilitas à Rome* [in:] *Histoire raisonnée de la philosophie morale et politique*, A. Caillé, C. Lazzeri, M. Senellart (ed.), Paris 2001, pp. 108–115.

Ducos M., *Les romains et la loi: recherches sur les rapports de la philosophie grecque et de la tradition romaine à la fin de la République*, Paris 1984.

Dulckeit G., *Öffentliches und Privatrecht im römischen Recht*, "Zeitschrift der Akademie für Deutsches Recht" 1935, vol. 2, pp. 277–282.

du Plessis, P. (ed.), *Cicero's Law: Rethinking Roman Law of the Late Republic*, Edinburgh 2016.

Dvorjetski E., *Leisure, Pleasure and Healing: Spa Culture and Medicine in Ancient Eastern Mediterranean*, Leiden 2007.

Dyck A. R., *A Commentary on Cicero, De Officiis*, Ann Arbor 1996.

Dyjakowska M., *Prawne aspekty relegacji Owidiusza*, "Folia Societatis Scientiarum Lublinensis: Humanistyka" 1993, vol. 34, no. 1, pp. 61–72.

Elvers R., *Romanorum de rebus religiosis doctrina*, Gottingae 1851.

Ernst W., *Justinian's Digest 9.2.51 in the Western Legal Canon: Roman Legal Thought and Mondern Causality Concepts*, Cambridge-Antwerp-Chicago 2019.

Fabry P., *Nomen iuris est autem a iustitia appellatum: Ulpien, l'étymologie, l'idée de justice dans la pensée juridique et politique de Rome*, "RHD" 2014, vol. 92, no. 4, pp. 489–515.

Fairweather J., *Seneca the Elder*, Cambridge 1981.

Falcone G., *Beneficia imperiali e "logica del sistema". Spunti di metodo tra le righe di Alberto Burdese*, "BIDR" 2015, vol. 109, pp. 207–223.

Falcone G., *D. 1.3.13 Pedio, Ulpiano e la "lex contractus"*, "Labeo" 1997, vol. 43, no. 2, pp. 133–176.

Falcone G., *Difesa del dominium e stabilità della res publica nell'orazione ciceroniana Pro Murena*, [in:] *Fides Humanitas Ius. Scritti in onore di Luigi Labruna*, C. Cascione, C. Masi Doria (ed.), Napoli 2007, pp. 1683–1710.

Falcone G., *Ricerche sull'origine dell'interdetto uti possidetis*, Palermo 1996.

Falcone G., *Ius suum cuique tribuere*, "AUPA" 2008, vol. 52, pp. 133–176.

Falcone G., *La formula "ut inter bonos bene agier oportet et sine fraudatione" e la nozione di "vir bonus"*, "Fundamina: A Journal of Legal History" 2014, vol. 20, pp. 258–274.

Falcone G., *La "vera philosophia" dei "sacerdotes iuris". Sulla raffigurazione ulpianea dei giuristi (D.1.1.1.1)*, "AUPA" 2004, vol. 49, pp. 41–147.

Falcone G., *L'attribuzione della qualifica "vir bonus" nella prassi giudiziaria d'età repubblicana (a proposito di Cato, or. frg. 186 Sbelnd. = 206 Malc.). Con un'Appendice su "optimus" "probus" 'fortis* [in:] *Vir bonus. Un modello ermeneutico della riflessione giuridica antica*, A. Lovato (ed.), Bari 2013, pp. 39–90.

Falcone G., *L'esordio del commento ulpianeo all'editto sui patti (D. 2, 14, 1 pr.) tra critica testuale e studio dei percorsi concettuali*, "AUPA" 2009, vol. 53, pp. 226–254.

Falcone G., *Sul c. d. Fragmentum Dositheanum*, "Specula iuris" 2021, vol. 1.1, pp. 203–227.

Falcone G., *Un'ipotesi sulla nozione ulpianea di ius publicum* [in:] *Tradizione romanistica e Costituzione*, vol. 2, L. Labruna, M. P. Baccari, C. Cascione (ed.), Napoli 2006, pp. 1167–1195.

Fargnoli I., *Studi sulla legittimazione attiva all'interdetto quod vi aut clam*, Milano 1998.

Fascione L., *Fraus legi: indagini sulla concezione della frode alla legge nella lotta politica e nella esperienza giuridica romana*, Milano 1983.

Fedeli P., *Commento e note* [in:] *Orazio. Tutte le poesie*, Torino 2009.

Ferrary J.-L., *Le discours de Philus (Cicéron, De re publica, III, 8–31) et la philosophie de Carnéade*, "Revue des Études Latines" 1977, vol. 55, pp. 128–156.

Ferrary J.-L., *Le droit naturel dans les exposés sur les parties du droit des traités de rhétorique*, [in:] *Testi e problemi del giusnaturalismo romano*, D. Mantovani, A. Schiavone (ed.), Pavia 2007, pp. 75–94.

Ferrary J.-L., Schiavone A., Marotta V., *Cnaeus Domitius Ulpianus Institutiones. De Censibus*, Roma-Bristol 2021.

Ferretti P., *Possessio, animus e corpus*, "forum historiae iuris" 2019 (available online at: https://forhistiur.net/2019-01-ferretti/).

Filippi C., *La causa curiana*, "Anuario de Derecho Civil" 2004, vol. 9, pp. 131–138.

Finazzi G., *La sostituzione pupillare*, Napoli 1997.

Fiori R., *Bonus vir: Politica, filosofia, retorica e diritto nel de officiis di Cicerone*, Napoli 2011.

Fiori R., *Eccezione di dolo generale ed editto asiatico di Quinto Mucio: il problema delle origini* [in:] *L'eccezione di dolo generale. Diritto romano e tradizione romanistica*, L. Garofalo (ed.), Padova 2006, pp. 51–89.

Fiori R., *Il vir bonus fra tradizioni romane e filosofia greca nel de officiis di Cicerone* [in:] *Vir bonus. Un modello ermeneutico della riflessione giuridica antica*, Andrea Lovato (ed.), Bari 2013, pp. 19–38.

Fiori R., *The vir bonus in Cicero's de officiis: Greek philosophy and Roman legal science* [in:] *Aequum ius. От друзей и коллег к 50-летию профессора Д.В. Дождева*, Moscow 2014, pp. 187–202.

Forzieri Vannucchi O., *Studi sull'interpretazione giurisprudenziale romana*, Milano 1973.

Fotheringham L., *Repetition and Unity in a Civil Law Speech: The Pro Caecina* [in:] *Cicero the Advocate*, J. Powell, J. Paterson (ed.), Oxford 2004, pp. 253–276.

Fraenkel E., *Orazio*, Roma 1993.

Franchani F., *Il diritto nei retori Romani: contributo alla storia dello sviluppo del diritto romano*, Milano 1938.

Franciosi E., *Gloriae et virtutis causa. Status sociale e giuridico degli atleti nel mondo romano* [in:] *Studi per Giovanni Nicosia*, vol. 3, Milano 2007, pp. 437–468.

Frezza P., *Ius gentium*, "RIDA" 1949, vol. 2, pp. 259–308.

Frezza P., *La cultura di Ulpiano*, "SDHI" 1968, vol. 34, pp. 363–375.

Frezza P., *La persona di Ulpiano (a proposito del volume di Tony Honore)*, "SDHI" 1983, vol. 49, pp. 412–422.

Frezza P., *Le garanzie delle obbligazioni. I. Le garanzie personali*, Padova 1962.

Frier B. W., *The Rise of the Roman Jurists. Studies in Cicero's pro Caecina*, Princeton 1985.

Gallo F., *'Ars boni et aequi' e ' ius naturale'*, "SDHI" 2009, vol. 75, pp. 7–52.

Gallo F., *Celso e Kelsen: Per la rifondazione della scienza giuridica*, Torino 2010.

Gallo F., *La riflessione di Papiniano sul "ius honorarium"* [in:] *Règle et pratique du droit: dans les réalités juridiques de la antiquité: Atti della 51° Sessione della SIHDA – Sociétè Internationale Fernand De Visscher pour l'Histoire des Droits de l'Antiquité (Crotone-Messina, 16–20 settembre 1997)*, I. Piro (ed.), Catanzaro 1999, pp. 31–53.

Gallo F., *L'officium del pretore nella produzione e applicazione del diritto: Corso di diritto romano*, Torino 1997.

Gallo F., *Sulla definizione celsina del diritto*, "SDHI" 1987, vol. 53, pp. 7–52.

Gandolfi G., *Studi sull'interpretazione degli atti negoziali in diritto romano*, Milano 1966.

García Garrido M. J., *Navarra, M., Ricerche sulla utilitas nel pensiero dei giuristi romani*, "Iura" 2003, vol. 54, pp. 288–293.

Garzetti A., *Floro e l'età adrianea*, "Athenaeum. Studi di letteratura e storia dell'antichità" 1964, vol. 42, pp. 136–144.

Gaudemet J., *Iustum matrimonium*, "RIDA" 1949, vol. 2, pp. 309–366.

Gaudemet J., *Utilitas publica*, "RHD" 1951, vol. 4, no. 29, pp. 136–144.

Gergely D., *Salus rei publicae als Entscheidungsgrundlage des römischen Privatrechts*, Budapest 2015.

Gerkens J.-F., *"Aeque perituris ...": Une approche de la causalité dépassante en droit romain classique*, Liège 1997.

Gerkens J.-F., *Selbsthilfe bei Brandgefahr. Überlegungen zu den Rechtsmitteln im Prinzipat* [in:] *Liber Amicorum Guido Tsuno*, P. Thomas, F. Sturm, J. Otto, H. Mori (ed.), Frankfurt am Main 2013, pp. 103–124.
Giaro T., *Absurditätsargumente in der römischen Jurisprudenz*, "OIR" 2006, vol. 11, pp. 31–61.
Giaro T., *Dogmatische Wahrheit und Zeitlosigkeit in der römischen Jurisprudenz*, "BIDR" 1987, vol. 29, pp. 1–104.
Giaro T., *Excusatio Necessitatis nel Diritto Romano*, Warszawa 1982.
Giaro T., *Geltung und Fortgeltung des römischen Juristenrechts*, "ZSS RA" 1994, vol. 111, no. 1, pp. 66–94.
Giaro T., *L'expérience de l'absurde chez les juristes romains* [in:] *Mater familias. Scritti romanistici per Maria Zabłocka*, Z. Benincasa, J. Urbanik (ed.), Varsavia 2016, pp. 243–268.
Giaro T., *Papinian und die reductio ad absurdum* [in:] *Argumenta Papiniani: Studien zur Geschichte und Dogmatik des Privatrechts*, J. D. Harke (ed.), Berlin, Heidelberg 2013, pp. 41–57.
Giaro T., *Prawda dogmatyczna i "ponadczasowość" jurysprudencji rzymskiej*, "CPH" 1988, vol. 40, no. 1, pp. 1–31.
Giaro T., *Römische Rechtswahrheiten. Ein Gedankenexperiment*, Frankfurt am Main 2007.
Glucker J., *Carneades in Rome: Some Unsolved Problems*, "Bulletin of the Institute of Classical Studies" 2001, vol. 45, no. 76, pp. 57–82.
Goldschmidt V., *La doctrine d'Épicure et le droit*, Paris 1977.
Gorczyca SJ J., *Zarys etyki fundamentalnej*, Kraków 2014.
Gordon W. M., *Translation and Interpretation* [in:] *Critical Studies in Ancient Law, Comparative Law and Legal History: Essays in Honour of Alan Watson*, J. Cairns, O. Robinson (ed.), Oxford-Portland Oregon 2001, pp. 61–72.
Górska M., *Łaciński genetivus possessivus (proprietatis) a modalność*, "Linguistica Copernicana" 2011, vol. 1, no. 5, pp. 63–75.
Gröschler P., *Actiones in factum. Eine Untersuchung zur Klage-Neuschöpfung im nichtvertraglichen Bereich*, Berlin 2002.
Gross A. G., *Why Hermagoras Still Matters: The Fourth Stasis and Interdisciplinarity*, "Rhetoric Review" 2004, vol. 23, no. 2, pp. 141–155.
Guarino A., *Il problema dogmatico e storico del diritto singolare* [in:] *Pagine di Diritto Romano*, vol. 6, Napoli 1995, pp. 3 75.
Guarino A., *L'ordinamento giuridico romano*, Napoli 1980.
Guarino A., *Res gestae divi augusti: testo critico, introduzione, traduzione e commento*, Milano 1968.
Guggenheimer E. H., *Rhyme Effects and Rhyming Figures: A Comparative Study of Sound Repetitions in the Classics with Emphasis on Latin Poetry*, Berlin-Boston 2018.
Günther H.-C., *Horace's Life and Work* [in:] *Brill's Companion to Horace*, H.-C. Günther (ed.), Leiden-Boston 2013, pp. 1–62.
Guzmán Brito A., *Caución tutelar en derecho romano*, Pamplona 1974.
Gwynn A., *Roman Education from Cicero to Quintilian*, Oxford 1926.
Hadot P., *Marius Victorinus: recherches sur sa vie et ses œuvres*, Paris 1971.
Harke J. D., *Actio utilis. Anspruchsanalogie im römischen Recht*, Berlin 2016.
Hassan R., *La poesia e il diritto in Orazio. Tra autore e pubblico*, Napoli 2014.
Hausmaninger H., *Subtilitas als juristische Wertung in den Codex-Konstitutionen Justinians* [in:] *Festschrift Fritz Schwind zum 65. Geburtstag: Rechtsgeschichte, Rechtsvergleichung, Rechtspolitik*, R. Strasser, M. Schwimann, H. Hoyer (ed.), Wien 1978, pp. 71–77.
Hausmaninger H., *Subtilitas iuris* [in:] *Iuris professio: Festgabe für Max Kaser zum 80. Geburtstag*, H.-P. Benöhr, K. Hackl, R. Knütel, A. Wacke (ed.), Wien-Köln-Graz 1986, pp. 59–72.

Heath M., *Hermagoras: Transmission and Attribution*, "Philologus" 2002, vol. 146, no. 2, pp. 287–298.
Heath M., *The Substructure of stasis-theory from Hermagoras to Hermogenes*, "The Classical Quarterly" 1994, vol. 44, no. 1, pp. 114–129.
Heineccius J. G., *Fundamenta stili cultoris. Nunc demum omnibus Io. Matthiae Generi animadversionibus, additamentis, et praefatione locupletata accuravit, digessit, suas quoque observationes adiecit Nicolaus Niclas*, Amstelodami 1761.
Herforth R., *Begründet die irrtümliche Zahlung einer fremden Schuld die condictio indebiti? Nach römischen und gemeinem Recht*, Zürich 1902.
Hibst P., *Utilitas publica, gemeiner Nutz, Gemeinwohl: Untersuchungen zur Idee eines politischen Leitbegriffes von der Antike bis zum späten Mittelalter*, Frankfurt am Main-New York 1991.
Hillgruber M., *"Scriptum" und "voluntas" in der Rechtswissenschaft der römischen Republik*, "Museum Helveticum" 1995, vol. 52, no. 3, pp. 170–180.
Himmelschein J., *Studien zu der antiken Hermeneutica iuris* [in:] *Symbolae Friburgenses in honorem Ottonis Lenel*, Leipzig 1931, pp. 373–424.
Honoré A. M., *Legal Reasoning in Rome and Today*, "Cambrian Law Review" 1973, vol. 4, pp. 58–67.
Honoré T., *The "Fragmentum Dositheanum"*, "RIDA" 1965, vol. 12, pp. 301–323.
Honoré T., *Ulpian, Natural law and Stoic influence*, "TR" 2010, vol. 78, no. 1–2, pp. 199–208.
Honoré T., *Ulpian: Pioneer of Human Rights*, New York 1982.
Honsell T., *Gemeinwohl und öffentliches Interesse im klassischen römischen Recht*, "ZSS RA" 1978, vol. 95, no. 1, pp. 93–137.
Honsell T., *In fraudem legis agere*, [in:] *Festschrift für Max Kaser zum 70. Geburtstag*, D. Medicus, H. H. Seiler (ed.), München 1976, pp. 111–126.
Horak F., *Rationes decidendi: Entscheidungsbegründungen bei den älteren römischen Juristen bis Labeo*, vol. 1, Insbruck 1969.
Horsmann G., *Die Bescholtenheit der Berufssportler im römischen Recht. Zur Bedeutung von "artem ludicram facere" und "in scaenam prodire" in den juristischen Quellen*, "Nikephoros" 1994, vol. 7, pp. 207–227.
Huelsenbeck B., *The rhetorical collection of the Elder Seneca: Textual tradition and traditional text*, "Harvard Studies in Classical Philology" 2011, vol. 106, pp. 229–299.
Humbert M., *Equité et raison naturelle dans les oeuvres de Celse et de Julien* [in:] *Testi e problemi del giusnaturalismo romano*, D. Mantovani, A. Schiavone (ed.), Pavia 2007, pp. 419–473.
Isaac B., *Army and Violence in the Roman World* [in:] *Empire and Ideology in the Graeco-Roman World: Selected Papers*, Cambridge 2017, pp. 69–81.
Insadowski H., *Prawo rzymskie u Horacego*, Lublin 1935.
Isnardi Parente M., *Techne: Momenti del pensiero greco da Platone ad Epicuro*, Firenze 1966.
Jong H. de, *Ἐντολή (mandatum) in den Basiliken*, Leiden-Boston 2020.
Jońca M., *Przestępstwo znieważenia grobu w rzymskim prawie karnym*, Lublin 2013.
Jory E. J., *Ars Ludicra and the Ludus Talarius*, "Bulletin of the Institute of Classical Studies" 1995, vol. 40, no. 66, pp. 139–152.
Jossa G., *L'"utilitas rei publicae" nel pensiero di Cicerone*, "Studi Romani" 1964, vol. 12, no. 3, pp. 269–288.
Jossa G., *L'"utilitas rei publicae" nel pensiero imperiale dell'epoca classica*, "Studi Romani" 1963, vol. 11, no. 4, pp. 387–405.
Kamińska R., *Ochrona dróg i rzek publicznych w prawie rzymskim w okresie Republiki i Pryncypatu*, Warszawa 2010.

Kamińska R., *Ochrona dróg publicznych przez urzędników rzymskich*, "ZP" 2017, vol. 8, no. 2, pp. 75–96.
Kamińska R., *Ochrona miejsc świętych w prawie rzymskim*, "ZP" 2016, vol. 12, no. 1, pp. 79–93.
Kamińska R., *Organizacja "cura urbis" w Rzymie w początkach Pryncypatu*, "ZP" 2013, vol. 13, no. 1, pp. 73–95.
Kamińska R., *Udział pretora w zarządzaniu i ochronie dróg rzymskich* [in:] *Prawne aspekty podróży i turystyki – historia i współczesność: prace poświęcone pamięci profesora Janusza Sondla*, P. Cybula (ed.), Kraków 2018, pp. 221–230.
Kamińska R., *W trosce o miasto. "Cura urbis" w okresie Republiki i Pryncypatu*, Warszawa 2015.
Kaser M., *Das römische Privatrecht. 1. Abschnitt. Das altrömische, das vorklassische und klassische Recht*, München 1971.
Kaser M., *"Ius publicum" und "ius privatum"*, "ZSS RA" 1986, vol. 103, no. 1, pp. 1–101.
Kaser M., *Zum römischen Grabrecht*, "ZSS RA" 1978, vol. 95, no. 1, pp. 15–92.
Kaser M., *Zur Geschichte des precarium*, "ZSS RA" 1972, vol. 89, no. 1, pp. 94–148.
Kaser M., *"Ius publicum" – "Ius privatum" (zugleich Besprechung von Nocera, 'Ius publicum')*, "SDHI" 1951, vol. 17, pp. 267–278.
Kaser M., *Restituere als Prozeßgegenstand. Die Wirkungen der litis contestatio auf den Leistungsstand im römischen Recht*, München 1968.
Kaser M., *Römische Rechtsquellen und angewandte Juristenmethode: ausgewählte, zum Teil grundlegend erneuerte Abhandlungen*, Wien-Köln 1986.
Kaser M., *Zur Methodologie der römischen Rechtsquellenforschung*, Wien-Köln-Graz 1972.
Kaser M., Krüger H., *Fraus*, "ZSS RA" 1943, vol. 63, no. 1, pp. 117–174.
Kennedy G.A., *A New History of Classical Rhetoric. An Extensive Revision and Abridgement of The Art of Persuasion in Greece, The Art of Rhetoric in the Roman World and Greek Rhetoric under Christian Emperors with Additional Discussion of Late Latin Rhetoric*, New Jersey 1994.
Kirschenbaum A., *Sons, Slaves, and Freedmen in Roman Commerce*, Jerusalem 1987.
Kleyn D., Niekerk G. van, *Ulpian's praecepta iuris and their role in South African law. Part 1: Historical context*, "Fundamina: A Journal of Legal History" 2014, vol. 20, no. 1, pp. 437–445.
Klinck F., *Erwerb durch Übergabe an Dritte nach klassischem römischen Recht*, Berlin 2004.
Knütel R., *Dolus tutoris pupillo non nocet* [in:] *Iuris professio: Festgabe für Max Kaser zum 80. Geburtstag*, H.-P. Benöhr, K. Hackl, R. Knütel, A. Wacke (ed.), Wien 1986, pp. 101–126.
Kodrębski J., *Rec. "Sententia legis", Bernard Vonglis, Paris 1967*, "CPH" 1972, vol. 24, no. 1, pp. 241–244.
Kolańczyk K., *O pochodzeniu i stanowisku społecznym prawników rzymskich*, "CPH" 1955, vol. 7, no. 1, pp. 227–284.
Könczöl M., *Law, fact and narratives in ancient rhetoric: The case of the causa Curiana*, "International Journal for the Semiotics of Law-Revue internationale de Sémiotique juridique" 2008, vol. 21, no. 1, pp. 21–33.
Koschembahr-Łyskowski I., *Coventiones contra bonos mores w prawie rzymskim*, Kraków 1925.
Kremer D., *Les Institutiones d'Ulpien. Premier manuel de droit romain*, "Index" 2021, vol. 49, pp. 64–87.
Kreuzsaler C., Urbanik J., *Humanity and Inhumanity of Law. The Case of of Dionysia*, "The Journal of Juristic Papirology" 2008, vol. 38, pp. 119–156.
Krokiewicz A., *Sceptycyzm grecki. Od Pirrona do Karneadesa*, Warszawa 2002.
Królczyk K., *Polityka dynastyczna cesarza Septymiusza Sewera (193–211 r.)*, "Klio" 2018, vol. 47, no. 4, pp. 181–201.

Krzynówek J., *Funkcje i stosowanie "precarium" w rzymskim prawie klasycznym*, "PK" 1993, vol. 36, no. 3–4, pp. 137–148.

Krzynówek J., *Granice praepositio przy actio exercitoria*, "PK" 1994, vol. 37, no. 3–4, pp. 175–189.

Kubiak P., *Kilka uwag na temat znajomości prawa u mówców sądowych republikańskiego Rzymu*, "Krakowskie Studia z Historii Państwa i Prawa" 2015, vol. 8, no. 1, pp. 1–24.

Kulawiak-Cyrankowska J., *The Death Penalty, the "Marriage Penalty" and Some Remarks on the Utility of Senecan Research in the Study of Roman Law*, "Studia Iuridica" 2019, vol. 80, pp. 197–214.

Kulawiak-Cyrankowska J., *Tłumaczenie niezbędne? Garść uwag na temat języka łacińskiego w świecie polskiej romanistyki prawniczej* [in:] *Translatoryka i Translacje. Przekład w XXI wieku: wyzwania, możliwości, trendy*, Ł.J. Berezowski (ed.), Łódź 2020, pp. 31–38.

Kunkel W., *Die römischen Juristen: Herkunft und soziale Stellung*, Köln 2001.

Kupisch B., *Der Sklave als Zwangs-Erbe, Ulpian/Julian 4 ad Sab. (D. 28,5,6,4): Eine Nach-Lese*, "TR" 2016, vol. 84, no. 3–4, pp. 379–400.

Kupisch B., *In integrum restitutio und vindicatio utilis bei Eigentumsübertragungen im klassischen römischen Recht*, Berlin 1974.

Kupiszewski H., *Pojęcie państwa w de republica Cycerona*, "PK" 1991, vol. 34, no. 1–2, pp. 163–169.

Kuryłowicz M., *'Leges aleariae' und 'leges sumptuariae' im antiken Rom*, "Acta Universitatis Szegediensis. Acta Juridica et Politica (=Studia in honorem Velimiri Polay)" 1985, vol. 33, pp. 271–279.

Kuryłowicz M., *'Leges sumptuariae' w państwie i prawie rzymskim* [in:] *Z historii państwa, prawa, miast i Polonii. Prace ofiarowane profesorowi Władysławowi Ćwikowi w czterdziestolecie Jego pracy naukowej*, J. Ciągwa, T. Opas (ed.), Rzeszów 1998, pp. 139–154.

Kuryłowicz M., *Prawo i obyczaje w starożytnym Rzymie*, Lublin 1994.

Kuryłowicz M., *Prawo rzymskie wobec przejawów luksusu i marnotrawstwa* [in:] *Zbytek i ubóstwo w starożytności i średniowieczu*, L. Kostuch, K. Ryszewska (ed.), Kielce 2010, pp. 131–140.

Kuryłowicz M., *Przestępstwa spekulacji contra annonam w prawie rzymskim*, "Folia Societatis Scientiarum Lublinensis" 1993, vol. 34, no. 1, pp. 5–14.

Kuryłowicz M., *Sacerdotes iustitiae* [in:] *Ecclesia et Status. Księga jubileuszowa z okazji 40-lecia pracy naukowej profesora Józefa Krukowskiego*, A. Dębiński, K. Orzeszyna, M. Sitarz (ed.), Lublin 2004, pp. 699–713.

Kuryłowicz M., *Wokół pojęcia aequitas w prawie rzymskim*, "Studia Iuridica Lublinensia" 2011, vol. 15, pp. 15–27.

La Bua G., *Cicero and Roman Education: The Reception of the Speeches and Ancient Scholarship*, New York 2019.

La Bua G., *Diritto e retorica: Cicerone iure peritus in Seneca retore e Quintiliano*, "Ciceroniana on line (Atti del XII Colloquium Tullianum, Salamanca, 7–9 ottobre 2004), vol. 12, pp. 181–203.

Lachmann K., *Kleinere Schriften zur classischen Philologie*, vol. 2, Berlin 1876.

Lachmann K., *Versuch über Dositheus*, Berlin 1837.

Lamberti F., *Per la datazione della Lex Iunia Vellaea al 26 d. C.*, "Rivista di diritto romano" 2018, vol. 18, pp. 175–186.

Lambrini P., *Capacità naturale e acquisto del possesso*, "Index" 1999, vol. 27, pp. 317–332.

Lambrini P., *L'elemento soggettivo nelle situazioni possessorie del diritto romano classico*, Padova 1998.

Lana I., *Il primo approccio degli studenti romani con la legge alla scuola del retore*, "Klio" 1979, vol. 61, no. 1–2, pp. 89–96.

Lanfranchi F., *Il diritto nei retori romani: contributo alla storia dello sviluppo del diritto romano*, Milano 1938.

Lausberg H., *Handbuch der literarischen Rhetorik. Eine Grundlegung der Literaturwissenschaft*. 3. Auflage mit einem Vorwort von Arnold Arens, Stuttgart 1990.

Leesen T.G, *Gaius meets Cicero: Law and Rhetoric in the School Controversies*, Leiden 2010.

Lenel O., *Das interdictum Quod legatorum utile*, "ZSS RA" 1932, vol. 52, no. 1, pp. 282–284.

Lenel O., *Das Edictum perpetuum: ein Versuch zu seiner Wiederherstellung*, Leipzig 1927.

Lepore P., *Rei publicae polliceri: Un'indagine giuridico epigrafica*, Milano 2012.

Leppin H., *Histrionen: Untersuchungen zur sozialen Stellung von Bühnenkünstlern im Westen des Römischen Reiches zur Zeit der Republik und des Principats*, Bonn 1992.

Leptien U., *Utilitatis causa. Zweckmässigkeitsentscheidungen im römischen Recht*, Freiburg 1967.

Leptien U., *"Utilitatis causa". Zweckmäßigkeitsentscheidungen im römischen Recht*, "SDHI" 1969, vol. 35, pp. 51–72.

Levy E., *Natural law in the Roman period*, "Natural Law Institute Proceedings" 1949, vol. 2, no. 43, pp. 43–72.

Licandro O, Palazzolo N., *Papirius Iustus. Libri XX de constitutionibus*, Roma 2021.

Liebs D., *Ricerche sulle Pauli Sententiae (= Quaderni di ‚Studi Senesi' 145)*, "ZSS RA" 2019, vol. 136, no. 1, pp. 465–479.

Lindsay W. M., *The Latin Language: An Historical Account of Latin Sounds, Stems, and Flexions*, Oxford 1984

Lintott A., *Cicero as Evidence: A Historian's Companion*, Oxford-New York 2008.

Lombardi L., *Saggio sul diritto giurisprudenziale*, Milano 1975.

Longchamps de Bérier F., *The praetor as a promoter of "bonum commune"*, "Legal Roots" 2014, vol. 3, pp. 217–231.

Longo G., *Sullo scioglimento del matrimonio per volontà del paterfamilias*, "BIDR" 1932, vol. 40, 201–224.

Longo G., *Utilitas publica*, "Labeo" 1972, vol. 18, pp. 7–71.

Loska E., *Kilka uwag na temat zeznań niewolników w procesie karnym*, "Zeszyty Naukowe KUL" 2017, vol. 60, no. 3, pp. 449–464.

Lotmar P., *Zur Geschichte des interdictum quod legatorum*, "ZSS RA" 1910, vol. 31, no. 1, pp. 89–158.

Lucifredi Peterlongo M. E., *Barbarius Philippus servus fugitivus praetor designatus est. Contributo all'esegesi di D. 1.14.3* [in:] *Contributi allo studio dell'esercizio di fatto di pubbliche funzioni.*, Milano 1965, pp. 1–113.

Luraschi G., *Il 'praemium' nell'esperienza giuridica romana* [in:] *Studi in onore di Arnaldo Biscardi*, vol. 4. F. Pastori (ed.), Milano 1983, pp. 239–283.

Łapicki B., *Etyczna kultura starożytnego Rzymu a wczesne chrześcijaństwo*, Wrocław 1956.

Łuka A., *Inque meo nullum carmine crimen erit. Owidiusza konflikt z prawem*, "Studia Prawnicze KUL" 2014, vol. 1, no. 57, pp. 85–118.

Maganzani L., *Il principio dell'utilitas contrahentium e il suo superamento nell'età del giusnaturalismo* [in:] *'Fides Humanitas Ius'. Studii L. Labruna*, vol. 5, C. Cascione, C. Masi Doria (ed.), Napoli 2007, pp. 3087–3095.

Mantello A., *Il sogno, la parola, il diritto. Appunti sulle concezioni giuridiche di Paolo*, "BIDR" 1991, vol. 94–95, pp. 349–416.

Mantello A., *Un illustre sconosciuto tra filisofia e prassi giuridica, Eufrate d'Epifania* [in:] *Sodalitas. Scritti in onore di Antonio Guarino*, vol. 2, V. Giuffrè (ed.), Napoli 1984, pp. 963–995.

Mantovani D., *Giuristi romani e storia dell'economia antica. Elementi per una dialettica* [in:] *Il diritto allo stato puro? Le fonti giuridiche romane come documento della società antica*, C. Buzzacchi, I. Fargnoli (ed.), Milano 2021, pp. 182–207.

Mantovani D., *Iuris scientia e honores. Contributo allo studio dei fattori sociali nella formazione giurisprudenziale del diritto romano (III–I sec. a.C.)* [in:] *Nozione formazione e interpretazione del diritto: dall'età romana alle esperienze moderne. Ricerche dedicate al professor Filippo Gallo*, vol. 1, S. Romano (ed.), Napoli 1997, pp. 617–680.

Mantovani D., *Inter aequum et utile. The Law as Economics in the Roman World?*, [in:] *Uomini, istituzioni, mercati. Studi di storia per Elio Lo Cascio*, M. Maiuro, G. D. Merola, M. De Nardis, G. Soricelli (ed.), Bari 2019, pp. 505–524 (= *Inter aequum et utile. Il diritto come economia nel mondo romano?*, [in:] *Diritto romano e economia. Due modi di pensare e organizzare il mondo (nei primi tre secoli dell'Impero)*, D. Mantovani, E. Lo Cascio (ed.), Pavia 2018, pp. 785–809).

Mantovani D., *L'aequitas romana: una nozione in cerca di equilibrio* [in:] *Quante equità?*, D. Mantovani, S. Veca (ed.), Milano 2017, pp. 15–60.

Mantovani D., Schiavone A. (ed.), *Testi e problemi del giusnaturalismo romano*, Pavia 2007.

Marotta V., *Iustitia, vera philosophia e natura: una nota sulle institutiones di Ulpiano*, "Seminarios Complutenses de Derecho Romano. Revista Internacional de Derecho Romano y Tradición Romanística" 2006, vol. 19, pp. 285–334 (=*Iustitia, vera philosophia e natura: una nota sulle institutiones di Ulpiano*, [in:] *Testi e problemi del giusnaturalismo romano*, D. Mantovani, A. Schiavone (ed.), Pavia 2007, pp. 563–601).

Marotta V., *Ulpiano e l'impero, vol. 1*, Napoli 2000.

Marrou H., *A History of Education in Antiquity*, London 1956.

Marsh D., *Lucian and the Latins: Humor and Humanism in the Early Renaissance*, Ann Arbor 1998.

Martens S. A. E., *Durch Dritte verursachte Willensmängel*, Tübingen 2007.

Martini R., *Antica retorica giudiziaria (gli status causae)*, "Diritto@Storia" 2004, no. 3 (available online at: https://www.dirittoestoria.it/3/TradizioneRomana/Martini-Antica-Retorica-Giudiziaria.htm).

Martini R., *Le definizioni dei giuristi romani*, Milano 1966.

Maschi C. A., *La conclusione della giurisprudenza classica all'età dei Severi: Iulius Paulus* [in:] ANRW, vol. 2.15, Berlin-New York 1976, pp. 667–707.

Masi Doria C., *Dalle basi culturali al diritto classico*, [in:] *Veritas e ius: per una storia della verità giuridica*, C. Cascione, C. Masi Doria (ed.), Napoli 2013, pp. 2–62.

Masi Doria C., *Linee per una storia della "veritas" nell'esperienza giuridica romana. I. Dalle basi culturali al diritto classico*, [in:] *Quid est veritas? Un seminario su verità e forme giuridiche*, C. Cascione, C. Masi Doria (ed.), Napoli 2013, pp. 1–64

Mastino I., *"Utilitas valuit propter honestatem": Cicerone e il principio giuridico dell'utilitas*, "Diritto@Storia" 2013, no. 11 (available online at: http://www.dirittoestoria.it/11/D&Innovazione/Mastino-Cicerone-Principio-giuridico-utilitas.htm).

Mayer-Maly T., *Gemeinwohl und Naturrecht bei Cicero* [in:] *Völkerrecht und rechtliches Weltbild: Festschrift für Alfred Verdross*, F. A. Frhr. vol. d. Heydte, I. Seidl-Hohenveldern, St. Verosta, K. Zemanek (ed.), Viena 1960, pp. 195–206.

Mayer-Maly T., *Gemeinwohl und Necessitas* [in:] *Rechtsgeschichte als Kulturgeschichte: Festschrift für Adalbert Erler zum 70 Geburtstag*, A. Fink et al. (ed.), Aalen 1976, pp. 135–145.

Mazurek T., *Self-Parody and the Law in Horace's "Satires" 1.9*, "The Classical Journal" 1997, vol. 93, no. 1, pp. 1–17.

McDonald I. R., *The "Vir Bonus" and Quintilian VI.3*, "Studies in Philology" 1975, vol. 72, no. 3, pp. 237–245.

McGinn T. A. J., *Satire and the law: the case of Horace*, "The Cambridge Classical Journal" 2001, vol. 47, pp. 81–102.

Meador P. A., *Quintilian's "vir bonus"*, "Western Speech" 1970, vol. 34, no. 3, pp. 162–169.

Meinhart M., *Die Datierung des SC Tertullianum, mit einem Beitrag zur Gaiusforschung*, "ZSS RA" 1966, vol. 83, no. 1, pp. 100–141.

Meinhart M., *Die Senatusconsulta Tertullianum und Orfitianum in ihrer Bedeutung für das klassische römische Erbrecht*, Graz 1967.
Menge H., *Lehrbuch der lateinischen Syntax und Semantik, Völlig neu bearbeitet von T. Burkard und M. Schauer*, Darmstadt 2000.
Mercogliano F., *Actiones Ficticiae – Tipologie e Datazione*, Napoli 2001.
Merle H., *Ars*, "Bulletin de Philosophie Médiévale" 1986, vol. 28, pp. 95–133.
Messana M. A., *Sui "libri definitionum" di Emilio Papiniano. "Definitio" e "definire" nell'esperienza giuridica romana*, "AUPA" 1998, vol. 45, no. 2, pp. 61–322.
Miller S. G., *Starożytni olimpijczycy*, trans. by I. Żółtowska, Warszawa 2006.
Molitor E., *Über öffentliches Recht und Privatrecht. Eine rechtssystematische Studie*, Karlsruhe 1949.
Mousourakis G., *A Legal History of Rome*, New York 2007.
Müllejans H., *Publicus und privatus im römischen Recht und im alteren kanonischen Recht: unter besonderer Berücksichtigung der Unterscheidung Ius publicum und Ius privatum*, München 1961.
Müller G. M., Zini F. M., *Philosophie in Rom – Römische Philosophie?, Kultur-, literatur- und philosophiegeschichtliche Perspektiven*, Berlin-Boston 2019.
Nadeau R., *Classical systems of stases in Greek: Hermagoras to Hermogenes*, "Greek, Roman, and Byzantine Studies" 1959, vol. 2, no. 1, pp. 51–71.
Navarra M., *Note in tema di "utilitas": Modestino e Coll. 10.2*, "Labeo" 2004, vol. 50, no. 1, pp. 84–134.
Navarra M., *Ricerche sulla "utilitas" nel pensiero dei giuristi romani*, Torino 2002.
Navarra M., *"Utilitas contrahentium" e sinallagma* [in:] *La compravendita e l'interdipendenza delle obbligazioni nel diritto romano*, vol. 2, L. Garofalo (ed.), Padova 2007, pp. 225–255.
Navarra M., *Utilitas publica-utilitas singulorum tra IV e V sec. d. C. Alcune osservazioni*, "SDHI" 1997, vol. 63, pp. 269–291.
Nelson H. L. W., *Überlieferung, Aufbau und Stil von Gai Institutiones*, Leiden 1981.
Nicgorski W., *Cicero's Paradoxes and His Idea of Utility*, "Political Theory" 1984, vol. 12, no. 4, pp. 557–578.
Nicosia G., *Studi sulla deiectio*, Milano 1963.
Niczyporuk P., *Bankierzy i operacje bankierskie w starożytnym Rzymie*, Białystok 2013.
Nocera G., *Il binomio pubblico-privato nella storia del diritto*, Napoli 1989.
Nocera G., *Ius naturale nella esperienza giuridica romana*, Milano 1962.
Nörr D., *Ethik von Jurisprudenz in Sachen Schatzfund*, "BIDR" 1972, vol. 14, pp. 11–40.
Nörr D., *Iurisperitus sacerdos* [in:] *Xenion: Festschrift für Pan. J. Zepos anlässlich seines 65. Geburtstages am 1. Dezember 1973*, vol. 2, E. von Caemmerer (ed.), Athens-Freiburg-Köln 1973, pp. 555–572.
Nörr D., *Rechtskritik in der Römischen Antike*, München 1974.
Nowicka D., *Quid enim si publica utilitas ex hoc emergit? Kilka uwag o informatorach w rzymskim* [in:] *Pro publico bono – idee i działalność*, M. Marszał, J. Przygodzki (ed.), Wrocław 2016, pp. 25–36.
O'Brien M., *Apuleius and the Concept of a Philosophical Rhetoric*, "Hermathena" 1991, vol. 151, pp. 39–50.
Ogórek J., *Quae ratio intercedat inter Ciceronis Paradoxis Stoicorum et Horati stoicismum, qui Satiris Epistulisque eius continetur*, Lemberg 1902.
Orestano R., *Ius singulare e privilegium in diritto romano: Contributo storico-dommatico*, Tolentino 1937.
Ormanni A., *Penus legata: contributi alla storia dei legati disposti con clausola penale in età repubblicana e classica*, Milano 1962.
Pallasse M., *Cicéron et les sources du droit*, Paris 1946.

Palma A., *Humanior interpretatio. "Humanitas" nell'interpretazione e nella normazione da Adriano ai Severi*, Torino 1992.

Parks E. P., *The Roman Rhetorical Schools as a Preparation for the Courts under the Early Empire*, Baltimore 1945.

Paturet A., *Ulpien D. 1.1.1.2 et la distinction ius publicum–ius privatum*, "Global Jurist" 2013, vol. 13, no. 2–3, pp. 115–126.

Pavese M. P., *Scire leges est verba tenere. Ricerche sulle competenze grammaticali dei giuristi romani*, Torino 2013.

Pellat C. A., *Exposé des principes généraux du droit romain sur la propriété et ses principaux démembrements et particulièrement sur l'usufruit: suivi d'une traduction et d'un commentaire du livre VI des Pandectes*, Paris 1853.

Perelman C., *Logika prawnicza: nowa retoryka*, Warszawa 1984.

Perozzi S., *Istituzioni di diritto romano*, Roma 1928.

Peters H., *Generelle und spezielle Aktionen*, "ZSS RA" 1911, vol. 32, no. 1, pp. 179–307.

Petrucci A., *Protección de quienes contratan con empresas comerciales en la experiencia jurídica romana. Aplicaciones de la acción institoria*, "Revista de Derecho Privado" 2007, no. 12–13, pp. 179–204.

Pikulska-Robaszkiewicz A., *Ustawowa regulacja obyczajów w prawie rzymskim*, "Studia Iuridica" 1999, vol. 37, pp. 213–219.

Pinkster H., *The Oxford Latin Syntax. Volume 1. The Simple Clause*, Oxford 2015.

Piscitelli T., *Dignitas in Cicerone. Tra semantica e semiologia*, "Bollettino di Studi Latini" 1979, vol. 9, pp. 253–267.

Platschek J., *Das Edikt De pecunia constituta: Die römische Erfüllungszusage und ihre Einbettung in den hellenistischen Kreditverkehr*, München 2013.

Plisecka A., *Definicja sprawiedliwości w filozofii Cycerona i prawie rzymskim*, "Studia Iuridica" 2002, vol. 40, pp. 131–140.

Pölönen J., *Religion in Law's Domain: recourse to supernatural agents in litigation, dispute resolution, and pursuits of justice under the Early Roman Empire*, "RIDA" 2018, vol. 65, pp. 163–194.

Pölönen J., *The Case for a Sociology of Roman Law* [in:] *Law and Sociology*, M. Freeman (ed.), New York 2006, pp. 398–408.

Powell J. G. F., *The Embassy of the Three Philosophers to Rome in 155 BC* [in:] *Hellenistic Oratory: Continuity and Change*, C. Kremmydas, K. Tempest (ed.), Oxford 2013, pp. 219–248.

Pringsheim F., *Bonum et aequum*, "ZSS RA" 1932, vol. 52, no. 1, pp. 78–155.

Pugliese G., *I principi generali del diritto. L'esperienza romana fino a Diocleziano* [in:] *Atti dei Convegni Lincei 96. Convegno sul tema: I principi generali del diritto (Roma, 27–29 maggio 1991)*, Roma 1992, pp. 69–87.

Pugliese G., *In tema di actio exercitoria*, "Labeo" 1957, vol. 3, pp. 308–343.

Pugsley D., *Causation and Confessions in the Lex Aquilia*, "TR" 1970, vol. 38, no. 2, pp. 163–174.

Quadrato R., *Retorica e giurisprudenza: da Quintiliano a Gaio.*, "SDHI" 2013, vol. 79, pp. 837–858.

Querzoli S., *Materia and officia of rhetorical teaching in Book II of the Institutio Oratoria* [in:] *Quintilian and the Law: The Art of Persuasion in Law and Politics*, O. E. Tellegen-Couperus (ed.), Leuven 2003, pp. 37–50.

Rainer M., *Julian und die cautio damni infecti*, "Fundamina: A Journal of Legal History" 2010, vol. 16, no. 1, pp. 359–365.

Ram J. J., *Disputatio iuridica inauguralis de interdicto quod vi aut clam*, Traiecti ad Rhenum 1738.

Rampazzo N., *Quasi praetor non fuerit. Studi sulle elezioni magistratuali in Roma repubblicana tra regola ed eccezione*, Napoli 2008.

Ravljen M., *Concept of Avoidance of the Law (Fraus Legis) through Roman and German Law History*, "Russian Law: theory and practice" 2018, no. 2, pp. 78–88.
Reale G., *Storia della filosofia antica. I sistemi dell'età ellenistica*, vol. 3, Milano 1997.
Riccobono S., *La definizione del "ius" al tempo di Adriano*, "BIDR" 1948, vol. 12, no. 53–54, pp. 5–82.
Riccobono S., *Stipulatio ed instrumentum nel Diritto giustinianeo*, "ZSS RA" 1922, vol. 43, no. 1, pp. 262–397.
Robleda O., *El matrimonio en derecho romano*, Roma 1970.
Robleda O., *Il divorzio a Roma prima di Costantino* [in:] ANRW, vol. 14.2, Berlin–New York 1982, pp. 347–391.
Rodríguez Diez J. E., *Potestas alienandi. Transfer of ownership by a non-owner from Roman law to the DCFR*, Oisterwijk 2016.
Rosillo-López C., *La corruption à la fin de la république romaine (IIe-Ier s. av. J.-C.): aspects politiques et financiers*, Stuttgart 2010.
Rotondi G., *Leges publicae populi Romani*, Milano 1912.
Rozwadowski W., *Etiam clarum ius exigit interpretationem* [in:] *W poszukiwaniu dobra wspólnego: księga jubileuszowa Profesora Macieja Zielińskiego*, A. Choduń, S. Czepita (ed.), Szczecin 2010, pp. 37–48.
Rozwadowski W., *Nauczanie prawa w państwie rzymskim*, "CPH" 2003, vol. 55, no. 1, pp. 9–28.
Rudorff A. F., *De iuris dictione edictum: Edicti perpetui quae reliqua sunt*, Lipsiae 1869.
Ruffini F., *L'actio spolii. Studio storico-giuridico*, Torino 1889.
Rüfner T., *Antritt der Erbschaft unter unsicheren Voraussetzungen: D. 29,2,21,3 (Ulp. 7 ad Sab.)*, "ZSS RA" 2010, vol. 127, no. 1, pp. 286–295.
Ruggiero I., *Ricerche sulle Pauli Sententiae*, Milano 2017.
Ryan F. X., *Rank and participation in the republican senate*, Stuttgart 1998.
Sadowski P., *Filozofia prawa w życiu i nauczaniu Ulpiana*, "ZP" 2008, vol. 8, no. 1, pp. 81–108.
Santoro R., *Aspetti formulari della tutela delle convenzioni atipiche*, [in:] *Scritti Minori*, vol. 1, M. Varvaro (ed.), Torino 2009, pp. 349–390.
Santa Cruz Teijeiro J., *Der Einfluß der rhetorischen Theorie des status auf die römische Jurisprudenz, insbesondere auf die Auslegung der Gesetze und Rechtsgeschäfte*, "ZSS RA" 1958, vol. 75, no. 1, pp. 91–115.
Santa Cruz Teijeiro J., *Influencia de algunas disciplinas no jurídicas en el derecho romano*, "Anuario de historia del derecho español" 1957, vol. 27, pp. 343–398.
Santa Cruz Teijeiro J., *Notas para un estudio expositivo sobre el influjo de la retórica en el Derecho romano*, "Revista de estudios políticos" 1952, vol. 64, pp. 109–124.
Santucci G., *'Utilitas contrahentium'. Note minime su una 'regula' che 'cacciata dalla porta rientrò dalla finestra'* [in:] *Modelli teorici e metodologici nella storia del diritto privato*, vol. 3, R. Fiori (ed.), Napoli 2008, pp. 277–312.
Scarano Ussani V., *L'ars dei giuristi. Considerazioni sullo statuto epistemologico della giurisprudenza romana*, Torino 1997.
Scarano Ussani V., *L'utilità e la certezza: compiti e modelli del sapere giuridico in Salvio Giuliano*, Milano 1987.
Scarano Ussani V., *Tra "scientia" e "ars". Il sapere giuridico romano dalla sapienza alla scienza nei giudizi di Cicerone e di Pomponio*, [in:] *Per la storia del pensiero giuridico romano. Dall'età dei pontefici alla scuola di Servio. Atti del seminario di S. Marino 7–9 gennaio 1993*, D. Mantovani (ed.), Torino 1996, pp. 229–262.
Scevola R., *"Utilitas publica", I. Emersione nel pensiero greco e romano*, Padova 2012.
Scevola R., *"Utilitas publica", II. Elaborazione della giurisprudenza severiana*, Padova 2012.

Schermaier M., *Ulpian als 'wahrer Philosoph'. Notizien zum selbstverständnis eines Römischen Juristen* [in:] *Ars boni et aequi. Festschrift für Wolfgang Waldstein zum 65. Geburtstag*, M. Schermaier, Z. Vegh (ed.), Stuttgart 1993, pp. 303–322.

Schiavone A., *Giuristi e principe nelle Istituzioni di Ulpiano. Un'esegesi*, "SDHI" 2003, vol. 69, pp. 3–56.

Schiavone A., *Ius: L'invenzione del diritto in Occidente*, Torino 2005.

Schiller A.A., *Roman Law: Mechanisms of Development*, Hauge-Paris-New York 1978.

Schindler K.-H., *Ein Streit zwischen Julian und Celsus*, "ZSS RA" 1957, vol. 74, no. 1, pp. 201–233.

Schittko M.P., *Analogien als Argumentationstyp*, Göttingen 2003.

Schofield M., *Cicero's Definition of Res Publica*, [in:] *Cicero the Philospher. Twelve Papers*, J.G.F. Powell (ed.), Oxford-New York 1995, rep. 2002, pp. 63–83.

Schulz F., *Storia della Giurisprudenza Romana*, Firenze 1968.

Schwarz A.B., *Das strittige Recht der römischen Juristen* [in:] *Festschrift Fritz Schulz*, vol. 2, H. Niedermeyer, W. Flume (ed.), Weimar 1951, pp. 201–225.

Schwarz F., *Begriffsanwendung und Interessenwertung im klassischen römischen Recht*, "Archiv für die civilistische Praxis" 1952, vol. 152, no. 3, pp. 193–215.

Schwarz F., *Die Funktion des Irrtums bei Erfüllung gänzlich Oder teilweise nicht geschuldeter Fideikommisse*, "ZSS RA" 1951, vol. 68, no. 1, pp. 266–319.

Seidl E., *Moderne zivilrechtliche Lehren als Erkenntnismittel der Rechtsgeschichte* [in:] *Das deutsche Privatrecht in der Mitte des 20. Jahrhunderts. Festschrift für Heinrich Lehmann zum 80. Geburtstag*, H.C. Nipperdey (ed.), Berlin 1956, pp. 97–112.

Seidl E., *War Begriffsjurisprudenz die Methode der Römer?*, "Archiv für Rechts- und Sozialphilosophie" 1957, vol. 43, no. 3, pp. 343–366.

Selb W., *Symbolae iuridicae et historicae Martino David dedicatae. Ediderunt J.A. Ankum, R. Feenstra, W.F. Leemans. Tomus primus: lus Romanum. Tomus alter: Iura Orientis Antiqui* [review], "ZSS RA" 1970, vol. 87, no. 1, pp. 550–556.

Senn F., *De la justice et du droit: explication de la définition traditionnelle de la justice suivie d'une étude sur la distinction du ius naturale et du ius gentium*, Paris 1927.

Siedlecki W., *Podstawowe pojęcia prawne*, Kraków 1948.

Sitek B., *Utilitas publica z perspektywy prawa rzymskiego i polskiego*, "Themis Polska Nova" 2014, vol. 1, no. 6, pp. 21–35.

Smiley C.N., *Ulpian ὁ Κειτούκειτος. The Influence of the Stoic Theory of Style in Athenaeus*, "The American Journal of Philology" 1908, vol. 29, no. 3, pp. 322–328.

Solazzi S., *La prestazione dell'auctoritas e la pluralità dei tutori*, "Atti della R. Acc. Di scienze morali e politiche di Napoli" 1935, vol. 57, pp. 212–235.

Sondel J., *Les 'leges sumptuariae' considérées comme l'expression des conditions sociales et économiques de la Rome antique*, "Archivum Iuridicum Cracoviense" 1973, vol. 6, pp. 101–124.

Sondel J., *Precarium w prawie rzymskim*, Kraków 1971.

Sondel J., *Ustawy przeciw luksusowi w starożytnym Rzymie*, "Sprawozdania z Czynności i Posiedzeń PAU" 1994, vol. 58, pp. 25–29.

Sorka K., *Interpolacje "Digestów" justyniańskich. Rys historyczno-metodologiczny*, "Forum Prawnicze" 2017, vol. 43, no. 5, pp. 54–68.

Sorka K., *Veritatem esse quaerendam. Prawda w rzymskim procesie cywilnym*, Kraków 2021.

Spagnolo B., Sampson J., *Principle and Pragmatism* [in:] *Principle and Pragmatism in Roman Law*, B. Spagnolo, J. Sampson (ed.), Oxford-New York 2020, pp. 1–26.

Spinelli E., *Justice, Law, and Friendship: Ethical and Political Topics in Epicurus* [in:] *Philosophie für die Polis*, C. Riedweg (ed.), Berlin-Boston 2019, pp. 379–408.

Staffhorst A., *Die Teilnichtigkeit von Rechtsgeschäften im klassischen römischen Recht*, Berlin 2006.
Stagl J.F., *Die Funktionen der utilitas publica*, "ZSS RA" 2017, vol. 134, no. 1, pp. 514–523.
Stagl J.F., *Camino desde la servidumbre: Escritos sobre la servidumbre en la Antigüedad, su derrota y la amenaza de su retorno*, Madrid 2021.
Stagl J.F., *Das "testamentum militare" in seiner Eigenschaft als "ius singulare"*, "Revista de estudios histórico-jurídicos" 2014, no. 36, pp. 129–157.
Stagl J.F., *Favor dotis: die Privilegierung der Mitgift im System des römischen Rechts*, Wien 2009.
Stein P., *Interpretation and Legal Reasoning in Roman Law*, "Chicago-Kent Law Review" 1995, vol. 70, no. 4, pp. 1539–1556.
Stein P., *Ulpian and the distinction between ius publicum and ius privatum* [in:] *Collatio iuris romani. Études dediées á Hans Ankum à l'occasion de son 65e anniversaire*, vol. 2, R. Feenstra, A.S. Hartkamp, J.E. Spruit, R.J. Sijpesteijn, L.C. Winkel (ed.), Amsterdam 1995, pp. 499–504.
Steinwenter A., *Utilitas publica–Utilitas singulorum* [in:] *Festschrift Paul Koschaker mit Unterstützung der Rechts- und Staatswissenschaftlichen Fakultät der Friedrich-Wilhelms-Universität Berlin und der Leipziger Juristenfakultät zum 60. Geburtstag überreicht von seinen Fachgenossen*, vol. 1, M. Kaser (ed.), Weimar 1939, pp. 84–102.
Stella Maranca F., *Il diritto romano nell'opera di Orazio*, "Annali della Facoltà di Giurisprudenza dell'Università degli Studi di Bari" 1933, vol. 2, pp. 71–89.
Stella Maranca F., *Le "duae positiones" dello "studium iuris"*, Bari 1936.
Stella Maranca F., *Orazio e la legislazione Romana* [in:] *Conferenze Oraziane in commemorizacione del bimillenario Oraziano*, Milano 1936, pp. 43–66.
Stella Maranca F., *Per lo studio del diritto romano nell'opera di Orazio*, Modena 1935.
Stepan S., *Scaevola noster. Schulgut in den "libri disputationum" des Claudius Tryphoninus?*, Tübingen 2018.
Stolfi E., *Studi sui "Libri ad edictum" di Pomponio. II. Contesti e pensiero*, Milano 2002.
Stroh W., *Cicero: Redner, Staatsmann, Philosoph*, München 2011.
Stroh W., *Taxis und Taktik: Die advokatische Dispositionskunst in Ciceros Gerichtsreden*, Stuttgart 1975.
Stroux I., *Summum ius summa iniuria. Ein Kapitel aus der Geschichte der interpretatio iuris*, Leipzig 1926 (=*Summum ius summa iniuria. Un capitolo concernente la storia della interpretatio iuris [versione dal tedesco di G. Funaioli con prefazione di S. Riccobono]*, "AUPA" 1929, vol. 12, pp. 639–691).
Sukačić M., *Pitanje aktivne legitimacije za primjenu interdikta quod vi aut clam u klasičnom rimskom pravu*, "Zbornik radova Pravnog fakulteta u Splitu" 2020, vol. 57, no. 4, pp. 1057–1078.
Sussman L.A., *The Elder Seneca*, Leiden 1978.
Szolc-Nartowski B., *Udział osób nieuprawnionych w wydaniu orzeczenia w postępowaniu cywilnym – uwagi na tle D. 1,14.3 i D. 41,3,44 pr.*, "ZP" 2006, vol. 6, no. 2, pp. 97–116.
Szpunar A., *Nadużycie prawa podmiotowego*, Kraków 1947.
Święcicka P., *Formalność topicznego myślenia: problem "reguł proceduralnych" dyskursu dogmatycznego rzymskich jurystów*, "CPH" 2011, vol. 63, no. 2, pp. 209–240.
Święcicka P., *Iurisconsultus et Auditores. Dialektyczna formuła poznania i rozwoju prawa w Rzymie republikańskim*, "Krakowskie Studia z Historii Państwa i Prawa" 2013, vol. 6, no. 3, pp. 193–227.
Święcicka P., *"Lex Aquilia de damno" – problemy z datacją ustawy*, "Krakowskie Studia z Historii Państwa i Prawa" 2008, vol. 2 , pp. 17–32.
Święcicka P., *Prawo jurysprudencyjne jako prawniczy dyskurs argumentacyjny (zarys problematyki)*, "ZP" 2011, vol. 11, no. 1, pp. 317–338.
Świrgoń-Skok R., *Beneficjum (beneficium) w źródłach prawa rzymskiego*, "Studia Prawnoustrojowe" 2007, vol. 7, pp. 229–239.

Świrgoń-Skok R., *Kategoria spadkobierców koniecznych (heredes necessarii) jako przykład zapewnienia ciągłości w rodzinie rzymskiej w okresie prawa klasycznego*, "Studia Iuridica Lublinensia" 2010, vol. 14, pp. 135–146.
Tafaro S., *Regula e ius antiquum in D.50.17.23. Ricerche sulla responsabilità contrattuale*, Bari 1984.
Talamanca M., *Per la storia della giurisprudenza romana*, "BIDR" 1977, vol. 80, pp. 195–344.
Talamanca M., *Rec. a V. Scarano Ussani*, "BIDR" 1988, vol. 91, pp. 864–881.
Tarn W. W., *La civilisation hellénistique*, Paris 1936.
Taylor L. R., *Horace's Equestrian Career*, "American Journal of Philology" 1925, vol. 46, pp. 161–170.
Tellegen J. W., *Savigny's System and Cicero's Pro Caecina*, "OIR" 1996, vol. 2, pp. 91–106.
Tellegen J. W., *The Reliability of Quintilian for Roman Law: On the Causa Curiana* [in:] *Quintilian and the Law: The Art of Persuasion in Law and Politics*, O. E. Tellegen-Couperus (ed.), Leuven 2003, pp. 191–200.
Tellegen-Couperus O. E., *Cicero and Ulpian: Two paragons of legal practice*, "RIDA" 2009, vol. 56, no. 1, pp. 485–497.
Tellegen-Couperus O. E., *Quintilian and Roman Law*, "RIDA" 2000, vol. 47, pp. 167–177.
Thiele G., *Hermagoras: Ein Beitrag zur Geschichte der Rhetorik*, Berlin-Boston 2019.
Thomas P., *Ars aequi et boni, legal argumentation and the correct legal solution*, "ZSS RA" 2014, vol. 131, no. 1, pp. 41–59.
Tondo S., *Aspetti simbolici e magici nella struttura giuridica della manumissio vindicta*, Milano 1967.
Trampedach F., *Die condictio incerti*, "ZSS RA" 1896, vol. 17, no. 1, pp. 97–154.
Ulrych K., *Res extra commercium*, Praga 2014 (PhD thesis available online at: https://dspace.cuni.cz/handle/20.500.11956/53795).
Urbanik J., *D. 24.2.4: … Pater tamen eius nuntium mittere posse: l'influsso della volontà del padre sul divorzio dei sottoposti* [in:] *Εὐεργεσίας χάριν. Studies Presented to Benedetto Bravo and Ewa Wipszycka by Their Disciples, Warsaw 2002 [= The Journal of Juristic Papyrology. Supplement no. 1]*, T. Derda, J. Urbanik, M. Węcowski (ed.), Warszawa 2002, pp. 293–336.
Urbanik J., *Dissolubility and indissolubility of marriage in the Greek and Roman tradition* [in:] *Mater familias. Scritti romanistici per Maria Zabłocka*, J. Urbanik, Z. Benincasa (ed.), Varsavia 2016, pp. 1039–1068.
Urbanik J., *Rozwód w papirusach. Studium przypadków*, "U schyłku starożytności. Studia źródłoznawcze" 2010, vol. 9, pp. 159–188.
Valiño E., *Actiones utiles*, Navarra 1974.
Vallar S., *Folie et droit romain – Quelques observations*, "Criminocorpus. Revue d'Histoire de la justice, des crimes et des peines" 2016 (available online at : http://journals.openedition.org/criminocorpus/3146).
Vallar S., *Perseverantia voluntatis e furor*, "Quaderni Lupiensi di Storia e Diritto" 2013, vol. 3, pp. 147–159.
Van Kędzierski D., *Metodologia i paradygmat polskich szczegółowych nauk prawnych*, "Transformacje Prawa Prywatnego" 2018, vol. 3, pp. 5–59.
Van Warmelo P., *Interdictum quod vi aut clam*, "Acta Juridica" 1962, vol. 15, pp. 15–37.
Varonese B., *L'utilitas contrahentium nei contratti reali gratuiti in diritto romano classico: un modello di responsabilità*, Padova 2012 (PhD thesis available online at: http://paduaresearch.cab.unipd.it/4367/1/Tesi_PDF_unita.pdf).
Vaughn J. W., *Law and rhetoric in the causa Curiana*, "Classical Antiquity" 1985, vol. 4, no. 2, pp. 208–222.
Viarengo G., *Studi sulla tutela dei minori*, Torino 2016.
Viehweg T., *Topica e giurisprudenza*, transl. G. Crifò, Milano 1962.

Voci P., *Ars boni et aequi*, "Index" 1999, no. 27, pp. 1–22.

Voci P., *D.1,14,3. Note in tema di esercizio di fatto di pubbliche funzioni* [in:] *Studi di diritto romano pubblicati a cura della Facoltà di giurisprudenza dell'Università di Padova*, vol. 1, Padova 1985, pp. 623–648 (= *D.1,14,3. Note in tema di esercizio di fatto di pubbliche funzioni* [in:] *Studi in memoria di Enrico Guicciardi*, Padua 1975, pp. 59–80).

Voci P., *Linee storiche del diritto ereditario romano I. Dalle origini ai Severi* [in:] ANRW, vol. 2.14, Berlin-New York 1976, pp. 392–448.

Volterra E., *Lezioni di diritto romano. Il matrimonio romano*, Roma 1961.

Volterra E., *L'ouvrage de Papirius Justus Constitutionum libri XX* [in:] *Symbolae iuridicae et historicae Martino David dedicatae*, vol. 1, J. A. Ankum, R. Feenstra, W. F. Leemans (ed.), Leiden 1968, pp. 215–223.

Volterra E., *Quelques observations sur le mariage des filiifamilias*, "RIDA" 1948, vol. 1, pp. 213–242.

von Jhering R., *Geist des römischen Rechts auf den verschiedenen Stufen seiner Entwicklung. Zweiter Theil*, Leipzig 1875.

Vonglis B., *Droit romain et rhetorique*, "TR" 1969, vol. 37, no. 2, pp. 247–256.

Vonglis B., *La lettre et l'esprit de la loi dans la jurisprudence classique et la réthorique*, Paris 1968.

Wacke A., *Das Rechtswort: Tenor*, "ZSS RA" 2020, vol. 137, no. 1, pp. 291–311.

Wacke A., *Gloria und virtus als Ziel athletischer Wettkämpfe und die Unbescholtenheit der Athleten sowie die erlaubten Sportwetten nach römischen Rechtsquellen.* [in:] *Kultur(en) – Formen des Alltäglichen in der Antike. Festschrift für Ingomar Weiler zum 75. Geburtstag*, P. Mauritsch, C. Ulf (ed.), Graz 2013, pp. 41–84.

Wacke A., *Ne occasio sit maioris tumultus faciendi: Absurditätsargument und Folgenberücksichtigung in römischen Rechtsquellen, Teil 2* [in:] *Een Rijk Gerecht, Opstellen aangeboden aan Paul Nève*, B. C. M. Jacobs, E. C. Coppens (ed.), Nijmegen 1998, pp. 585–602.

Wacke A., *Sul concetto di "dolus" nell'"actio de dolo"*, "Iura" 1977, vol. 28, no. 11–39.

Waldstein W., *"Aequitas" e "summum ius"*, [in:] *Saggi sul diritto non scritto*, Milano 2002, pp. 131–163.

Waldstein W., *Bemerkungen zum ius naturale bei den klassischen Juristen*, "ZSS RA" 1988, vol. 105, no. 1, pp. 702–711.

Waldstein W., *Equità e ragione naturale nel pensiero giuridico del I secolo d. C.* [in:] *Testi e problemi del giusnaturalismo romano*, D. Mantovani, A. Schiavone (ed.), Pavia 2007, pp. 249–269.

Waldstein W., *Ius naturale im nachklassischen römischen Recht und bei Justinian*, "ZSS RA" 1994, vol. 111, no. 1, pp. 1–65.

Waldstein W., *Römische Rechtswissenschaft und wahre Philosophie*, "Index" 1994, vol. 22, pp. 31–45.

Waldstein W., *Zum Problem der 'vera philosophia' bei Ulpian* [in:] *Collatio Iuris Romani. Études dédiées á Hans Ankum à l'occasion de son 65e anniversaire*, R. Feenstra, A. S. Hartkamp, J. E. Spruit, P. J. Sijpesteijn, L. C. Winkel (ed.), Amsterdam 1995, pp. 607-–617.

Waldstein W., *Zur Ulpians Definition der Gerechtigkeit (D. 1,1,1pr.)* [in:] *Festschrift für Werner Flume zum 70. Geburtstag, 12. September 1978*, vol. 1, K. Ballerstedt, F. A. Mann, H. H. Jakobs, B. Knobbe-Keuk, J. Wilhelm (ed.), Cologne 1978, pp. 213–232.

Walsh P. G., *Introduction* [in:] Cicero, *On Obligations (De officiis)*, translated by P. G. Walsh, Oxford–New York 2000, pp. IX–XLVII.

Walter M., *Introduction* [in:] *Cicero. On Duties*, translated by Walter Miller, Cambridge 1913, pp. XI–XIV.

Walzer A. E., *Quntilian's "Vir Bonus" and the stoic wise man*, "Rhetoric Society Quarterly" 2003, vol. 33, no. 4, pp. 25–41.

Watson A., *Mandate and the Boundaries of Roman Contract*, "BIDR" 1991, vol. 33, pp. 41–48.

Watson A., *Narrow, Rigid and Literal Interpretation in the Later Roman Republic*, "TR" 1969, vol. 37, pp. 351–368.

Watson A., *The Law of Property in the Later Roman Republic*, 1968.

Watson A., Abou El Fadl K., *Fox Hunting, Pheasant Shooting and Comparative Law*, "The American Journal of Comparative Law" 2000, no. 48, pp. 1–37.

Wesel U., *Rhetorische Statuslehre und Gesetzesauslegung der römischen Juristen*, Köln-Berlin-Bonn-München 1967.

Wesel U., *Zur Deutung und Bedeutung des Status Scriptum et Sententia*, "TR" 1970, vol. 38, no. 3, pp. 343–366.

Wibier M., *Transmitting Legal Knowledge: From Question-and-Answer Format to Handbook in Gaius' Institutes* [in:] *Between Orality and Literacy: Communication and Adaptation in Antiquity: Orality and Literacy in the Ancient World*, vol. 10, R. Scodel (ed.), Leiden-Boston 2014, pp. 356–373.

Wieacker F., *Offene Wertungen bei den römischen Juristen*, "ZSS RA" 1977, vol. 94, no. 1, pp. 1–42.

Wieacker F., *The "Causa Curiana" and Contemporary Roman Jurisprudence*, "Irish Jurist" 1967, vol. 2, no. 1, pp. 151–164.

Wieacker F., *Vom romischen Recht: Zehn Versuche*, Stuttgart 1961.

Wikarjak J., *Gramatyka opisowa języka łacińskiego*, Warszawa 1978.

Winkel L., *Die stoische οἰκείωσις-Lehre und Ulpians Definition der Gerechtigkeit*, "ZSS RA" 1988, vol. 105, no. 1, pp. 669–679.

Winterbottom M., *Quintilian and the Vir Bonus*, "The Journal of Roman Studies" 1964, vol. 54, no. 1–2, pp. 90–97.

Wischmeyer T., *Zwecke im Recht des Verfassungsstaates: Geschichte und Theorie einer juristischen Denkfigur*, Freiburg 2015.

Wlassak M., *Die prätorischen Freilassungen*, "ZSS RA" 1905, vol. 26, no. 1, pp. 367–431.

Woerther F., *Hermagoras. Fragments et témoignages*, Paris 2012.

Wubbe F., *Ius singulare quid sit* [in:] *Ars boni et aequi. Festschrift für Wolfgang Waldstein zum 65. Geburtstag*, M. Schermaier, Z. Vegh (ed.), Stuttgart 1993, pp. 451–469.

Wycisk T., *Quidquid in foro fieri potest – Studien zum römischen Recht bei Quintilian*, Berlin 2008.

Wyrwińska K., *Grecka myśl filozoficzna i jej wpływ na kształtowanie się rzymskiego kanonu wykształcenia prawniczego. Przyczynek do studium* [in:] *Vetera novis augere: Studia i prace dedykowane Profesorowi Wacławowi Uruszczakowi*, S. Grodziński, D. Malec, A. Karabowicz (ed.), Kraków 2010, pp. 1179–1187.

Zabłocka M., *Rzymskie źródła techniki legislacyjnej*, "Palestra" 2016, vol. 1–2, pp. 15–20.

Zajadło J., *Cyceron dla prawników*, Gdańsk 2019.

Zajadło J., *Oratio pro Aulo Caecina Cycerona – prawo pomiędzy jurysprudencją a retoryką*, "Ruch Prawniczy, Ekonomiczny i Socjologiczny" 2019, vol. 2, pp. 35–49.

Zamorski K., *Historia jako przedmiot poznania* [in:] *Przedmiot poznania politologii: podstawy dyscypliny nauki*, R. Skarzyński (ed.), Białystok 2014, pp. 89–138.

Ziembiński Z., *Problemy podstawowe prawoznawstwa*, Warszawa 1980.

Zülch C., *Der "Liber singularis responsorum" des Ulpius Marcellus*, Berlin 2001.

Greg Woolf / Ilaria Bultrighini /
Camilla Norman (Ed.)

Sanctuaries and Experience

Knowledge, Practice and Space in the Ancient World

POTSDAMER ALTERTUMSWISSENSCHAFTLICHE BEITRÄGE – VOLUME 83

2024. 474 pages with 29 b/w illustrations and 68 colored photos
978-3-515-13399-9 SOFTCOVER
978-3-515-13407-1 E-BOOK

Ancient religion is traditionally understood in terms of myths, rituals and institutions, as transmitted in ancient texts. The studies gathered here focus instead on the lived experience of ancient cult and the places in which that experience was formed. They build on recent explorations of Lived Ancient Religion and also on new approaches to Material Ancient Religion. All ancient societies constructed elaborate sanctuaries. Their architecture and the collective rituals that took place there shaped collective experiences. Through case studies drawn from Ancient Egypt, the Greek World and the Roman Empire these themes are explored and elaborated. Together they indicate new ways of approaching ancient religious experience, collective and individual.

THE EDITORS

Greg Woolf has since July 2021 been Ronald J Mellor Professor of Ancient History in the University of California, Los Angeles. His research focus is Cultural change in the Roman World, Seasonality and Roman Society as well as Migration and human mobility in antiquity.

Ilaria Bultrighini studied Ancient History, Archaeology, and Classics at the Universities of Urbino and Rome La Sapienza and received her PhD from G. d'Annunzio University of Chieti-Pescara (2012). In 2021 she was awarded the National Scientific Habilitation as Associate Professor of Ancient History and is currently an Honorary Research Fellow in Ancient History at UCL.

Camilla Norman completed a Bachelor of Arts (honours) and Doctor of Philosophy (archaeology) from the University of Sydney, and a Masters of Cultural Materials Conservation at the University of Melbourne. She specializes in the archaeology of pre-Roman Italy, with a focus on the indigenous populations of Apulia and Basilicata.

Franz Steiner Verlag

Order online at:
service@steiner-verlag.de